The Harley-Davidson Motor Company

• A 100-Year History •

David K. Wright

CarTech®
Auto Books & Manuals

CarTech®, Inc.,
39966 Grand Avenue
North Branch, MN 55056
Telephone (651) 277-1200 • (800) 551-4754 • Fax: (651) 277-1203
www.cartechbooks.com

ISBN 1-884089-59-3
Item CT959

Printed in China

Library of Congress Cataloging-in-Publication Data

Wright, David K.
    The Harley-Davidson Motor Company : a 100-year history / David K. Wright.
       p. cm.
Includes index.
    ISBN 1-884089-59-3 (hardcover)
    1. Harley-Davidson Motor Company--History. 2. Motorcycle industry--United States--History. 3. Motorcycle racing--History. I. Title.
    HD9710.5.U64 H378 2003
    338.7'6292275'0973--dc21
                                    2002012047

On the front cover: *Elmer Ehnes, of Kokesh Motorcycles in Spring Lake Park, Minnesota, restored the rare 1937 Harley-Davidson EL shown here. Its classic lines are a nice complement to the modern lines of the new Harley-Davidson V-Rod owned by Ed Collova. A big thanks to Rob Carlson of Kokesh Motorcycles for locating the bikes and for moving them around at a photographer's whim on a very hot, humid afternoon.* (Steve Hendrickson)

On the back cover: *The FLH family of bikes, including this '03 Road King, is the only series that got substantial mechanical changes for 2003. All of the FLH models, from Road King to Electra Glide Classic, benefit from larger and stronger swingarms, a wider-diameter rear axle, and a stiffer chassis for a more controlled ride. All FLH models also have CD players now, and their EFI system has been improved.* (Dain Gingerelli)

On the title page: *The three Big Twin platforms are the Dyna Glide series, the Softail series, and the FLH Touring series, represented in this shot by a Low Rider, a Fat Boy, and an Electra Glide Classic – All decked out in Anniversary Sterling Silver and Vivid Black two-tone paint.* (Dain Gingerelli)

Table of Contents

Introduction

Preface

I liked Harley-Davidson better when the company was on its ass. That was in the early 1980s, when I was writing the first edition of this book. The 13 men who would come to be known as the buyback team were so busy trying to save the corporation that they hardly noticed a guy who was asking lots of questions, rooting in the archives, and keeping at least one photocopy machine perpetually busy. It was a tough time at the big brick structure on Juneau Avenue, as 40 percent of the workforce suffered wage reductions, then lay-offs, in the face of the Japanese bike onslaught.

Nowadays, most of the original buyback leaders are gone and Harley-Davidson is run by the kinds of corporate loyalists you would find in any big business. They produce slick news releases that do not always answer the public's most pressing questions, they influence unpopular decisions such as disbanding the admittedly non-competitive VR 1000 Superbike team, and they make a great deal of money. The company talks the talk, handing out money for Vietnam veterans' causes, for example, but it shows no favor when actually dealing with the next vet in the door. There are fewer H-D employees who are bike riders, proportionately, than in the bad old days. With that in mind, one wonders who will actually wallow with bike owners at places like Sturgis and Daytona Beach when Willie G. hangs up his helmet.

Longtime dealers remain the company's biggest asset. It is heartening to see people who hung on through thick and thin grow rich. So long as Harley-Davidson, Inc., listens to its dealer network rather than overwhelming it, the company should not only survive, it should prosper.

Introduction

The air was warm that May evening in 1966. College graduation and my draft notice were a month down the road. Although I didn't know it, Vietnam lay only ten months down the road. The road on that particular May evening led to a drive-in movie outside Springfield, Ohio. Five couples took up three parking places with a Chevrolet, a Volkswagen Bug, and a Harley-Davidson. We spread blankets on car hoods and on the gravel, popped tab tops, and watched Frankie Avalon pursue Annette Funicello. After the show, the guy with the H-D staggered a bit under the weight

The Heritage Softail is one of the 100th Anniversary Harleys that are identified by their distinctive tank badge, along with anniversary logos on the ignition cover and derby cover. (Dain Gingerelli)

of a 12-pack consumed. We eased him into the back seat of the Chevy and I was elected to ride his bike home. Why me? I owned a small Italian bike, and all cycles were alike, right?

The first kick nearly tossed me into the next row of cars. Fiddling in the glare of an occasional headlight, I somehow got the Harley running. My girl climbed nervously aboard and we eased off. Three feet later, I noticed a pronounced lurch that shook the handlebars; it went away as quickly as it had appeared. We moved into traffic and somehow made it through the Midwest midnight to the bike owner's apartment. The next day, the guy with the Volkswagen called, upset. Somehow, in the darkness, the footpeg or the safety bar had caught his front fender, ripping it half off his car. That accounted for the momentary handlebar twitch, all right.

When the idea of writing about Harley-Davidson was suggested, the fender assault came immediately to mind. No one thinks of stuff like that when you mention Harley, I believed. However, I was wrong. Everyone conjures up his or her own mental image whenever H-D is brought up. Except for maybe gun control or Prohibition, nothing fosters a stronger reaction, one way, or the other. If most bikes are decaf, a Harley-Davidson is a rich, thick cappuccino. If some exhaust notes resemble elevator music, a Harley-Davidson makes a noise like the Grateful Dead. If a confab of other riders seems to be a current event, a get-together of Harley Owners Group (H.O.G.) members represents the sweep of human history. Who wouldn't want to write about something as up-front as a Harley-Davidson? Everybody knows—you don't just show up on a Harley. You arrive.

I never did pay for that fender.

Acknowledgements

With the first edition of this book in 1982, I tried mightily to thank every friend, bankrupt racer, unindicted co-conspirator, Harley-Davidson owner, corporate poobah, ex-girlfriend, and ancient seer who gave me any sort of warning or advice. This time, I'll confine the names to those who aided me with this edition.

They include: Adam at Capital City Harley-Davidson, Lonnie Anthony, Dave Arnold, Al Doerman, Pat Doerman, Jim Dricken, Werner Fritz, Dain Gingerelli, Chris Haynes, Steve Hendrickson, Susan Kennedy, Molly Koecher, Michael Lange, Carl Leiterman, Vicki Libis, John Mancuso, Linda Minash, Jo Ann Newbury, Mary Ann Thurber, Buzz Walneck, Austin Wright, Monica Wright, Jessie Wright-Minash.

David K. Wright
Summer, 2002

David K. Wright (on right) with Jessie. Besides writing the first three editions of this work, David recently wrote Great Minnesota Taverns from Trails Books. He is also a Vietnam veteran and has written several books on the Vietnam war. Jessie, to date, has no literary aspirations.

The Springer Softail, along with some other Softail models, got an upgrade in the tire department for 2003, with a larger 150mm rear tire. (Dain Gingerelli)

Chapter 1

Beginnings

The years 1903 and 2003 are similar in at least one important aspect: People in the early twentieth century continued to be amazed at the scope and importance of the Industrial Revolution, just as folks now remain dazzled by the Computer Age. It isn't difficult to think of Arthur and Walter Davidson and Bill Harley as having the same sense of adventure as today's dot-com pioneers. They and a German immigrant whose name is lost all were employees of the Barth Manufacturing Company in Milwaukee when the four decided, shortly after 1900, to build a motorcycle. They spent hours after work studying French blueprints and other designs before producing a spindly machine with a DeDion-type, single-cylinder engine.

The three-horsepower motor compressed and detonated air mixed with gasoline to move a piston, a crankshaft, a chain, and a belt that resulted in power to the rear wheel.

This early photo of founders and employees proves that some very young men started Harley-Davidson. That's Bill Harley sitting with arms crossed. Behind him is Bill Davidson and behind them is Walter Davidson. Sherbie Becker, far left, and Bill Manz, left; Oscar Becker is astride the bike, with Max Kobs behind him. The two over Sherbie's shoulder are John Pfannerstill, left, and Charles Menzel. The two at right are not identified.
(William H. Davidson collection)

Ole Evinrude, who lived in the same Milwaukee neighborhood as the founders, is said to have taught them how to make a carburetor work. (Outboard Marine Corporation)

The four founders with three unidentified employees in 1910. Walter is second from left, Arthur is in the middle, William A. is second from right, and William Harley is at right. (William H. Davidson collection)

These were shade-tree mechanics; though barely out of their teens, they could figure out how things worked. They were savvy enough to find friends who could machine or fabricate the parts they could envision, but did not have the equipment to make themselves, when production began in the Davidson parents' garage.

That 1903 cycle was painted gloss black, as were two identical machines that the Davidsons and Harley managed to construct—and sell—the following year. Aunt Jane Davidson hand-applied red striping and created the original "Harley Davidson Motor Company" logo seen on the fuel tanks. The initial bike not only looked good, it had several things going for it that would separate it from the many other powered cycles then under construction in garages, barns, and basements across the country.

Superior Design

Perhaps through luck, the Davidsons and Harley had hit upon internal dimensions that proved reliable, if not very quick, the first time the engine was produced. Bill Harley realized that the spidery bicycle frame would soon be obso-

lete, so he designed a loop frame that eliminated many of the stresses to which diamond-shaped frames were subjected. The crucial factor, though, may have been economic: none of the three left his day job immediately to embark on a career as a motorcycle manufacturer.

Rather, they worked evenings and weekends on their creations. That accounted for the fact that the pair of bikes made in 1904 was followed by just eight machines in 1905. By 1906, 50 Harley-Davidsons were made and quickly sold. One man (neither a Harley nor a Davidson) was hired to work in the 10-by-15-foot shed bearing the Harley-Davidson Motor Company name. The Davidsons' father, a cabinetmaker who must have been confident of their future, built that structure for the young men. The hum of machinery echoed daily from the Davidson back yard at 38th Street and Highland Boulevard, on land now owned by the Miller Brewing Company. Among local residents was Ole Evinrude, who was working on a reliable marine engine and who imparted to Harley and the Davidsons vital carburetor knowledge.

Joined by the eldest Davidson brother, William A., the four filed incorporation papers after constructing approximately 150 machines in 1907. Walter was transformed from machinist to president, Bill Harley from draftsman to chief engineer, Arthur from patternmaker to secretary and general sales manager, and latecomer William ceased being a railroad tool room foreman for the superior title of works manager.

Bill Harley decided at this time to pursue a degree in automotive engineering at the University of Wisconsin and left for Madison, 75 miles west. The three Davidsons, living modestly in flats near their work, put in long, grimy hours in the shed. Arthur and Walter, still bachelors, lived with their parents, keeping the proceeds from sales of cycles in a large jar in a medicine cabinet. Their mother, appalled at the oil and grease they tracked in each night, hired a maid to clean up after them. Unfortunately, the maid learned where the company treasury was stored. Somehow, her repeated trips to the jar did not cause the company to founder.

Some 450 Harley-Davidsons were built to run America's rutted roads in 1908. Eighteen people were employed and a 2,380-square-foot brick building was erected for production purposes. The late William H. Davidson, president of the company from 1942 to 1971 and son of William A., remembers his father putting machinery in place and starting production as soon as the cement was dry on the just-poured floor of an H-D factory. Production grew every year but one through 1920, when 28,189 cycles were delivered to a network of domestic and foreign dealers recruited largely by Arthur Davidson.

Just 13 years after incorporation, sales had increased 5,000 percent! What kind of men could parlay a shed, borrowed tools, and some metal into the largest motorcycle company in existence at the time? They were conservative, as their 1908 letterhead indicated: The company hedged its bets by offering not only motorcycles but such items as "automatic float feed carburetors, marine motors, and reversible propellers." Merely attaching labels such as practical or industrious doesn't do these very human people justice.

Arthur Davidson

Arthur Davidson, originally a pattern maker, was the most outgoing of the four founders. A small man, he served Harley-Davidson as secretary and general sales manager until his death in an automobile accident in 1950. His biggest contribution to the company, besides working with Bill

Author Steven Wright owns this very early twin. (David K. Wright)

Harley to build the first motorcycle, was to recruit a nationwide dealer network. Beginning in the northeast around 1910, Arthur persuaded a number of persons to become H-D dealers at a time when the company's sole claim to fame was Walter Davidson's 1908 victory in a nationally sanctioned endurance run in New York.

A very early single, from about 1912, is displayed at a recent Antique Motorcycle Club of America meet. (David K. Wright)

A good storyteller, Arthur took a strict approach to his job only when absolutely necessary. He and brother Walter were able riders, but his first love may have been the out-of-doors. In later years, he became a gentleman farmer in Waukesha County, west of Milwaukee, raising prize Guernsey cattle. Ironically, some of his best stock came from the Hendee farm in Massachusetts, owned by a founder of the Indian Motocycle Company. He contributed time and money to the Boy Scouts, establishing a trust fund and donating land for a camp. He was also interested in and gave money to a local home for the blind.

Arthur was usually charitable to his dealers, too. "A Harley-Davidson dealer must make money," he stated repeatedly in meetings with dealers and factory personnel alike. Former H-D President William H. Davidson said

William S. Harley on the cycle, William A. Davidson in the sidecar, on a trip through New England in the early 1920s. They crashed the rig on a steep, freshly oiled gravel road. Harley gashed his head and Davidson suffered a broken kneecap. (William H. Davidson collection)

Arthur firmly believed that the well being of dealers was crucial to the success of the company. Arthur also believed the American Motorcyclist Association (AMA) was important to the company, and so became a pillar of that organization. "We didn't do it (assume control of the AMA in the early days) because we wanted to," according to William H. "We did it because there was no one else around." Ever the salesman, Arthur was instrumental in signing dealers as far away as Australia and New Zealand while he recruited corporate members in the U.S. for the AMA. "Look, you make our castings, we want your support." That, said William H., was Arthur's approach when all else failed.

Following World War II, he spent an increasing amount of time on his farm. A visitor recalls the satisfaction Arthur could not conceal as he ducked through a fence, walked up to the largest bull in his herd of cattle, and, grabbing it by the nose ring, led it like a puppy around the barnyard. The zest he showed for life ended on the evening of December 30, 1950, when he and his wife were killed in a two-car crash in Milwaukee. Arthur was 69 years old. Like his brothers and Bill Harley, he remained active in the company until his death. He could not know that his son James, and James's wife, also would lose their lives in an automobile accident, in 1966.

William S. Harley

If there is one photo in the Harley-Davidson archives that reveals Bill Harley, it is the picture showing him with William A. Davidson after a day of fishing. Harley is at the helm of the motorcycle, with William A. in the sidecar. The two had just returned, on this summer day, from a successful trip, as the pike draped over the sidecar indicate. In addition to being a highly skilled rider, Bill Harley was an outdoorsman of the first rank. A draftsman at the time he and Arthur Davidson produced the first bike, Harley served as the company's chief engineer and treasurer until his death from heart failure on September 18, 1943. He may have enjoyed hunting, fishing, and golf even more than motorcycling. The sole college graduate among the four founders, he was prevented from much recreation until well into the 1920s, after company growth stabilized. While he had many friends, he preferred the solitary sports that would take him into the pine- and birch-studded Wisconsin lake country.

Walter Davidson and an early single, similar to the model he used to win a New York endurance run in 1908. His performance in that event boosted H-D's early reputation.
(William H. Davidson collection)

Bill Harley earned his recreation, having started work at the age of 15 in a Milwaukee bicycle factory. He ran some of the first Harley-Davidson motorcycles in endurance contests, finishing consistently and well. More important, his talent as an engineer resulted in many of the classic H-D models introduced during his tenure. In both world wars, Harley was responsible for contact between the factory and the War Department. He had the foresight in 1939 to realize that war was inevitable; prototype H-Ds were in the hands of the military at Fort Knox, Kentucky, more than a year before Pearl Harbor. It is a tribute to him that the H-D 45-ci bike needed only a crankcase plate and extended forks to become virtually indestructible in the hands of GIs fighting from Germany to Japan.

Despite his work with the military, he found time to retreat to the woodlands. He purchased a Leica 35 mm camera, mounted it on a gunstock, and stalked ducks and other birds, pulling the trigger and capturing them on film. After examining his prints, Harley would sketch the birds and other animals he had seen and photographed. His interpretations of wildlife etched on copper often were given to his friends. Harley continued to play a vigorous game of handball and participate in AMA activities until his death. He died before he could know that his efforts on behalf of the military contributed to the successful outcome of the Second World War.

Walter Davidson, Sr.

Harley-Davidson's first president probably was not aware of his future when he crawled from beneath a locomotive in Parsons, Kansas, to receive a letter from Arthur inviting him to ride a new motorcycle. Walter was headed for Milwaukee anyway, to attend elder brother William's wedding, so he looked forward to the bike ride. On arrival in the Brew City, he discovered that the cycle was in pieces and that brother Arthur and Bill Harley had hoped he would precede his ride by putting the machine together. That delayed, probably shaky ride changed his life, fascinating him in two ways: As a machinist, he appreciated the close tolerances of the small, DeDion-type engine, and he quickly discovered that he was a natural rider. Walter went

William A. Davidson, left, and William S. Harley mope following poor results at the 300-mile road race in Dodge City, Kansas, in 1914. The factory was winning consistently by the following year. (William H. Davidson collection)

immediately to the Chicago, Milwaukee & St. Paul Railroad and secured a machinist's post so that he could assist Arthur and Bill Harley with their hobby.

"Harley-Davidson was his life," said William H. Without formal business training of any kind, Walter grew with his title. He was extremely generous, giving disproportionately to charity, but his honesty was almost excessive. At a business luncheon once, in a swank New York hotel, Walter looked at the tab, deducted his own meal, and listed as a business expense only the meals consumed by his fellow diners. Hank Syvertson, who ran the H-D racing department in the 1930s, once wanted to ride to an assignment in Los Angeles aboard the luxurious Super Chief train. Walter examined railroad rates and then informed Syvertson he was welcome aboard—if the extra $12 came out of Syvertson's own pocket.

Toward the end of his life, Walter became broadly recognized for his business ability. He was a trustee of Milwaukee's highly successful Northwestern Mutual Insurance Company and a director of First Wisconsin, the state's largest bank. He died at the helm of Harley-Davidson on February 7, 1942, at the age of 65. While he will be remembered as the first president of H-D, his 1908 win in that New York endurance run may have been his most important contribution. Many believe his perfect score on one of only three H-Ds entered put the motorcycle on the map.

William A. Davidson

If Walter was the head of the company, William was the heart. A rider only briefly, he quit a responsible job as a Milwaukee Road railroad toolmaker and foreman to join his younger brothers and Bill Harley. A family man at the time, William became works manager in a motorcycle company during a decade when even the automobile industry was considered a question mark. He purchased the presses and other machines necessary to meet production needs that increased at a bewildering rate.

His employees called him "Old Bill," and he apparently relished his paternal role. One of his numerous pockets held a small black notebook filled with the names of employees who borrowed money from him "just till payday." He seldom collected any of the debts from the lengthy list of machinists, tool-and-die makers, welders, and assemblers. A large man who enjoyed hunting and fishing, he liked to tell employees and visitors alike "my office door is always open." However, anyone who took too much of his time was aimed toward a barrel of peanuts and told to "help yourself on the way out."

The fatherly feeling William possessed was tested on April 19, 1937, when Harley-Davidson and its employees signed the first union contract. William H. believed that the fight to keep out the union, and the subsequent defeat his father took personally, hastened his death, though William A. was afflicted with diabetes. Known among fellow founders and the Davidson and Harley families as an employee's friend, William A. Davidson died at the age of 66, two days after signing the agreement admitting a union to his shop.

Major Shareholders

Incorporation papers, filed on September 17, 1907, indicate that Walter was the largest shareholder, followed by Arthur. Bill Harley and Bill Davidson were third, perhaps because Harley was spending most of his money on education and Davidson had a family to support. Davidson's sister, Elizabeth, was an early investor and ended up with a sizeable share of the fledgling corporation.

Bill Harley returned to Milwaukee during his studies long enough to design H-Ds first twin, in 1909. His concept was light on theory and heavy on practicality: He grafted a second cylinder onto a single-cylinder engine, and then modified the lower end to withstand the added power. In 1912, Harley created the first commercially successful motorcycle clutch, a rear-hub, free-wheel unit. In 1914, he introduced the "step-starter," which allowed a machine to be kicked over by pushing either foot pedal. New that same year were an internal expanding rear brake, a carburetor choke, and a two-speed transmission. In 1915, a three-speed transmission was offered.

While Harley and fellow engineers were at work, the Davidsons were taking care of other facets of the business. Walter studied heat-treating and taught it to employees, William mastered oxy-acetylene welding and passed it on, and Arthur learned advertising techniques while he recruited dealers. Such efforts were needed because there were an estimated 150 cyclemakers in the U.S. alone during the second decade of the twentieth century.

The physical plant continued to grow, with 297,110 square feet devoted to manufacturing, staffed by 1,574 employees—just ten years after the first H-D was assembled. The founders were so pressed to expand that they once built a 2,400-square-foot brick structure, only to raze it six months later to make room for a larger building.

During the early years, the company relied heavily on two Milwaukee financial institutions, Marshall and Ilsley (M&I) Bank and First Wisconsin National Bank. The firm's first commercial loan originated at M&I, which maintained a close relationship with H-D until Harley-Davidson's acquisition by American Machine and Foundry (AMF) in 1969. When World War I orders for motorcycles came in, M&I provided crucial dollars that helped make Harley-Davidson the world's largest motorcycle company by 1918.

Everything the Milwaukee cyclemakers touched seemed to turn to gold. Therefore, they introduced sidecars and other motorcycle accessories, which sold well, and bicycles, which did not. "Motorcycles and bicycles appeal to two different customers," said William H. Davidson, pointing out that the dealers were so busy offering motorcycles that they let the nine different bicycle models, introduced in 1917 and produced for H-D by the Davis Sewing Machine Company, gather dust. To accommodate the ravenous public appetite for their motorized products in the late 1910s, the founders leased warehouse and production space wherever it was available. Prohibition dealt a nasty blow to Milwaukee because it forced the major breweries to close; Harley-Davidson quickly leased idle facilities at the Pabst Brewing Company to house parts.

Early twins, early singles. The first H-D twin was produced late in 1907 but could not be made to run well with its suction valves. Mechanical valves on the 1911 and ensuing models solved the problem. (William H. Davidson collection)

The Harley-Davidson endurance team; date and place unknown. The rider at far right is Lacy Crolius, the company's first advertising director. Next to him is Walter Davidson. (William H. Davidson collection)

Victory followed victory on dusty racetracks at places such as Dodge City, Kansas, and Marion, Indiana, and even in the halls of Washington, D. C., where H-D led a successful fight for approval of sidecars for use by rural letter carriers. Not even Yellowstone National Park was safe from Harley-Davidsons: The Department of the Interior purchased H-Ds to patrol its vast facility in northwest Wyoming. While the racetrack successes were to continue, the economic trophies would temporarily tarnish.

A brief but severe depression occurred worldwide beginning late in 1920. Walter Davidson, addressing a national dealer meeting in the fall of that year, correctly attributed the economic stagger to readjustment following a post-World War I boom. The nation and the world recovered gradually in 1922, enjoying more prosperity than would be known for the next seven years. Unfortunately, the motorcycle industry did not fully share in the good times. Henry Ford had his Dearborn, Michigan, assembly line in high gear by 1920. Paying premium wages, he was able to produce a reliable automobile for as little as $245, a price that compared very favorably to the two-wheelers.

Cars Versus Cycles

Harley-Davidson sales reflected the fact that many increasingly affluent Americans were turning their backs on motorcycles. The 1920 model year saw H-D produce 28,189 motorcycles. The recession of the next year saw only 10,202 come off the Juneau Avenue assembly line. The economy soared, but cycle sales did not. Harley-Davidson's best sales year during the 1920s was 1926, when 23,354 bikes were sold. The company would not exceed 1920 sales figures until 1942. Meanwhile, few houses were being built without garages, because everyone was acquiring a car.

The decision to drop factory support of racing after the 1921 season was only in part economic. Throughout its history, Harley-Davidson's attitude toward competition has swung from one extreme to the other. As early as 1913, Arthur Davidson was using racing results in sales literature, despite descriptions of cycle racing gore in the daily papers. During the period 1914–1921, H-D assembled a group of supremely talented riders who swept most of the significant events. "The Wrecking Crew," as it was known, altered Harley-Davidson's reputation from reliable and slow to reliable and virtually invincible. To the credit of the factory, when it did go racing the factory provided a lot of support.

William H. Davidson remembers being put on a train at age 14 in 1920 with just-produced cams clattering in his suitcase. He was to deliver said cams to racer Jim Davis in time for the 300-mile road race in Dodge City, Kansas. Cams in place, Davis provided H-D with its fifth consecutive Dodge City win. That same year, Otto Walker mounted his Harley and became the first rider ever to exceed 100 mph in competition. Walker's achievement was a fitting finale to racing for the time being.

A source of strength during the 1910s and 1920s was the acceptance of Harley-Davidson models overseas. By 1921, H-D dealers were in 67 countries, a figure not equaled since. The following year, export brochures were printed in seven languages: Danish, Dutch, English, French, Italian, Spanish, and Swedish. As early as 1913, the company produced catalogs and owner's manuals for "Los Entusiastas Latinos." By 1920, there were dozens of South American dealers. *The Enthusiast* magazine, an official publication, began in 1916 and was briefly offered in Spanish. Even earlier, matching "Factory Facts" flyers were created for the U.S. and Canada, the

Douglas Watson, son of English distributor Sir Duncan Watson, sat on the H-D board until a short but severe depression in the early 1920s. Harley-Davidson exported as many as one bike in three before the Great Depression.
(William H. Davidson collection)

The four founders. From left are Arthur Davidson, Walter Davidson, William S. Harley, and William A. Davidson. This photo was taken in 1915. Note that the fellows were still quite young, though they had been making H-Ds for more than a decade.
(William H. Davidson collection)

only difference being in the price of the bikes. The 1913 Model 9-E, for example, was $285 fob Milwaukee and $350 fob Milwaukee if shipped to a Canadian buyer.

In 1919, Englishman Duncan Watson was selected as the H-D distributor, and was made a company director. Despite the fact that cycles outnumbered cars in the United Kingdom at the time, Watson was forced to relinquish his distributorship just four years later because of a new 33 percent British import tariff. To meet the European riders' hunger for big V-twins, firms such as Italy's Anzani and Britain's JAP created H-D look-alikes. Throughout the 1920s, accounts of races, brave deeds, and tours of faraway places poured into *The Enthusiast* offices and were reported to readers.

Experimental Bikes

Never reported during this time were the workings of the research and development (R&D) department. Less active following the 1920–1921 recession, R&D employees nevertheless constructed—and then destroyed, without so much as taking a photo—everything from a V-4 to variations on the V-twin theme. Four-cylinder Hendersons, popular at the time with police, interested H-D enough to explore a de-

A Harley-Davidson bicycle, in original condition. These bikes were offered from 1918 to 1924 and were made for H-D by the Davis Sewing Machine Company. (David K. Wright)

sign, but not enough to tool up for such an in-line machine. No sooner was one lightweight phased out than another was conceived, constructed by hand, tested, then assembled in quantity.

Less exotic experiments involved sidecars. Produced by the factory and for Harley-Davidson by the Seaman Body Company (later a part of Nash Motors), sidecars were seen as the answer to all sorts of pickup and delivery problems. They were created with bodies in the shape of cameras, shoes, sheds, and more, not as jokes but to fit the needs of different kinds of businesses. Again, the inventiveness displayed by the H-D developers was thwarted by the rock-bottom price of automobiles. R&D people have always come in handy, however. During the 1930s, when National Screw Company in Cleveland was hit by a strike, Harley-Davidson engineers quickly devised machines that would pump out the spokes for wheels formerly supplied by the struck company.

In the 1920s, and well into the 1930s, for that matter, Harley-Davidson passed up annual cosmetic changes, preferring instead to refine the product. An illustration of this emphasis can be found in the electrical system. Before World War I, H-D installed Bosch electrical equipment, known for its reliability. However, the German-designed units were replaced with U.S.-made Remy parts after war was declared. Dissatisfied with Remy, Harley-Davidson engineers created ignition coils that were the envy not only of the motorcycle industry, but of automakers, as well. The increasing reliability of H-Ds made up for the fact that the same olive-drab color scheme, with striping variations, was used on machines produced from 1918 through 1932.

Meanwhile, consumers with experimental blood in their veins were using Harley-Davidson motors in other ways. A fellow by the name of Harvey Mummert constructed a light plywood airplane powered by an 18-horsepower H-D motor and bravely entered it in the first national air races, over Dayton, Ohio, in 1924. He won the speed and efficiency contests in spite of one forced landing. None of his competitors finished the races, local news accounts reported; their motors quit, both on the ground and in the air. Less than a decade later, in 1932, Fawcett Publications' *Flying and Glider Manual* showed plans for building a propeller for a Harley-Davidson 74-ci engine. Designed to power an iceboat, the motor was one of six (others included the Indian Chief, the

A two-cam racer from the 1920s. (David K. Wright)

Lawrence 28, and the Heath Henderson) deemed suitable for a hydroglider. However, the most popular use of H-D on water or in the air proved to be the Harlequin airplane.

Several hundred Harlequin-powered light planes took to the skies in the mid-1930s, sporting a horizontally opposed, two-cylinder engine that used cylinder jugs from an H-D 74-ci engine. According to the 1933 edition of the Fawcett manual, the H-D parts were "noted for long life and are low priced and available. The valves are large and the valve chamber allows the best cooling possible to obtain in any design." The motor weighed 90 pounds and delivered 30 horsepower. Total cost to power a light plane was "way below $100." Before the introduction of light, four-cylinder engines by Cessna and others, home-built Harlequins could be found in hangars across the country.

Classic Cycles

Harley-Davidson produced a number of truly classic machines during the 1920s. The very first 74-ci model, the JD, came out in 1921. The for-and-aft, horizontally opposed, 37-ci Sport Twin, introduced in 1919, hung on into the early 1920s, and was well received overseas. Especially desirable in the U.S. were the two-cam 61-ci and 74-ci road bikes of 1928 and 1929, developed from successful board-track racing ma-

chines and capable of outrunning anything street legal, on two wheels or four. Also highly regarded was any H-D single produced at the time. Significant models included the 21-ci side valve and overhead valve singles, offered from 1926 into the early 1930s, and the "Peashooter," the racing version of the overhead valve motor. The latter became a force on English, Australian, and New Zealand speedway tracks and even competed successfully in the U.S. in hillclimb events—against machines with more than twice the displacement.

Due in large part to the appeal of the smaller displacement Sport Twin and the magneto- or coil-equipped singles, sales in foreign lands accounted for much of Harley-Davidson's revenue. Of 13,942 machines produced in 1924, for example, 6,194 were exported. Another important source of income was the sidecar; 3,257 were sold in 1924, or approximately one for every two of the V-twins created that year. An Indiana dealer at the time reported annual sales of 41 V-twins; 40 were sidecar-equipped. To make acquisition of a bike easier, the company formed a financing company in 1923 that evolved into Kilbourn Finance Corporation, an important H-D subsidiary that exists today as a dealer resource. Not even easy payments helped in 1924, however: H-D stockholders learned of the company's $119,143 loss, the only negative year before the Great Depression.

"The real beginning of our decline in this country," according to President Walter Davidson, addressing the board

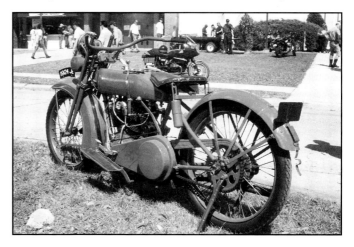

A 1924 Model JE 61-ci V-twin. (David K. Wright)

William H. Davidson aboard the first 1930 Big Twin off the assembly line. This model, the VL, suffered mechanical woes that took a year to remedy. Davidson, to his credit, rode this bike from Milwaukee to Denver and back. (William H. Davidson collection)

of directors in 1927, "began several years ago when we found it difficult to secure new dealers in territories where our old dealer either quit or for some reason had the agency taken away from him." To recruit new dealers, the company ran advertisements not only in *The Enthusiast* but also in such high-buck national magazines as *The Saturday Evening Post*. Prior to the *Post* ads, national exposure was confined largely to mechanically oriented monthlies and to bicycle-motorcycle magazines. From the start, H-D provided its dealers with a variety of in-store signs and other trinkets. Because Milwaukee is a center for quality printing, the banners, posters, and so on sent to dealers as early as the mid-1910s had a consistently professional look.

In addition to recruiting dealers (for as little as $1,200 seed money to open a shop in Clarksburg, West Virginia, for example), H-D endorsed the American Motorcyclist Association (AMA) as a means of maintaining public interest. Walter Davidson joined Louis Bauer of Indian and Frank Schwinn of Excelsior in 1928 to retrieve the AMA from a deficit position. That backing, primarily by Harley-Davidson, led to a solid

(and very rigid) race sanctioning, lobbying, and social organization. The AMA joined H-D dealers throughout the period in putting together annual Memorial Day weekend gypsy tours and other cycle-oriented events.

Dealers did not have much leeway in their relations with the factory, as a 1925 contract signed by Walter Davidson and Emil Schott of Lewiston, Maine, attests. While Schott, who ordered 15 bikes and 6 sidecars for the 1926 model year, could not sell outside his assigned territory, the contract was "not to be construed as granting . . . exclusive sale of Harley-Davidson Motorcycles in the territory herein described." In addition, a part of the pact was this reminder: "The dealer agrees not to sell imitation component parts … and will not use imitation component parts in repairing Harley-Davidson Motorcycles and Parcelcars."

The 1920s also saw the second generation of Harleys and Davidsons join the company. William H. Davidson came aboard in 1928 after completing work for his degree at the University of Wisconsin. He learned the business by starting out in the factory and was followed in the next few years by

Gordon Davidson in sales and by William J. Harley and Walter Davidson, both of whom were assigned initially to the shop. John Harley, brother of William J., began work in the office. The Davidsons, through birth, marriage, and death, greatly outnumbered the Harleys on the stockholder rolls. Seventeen Davidsons, versus just three Harleys, held stock at the eve of World War II.

1920's Progress

Mechanical and styling advances continued throughout the 1920s. Balloon tires, front brakes, streamlined gas tanks, Alemite lubrication, the beginning of parts standardization,

greatly improved metallurgy, and related steps forward, made H-D riders forget about oil on pant legs from the total-loss system. Theodore A. Hodgdon, Jr., whose father was one of the guiding lights of the Indian Motocycle Company, portrays this period quite accurately.

"It is not generally remembered today," Hodgdon said, "but of the hundreds of U.S. cycles during the 1910s, 1920s, and 1930s, only a handful were worth their weight in scrap. Unreliability and simply shoddy workmanship were the norms of the period. It was rare for most makes to exceed 5,000 miles in actual service before some catastrophic failure prematurely retired them. The buyer of an Indian or a Harley-Davidson did not generally suffer these indignities,

William J. Harley, foreground, and William H. Davidson, in the sidecar, meet (from left) Allan, Gordon, and Walter C. Davidson following a trip by the latter three from Milwaukee to the Pacific Northwest and return in 1929. The trio rode 45-ci bikes; Harley and William have chosen a 74-ci VL. (William H. Davidson collection)

and could expect his mount to perform as advertised. In addition, extensive dealership networks enabled him to ride anywhere, anytime, with reasonable confidence that he might return on the same machine that he started out on." With these comments in mind, it is easy to see how the 1920s rider might buy an off brand and become permanently disillusioned with motorcycling.

Neither disillusionment nor despair but rather indignation was the emotion felt by Harley-Davidson principals in February 1929, when a federal judge ruled that H-D owed the Eclipse Machine Company of Elmira, New York, $1.1 million for three patent infringements. Eclipse, formerly a bicycle manufacturer, had perfected and patented the design for a very sound motorcycle transmission component. The suit, filed in 1924, dragged on in various courts for five years. Harley-Davidson, following approval in a lower court, continued installation of the clutch-actuating device in question until the final judgment was received. Fortunately, 1929 model year sales of 20,946 motorcycles resulted in sufficient revenue to pay off the New York firm and still turn a profit. However, the infringement can now be seen as a hint of things to come, not only for Harley-Davidson but also for the whole, Depression-ridden world.

The 1930 models had been unveiled less than two months when the stock market plummeted in the autumn of 1929. Oddly, sales did not suffer markedly that first year, slipping only to 17,662 units. Much of the decrease was due to the further decline in popularity of single-cylinder machines, which dropped from 3,882 units to 1,989. The big twins were only negligibly less popular, going at the rates of 10,842 in 1929 and 10,727 in 1930. A precipitous skid occurred the following year, as the economy continued its decline: 10,500 cycles rolled out of Juneau Avenue, and of those 3,831 went overseas.

1930's Despair

"We may be able to keep you on until spring," William A. Davidson told employees in the fall of 1930. As works manager, it was his unpleasant duty to lay off not only hourly employees but foremen as well. Those fortunate enough to stay on gladly accepted a 10 percent pay cut in November 1930. Gross revenues during the period 1930–1932 slid from $6,562,000 to $4,173,000 to $2,389,000. Sales in 1932 totaled just 6,841 cycles, of which 1,974 were exported. In other words, only 4,867 new H-Ds were purchased in the entire U.S. in 1932. Board meeting minutes tell of extended, serious talks about whether Harley-Davidson should remain in business.

Not willing to throw in the towel, the Harleys and the Davidsons emphasized sales to police departments (more than 2,900 state and local departments were riding Harleys at the start of the Depression), personally won races (William H. Davidson, wearing a tie and boots, won Michigan's Jack Pine Enduro in 1930), and devised new

President Walter Davidson, with young William H., tries on the CAC cinder-track racer at a New York auto show in late 1933 or early 1934. No more than a dozen of these highly specialized bikes were sold. (William H. Davidson collection)

The founders size up the first 61-ci overhead valve E, which first rolled off the assembly line for the 1936 model year. This bike became known to H-D enthusiasts as the Knucklehead. Harley-Davidson's major rival, Indian, made nothing that could compete with the overhead valve 61- and 74-ci Harleys. They were produced with few changes through 1947. (William H. Davidson collection)

ways to sell. The latter involved creation in 1931 of coupon books for H-D riders. The enthusiasts were to jot down prospects and give them to dealers. If the tip led to a sale, the coupon provider earned points. Two sales garnered the rider a bronze medal, four sales meant silver, and eight sales meant gold. Anyone who snagged eight sales for his dealer also received $500 in cash from the factory and a commission on each sale. It was a sign of the times that just one person earned gold.

Sales in 1933 were 3,703 bikes, the lowest since 1910. It is a credit to the company that it turned a slight profit that year. Through all of it, there was one bright spot, a spot that moved hurriedly and consistently to the front. That spot was Joe Petrali. The slightly built Californian provided the factory with a morale booster by winning virtually every board-track, dirt-track, and hillclimb event he entered for more than a decade. A quiet man who would not give an inch in a race, Petrali also was a technical conduit, telling William S. Harley and his engineers what worked and what did not.

Petrali's input was one of the reasons the H-Ds from the Knucklehead on (1936–1947) were state of the art.

Petrali capped a brilliant career by running one of the new 1936 61-ci V-twins to a speed of 136.183 mph on the sands of Daytona Beach. Fewer than 100,000 cycles were registered in the U.S. at one point in the 1930s, but Petrali's victories played a part in making Harley-Davidson a two-to-one choice over Indian, the only other U.S. cycle company still in business. By 1935, Indian was reduced to making 3,000 coaster wagons under subcontract to the Fisk Tire and Rubber Company.

Harley-Davidson looked for subcontract work, too, but without much success. One source of income from 1933 through 1937 was a licensing agreement arranged by one of its overseas representatives, Alfred Child. Child and a Japanese businessman signed a contract late in 1932 that turned over blueprints for current H-D models to a Japanese consortium. The factory received $3,000 for the prints in 1933, followed by sums of $5,000, $8,000, and $10,000 in 1934, 1935,

This shapely tank is from the 1931 model year, the first affected by the Depression. Economic hard times hung on, and paint and decals became more stylized, as the company tried hard to attract buyers. (David K. Wright)

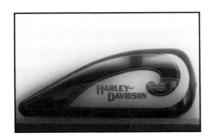

Compare the paint job on this 1932 tank with the 1931, at left. Although the company eased away from the olive drab for 1931, nothing offered that year approached the 1932 scrollwork. (David K. Wright)

A 1933 model year gas tank. There were no stylists per se at the factory at the time, but there were people who knew what looked good on a bike. (David K. Wright)

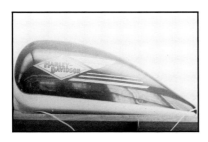

The early stages of Art Deco design can be seen on this 1934 model year tank. Paint quality and careful application have been Harley-Davidson selling points through the years. (David K. Wright)

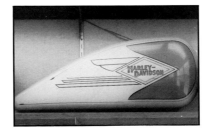

A 1935 tank. Beginning with the 1933 models, the V-series and 45-ci Harley-Davidsons took on beautifully stylized tanks and color schemes. (David K. Wright)

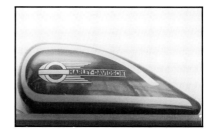

This tank, from 1936, sat atop the big flathead motors. The decal is considered a classic, a variation on a theme used throughout the mid-1930s. (David K. Wright)

and 1936, respectively. Precision machinery, idled by the lack of orders, also was sold to the Asian concern, which created two- and three-wheelers under the Rikuo nameplate. President Walter Davidson grumbled over what he believed to be a real steal by the Japanese, but conceded that H-D would have lost the market anyway due to an unfavorable exchange rate. In all, the factory received $32,320 for tools, dies, and machines sold to Child and his Japanese friend. The money was put to good use, no doubt, since in November 1933 Walter observed the "complete collapse of the [U.S.] banking system." Equally auspicious, the deal with the Japanese helped turn that nation on to motorcycles.

Fewer than 300 motorcycle clubs existed in the country in the early 1930s. In some parts of the U.S. it was difficult to find any kind of organized group of riders whatsoever thanks to the declining popularity of motorcycles, caused primarily by lack of money. Those who were in clubs became increasingly a subculture, wearing clothing available only from a motorcycle dealer. The mid-1930s rider, done up in cycling attire, appeared to be wearing all of the worst features seen on equestrians, police, delivery boys, and bellhops. Harley-Davidson parts and accessories catalogs offered a wide selection of clothing and accessories. It's only a slight exaggeration to state that clothing and various extras offered through H-D dealers helped many dealers survive the Depression.

Low Profits, Low Prices

While the company realized $373,000 net profit in 1934, $300,354 in 1935, and $381,227 in 1936, prices were very low on a new bike. The profit margins for garb, add-ons, and parts, however, have always contributed a higher percentage than have the cycles. Production during the 1934–1936 period totaled 10,231, 10,368, and 9,812, respectively. Since low inventory was next to godliness with the conservative Davidsons, the factory produced no more cycles each year than it could sell. Many years later, lack of inventory would prove a problem.

A larger problem surfaced on March 11, 1937, when nine employees asked to represent H-D wage earners under the banner of the United Auto Workers. Taking their cue from historic auto industry organizing, Harley-Davidson employees realized that the Depression was gradually lessening and that the company would survive. Neither H-D nor most other major manufacturers in Milwaukee had a sweatshop reputation; the hourly employees sought job security and more say in such matters as safety, working conditions, vacations, and compensation. Company officers were so unfamiliar with unionism initially that they failed to understand the employees' request. It became immediately evident in the form of a demand for a union election. Once organized, the wage earners sought and received 45 cents per hour for women, 60 cents per hour for men, and a week of paid vacation each year. Today, four labor unions represent various skills and jobs.

During this period, working with a minimum of capital, H-D managed to create several exciting models. In 1936, the 61–ci overhead valve model was introduced. It featured a circulating pressure oil system that was seen the following year on the 45-ci models and on the 74- and 80-ci side-valve cycles, plus a new and improved four-speed gearbox. The big 1937s all featured full roller bearing motors, chrome molybdenum tubular front forks, complete instrument panels, and interchangeable wheels. The results were encouraging: 1937 sales hit 11,674 units, the most since the Depression set in. Many longtime Harley-Davidson fans believe the mid-1930s bikes are the best looking machines ever to come out of Milwaukee. The streamlined, teardrop tanks with their Art Deco decals blend perfectly into the rear portion of the frame running to the back axle. The 45-ci model received the full styling treatment, even though some viewed it as a utility machine. The 45, however, was about to become the star of the show.

Secure in the knowledge that this trusty solo motorcycle would fit Allied needs, William S. Harley and Walter Davidson departed for Camp Holabird, Maryland, on October 30, 1939. The military buildup had begun and Harley-Davidson was in the running to create a shaft-drive, three-wheel vehicle for sandy and mucky terrain. Also under consideration for the project were Indian and General Motors' Delco division. Delco's prototype used a BMW 750-cc flathead engine in its three-wheeler, and while cost estimates were a soaring $4,600 apiece, the merits of the German power plant impressed the military. The three-wheel project was dropped but was followed by an order for 1,000 two-wheel, shaft-drive cycles, to be built by H-D. To the credit of the factory, delivery of the last of these BMW copies was completed by July 1942, as promised.

The two Army-Navy "E" awards given to Harley-Davidson in 1943 and 1945 for supporting the war effort were due in large part to the performance of thousands of 45-ci machines, to the feeling among employees that victory over the Axis hinged on the quality of their work, and to the second generation of management. In addition to turning out a reported 88,000 cycles on which soldiers could depend during the period 1942–1945, the company performed such one-shot projects as secretly taking apart, assessing, and somehow reassembling a Russian motorcycle for Army intelligence.

New Leadership

Walter Davidson died in 1942 and William S. Harley followed just over a year later. William H. Davidson, son of works manager William A., was named president on February 23, 1942. Like the founders, there was more to him than the initial impression of a shrewd, conservative, and low-key man of intellect. This second-generation Davidson went to work for the company as a laborer in 1925, during summer off from college. He performed the most menial tasks and learned to ride well enough to capture the prized Jack Pine Enduro on a 45-ci bike in 1930.

Davidson's recollection of that event showed just how well the Harleys and the Davidsons got along. "On the final day, I had a good chance of winning," he remembered. "But the stopwatch I wore around my neck on a lanyard had hit my tank and shattered. So Bill Harley (William J., also competing on a factory bike) gave me his watch. With a working timepiece, I was able to win." That's the kind of support the two families provided one another down through the years, enabling William H. to remain at the helm of a viable company until almost 1970.

Founder Walter Davidson's two sons, Walter C. and Gordon, served in the positions of vice president/sales and vice president/manufacturing, respectively. Young Walter was instrumental during World War II in procuring raw materials that other factories could not seem to get. Never one to let strong language stand in the way of a good story, he did battle with an increasingly rebellious dealer network during the late 1940s and into the 1950s. An excellent rider and a duck-hunting fanatic, he retired when AMF took control. Gordon also had a sense of humor but was more temperate with his adjectives. He mixed easily with hourly employees and supervisors alike, and, according to at least two veteran employees, was incredibly tight with the company's money. He died of lung cancer in 1967. Founder William A. Davidson's son, Allan, briefly worked for the company but died prematurely. Arthur's son, also named Arthur, found a successful career outside the company.

The Harleys made important contributions, too. William J. Harley succeeded his father, William S., as vice president/engineering. He worked his way through the ranks to the position, acquiring riding skill in connection with his job and swimming and duck hunting abilities with the Davidsons along Wisconsin's great Mississippi River flyway. In later years, William S. became a connoisseur of wine and cheese, due in part to his frequent trips to Varese, Italy, in connection with H-D business there. Assuming the title of chief engineer immediately following his father's death, Harley was named to a vice presidency in 1957, 14 years before his death in 1971 from diabetes.

John E. Harley, younger brother of William J., successfully ran the parts and accessories division for many years. Gentle, quiet, and well liked, John's military school background propelled him into the U.S. Army during the World War II, immediately after graduation from the University of Notre Dame. He rose to the rank of major, calling upon his years as an accomplished rider to help direct training of armored division motorcyclists at Fort Knox, Kentucky, and Fort Benning, Georgia. Like his brother and the Davidsons, John was a member of H-D's board of directors. Ironically, he was never an officer in the company. A golfer, sailor, and duck hunter, John died of complications caused by cancer in December 1976.

John Davidson tries on a racer while Willie G. tugs at a tooth during the 1938 Milwaukee AMA flat-track races. How many kids ever got this close to a competition Harley-Davidson? (William H. Davidson collection)

Postwar Events

Not even then-monthly copies of *The Enthusiast* were produced in October 1945 as a 40-day strike descended upon the company. The job action delayed the 1946 models until

February 6, 1946, five months later than planned. Not that the 1946 H-Ds were anything new—the familiar 45-, 61-, and 74-ci models were mechanically identical to their prewar brethren. Addressing the board of directors, President Davidson noted, "We will not be able to produce any radically new, postwar models until the beginning of 1948." Despite materials shortages that plagued the company until after the Korean War, 15,554 bikes were produced in 1946. Some 20,392 units were made in 1947, the last year of the 61- and 74-ci hemispheric combustion chamber Knuckleheads, as they were known.

Ambitious plans for new models were announced repeatedly to directors during the 1940s, but they failed to pass the prototype stage. Among them:

- A Servi-Car with the horizontally opposed XA motor and driveshaft.
- Hydraulic front forks throughout the line by 1948.
- A vertical twin with shaft drive, hydraulic forks, rear suspension, rubber-mounted handlebars, foot shift, hand clutch, and more.

The latter was a response to the introduction in some quantity of British twins, ridden by GIs who had been stationed in England. The sieve-like motors and marginal quality control of the British bikes were a tradeoff for handling that made Harley-Davidsons seem agricultural by comparison. Dealers, particularly along the West Coast, who sought to take on a line of British cycles, increasingly popular scooters, or motorbikes such as the U.S. -made Servi-Cycle, were all but terrorized by old Arthur Davidson. "If they divide their time," he told directors in 1947, ". . . we'll eventually replace them with exclusive dealers." Any thoughts concerning production of a vertical twin in Milwaukee were shelved after the experience of the Indian Motocycle Company, H-D's only remaining domestic competitor.

Indian appears to have had the same hot-and-cold fascination with middleweight bikes. The fascination eventually proved fatal. According to Ted A. Hodgdon, Jr., son of a long-time Indian executive, "Since 1930, Indian had been examining lighter English design engineering. The experimental shops at Springfield (Massachusetts) contained examples of these machines, such as Norton, Matchless, Velocette, and

Triumph. These products . . . influenced the Prince single of the 1930s. While a good enough little motorcycle, it did not sell well. It should have been a warning, but the lessons of the Prince went unheeded in Springfield." Following World War II, Indian emphasize middleweight vertical twins, with the traditional, heavyweight Indian V-twin carried only as an afterthought.

"Nearly all of the 'new' machines failed quickly and resulted in massive warranty claims," Hodgdon said. "The small displacement and fragile Arrow and Scout rewarded rough treatment by promptly reducing themselves to junk . . . Word quickly spread and diehard devotees switched their loyalties overnight. The traditional V-twins, carryovers from prewar design, were good motorcycles and enjoyed some success, but the damage had been done . . . Production on the offending designs ceased and stopgap imports were sold under the Indian name for a few years. It was not enough and the wigwam folded." An echo occurred in 1970, when Taiwanese bikes with the Indian nameplate were offered to Harley-Davidson. H-D did not seriously consider selling such cycles.

Plant Expansion

By the end of 1948, the company was installed in the former A. O. Smith propeller plant on Capitol Drive in west suburban Wauwatosa, Wisconsin. The 269,000-square-foot, single-story facility was purchased two years earlier for $1.5 million to meet anticipated demand for postwar models, such as the 1948 big twins with hydraulic lifters and the 1949 Hydra-Glide, the first Harley offered with hydraulic forks. For a couple of years in a row, the company badly misjudged public appetite for cycles; sales in 1949 totaled 23,740 units, compared to a predicted 43,250.

A year later, Harley-Davidson pointed out to the U.S. Tariff Commission that foreign cycle sales amounted to nearly 40 percent of new registrations. The company requested a 50 percent hike in the tariff on foreign makes. Joined by the United Auto Workers and by Cushman scooter executives, H-D principals argued their case in Washington, but to no avail. The commission voted four-two to allow trade to go on as before, in part because the former Japanese distributor for H-D, Alfred Child, provided damaging testimony concerning Harley-Davidson's inability to accurately gauge the domestic market or to placate its dealers. The importer of British BSA bikes at the time, Child apologized years later. "Sorry, Bill," he wrote William H. Davidson, "but my future depended on being able to carry on my business."

Other phenomena were occurring beyond the company's control. In 1947, members of a Hollister, California, fraternal organization playfully dumped a questionable liquid out a second-floor window onto a group of cyclists in town for a race. The riders overreacted, squaring off with the town toughs, then turning on anybody who was on the street. The wire services and *Life* magazine picked up the story, complete with vivid photos. That riot, immortalized in Stanley Kubrick's 1953 movie, *The Wild One*, starring Marlon Brando, made cyclists paranoid and appeared, to non-riders, to split all cyclists into two camps. One side seemed determined to improve cycling's image; its trademark was a large, full-dress touring bike. The other side struck the public as an outlaw element, riding noisy bikes in various stages of modification, ready for violent or outrageous behavior. Motorcycling needed fresh air. It blew in unexpectedly from the Far East.

The U.S. very generously primed Japan's obliterated economy after World War II. Following a period when Japanese trinkets were scorned as shoddy and in poor taste, a number of quality products were exported worldwide: cameras, tape decks, television sets—and motorcycles. The Japanese cycle invasion began innocently enough around 1960 with a 50-cc Honda: the opposite end of the spectrum from either brittle British sport bikes or rock-solid Harleys. The Asian machines found favor with housewives, students, and others who might or might not graduate to larger, faster, two-wheel transportation. When riders who wanted more were ready, so were the Japanese, producing larger, speedier, and more expensive motorcycles with each succeeding year.

Earlier, following introduction of the K model in 1952, which competed without success with the British vertical twins, Harley-Davidson was in dire economic straits. Consultants confirmed Gordon Davidson's contention that, "unless we lower the boom in very drastic fashion on every phase of our operation, we are headed for very serious trouble." Part of the problem appears to have been an unwillingness to sink a large share of the profits back into the company. Executive salaries were very low (only four com-

pany officers were paid more than $20,000 in 1950, for example), but shareholders were rewarded with dividends that frequently exceeded 10 percent of the value of the stock.

Eve of the Boom

A retired Harley-Davidson employee guessed that this was a method of keeping everybody's wages and salaries in line. "You couldn't very well ask for more money than the president of the company was making," he said. Meanwhile, a variety of possibilities was explored, including consolidating all operations in the Capitol Drive plant, then moving everything back to Juneau Avenue, diversifying into such areas as snowblowers and lawn mowers, manufacturing a motor scooter for Sears, even building air conditioning compressors. Production slid to 12,250 cycles in 1954 and to 9,550 in 1955. H-D continued to turn a modest profit throughout the 1950s before officers realized there was a bike boom— and that it was worldwide and growing.

Harley-Davidson's Post-War Models Committee, renamed the Development Committee, concluded on June 17, 1959, that the best way to introduce a middleweight motorcycle was to import. Of more consequence, the committee agreed to "give consideration to the 250-cc model motorcycles produced by the motorcycle division of Aeronautica Macchi, SpA, of Varese, Italy." The committee decided against putting Aermacchi engines in Sportster chassis, but to explore instead a joint venture with the firm.

William H. Davidson and his wife traveled to Varese in a circuitous route, visiting Europe's leading motorcycle manufacturers on the way. Following negotiations with Aeronautica Macchi (constructors during World War II of the respected Macchi fighter plane), H-D purchased half of the profitable Aermacchi cycle division for $247,209, a bargain even in those days. Financing was arranged through a Swiss bank and was expedited when a bank director confessed that he was a long-time H-D admirer. Net profits were estimated at $57,000 annually, based on the sale of 4,500 units in the 175–250-cc class and 1,000 units in the 125–150-cc class, plus spare parts.

The long-sought, in-between Harleys were introduced in September 1960 for the 1961 season. Chief Designer Wilbur Petri, whose father had run the H-D tool room from

1914 to 1944, was sent to Italy as technical consultant and administrative advisor. Promised that he would spend just two years in the picturesque village separated from Switzerland by an Alpine mountain, Petri had to plead with management to bring him back to Milwaukee in 1967. During his tenure, he confronted electrical systems that never lived up to expectations and the complications of fitting U.S. handlebars, grips, levers, and cables to the machines. With the company for 43 years, the mechanical engineer believed in the Aermacchi line. Despite his trials, Petri believed the bikes to be "well designed."

The Italian bikes failed in this country for several reasons. Petri noted that the machines became dated in comparison to their Japanese competitors. Harley-Davidson's answer was to put more on the midweight bikes without raising prices. The result was that no one made any money from a sale. In fact, dealers were as responsible as anyone for the demise of Aermacchi. They didn't care much for the switch to two-stroke motors, and they found it more profitable to steer a prospect from a smaller to a larger bike. Petri asked rhetorically, "Would you rather sell a bike that nets $400 or $1,000?" John A. Davidson, son of William H. and the president of the company at the time, announced on June 14, 1978, the closing of the lakeside plant near Varese.

These are the post-World War II single-cylinder 125-cc two-strokes on the assembly line in late 1947. Like the English BSA Bantam, this model was copied from a German DKW cycle. (William H. Davidson collection)

Going Public

Meanwhile, momentous events were taking place in Milwaukee and beyond. The first baby boomers had, by 1965, reached the age of 19—a point at which many post-high school kids might acquire their first motorcycle. Demand for bikes of all kinds began to grow, aided by an economy that kept cooking, in part because of events in the Republic of Vietnam. At Harley-Davidson, company stock that once was held by a few Davidsons and Harleys was now in the hands of 326 individuals. To pay off these individuals, who might have had different interests, and to create investment capital for the coming cycle boom, the directors made their first public stock offering in 1965.

Several chances to buy H-D stock took place during the period 1965–1969, with more than 1.3 million shares ultimately made available. The company looked like a good investment, despite the fact that Harley-Davidson had just 12–16 percent of the total motorcycle market: Accessories were blossoming, riders queued up with money in hand at the dealerships, and H-D had a reputation for being soundly managed. In addition to attracting individual investors, the company was noticed by such firms as AMF, Bangor Punta, Chrysler, International Harvester, and White Motor. These and other corporations made at least informal inquiries about purchasing the company—lock, stock, and barrel. All were politely turned down.

Harley-Davidson could do very little about sales of foreign bikes, but for several years was able to prevent British machines from becoming too uppity on America's flat tracks and road-racing courses. Until 1969, H-D personnel and allies of the AMA's Competition Committee preserved the 750-cc

The handsome but sluggish 1952 K model is checked out by, from left, Gordon Davidson, vice president manufacturing; Walter C. Davidson, vice president sales; William J. Harley, vice president engineering; and William H. Davidson, president. (William H. Davidson collection)

flathead side valve engine by permitting overhead valve engines with a maximum displacement of only 500 cc. Earlier, the committee had further thwarted efforts of Triumph and BSA by limiting compression ratios. The trusty American flathead would run at relatively low compression, say 7.5:1, while the British vertical twins could not pull the higher RPM needed to pass the Harleys without a ratio of 9.5:1 or higher.

The late Floyd Clymer, a pioneer racer, Indian dealer, and publisher, reported in 1956 on an AMA competition committee meeting that was orchestrated by H-D's favorite AMA official, E. C. Smith. Sensing that the compression ratio rule was in trouble, AMA officials waited until a proponent of British bikes angrily left the room to take the compression vote. It failed by a single ballot!

An increasing number of racers were astride foreign machines. Riders including Dick Mann, Gary Nixon, and, a bit later, Kenny Roberts, won national championships aboard Matchless, BSA, Triumph, Honda, Yamaha—anything but the Milwaukee bikes. Immediately after the rules were liberalized in 1969, Triumphs and BSAs temporarily blew the iron-head XRs into the hay bales, spending themselves into oblivion when they should have been casting a

nervous eye toward the Far East. Honda motorbikes arrived and were followed by wickedly quick 250-cc Suzuki X-6 Hustlers, which were in turn followed by vile-handling but fast Kawasaki 500-cc triples and the milestone Honda 750-cc four-cylinder.

Coincidentally, Harley-Davidson worked with the transverse-four configuration several years prior to the introduction of the bigger Honda. Very little is known about the machine, although photos of a non-running model still exist in company archives. The engine carried double overhead cams and was labeled the X1000. Many H-D employees with archives access are aware of the photo, but few seem to know why the mockup was created. According to one retired employee, the X1000 was only a styling exercise and never got as far as a prototype. Work on more familiar models continued, supplemented by the smaller machines that arrived from Varese, Italy.

Merger mania swept the corporate world in the late 1960s, as such conglomerates as Litton, LTV, TRW, and others devoured smaller companies by the hundreds. There were, it seemed, just two kinds of corporations in Vietnam War-era America: those about to be consumed and those doing the digesting. One of the corporations eager to grab a merger meal ticket was Bangor Punta, an East Coast firm with roots in the railroad business. A neighbor of Harley-Davidson, Waukesha Engine Company, was acquired by Bangor Punta, which then cast a covetous eye at H-D. Anxiety among Harley directors grew in direct proportion to the amount of Harley-Davidson stock the conglomerate was acquiring. Prompted in part by rumors that Bangor Punta had a reputation for exploiting its acquisitions, in 1968 President William H. Davidson re-opened talks with another conglomerate, American Machine and Foundry (AMF).

The AMF Years

A bidding war for outstanding shares ensued, with H-D principals urging shareholders to peddle their stake to AMF. There were, William H. Davidson saw, "substantial benefits to the shareholders of both companies. . . . The merger will be a tax-free reorganization and will give the shareholders of H-D participation in a large and more di-versified enterprise with greater financial resources for fur-ther development and growth." Unfortunately, one H-D board member almost ruined the deal by passing to Bangor Punta some of Harley-Davidson's most private anti-merger thoughts. Despite filing a lawsuit, Bangor Punta lost the bid for America's only motorcycle. Shareholders expressed their confidence in William H. by voting overwhelmingly on December 18, 1968, to merge with American Machine & Foundry. For the record, 713,554 shares in H-D became 1,020,331 shares in AMF. Had it been a cash deal, the con-glomerate would have paid more than $30 million for Harley-Davidson.

AMF shareholders approved the merger on January 7, 1969. At the time, H-D was selling 15,475 domestically pro-duced cycles per year. A dozen years later, the company would be selling more than 50,000 machines annually—all U.S. -made heavyweights. In additional to dollars, AMF brought diverse engineering skills, modern management techniques, and marketing, advertising, and promotional ideas that heightened recognition almost overnight. The red, white, and blue No. 1 insignia, Michael Parks astride a Sportster in TV's *Then Came Bronson*, Robert Blake enforcing the law on the big screen in *Electra Glide in Blue*, Evel Kniev-

el's death-defying leaps—all were calculated to make the public more aware of Harley-Davidson during a period of incredible increases in U.S. cycling registrations.

The more Harley-Davidson shareholders thought about the transaction, the more they liked it. One employee, who bought 100 shares of H-D stock at $7 per share when it first went public in 1965, was confronted with the happy prospect of receiving 150 shares in AMF. At that time, AMF shares were selling for $28 per share. The value increased rapidly to $35 per share, allowing the shareholder to realize $5,250 on his $700 investment in less than five years. It did not take long for many Harley and Davidson relatives, who wanted more liquidity, to liquidate, much to their financial benefit.

Among the first to depart was Walter C. Davidson, vice president of sales. He became disillusioned with his position in the scheme of things. William H. Davidson was named chairman in 1971, though he no longer had a board to chair. "They pulled my teeth," he complained to an employee. In a company marked previously by stability, a succession of lead-ers came and went. William H. Davidson, John H. O'Brien, John A. Davidson, Vaughn L. Beals, E. Gus Davis, and Charles K. Thompson all took their turns in the president's chair—in a single decade. O'Brien departed after displeasing AMF with some sort of deal he had in mind in Europe. Davis left in less than 18 months, a victim of his own bombast, according to as-sociates. And William H. and son John had the outrageous (to AMF) idea that the president of Harley-Davidson should make decisions affecting the company.

Reconfiguring York

Not all of AMF's moves proved to be of long-range ben-efit. The company's massive York, Pennsylvania, defense and bowling equipment plant lay all but idle in 1972, just when H-D needed more assembly space and when Milwau-kee's unionized assemblers were more militant than ever. The decision was made to refurbish the York facility, con-verting it to final assembly and relying on Capitol Drive only for the production of engines and transmissions. Con-firmed reports of sabotage of a few 1972 models on the Capitol Drive assembly line hastened the move, allowing the first bike produced in York to bob down the overhead conveyor system in February 1973. Quality problems affected the 1973s, but those ills were minute compared to a world news event the following year.

The Middle East War in October 1974 caused American drivers and riders to become aware of the price and availability of gasoline. H-D and fellow bike makers rejoiced—here at last was a prudent reason to buy a motorcycle! However, the oil crisis also was a blow to AMF, because it greatly increased the cost of hauling engines and transmissions from Milwaukee to York, a distance of 700 miles, for final assembly. At a time when the price difference between a Harley-Davidson and a Japanese bike was already noticeable, this added expense was troubling.

AMF President Rodney C. Gott indicated in the 1975 annual report that the conglomerate was less than enthralled with bicycles, sailboats, tennis rackets, skis, golf clubs, rubber balls, and motorcycles. The disillusionment with H-D stemmed in part from a 101-day strike in 1974 that had idled York and Capitol Drive assembly lines. Fourteen weeks of production were lost before AMF acceded to worker demands. Actually, the strike helped H-D work off an inventory created by a 25 percent drop in U.S. cycle registrations, combined with intensified Japanese production of cycles with engines larger than 750 cc.

Those additional Japanese bikes, introduced just as the post-Vietnam War economy declined, led to charges by AMF of "dumping," that is, sending excess production here. The U.S. Treasury Department agreed in August 1978 that three of the four Japanese bike makers had indeed offered their cycles here for less than their prices on the domestic market. Nevertheless, just three months later, the nonpartisan International Trade Commission ruled that the dumping had not damaged sales of Harley-Davidson motorcycles.

"The law says dumping is selling products at less than fair market value," said John A. Davidson, H-D's president at the time. AMF had picked him to lead the fight in Washington against the Japanese. "In the early 1970s, when the motorcycle business was doing well worldwide, the Japanese established production schedules that were much higher than the mid-1970s demand for their products. We contended that they chose the U.S. to unload their excess production."

Fair Market Value

The AMF charges were not based on manufacturers' costs, even though the conglomerate did hire consultants to check the cost of Japanese cycle making. Rather, Davidson reported, those numbers were used as guidelines to compare U.S. selling prices with prices in Japan and were adjusted for such factors as shipping costs and the value of the Japanese yen relative to the dollar. AMF decided to pursue matters with the Treasury after totaling all of the figures and coming up with what appeared to be less than fair market value. This conclusion led AMF to believe that federal anti-dumping statutes had been violated.

Davidson said the case was unusually complicated because no Japanese manufacturer was allowed to sell motorcycles larger than 750 cc in Japan. Investigators thus had to look at other free-market economies such as France and Canada for model comparisons with the big bikes offered in the U.S. The Japanese muddied the waters with minor model differences and designations, which made comparisons difficult. Nevertheless, weighted average dumping margins for each of three Japanese manufacturers were:

Arthur Davidson congratulates Joe Weatherly after the latter won the 100-mile national road race at Laconia, New Hampshire, in 1949. Arthur remained active with the company until his death in an auto accident in 1950. (William H. Davidson collection)

Honda, 2.9 percent; Kawasaki, 7.26 percent; and Yamaha, 1.98 percent. Suzuki was guilty of so tiny a margin that the Treasury dropped charges against it, Davidson said.

AMF and Harley-Davidson evidently looked at the percentages, realized they were not that dramatic, and began producing news releases commenting on the Treasury decision. Davidson was quoted as saying that "the dumping margins were very much higher on certain models. Some ranged as high as 54 percent." There was no indication which models he meant. In any event, a finding favorable to H-D by the nonpartisan International Trade Commission would have meant that the Japanese had the unenviable choice of either increasing prices in the U.S. or paying duty on the bikes they shipped to this country.

Late in 1978, the commission delivered its decision: Although the Japanese had indeed dumped products on these shores, the practice had not injured Harley-Davidson. AMF and H-D employees not directly involved with the proceedings probably were stunned by the decision. However, those who spent countless hours preparing the material sensed trouble when the commissioners requested and received permission to query Harley dealers about the problem.

Dealers' Views

"We told our dealers to be frank with the commission, and that's where our case was lost," Davidson said. Harley-Davidson dealers, plagued with real and imagined problems with the Aermacchis, told the commission that the smaller H-Ds were obsolete and could not compete with the state-of-the-art Japanese bikes. "So they ruled that we injured ourselves by failing to keep our production up to date," Davidson said.

Despite months of work without reward, Davidson believed the whole process was worthwhile. "It stabilized prices and made everyone—us and the Japanese—take a closer look at production." The big loser in the proceedings may have been Yamaha. That company petitioned to have its case dropped due to the small difference between U.S. and Japanese pricing. The Treasury Department agreed to drop the matter if Yamaha would permit it to monitor pricing. "This drove Yamaha nuts," Davidson said. The other big loser was the troubled Aermacchi operation in Italy. If anyone at AMF or Harley-Davidson had any doubts about what dealers thought of the H-D lightweights, they knew after the commission recessed.

A former AMF corporate employee who prefers anonymity believes pursuit of the Japanese was not only a waste of time, but was hideously expensive in terms of the number of well-paid executives who commuted between Milwaukee and Washington, D. C., for weeks at a time. "AMF's bankroll was of great value to Harley-Davidson," he contended. "But the dumping thing proves that not all of the money was wisely spent."

All this is significant, as we'll see later. For now, though, let's take a look at how today's Harley-Davidsons go together.

A Harley and three Davidsons surround the first Topper scooter. (William H. Davidson collection)

Chapter 2

Construction

At the present time, nine Harley-Davidson facilities in four states work to produce hundreds of thousands of new Harley Davidsons and related products and services each year. The facilities include:

- Headquarters, the Juneau Avenue complex in Milwaukee, where all things are administered.
- The Willie G. Davidson Product Development Center in the Milwaukee suburb of Wauwatosa. New and/or improved models are conceived here.
- The Capitol Drive Powertrain Operations plant in Wauwatosa, where XL engines and transmissions are crafted.
- The Pilgrim Road Powertrain Operations plant, in northwest suburban Menomonee Falls, where FL engines and transmissions go together.
- The southwest suburban Franklin Distribution Center, which stocks and ships parts and accessories.
- The Tomahawk Fiberglass Manufacturing plant, a couple of hundred miles north, but also in Wisconsin.
- The York Final Assembly Plant, in York, Pennsylvania, site of the FL and Softail lines assemblages.
- The Kansas City Final Assembly Plant, where the XLs, the Dyna Glides, and the dramatic V-Rod go together.
- The Talladega Test Facility in Talladega, Alabama; the super speedway is the site of H-D's road testing program.

The most interesting facility, and the site usually open to tour, remains the big plant in York. It employs 3,000 people, covers more than 200 acres, and has a million square feet-plus under one roof. At one time, a bomb-making facility owned by AMF, the sprawling site on the city's north side went through a stage from 1973 to the late 1980s wherein parts moved along a 3.5-mile overhead monorail, servicing

The most expensive piece of machinery ever purchased by AMF, worth $4.5 million, takes up hundreds of square feet in the Capitol Drive plant. This machinery makes five-speed transmissions. (David K. Wright)

Five-speed transmissions await shipment at the Capitol Drive plant. (David K. Wright)

gins a dangling ride down an assembly line, visiting 24 different stations for an average of less than six minutes per station. In just over 2.5 hours, a new Road Glide, Road King, or Electra Glide is ready to be kicked over for the first time.

Softails pick up a crew of three, who move with the bike as parts are connected to the frame. The trio of workers knows every job along the line; consequently, an assembler may attach a front wheel on one bike, a rear wheel on the next, and controls on the next. More Softails are needed than touring bikes. That is the reason for the plant addition, which produced its first machine in the summer of 2002 in a 350,000-square foot shop that cost $145 million.

Preassembly

Before assembly of anything anywhere, the 1,200 or more parts that make up a bike must be made ready to join all other parts for a complete machine. A number of preassembly jobs are accomplished throughout the York facility. Among them:

400,000 square feet of manufacturing. That system became outmoded with the introduction of just-in-time (or material-as-needed) manufacturing methods. Nowadays, minimal inventory, delivered as it is required, keeps parts flowing to the assembly line. In addition to improving efficiency, the system has freed up money for other projects. Among those other ventures is a just-completed addition to the York complex, where Softails are assembled.

Moving the Softail line into its own assembly area is part of the ambitious capital expenditure program underway at Harley-Davidson, Inc. The company spent approximately $1 billion on capital improvements during the period 1994–2000, and could afford to part with $250 million in 2001. Small wonder that the firm was named America's outstanding company by *Forbes* magazine in 2002.

However, back to the Softail—it is assembled differently than the touring bikes put together in York. A touring machine begins life by having the frame hooked to a moving conveyor. The engine is quickly fitted and the machine be-

- **Chrome plating.** Hardware is buffed and polished, then loaded in racks. The process, from bare metal to completion, takes 90 minutes, beginning with a coat of nickel and ending with glistening chrome. Tank probes sense temperature, pH content, and contaminants as parts are lowered into and raised from the toxic solutions. Monitored on a console, this system of reverse osmosis units and scrubbers allows for 99 percent use of the heavy metals in the solution. Polishing is done with automatic machines, polishing jacks, and tumblers.
- **Machining.** A bewildering array of pieces is machined, often in widely separate areas, throughout the plant. Parts involved include primary chain housing, brake discs, and starter components. Housings arrive in York as rough castings and are machined and surface finished. Brake discs show up as blanked, circular pieces of metal and are turned to precise diameters, then hardened using magnetism and extremely high temperatures. After that, they are machined and ground for porosity and hardness. As many as 16 distinct operations are performed on starter components by numerically controlled machines that preclude having to adjust or remove the components.

- **Screw machining.** Steering head bushings, axles, linkages, and special screws are created from lengths of steel bar or hex stock, with automated machinery.
- **Grinding.** Surface, cylindrical, and centerless grinders precision machine such hardware as starter shafts, axles, and crankpins.
- **The presses.** A battery of 60-ton presses, many equipped with automatic feeders, stamps out components such as brackets, gussets, shims, battery clamps, and tank and fender blanks. Even larger presses, rated as high as 1,000 tons, deep-draw such items as gas and oil tanks, fenders, and air-cleaner housings. Blanking presses stamp out parts such as drive sprockets from stock as thick as 5/16 inch.
- **Wheel assembly.** Wire wheels, consisting of hubs, rims, and spokes, are laced and tightened by hand. They are then torqued in concentric holding fixtures and trued to specifications in indicator fixtures. Brake discs, drive sprockets, tubes, and tires are installed before final balancing.
- **Welding.** If one thing has changed since York began producing motorcycles more than 20 years ago, it is the welding department. The process is the same, but robots that move around a part quickly, often amid conditions that would quickly wear down a person, have replaced the vast majority of humans. Yes, some subweldments are still fabricated by hand. However, the gas metal-arc process applied automatically to the mild-steel frames is quick, quality work.
- **Paint.** Harley-Davidson is by now comfortable with a $26 million paint system that probably is as good as they say it is. If the finished bike is the standard, then paint standards are uniformly high. "If American automobiles have a Class A finish, Harley-Davidsons are Class Triple-A," says an employee for the paint supplier, PPG. The praise is based on an eight-stage zinc phosphate pre-treatment that is followed by a coat of epoxy, followed by robotically controlled application of PPG acrylic, followed by a powder clear coat. The latter step—powder clear coat over acrylic—is new technology. Details such as hand striping and silk-screening then take place.

Obviously, there are a huge number of operations before a bike moves down the assembly line …

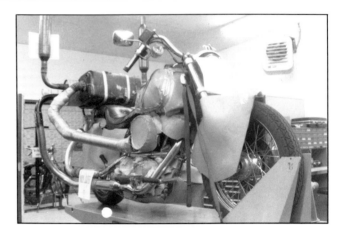

Shielded in layers of lead-impregnated plastic foam, this H-D undergoes noise emission analysis at the Capitol Drive facility. (Buzz Buzzelli)

Visitors assemble out front and are then escorted through the plant by an employee who has an electronic microphone. His signal goes to small earpieces worn by the visitors so that they can hear him above the noise of assembly activity. The greatest impression on the visitors is the number of robots that are used to eliminate the former manual jobs of cutting, welding, brazing, and buffing (though a few of these operations are still performed by hand).

The system is especially impressive when a visitor realizes that some 1,250 parts have to come together at the right time for complete assembly to take place. In manufacturing facilities all over America (and in Latin America, Europe, and Japan, for that matter), the right number of Harley parts are funneled into York, to emerge as a finished motorcycle. More and more parts these days are U.S. -made, though such things as wheels and electrical items show up in containers indicating Japanese or other manufacture.

Following startup and the artificial drive on rollers once a motorcycle is fully assembled, it is packed for shipping. These days the bikes take much less time to get running once they reach the dealer, a fact that every H-D retailer on earth no doubt appreciates. Because of modern manufacturing techniques, there are fewer post-assembly inspections in search of fewer and fewer flaws.

On Capitol Drive

This drive for quality is company wide, as a visit to the Capitol Drive engine plant in Wauwatosa reveals. Dynamometers worth $122,000 apiece test batches of engines for about 30 minutes. Two engines each day will be run longer for horsepower checks before being fully disassembled. Some engines are tested in the frame so engineers and technicians can see how the engine, transmission, and frame interrelate. The tests are complete to the point that employees can tell when a drill is getting dull.

Harley-Davidson engines and transmission, plus a few specialized parts such as clutch and powertrain components, are created and subassembled here. Engine assembly has taken place here since 1972 (it was done in the Juneau Avenue building earlier), before the assembly line was created in York. Continuous investment in the Wauwatosa facility has resulted in today's oil-tight, rattle-, and trouble-free H-Ds. A typical investment is the $4.5 million apparatus that automatically machines the cases for the five-speed transmission.

The Tomahawk Plant

Quality control programs are in place in H-D's Tomahawk plant, where fiberglass and ABS side covers, windshields, sidecars, and the electronics in fairings are crafted. When Harley-Davidson purchased the Tomahawk Boat Company in 1963, fiberglass was laid up by hand in a female mold. The following year, the use of compression

Pushrods and rocker boxes are put together by Jim Depka on the Capitol Drive plant assembly line. (Buzz Buzzelli)

Assembler Gloria Cruz installs cam gears and cam covers on the Capitol Drive assembly line. (Buzz Buzzelli)

The Big Twin assembly line at H-D's Capitol Drive plant in Wauwatosa, on Milwaukee's west side. (Buzz Buzzelli)

Harley-Davidson disc brakes are attached to wheels before assembly of the motorcycle. (David K. Wright)

A welder completes the construction of a frame at the York facility. (David K. Wright)

molding equipment, which involved injection of fiberglass-reinforced plastic into male and female molds and heat curing, was begun. The $250,000 in equipment paid for itself in six months, despite the fact that the products created in those early years would not stand up to close scrutiny today.

Purchased primarily to create golf car bodies and for sidecars and Servi-Cars, the equipment was first used for saddlebags and fairings in 1969. Compression molding and the consequent heat curing caused the product to shrink by about 6 to 8 percent. That shrinkage exposed the fibers in the material. The molded components were painted a matte finish, either black or white, that effectively concealed the minute fiber strands. So far, so good—until the late 1970s.

Around this time, Harley-Davidson began offering TourPaks, saddlebags, and fairings to match bike colors. Dealers and customers alike complained with validity that

A quality audit is performed on an Electra Glide Classic. The audit involves 2.5 hours of testing and inspection. (David K. Wright)

Consequently, not even metallic colors cause problems, despite the fact that they formerly showed a lot of "flip." That means the paint appears to change color depending on the amount of light and the angle from which it is seen. Every color comes from a target paint sample created by the styling department. Each paint company then has to match the sample. The goal of styling, construction, and assembly is to create a finished product that looks uniform, even if tiny formula adjustments have to be made in York or in Tomahawk.

All of the motorcycle products that emerge from the plant are styled by vice president Willie G. Davidson and his associates. The styling VP has worked with mold makers to create distinctive parts and accessories for the bikes. Initially, Willie G. even created some new boat designs for the

the adornments were not as well finished as either the competition's accessories or the many aftermarket products available.

It wasn't orange peel, but it didn't look right, according to a former employee. Then, in 1980, the Japanese entered the touring-bike market with rim-molded fairings and bags. The only way H-D could compete was to use lots of sandpaper and primer. Results were expensive and inefficient. The company then took its new stance regarding quality with the introduction of low-profile fiberglass resin.

Shrinkage of the material is about 2 percent, effectively concealing the hairlike pieces of fiberglass. Efforts to make the accessories more closely match the bike were redoubled, with the result that criticism has come 180 degrees. A H-D executive says finish is no longer a problem. He adds that a state-of-the-art paint facility now applies urethane produced by Cook, PPG, or Sheboygan Paint Company to a greatly improved surface. The urethanes take clear coats well. In addition, paint specifications are subjected to the statistical control program instituted by the company in the late 1980s.

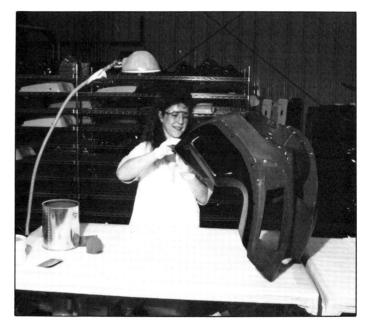

Some detail work in Tomahawk is still done by hand. (David K. Wright)

Tomahawk division. Weather permitting, a local resident may spot one of Willie G.'s personal machines parked near the building on the east side of town.

One more Harley-Davidson installation should be noted. Since 1981, the company has operated road-testing facilities at the Talladega (Alabama) International Motor Speedway. Durability, federally mandated emissions testing, and high-speed handling tests are carried out. More important, prototype models are run over railroad ties and concrete rub strips to test new frame designs. Testing takes place rain or shine by about 40 employees. Much of the fieldwork on the V-Rod went on in and around Talladega.

Here's the most amazing thing about the entire manufacturing process: Ever since the buyback, motorcycle quality has improved while the company has produced a great many more bikes. That's quite an accomplishment, when you think about it. Qualified people and big money made it all happen.

Final touches go on an FXRP police bike fairing in Tomahawk.
(David K. Wright)

Glenn Christianson, manager of inventory control, looks over a sidecar before it leaves Tomahawk. Sidecars may go to York, to a dealer, or to an overseas customer.
(David K. Wright)

Chapter 3

Iron

The very first Harley-Davidson model was manufactured from 1903 through 1908. It featured a 25-ci, 3-horsepower motor that drove the rear wheel directly via a single loop of leather strap. In 1909, cubic inches climbed to 35 and horsepower to 4 by way of a larger bore and stroke. The year 1907 marked the appearance of the first bottom-link springer front end. Crude as this suspension may have been, it was hailed in the young transportation industry as a breakthrough in combating the country's rutted roads and was grafted onto all kinds of racers. A battery ignition was seen as early as 1908, offered on the single as an alternative to the Bosch magneto.

There is proof positive that Harley-Davidson had a working V-twin as early as 1907. However, the twin was not perfected until 1911. An exhaust valve on the side of the cylinder created an exit for spent fuel, giving rise to the term "IOE" or inlet-over-exhaust configuration. Many have speculated on

the 45-degree arrangement of the initial twin. The silhouette of the motor may well have been determined because it was the ideal depth to fit between the frame's front down tube and the seat tube. As for eventual capacity, engineer William

A 1914 61-ci twin, owned by Harley-Davidson, Inc. (David K. Wright)

The first production V-twin, measuring less than 50 ci, was offered in 1909. This model featured suction exhaust valves, an idea that worked only in theory, before mechanical valves replaced them from 1911 onward. (F-22 Photography)

S. Harley probably picked 61 ci because it could be constructed by modifying two of the single cylinder heads and because the displacement worked out to 1000 cc. Sixty-one cubes was viewed as the ultimate reasonable size for a motorcycle engine at the time.

The company has shown a willingness to continuously improve its products down through the years. Call that evolutionary if you will. H-D made its single and V-twin cycles more comfortable in 1912 by offering the first cushioned seat post, a patented "Ful-Floteing" device that suspended the saddle by way of a spring inside the seat tube. In rapid succession, Harley-Davidson offered a clutch (1912), chain drive, and a single-speed transmission (1913), internal expanding rear brake, gaslight, sidecars, and a two-speed transmission (1914), an electrical lighting system (1915), and a three-speed transmission that same year.

World War I was but a pause in technological terms. The 1918 models displayed optional, hand-operated rear brakes, while 1920 bikes featured Harley-Davidson's own electrical system. The latter was created as an answer to the dampness-prone Remy units and set the standard for quality electrics for a decade. Few of the latest features were found on the direct-drive racers of the day, indicating that looking after the street rider was the company's priority. Harley-Davidson emerged from the 1910s as the world's largest motorcycle company simply because its products worked better than those of the competition.

Motorcycles, like all mechanical contrivances, reach plateaus, and such a leveling off seems to have occurred in 1922. That was the year before the demise of H-D's unique 37-ci, 180-degree, opposed-twin Sport model, created in 1919. The company produced a new series of 74-ci motors, the JD, in 1921, and then opted for refinement rather than revelation through 1925. Styling became a factor, evident in 1925 when the then-new H-D's sported teardrop gas tanks. This new look worked especially well in 1926, when the company re-entered the lightweight field in a burst of new technology with the 21-ci models in either flathead or overhead valve configuration. Both models offered detachable heads. The experience with the flathead would soon pay off.

Two-cam Power

Meanwhile, the company produced a high-output motor, even though H-D no longer financed a factory racing team. The 61-ci two-cam began showing up in hillclimb and flat-track winner's circles in 1925. Its success resulted in production in 1928 and 1929 of 61- and 74-ci two-cam street models for very sporting riders (specifications for the two-cam appear in chapter 8). The first production front brake appeared in 1928, too, and there was even bigger news the following year. Announced with twin headlights, the 1929 models included the 45-ci V-twin and the 30.50-ci single. Singles stuck around in various forms—speedway racer, utility machine—until 1934, but the descendents of that first 45 flathead are with us still.

The 1930 bikes reverted to a single headlight and so were featured on the new VL series. The VL's most interesting technical innovation initially was wheel interchangeability. By 1933, the full line of bikes sported incredibly colorful Art Deco gas tanks as the factory tried desperately to sell

A 1913 Harley-Davidson single. This example is on display at the Smithsonian Institution in Washington, D.C. (Smithsonian Institution photo by Rolfe Baggett)

Another look at the Smithsonian's 1913 single. (Smithsonian Institution photo by Rolfe Baggett)

The first 74-ci machine was introduced in 1921. If the 1936 Knucklehead is the father of today's Big Twins, this motorcycle is the grandfather. (F-22 Photography)

lowed in 1939 by a streamlined dash panel and in 1940 by the first metal nameplate and 16-inch wheels. This prewar burst of innovation culminated in 1941 with the introduction of the 74-ci Knucklehead, a classic among classics. Accented with metal tank strips, the 1941 Knuckler is among the most sought-after antique Harleys.

Paramilitary organizations and the police were the sole recipients of new civilian cycles during the war years. The ULH series 80-ci motors were last produced in 1941. Civilian production resumed in November 1945, nearly three months after the surrender of the Japanese. The public had to be content through 1947 with very minor alterations (such as cast alu-

bikes to an unemployed public. The Servi-Car, powered by the 45-ci motor, came out in 1932 and was offered a year later with a reverse gear added to the three-speed transmission. This innovation was optional on all V-twins with sidecars from 1933 through 1974, when Servi-Car production ceased.

Since times were tough, the introduction of several new models in 1936 was something of a gamble. Foremost among them was the model E, nicknamed the Knucklehead, the first overhead-valve V-twin. The new, hemispherical-head motor showed a recirculating oil system and a greatly improved, welded fuel/oil tank. Companion models that memorable year included an 80-ci flathead, the VLH, and the last VL, available with H-D's first four-speed transmission. Encouraged, the factory offered 74- and 80-ci UL flatheads the following year, together with the first WL in the 45-ci series. Generator and oil-indicator lights showed up in 1938, fol-

minum tail lights and a new nameplate), but 1948 was an exciting year indeed. Hydraulic lifters beneath 74-ci Panhead cylinders created interest, as did the all-new, 125-cc two-stroke machine with the three-speed, foot-shift transmission. Few took note of the demise of the 74-ci UL series after 1948. Another surprise was in store in 1949, as H-D swapped the venerable springer front end for hydraulic suspension, dubbing such models Hydra-Glides and introducing the soft ride on a 61-ci version of the Panhead. A smaller version of the same principle appeared in 1951 on the 125-cc bikes and was dubbed the Teleglide.

Foot-shift Panheads

The evolutionary process was at work in 1952, as foot shift was offered optionally on FL Panheads and on the EL, even though 1952 was the last year for that 61-ci series. More important, the new K model blended the heritage of the 45-ci motor with European styling and a four-speed foot-shift transmission in a dramatic departure in thinking for the utilitarian W series engine. The company's first off-the-shelf scrambler, the KRM, followed in 1953; it was the final year for the 45-ci engine aboard a two-wheeler. The 1951 KH ran a 55-ci (883 cc) motor, making the sporting bikes as fast as it was stylish. Meanwhile, H-D continued to produce several 125–165 cc machines, but the stage was set for a pair of momentous mid-1950s motorcycles.

The 74-ci FLH came out in 1955 and, even with its rigid frame, was the ultimate two-wheeled choice for touring enthusiasts. The FL series has evolved dramatically in its 48 years of existence, yet its long-haul luxury essence remains unchanged. Equally momentous was the introduction of the Sportster in 1957. If the FLs were the kings of the highway, the XLs were the studs of the street and strip. Overhead valves were the secret to the Sportster's thunderous performance. The following year, H-D made both the F and X series even more desirable: The former received a swingarm frame and automotive type shocks to become the Duo-Glide, while the latter was joined by the magneto-equipped XLCH (CH stood for "Competition Hot"). Overlooked at the time were such amenities as the new hydraulic brake on the 74-ci cycle.

Nineteen fifty-nine marked the final year of domestic small-engine production, with the exception of the Topper scooter, which made its debut in 1960; the golf cart, produced initially in 1963; and the snowmobile, offered from 1971 to 1975. Henceforth, all of the smaller power plants were to come from the Aermacchi/H-D plant in Italy. The mainstay bikes continued to evolve, with the Sportster receiving a full-width front brake drum in 1964 and the FL series acquiring a 12-volt battery, electric starting, a 5-gallon gas tank, and a new name, the Electra Glide, in 1965.

The Shovelhead motor was created for the Electra Glide in 1966, displaying a top end visually reminiscent of the Knucklehead. This evolutionary step disposed of several external oil lines, trading iron for aluminum in the process. To celebrate an increasingly oil-tight motor, H-D created the 74-ci King of the Highway bike, a machine that redefined the term "full dress." By 1967, Tomahawk fiberglass technology was used to produce the Servi-Car with a glass body. The

A 74-ci machine in the V series, from 1934. (David K. Wright)

first fiberglass-bodied sidecar came along in 1968, followed by similar treatment in 1969 for the golf car. (Incidentally, the first non-leather H-D saddlebags were white plastic and were seen on the 1953 K model, just one of several special offerings during that Golden Anniversary year.) The classic FLH, with its bar-mounted fairing, first appeared in 1969.

Servi-Cars, with their 45-ci side valve motors, came in many colors. This restored example is yellow and black. (David K. Wright)

From the seat forward, the Servi-Car looks a lot like any 45.
(David K. Wright)

government. By the following year, the 12-year-old motor was producing 58 horsepower at 6800 rpm.

Mid-year 1970 models bore the AMF logo, even though the designs were executed before the conglomerate acquired Harley-Davidson. The first model to be recognized by Harley-Davidson as an AMF bike was the 1971 Super Glide. More important, Willie G. Davidson did at the factory what riders themselves had been doing—he mated the XL front end to the FL frame and motor, producing an electric- (FXE) or a kick-start (FX) machine. Both are benchmarks among H-D fans. The Super Glide proved that Willie G.'s idea of a dream bike was on target and that such a machine could proliferate models even more distinctive than the initial (optional), red-white-blue bedecked Super Glide. The model carried the FX designation, indicating its descent from both series of machines.

Discs for the FL

Disc brakes up front became standard on FL models the following year, while the Sportster reached 61-ci (1000 cc) capacity. If Harley-Davidson clutches and transmissions had by then become trouble free, shifting required some thought: Governmental insistence placed all shifting mechanisms on the rider's left for 1972. XL machines ran discs up front initially in 1973, whereas FX and FL models sported disc brakes front and rear. "King of the Road" replaced "King of the Highway," and included such items as windshield, spotlights, front and rear safety bars, "Pak King" fiberglass bags, bag guards, and a windshield bag. The 738-pound dry weight made for rock-steady travel during the last full year of federally mandated 70-mph interstate highway speeds.

Motorcycles generally and H-Ds specifically were becoming so desirable that leaving a bike unattended was risky. Therefore, in 1974 the factory installed alarm systems on all domestically produced machines. The Sportster, said a magazine, was its own worst enemy; the bike had become so reliable that owners were neglecting routine service! Juneau Avenue did not neglect the 1976 U.S. Bicentennial—both the FX and FXE Super Glides were available with special commemorative paint, and the Electra Glide could be had in a Liberty Edition.

The Sportster did not sit idle during the years preceding the merger with American Machine & Foundry (AMF). In 1968, the XLH received electric start, and a Fairbanks-Morse magneto helped launch the XLCH. Both XL models showed 150-mph speedometers, and the large oval air cleaner was first affixed, courtesy of emissions experts inside the federal

Several new models were unveiled in 1977. The FXS Low Rider was a styling sensation, as Willie G. indicated once again that he and his cohorts were on the cutting edge of machinery with a custom look. In contrast, the Sportster was made available as a striking black XLCR Café Racer, complete with canyon-running amenities such as rearset footpegs, a bikini fairing, and low bars. While the Japanese were calling on a cadre of stylists and engineers, one small department in one factory was beating them to the styling punch by several years. Also on tap in the years immediately following were XLTs, XLT Huggers, XLS Roadsters, XLXs, and XRs. Each of these Sportsters catered to a particular kind of rider.

80 Cubes

The 1978 FLH became the first modern H-D with the 80-ci (1340 cc) motor, just in time to join an optional XLH as a 75th anniversary model. The Classic followed in 1979 and the successor to the touring crown, the FLT Tour Glide, in 1980. The FLT, with its five-speed transmission, vibration-isolated motor, improved frame, and frame-mounted fairing, contrasted well with the Low Rider, which acquired the 80-ci motor in 1979, and with the FXEF Fat Bob running the 1200-cc motor during its inaugural year in 1979 and switching to 80 cubes the year after. The laid-back Wide Glide, also running 80 ci, came aboard in 1980, as did the dramatic belt-drive FXB Sturgis.

The FXR was introduced, winning respect from bike magazines and luring Brand X touring riders into H-D showrooms with its European-style fairing. Riders bade the Shovelhead motor adieu after the 1984 model year, welcoming the Evolution and the 1100-cc Sportster engines for 1985. Special model introductions included the 1985–1/2 FXRC Low Glide Custom. Harley continued to prove that beauty was more than sheet metal deep by offering demo cruises wherever a rider could plunk down a valid operator's license. All this caused the media and the public to respond, here and abroad.

That same year, 1984, the Softail was introduced and the XR1000 was created in sufficient quantity to make it legal for AMA-sanctioned road racing. The bike was an XLS chassis with a special XL1000 engine that featured alloy heads. A pair of Dell'Orto carburetors fed the swift, hungry beast.

Also in 1984, the Evolution engine was introduced on the F bikes. Three years after that, the Sportster got its Evolution engine, with 883-cc capacity. It was followed in 1988 by a booming 1200-cc Evo for the Sporty. In a complete surprise, springer forks returned in 1988 on the FXST Softail. Two years later, the FLSTF Fat Boy rolled up with a pair of snazzy disc wheels. In 1991, the Sportster was first offered with a five-speed transmission, and a year later belt drive became standard on all Harley-Davidsons.

With money for development, the bikes became less prone to constant maintenance in the 1990s. In this new, more reliable breed was the 1992, limited edition FXDB Daytona, the first Harley-Davidson to take advantage of computer-aided design and to offer true pearl paint. Dual front brakes were standard. The FXDWG Dyna Wide Glide provided the most laid back posture ever seen on a factory H-D. The company quickly trademarked the elevated handlebars as Ape Hangers, a familiar term from a couple of decades earlier.

An 80-ci side valve produced in 1936 and designated the VLH. These bikes greatly resemble the 45s of the same year. However, the heads are larger, with deeper finning. This model is part of the H-D collection in York. (David K. Wright)

"A Historical Portrait"

In 1994, Willie G. and the stylists created the FLSTC Heritage Softail Classic, a machine that was nothing if not nostalgic. Fishtail pipes, studded bags, a full windshield—one writer called it "a historical portrait," but noted that it offered contemporary reliability. A year earlier, H-D had purchased part of the Buell Motorcycle Company, founded by racer and former Harley engineer Erik Buell. The small, racing-oriented company responded to the infusion of money with the 1994 Buell Thunderbolt. The 'bolt combined saddlebags and an H-D engine with racing hardware, siamesed exhausts and a bikini fairing. A neat package.

The FLHR Road King, which debuted in 1995, looked like an Electra Glide but provided its owners with all the toys: five-speed transmission, belt drive, discs front and rear, and air-adjustable front forks. The FXSTC, a 1996 model, combined a spoke front wheel and a solid rear for one of H-D's periodic tips of the hat to the chopper look. The FLHTC showed up with fuel injection that same year. The "B" attached to the Twin Cam 88 engine beginning in 1998 indicated that the Dyna line had an engine as smooth as a sunset lake, thanks to a counterbalancing system that let the Harley-Davidson sound and abundance of torque shine through.

The 2002 Harley-Davidsons were upstaged by the VRSCA V-Rod, the silver cycle with the drag bike look, a collaboration with Germany's Porsche designers. Lean and muscular, the V-Rod put out 115 horses and wound the 60-degree V-twin far higher than any street Harley in the last 100 years. Surprises are in store for 2003, among them that Dyna Glide will be the first to get the new V-twin. On the other hand, will a series of new bikes have to be designed to accept this magnificent motor? Moreover, will the touring folks be patient, or will they insist on affixing their saddlebags to a new bike/engine combination? As they say, stay tuned.

The First Singles, 1903–1911

The first Harley-Davidson was made entirely by hand. There simply were no engine blocks, transmissions, or carburetors, aftermarket or otherwise, available. That first engine was a copy of the French DeDion motor, a single-cylinder device with a capacity of approximately 25 ci (400 cc) that put out 2 horsepower—the equivalent of a fast walk on level ground. There was no gearbox; drive was direct to the rear wheel by means of a two-ply leather belt hooked to a pulley. The belt encircled the rear wheel rim. To get the vehicle moving, the rider pushed up to compression, then jumped on and pedaled frantically till the engine fired. Despite the exertion and the lack of hill climbing ability, Arthur Davidson and Bill Harley sold all they could create.

The head was permanently attached to the cylinder and was characterized by an induction valve stop. The downward movement of the piston sucked open this valve, admitting fuel, before the valve closed with the help of a spring. The exhaust valve opened and closed via cam action.

The next step, in late 1909, was to enlarge the motor to about 35 ci (435 cc) and to double the size of the flywheel, which Davidson and Harley knew affected the power plant's inclination to keep turning. This single design element added greatly to the longevity of the early H-Ds, while Harley's single-loop frame looked increasingly like a motorcycle and less like a bicycle.

By 1908, the company had conceived its own model identification system based on years in operation. The 1908 machines were considered fifth-year models, since true production had not commenced until 1904. Earlier, in 1906, H-D came up with its very first option: color choice. The standard, piano-finish black was supplemented with a Renault

A 1936 74-ci flathead. (David K. Wright)

gray/carmine striping combination that was the basis for the "Silent Gray Fellow" impression. Harley-Davidson realized quickly that many riders and the public alike appreciated quiet mufflers.

Here is the lowdown on a very early H-D single, taken from company archives. Because Harley-Davidson seldom fooled with success, the 35-ci motor was unchanged, except for valve design, from its creation through 1918, when it became available only on special, commercial order. A careful reading of the specs indicates that the writer was trying hard to differentiate motorcycles from bicycles!

Specifications *(From a brochure believed to have been printed in 1905. List price was $200, fob Milwaukee.)*

Motor: One-piece cylinder, large-diameter flywheel, starting by means of pedaling or by crank, crankshaft covered by aluminum cap when not in use.
Frame: Wheelbase is 51 inches, frame height is 21-1/2 inches, extension front forks, 2-1/4 inches detachable tires, spring seat post, three-coil suspension motor cycle saddle.
Carburetor: Automatic float feed enables engine to run from 5 to 45 mph without adjustment.
Grip control: Allows the cyclist to control engine speed without removing his hands from the handlebars.
Transmission: A 1-1/2-inch endless flat belt is used to drive the machine and is furnished with a 20 inch rear-drive pulley and either a 4-1/2-, 5-1/4-, or 6-inch leather-lined front pulley idler so constructed that the belt can be tightened by the rider while the machine is in motion.
Tanks: Gasoline tank holds 1-1/2 gallons, which is sufficient for 100 to 150 miles running. The lubricating oil tank holds two quarts and one filling is good for 750 miles. The oil is fed into the motor through a sight feed (gravity) oiler.
Muffler: Large enough to be noiseless with a minimum of back pressure.
Batteries: Three standard dry cells and a regular motorcycle coil 3 x 6 inches furnish the current.
Spark plug: 1/2-inch standard pipe thread; either mica or porcelain plug is furnished.
Tire and wheels: 2-1/4-inch G&J detachable motor cycle tires are used, and the wheels are built up with steel rims and extra heavy motor cycle spokes.

Here is an 80-ci Sport solo, designated a VLH in 1936. (David K. Wright)

Hubs: The front is 3/8 inch in diameter and the coaster brake is 1/2 inch in diameter.
Guards: Both braced by 1/4-inch steel rods.
Finish: In black, grip control and all bright parts nickel-plated. The aluminum casing is scraped and buffed to a high polish that does not tarnish or turn dull.

The V-Twin, 1907–1921

The 45-degree V-twin, the very essence of Harley-Davidson down through the years, was first offered publicly in 1909 (the first printed specs were done for the 1910 model year). A response to the creation of multiple-cylinder models from Thor, Reading-Standard, and other long-gone makes, the 7.2-horsepower behemoth was the forefather of decades of V-twins with Milwaukee origins.

The most important engine difference between the very first V-twin, originally seen at a cycle show in 1907 and produced through 1909, and the twins from 1911 onward was the inlet valves. Suction valves were tried repeatedly and without success from 1907 to 1909, whereas mechanical valves were used for the later twin. There were no twins offered in 1910, a year devoted to solving the valve problem. Careful attention to the specs will show that the first V's did not in fact measure up to the true 61-ci capacity in the early years.

However, the "6-D," as the model was initially dubbed, measured up in every other way. It included a precision Bosch magneto (replacing a trio of dry-cell batteries, coil, and points), a choice of 26- or 28- inch wheels (to accommodate riders of different heights), and the Renault gray finish (a light gray), all standard. The founders were sufficiently confident of the new machine to provide the same guarantee against defective parts and workmanship enjoyed by owners of H-D singles. In addition, while production was halted briefly in 1910, a "7-E" model, the very first all-out racer, was sold to a few select customers.

In 1911, Harley-Davidson introduced its patented idler. A lever and gears replaced a rod and harness to uncouple the direct drive, providing clutch-like disengagement between the pulley and the new, larger, 1-3/4-inch belt. No longer did riders have to overcome direct drive in order to stop; nor did they have to repeatedly restart a balky motor afterward. The 1911 model also featured a new fuel/oil tank, superseding separate tanks and storing three quarts of oil for the total-loss lubrication system.

A pre-war Knucklehead, restored and on display. (David K. Wright)

The oil traveled by gravity through a glass sight-tube to the crankcase, where it bathed the flywheel and the crank and was fed directly to the bearings. The force of the moving parts pushed oil to the piston and the lower cylinder wall. Oil not burned in combustion fell to the bottom of the case, where it was drained by hand. A hand-operated oil pump, standard for 1912, supplemented the gravity system, which could be adjusted but which most often ran at about one drop of oil every 2.5 seconds. Since the motor had been increased to 61 ci for 1912, more lubrication was required.

Specifications *(From a 1911 brochure.)*

Motor: Twin-cylinder, 6-1/2 horsepower, bore 3 inches, stroke 3-1/2 inches. Piston displacement, 49.48 ci.

Cylinders: Close-grained gray iron, heat-treated prior to machining. Cylinder and cylinder heads each one piece, eliminating all chances of leakage through gaskets or joints.

Piston rings: Eccentric-turned and step-cut.

Connecting rod: Modified "I" beam section of chrome vanadium steel, bushed at both ends with phosphor bronze; lower bearing is adjustable.

Inlet valve: Made of nickel steel.

Exhaust valve: Two-piece type with cast iron head and nickel steel stem.

Mechanical inlet valves: Featured on the twin-cylinder models only at this time.

Crankcase: Aluminum.

Crank pin and shafts: Special tool steel, hardened and ground to exact size.

Crankshaft bearings: Made of phosphor bronze.

Ignition: Bosch magneto.

Lubrication: Semi-automatic, vacuum-feed oiling system. Overflow valve fitted to prevent flooding the crankcase; same valve maintains partial vacuum in the crankcase while motor is running to ensure lubrication in direct proportion to requirements.

Carburetor: Schebler.

Transmission: Flat belt with shield and idler. Belts are 1-3/4 inches, two-ply, flat, waterproof.

Frame: Double bar loop, running continuously from steering head to seat mast. Steering head made of vanadium steel. All joints brazed.

Forks: All bearings provided with ball oilers. The main springs are 16-1/2 inches long and 1 inch in diameter. The recoil springs are 4-1/2 inches long and 1 inch in diameter.

Handlebars: Made of seamless steel tubing. Double grip control entirely enclosed within handlebars.

Oil and gasoline tanks: Individual units; top and lower frame bars are completely covered by the tanks. Gasoline tank capacity is 2-1/2 gallons, oil tank 1 gallon.

Toolbox: Standard.

Mud guards: 3-3/4 inches wide with a raised center front. Front fitted with large splasher.

Muffler: Cutout provided.

Wheelbase: 56-1/2 inches.

Front hub: Equipped with knockout-type axle.

Rear hub: Coaster brake.

Equipment: Either Troxel, Mesinger, or Persons saddle. G&J, Morgan & Wright, Goodyear, or Goodrich tires. Studded or corrugated tread may be had at regular prices, but if any other special tread is wanted, extra charge will be made. Tires are 2-1/2 inches. Large, rubber-tread motor cycle pedals are regular equipment. A canvas tool roll containing a complete set of tools is supplied with each machine, together with instruction book carefully written.

Single-cylinder Models, 1913–1918

This series of single-cylinder, four-cycle machines was known collectively as the 5-35, which stood for 5 horsepower and 35 ci (or 3500 rpm). Like virtually all H-Ds past and present, the stroke (4 inches) was bigger than the bore

(3–5/16 inches). The cylinder and integral head were of gray iron and featured a heat-treated steel piston with three rings and a hollow steel wrist pin. A chrome steel I-beam served as the connecting rod and there were separate camshafts for the inlet and exhaust valves. The crankcase was aluminum with a tool-steel crankshaft riding on phosphor-bronze bushings. A Bosch high-tension magneto provided ignition.

A Schebler carburetor was standard equipment, with a priming petcock on the left side of the cylinder head. The tank between the "Ful-Floteing" seat and the steering head held both gasoline and oil, with separate screw-type filler

Panhead with sidecar attached. (David K. Wright)

caps. Lubricants for the engine descended through a sight glass that told the rider how many seconds elapsed between drops of oil. One drop every five seconds was sufficient to lube the motor without throwing out a blue exhaust cloud, according to Bill McMahon, owner of a running 1914 model.

The shock of hitting a chuckhole was mitigated a bit by the front suspension, which featured main and recoil springs, but with only about 2 inches of travel. The tires measured 2.5 x 28 inches and therefore did little to cushion bike or rider. Rear suspension was of course nonexistent, though the spring beneath the patented seat was of some consolation to the owner's posterior. Drive was by roller chain and a sprocket on the crankshaft to a sprocket on the rear hub. The clutch, also on that hub, was engaged by moving a lever on the left side of the machine. The same pedals used to start the motor (with the rear wheel on the stand) activated the internal expanding rear coaster brake by backward force. With the clutch disengaged, the machine could be pedaled forward when all else failed.

Top speed in low gear was approximately 35 mph, with speed exceeding 60 mph in high. The two-speed transmission made its appearance on one single and one V-twin in 1914. By 1915, singles and twins alike were hooked to the H-D three-speed. This sliding-gear unit allowed the step starter to be routed directly through the transmission instead of its former attachment to the frame. A single, backward kick could turn the motor over.

Except for commercial use, no singles were produced from 1918 until 1926. Some confusion has arisen over the serial numbers on the early bikes, since the 1915 models began with "12" and the 1916 models bore the "16" designation. Harley-Davidson merely brought its serial numbers in line with the current year from 1916 onward. For example, "C16S10115" indicates that the model in question had a two-speed transmission with chain drive, was made during the 1916 model year, was a single, and was one of at least 10,115 motorcycles produced that year. This system continued through 1969.

The Sidecar, 1914–

There were sidecars before there were Harley-Davidsons. The first consisted of a large wagon towed by the bike, but this school of sidecar thought ended when passengers complained of oil, gravel, and mud showers. A seat between two wheels up front followed, but this arrangement prevented the rider from seeing around the passenger. The English came up with the first true sidecar, as we know it, a wicker-bodied unit, built in 1913.

An early H-D sidecar began life as a sheet of steel on which a pattern had been marked. Following trimming, the sheet was shaped into a pointed cowl. Reinforcement was provided by a 1/4-inch rod that was enclosed around the perimeter of the cowl, which was joined to the scoop-shaped body via the rods and spot welding. Metal braces and supports were added, since the pieces were subjected to torsion. A triple-veneered hardwood floor was added and rough edges hand-sanded before receiving a coat of primer and baking in a 225-degree oven. The bodies then were spray painted by hand. The seat consisted of a wood base, springs, and a leather cover. It was sewn on electric machines, a rarity for the time. The only screws on the car—two dozen of them—were used to attach the seat to a body flange. The frame consisted of 1-1/4-inch steel tubing and was shaped on a series of jigs and fixtures. Since no early photos show finished sidecars within the factory, it can be assumed that the frame, body, axle, wheel, and tire were shipped as a ready-to-assemble package to dealers. The price was $85.

How times change. The modern sidecar consists of a one-piece body laid up in a mold. The frame carries the body lower, just inches above the car's fender. The passenger, with no plastic windscreen for protection, formerly sat as high as the rider; today, he or she is seated about 18 inches below the bike's saddle for added stability and so the driver can see to the right. A long leaf spring carries the Big Twin body (sidecars with sprung wheels were made by Goulding prior to World War II but were available only for 45-ci models).

With nearly 90 years of sidecar experience, H-D sets up bikes for sidecar use quite differently from its solo mounts. The forks have slightly less trail, the steering damper is snugged up a bit, ball joints long ago replaced nuts and bolts as the means of affixing the car to the bike's special braces, the wiring connection for the sidecar tail light is made, and the hydraulic brake system is filled and adjusted. Only at this point, and if the rider is experienced, does

A 1952 Model K. This sports bike employed the 45-ci side valve motor. (David K. Wright)

the factory advise motoring off into the sunset. The current sidecar manual, complete with directions for finding the VIN, lists all of the quirks peculiar to riding a three wheeler: Reduced acceleration and lower gas mileage, pulling to the right under acceleration and to the left when decelerating, increased wear on tires and belts, and the necessity of steering rather than leaning into a turn. Finally, the bike will appear to be canted away from the car when viewed from the front or rear.

The golden age of the "chair" began in 1915. Cycles were authorized for Rural Free Delivery; the sidecar was a natural for carrying the mail. That same year, H-D produced the first van body on a sidecar chassis, and by 1918 the company was offering vans with capacities of as much as 600 pounds. By 1919, some 16,400 sidecars were constructed—more than 7 sidecars for every 10 Harley-Davidsons. Export literature first appeared in 1917, with left-hand body features for the English market. In the 1920s, sidecars constituted the main thrust in advertising and were sufficiently popular to necessitate fliers written in German, Spanish, and Japanese.

Goulding created its first sidecar in 1929 for the new 45-ci models. Seaman, a Milwaukee firm later absorbed by Nash (American Motors), made the bodies during the 1920s

The K was the first Harley-Davidson with swingarm rear suspension. (David K. Wright)

37-ci Flat Twin Sport Model 1919–1922

"This new motor has the distinction of developing the highest motor speed of any gasoline engine motor ever built, so far as we know. We are not going to tell you what it is, you would not believe it."

The new motor, a front-to-rear opposed Sport Twin, *had* to turn over rapidly; otherwise, it pumped out so little power that the lightweight cycle was left in the dust by more powerful competition, namely, the Indian Scout. The lightweight, conceived during World War I and introduced late in 1918, carried its 37-ci engine and three-speed transmission low in the frame. Equipped with 26-inch tires, only the handlebars and springs protruded above the level of the fenders. In addition to a fully enclosed drive chain that ran in a spray of oil emitted from a breather pipe, the Sport could be had with full electric lights and coil ignition, or magneto ignition and accessory gaslights. The machine was quiet, provided good fuel economy, displayed a distinct lack of vibration—and was slow. "What will it do on the road?" asked a copywriter. "Let's say 50 miles an hour and let it go at that—it will do better." Let's forgive the ad man, who probably pushed a pencil better than he rode.

The Speed Twin was offered for four years, from 1919 through 1922. In addition to being down on power, it represented very little that the Roaring Twenties rider wanted—the thump of the traditional V-twin, eye-watering acceleration, and a top end of more than 45 or 50 mph. Nevertheless, the bike contributed important income from the export market, where the opposed twin found favor with European riders before the creation of autobahns and such. The electrically equipped 22WJ sold for $340, while the magneto 22WF was offered for $310 during its final year of production.

Specifications (From a 1922 brochure)

Motor: 6 horsepower, opposed (front to rear) twin, 2-3/4-inch (68.94-mm) bore, 3-inch (76.20-mm) stroke, displacement 35.64 ci (584 cc).
Carburetor: Schebler.
Transmission: Three-speed sliding gear transmission, multiple

and earlier. Abresh Body Shop introduced a new design in 1936, and steel body production continued through 1966 at Abresh in Milwaukee. The latter had for years created special-order sidecar and van bodies for the factory. Fiberglass bodies, laid up in the former boat-building facility in H-D's Tomahawk plant, were introduced in 1967.

Virtually all H-Ds headed for the front in World War I were three wheelers, in contrast to the virtual absence of sidecars in World War II. A small exception was the batch of military "U" models ordered by the U.S. Navy. According to a notation found in the Harley-Davidson archives, only 136 such machines, attached to 74-ci side valve bikes, were ordered, all in battleship gray.

Harley-Davidson is the only major manufacturer that makes its own sidecars. For 2003, there are two models, the Standard and the Ultra Classic. The latter offers a plush interior and a premium sound system. Either 'car will fit any FL model since 1993, and can be had in matching stock paint. Both sidecars feature a disc brake on the third wheel, carpeted interior, tonneau cover, four wheel/tire combinations, and quick disconnect. There are no sidecars created by the factory for Softail, FLSTS, or for models with the springer front fork.

disc steel plate clutch running in oil.

Lubrication: Automatic oil pump.

Step starter: Rear stroke, mechanical, spring return.

Handlebars: One-piece welded, 1-inch tubular steel, double stem.

Controls: Grip, double-acting wire control entirely enclosed within handlebars.

Frame: Keystone.

Driving chain: Duckworth roller, 3/8 inch wide, 5/8-inch pitch.

Brakes: Internal expanding, double-acting band brake, 7-15/16-inch diameter, 1-inch face. Front external contracting brake available where required by law.

Saddle: Mesinger, Ful-Floteing seat post.

Tires: 26 x 3 inches.

Wheelbase: 53-1/2 inches.

Tanks: Capacity 2-3/4-gallon capacity for gasoline, 2 quarts for oil.

Mudguard: Pressed steel.

Finish: Brewster green, striped in gold.

74-ci Twin, 1921–1929

The first 74-ci twin, introduced in 1921, remained essentially unchanged through 1929. Dubbed the Superpowered Twin, the new motor was first featured in quantity in the 22JD, which was electrically equipped, and in the 22FD, which ran a magneto. Prices (fob Milwaukee) were $390 and $360, respectively. That was only $25 more than the 61-ci J and F models offered the same year. Harley-Davidson claimed 18 horsepower from the new, bigger twin. The bore was 3-7/16 inches (86.97 mm) and the stroke was an even 4 inches (101.60 mm). The machine was advertised as ideal for sidecars, "especially for use with the two-passenger sidecar (Model 22QT) and where traveling conditions are the worst," a 1922 brochure stated. The big twin was a response to four-cylinder Hendersons in particular, which had more, if less dependable, power than the trusty 61, which by then was a 13-year-old design.

The company noted that the new model was capable of 40–60 miles on a gallon of the low-octane gasoline almost universally available by 1920. The lighting and ignition system consisted of a 6-volt generator-ignition unit, a storage battery, headlight, taillight, and motor-driven oil warning signal. The ignition system consisted of a circuit breaker, a distributor, and a high-tension spark coil. The system was mounted directly behind the motor, probably to reduce the chance of contact with water.

Two important non-cosmetic changes on the 74 were introduced in 1924 and were the kinds of amenities riders had on Harleys and wanted on other bikes. Alemite lubrication on all bearing surfaces except within the motor greatly extended the life of the running gear. The cap of the Alemite gun was hooked over the fitting and the handle turned, forcing grease onto the surface with 500 pounds of pressure. An Alemite gun and a one-pound can of grease were furnished gratis with each new twin.

The second improvement was the use of aluminum for the 74's pistons. This lightweight metal with superior heat-dissipating properties meant more power and less chance of seizing. Additions that were more obvious included the handsome teardrop tank in 1925, balloon tires in 1925, and throttle regulated oil pressure and a front brake standard on 1928 models. Performance, by all accounts, was excellent. In fact, J models intended for sidecar use carried a spacer plate between the cylinders and the lower end. This 1/8-inch plate prolonged engine life by slightly lowering compression.

This 1958 Sportster is either an XL or an XLH (high compression). The engine measured 55 ci. (David K. Wright)

Willie G. Davidson with his café racer, the first XLCR produced. The vice president of styling personalized his machine by adding pinstriping, trading the original Goodyear tires for Continentals, and porcelainizing the exhaust.
(David K. Wright)

Specifications (From a 1922 brochure)

Motor: Air-cooled, high-speed, high efficiency, two-cylinder, four-cycle "L" head, pocket valve "V" type motor. For sidecar use, motors are fitted with 1/8-inch compression shims. Letter "S" in model number designates sidecar motor.
Carburetor: Schebler.
Battery: Exide.
Three-speed transmission: Sliding gear type, gears of chrome nickel steel, transmission box of aluminum. Transmission main shaft mounted on large, heavy-duty roller bearing on the left or drive side and a ball bearing on the right side. Main drive gear runs on a high-duty phosphor-bronze bearing. Uses same type lubrication oil as the motor.

Lubrication: Automatic oil pump. Average 800–1,000 miles per gallon of oil.
Step starter: Rear stroke mechanical starter, spring return.
Clutch: Multiple dry disc.
Handlebars: One-piece, welded, 1-inch tubular steel, double stem.
Controls: Grip, double-acting wire control entirely enclosed within the handlebars.
Frame: Extra heavy duty gauge high carbon steel seamless tubular loop, rigidly reinforced.
Driving chain: Duckworth roller, 3/8-inch width, 5/8-inch pitch.
Brake: Controlled by lever on right footboard. Internal expanding, double-acting band brake, operating on a steel drum 7-5/16-inch diameter with 1-inch face. Where the law calls for two brakes, an external contracting brake can be furnished in addition.
Saddle: Mesinger saddle, Ful-Floteing seat.
Suspension: Double spring front fork.
Tires: 28 x 3 inches.
Wheelbase: 59-1/2 inches.
Tanks: Gasoline capacity 3-1/4 gallons, lubricating oil 1 gallon.
Mudguards: Pressed steel, extra wide and substantial. Flat military front mudguards available.
Finish: Brewster green, tastily double striped in gold.

21-ci Single, 1926–1935

The 21-ci single was produced for ten years, though the average U.S. Harley-Davidson rider was hardly aware of its prolonged existence. The dependable little machine, available in side valve or overhead valve configurations, was infinitely more popular in Europe, Australia, and New Zealand than in its native land. Again, the ribbons of long, straight North American highways beckoned the rider astride large, slow-turning motors.

Created simultaneously with similar Indian models, the single helped lure racer Joe Petrali from Excelsior to run the Peashooter—the nickname for H-D's overhead valve model—in competition. And run it he did! Petrali swept every major dirt-track event in the country in 1935, 13 races in all. His success on the little machine prompted the AMA to create a new competition class made up of larger, more nearly stock, motorcycles.

The Harley-Davidson single was offered initially in four versions, a side valve magneto model, a side valve generator model, an overhead valve magneto model, and an overhead valve generator model. The side valves featured iron alloy pistons, while the overheads ran lightweight, racing-type aluminum. The side valve A and B singles were created with patented, aircraft-type Ricardo heads that squeezed the air-fuel mixture toward the plug for better combustion. All models were fully equipped and appeared to be scaled-down, singles versions of the big bikes. While the overhead valve had plenty of punch, the side valve was slow. Top end on the overhead, produced as a 21-ci bike through 1929, was a reported 65 mph in stock form. The side valve struggled to exceed 50. Prices ranged from $210 to $275 in 1926.

Specifications (From a 1926 brochure)

Motor: Four-stroke cycle, single cylinder, air-cooled, 21.098-ci (350-cc) displacement, 2-7/8-inch bore, 3-1/4-inch stroke. Side by side valves in models A and B. Overhead valves in models AA and BA.
Carburetor: Schebler DeLuxe.
Transmission: Three-speed progressive sliding gear, supplemented by hand pump. Transmission lubricated by separate oil splash. Nine-place Alemite fitted.
Ignition: Harley-Davidson generator-battery on electrically equipped models. Robert Bosch magneto on magneto models.
Electrical equipment: (On electric models only) Harley-Davidson generator, coil, timer-distributor, four-plate storage battery, vibrator horn, two-bulb headlight, standard tail lamp, ignition and light switch panel located back of steering head. Relay cutout that automatically opens and closes battery-generator circuit.
Starter: H-D rear stroke on right side.
Clutch: Single-plate dry disc, foot operated.
Handlebars: One piece, 1-inch tubular double stem with closed end grips.
Frame: High carbon, seamless, tubular steel with wide trussed loop. Drop forged head.
Controls: Grip, double-acting wire controls entirely enclosed within handlebars. Toe operated compression relief.

Brake: External contracting, foot operated. Drum 5-3/4-inch diameter, 3-3/16-inch x 1-inch lining.
Driving chains: Roller 5/8-inch pitch and 1-1/4 inch wide.
Seat: Mesinger top. Full spring seat post.
Tires: Full Balloon, 26 x 3.30 inches.
Wheelbase: 55 inches.
Tanks: Gasoline capacity, 3 gallons. Lubricating oil, 3 quarts. Reserve gasoline tank.
Mudguards: Pressed steel.
Footboards: Standard Harley-Davidson.
Tool equipment: Tool and tire repair kit.
Finish: Harley-Davidson olive green. Tanks, wide maroon striping with center gold stripe.

45-ci V-Twin, 1929–1951

Nineteen twenty-nine may have been a bad year for the stock market, but it was a vintage year for Harley-Davidson. The 30.50-ci single was introduced, the powerful two-cam was in its second year of road bike production, and—most meaningful of all—the 45-ci motor made its debut. Had anyone at H-D seen the Great Depression coming, the company probably would have saved the development dollars spent on the splendid 45.

Fewer than 3,400 of the XLCR café racer bikes were produced. (David K. Wright)

Three 45 models for 1929 indicated that the factory was serious about this bike. A low-compression D model was available for sidecar work, as well as a standard DL, and a high-compression DLD. Aluminum or magnesium pistons were provided for all 45's that year. The machines, with "R" added to their initials, remained essentially the same through 1936. Then they received a new letter, "W," displaying the recirculating oil system introduced on the 1936 Knucklehead. Special alloy heads for the WR and WLDR were the only other 1930s mechanical innovations. The W series dominated U.S. racing until two-wheel 45 production ceased in 1951.

The motor evolved into a real winner. Throughout its 45 years of production (the last 22 in the Servi-Car only), the 750-cc side valve V-twin was characterized by massively over-sized cooling fins on the heads, which allowed a machine to idle all day without seizure from overheating. Charles Darling, Sodus, New York, rode 45s from 1930 through 1951. Here are his impressions of those models through the years.

"The model years 1930–1935 had quite acceptable handling characteristics. … Even the deeply rutted dirt roads, which were fairly common in those days, did not represent much of a problem when negotiated at reasonable speeds. However, beginning with the 1936 model year and continuing through the last 1951 WL models, the steering head angle was decreased a few degrees, making the fork assume a more nearly vertical position. This decreased the 'caster' angle and had a decidedly negative effect on stability. It was even worse when the machines were equipped with 5.00 x 16 tires.

"Another handicap of the 45 R and W series was the three-speed transmissions. They had a wide ratio gap between second and third, making it necessary to really wind out the motor in second so it wouldn't bog down when the clutch was engaged in third gear. … The transmission itself on these models was notoriously weak, too. Despite this, the Harley 45 was a nice little machine to ride and provided economical transportation for thousands of people."

Police aboard Servi-Cars and soldiers aboard WLA 45s in World War II would agree with Darling's assessment. U.S. riders, accustomed to the power of the 61- and 74-ci bikes, frequently abused the 45 to make it run with the big twins. The motor refused to react in any negative way except to leak a bit of oil from around the head gaskets, though this may have been aggravated by the owner or dealer, who inadvertently scratched the gasket after cleaning carbon from the heads or grinding the valves.

A low-compression (6.5:1) motor, the 45 ran faultlessly on either regular or leaded gasoline; it continued to do so in the 1930s, when several compression choices were offered for those desiring more speed or pulling power for sidecar work. In addition, because the factory produced as many as 20 sets of spares for each WLA (Army) model, 45-ci parts remain available. Harley-Davidson certainly made faster and flashier bikes. It has yet to produce a machine that endeared itself to more people.

A test rider takes out a 2002 Sportster. (David K. Wright)

Specifications (From a 1929 dealer brochure)

Motor: V type twin cylinder air-cooled four-stroke cycle—bore 2-3/4 inches, stroke 3-15/16 inches, displacement 45.32 ci. Side by side valves, independent cam action on each valve. Dow metal pistons. New, plunger-type crankcase oil drain.
Carburetor: Schebler DeLuxe with self-cleaning air cleaner.
Muffler: Four tubes.
Lubrication: Throttle-controlled motor oiler that provides proper lubrication at all speeds. Transmission lubricated separately. 13 Alemite fittings.
Ignition: Harley-Davidson generator-battery with output controller.

Electrical equipment: Harley-Davidson generator with instantaneous output controller; weather and waterproof coil and timer; five plate, 22-amp/hr. storage battery; high-frequency horn; two bullet headlights; standard tail lamp; ignition and light switch panel with built-in ammeter and hooded parking light located back of steering head. Relay cutout automatically opens and closes generator-battery circuit.

Starter: Harley-Davidson rear stroke, right side.

Clutch: Multi-plate, multi-disc, foot operated.

Handlebars: One piece, 1-inch tubular, double stem with closed end twist grips.

Controls: Grip, double-acting wire controls, enclosed in handlebars and cables.

Brakes: Foot-controlled contracting rear brake and built-in, hand-controlled expanding front wheel brake.

Frame: High-carbon, seamless, tubular steel, strongly reinforced with wide trussed loop. Dropforged head and gearbox bracket.

Driving chains: Duplex engine chain 3/8-inch pitch, 3/4 inch wide. Large cushion motor sprocket.

Saddle: Mesinger form-fitting top. Adjustable spring seat post.

Tires: Standard make, 25 x 3.85 inches, full balloon.

Wheelbase: 56-1/2 inches.

Tanks: Saddle type. Gasoline capacity 3-3/4 gallons; oil capacity, 7-1/2 pints. Reserve gasoline tank.

Mudguards: Extra wide valanced, rear guard hinged for easy access to wheel.

Finish: Harley-Davidson Olive Green with maroon striping with center gold stripe. Rims and handlebars black.

30.50-ci Single, 1929–1936

In 1929, Harley-Davidson did what racers had been doing for more than a decade: It created a single from half of a 61-ci V-twin. Unlike the go-fast guys, who yanked the head and covered the gaping hole with a steel plate, H-D engineers grafted a head of very similar dimensions onto the lower end first produced in 1926 for the side valve and overhead valve singles. A dissimilar 500-cc (30-ci) single, the CAC, was raced in the early 1930s but, except for export, was not offered as a street bike. It appears that American riders at that time would accept nothing smaller than a 750-cc motor. They may have preferred a twin if their memories were long, since the first

The Panhead motor was first produced for the 1948 model year. It superseded the Knucklehead and offered the advantages of better oil passage and lighter weight—the Knucklehead was all iron, whereas the Panhead, produced through 1965, had numerous aluminum upper-end parts. (David K. Wright)

bikes on U.S. roads were singles that spewed oil and frequently needed leg power on steep grades.

The C, as it was known, used the 45-ci frame in 1929. From 1930 through 1934, the C used the same frame as the 1930 and 1931 45s. In 1932, the R 45 with the horizontal generator required a bowed front down-tube, which the singles did not need. Much of the rest of the C frame was from the 45. Forks, tanks, fenders, and the 18-inch drop wheels were shared with the 45; the 21-ci singles retained the 20-inch clincher rims throughout their production.

Not many H-D riders realize it today, but the single once was as much a part of the picture as the V-twin. Until the mid-1930s, the company continued to attempt to make single-cylinder Harleys popular. Among their last major efforts was a prototype single from 1934 that looks like half a

Knucklehead head, attached to a lower end appearing nowhere else in the motorcycle lineup. A photo of the one-of-a-kind motor recently surfaced on the Internet.

Specifications *(From a 1929 brochure)*

Motor: Four-stroke single-cylinder side valve. Bore 3-3/32 inches, stroke 4 inches; piston displacement, 30.50 ci.

Muffler: Four-tube "Pipes of Pan."

Carburetor: Schebler DeLuxe with self-cleaning air cleaner.

Transmission: Three-speed progressive sliding gear.

Lubrication: Throttle-controlled motor oiler. Transmission lubricated separately. 14 Alemite fittings.

Ignition: Harley-Davidson generator-battery with output controller.

Electrical equipment: H-D generator with instantaneous output controller; waterproof coil and timer; five plate storage battery; high-frequency horn; two bullet headlights; standard tail lamp; ignition and light switch panel with built-in ammeter and hooded parking light located back of steering head. Relay cutout automatically opens and closes battery-generator circuit.

Starter: Rear stroke, right side.

A Harley-Davidson employee astride a 2002 Sportster. (David K. Wright)

Clutch: Single-plate dry disc, foot operated.

Handlebars: One piece, 1-inch tubular, double stem with closed end twist grips.

Controls: Grip, double-acting wire controls enclosed in handlebars and cables. Toe-operated compression relief.

Brakes: Foot-controlled contracting rear brake and built-in hand controlled expanding front brake.

Frame: High-carbon, seamless, tubular steel, strongly reinforced and with wide trussed loop. Dropforged head and gearbox bracket.

Driving chains: Duplex engine chain 3/8-inch pitch, 3/4 inch wide, each sprocket 3/16 inch wide. Rear chain, roller 5/8-inch pitch, 3/8 inch wide. Large cushion motor sprocket.

Saddle: Mesinger form-fitting top. Adjustable spring seat posts.

Tires: 25 x 3.85 inches.

Wheelbase: 56-1/2 inches.

Finish: Harley-Davidson Olive Green with maroon striping with center gold stripe. Rims and handlebars black.

74-ci VL, 1930–1940

Harley-Davidson billed the 1930 74-ci big twins as "the greatest achievement in motorcycling history." Actually, the new design may have been one of the most poorly developed H-Ds ever to roll down Juneau Avenue. "Originally, it had a bad engine, a bad clutch, the flywheels were too small, the frames broke, and the mufflers became so clogged with carbon that the engines lost power," said William H. Davidson. He recalled a frantic trip he made to New York State in late 1929, only days after the Buffalo police took delivery of a fleet of new 74s. "We replaced mufflers, valve springs, pistons, everything we'd carried from Milwaukee. The shop mechanic took one out and it ran 90 miles an hour. Then I took one of their police officers out in a sidecar and wound it up to 75. He yelled to me that 75 was fast enough, which was fortunate, because it wouldn't go any faster."

The late company president also pointed out that the initial poor performance could not have come at a worse time. The stock market's nosedive took place just three months after the new model introduction in July 1929. Dealers were asked to sell a high-priced bike with big problems to riders facing even bigger problems, such as unem-

The ST was a 165-cc two-stroke. This is a 1957 example.
(David K. Wright)

ployment. To Harley-Davidson's credit, the early woes were corrected quickly.

There was no single spec on the new 74 that would arouse suspicion. The bore was 3-7/16 inches and the stroke was 4 inches. The Ricardo heads had been proven in earlier models. Combined with side-by-side valves and a 1-1/4-inch Schebler carburetor, the motor developed at least 15 percent more horsepower than previous 74s. It also featured a new, plugger-type crankcase oil drain and a cam gear case vacuum that was touted as keeping the motor cleaner (spewing less oil on bike or rider). The few affluent buyers soon wished they could trade their new machines for 61-ci J models, even if it meant well-lubricated boots and trousers.

By no means were all of the new ideas on the 74 bad. The primary chain was extra-heavy duplex. By loosening a single nut on either axle, a wheel could be quickly removed for service. Wheels were interchangeable, not only for the VL, but for the sidecar and Package Truck options as well. Full balloon 27 x 4.00 tires were featured on the new model. The new frame, while heavier than the J model, allowed for a lower riding position. As early as 1930, then, Harley-Davidson was touting a low and distinctive way to travel. Other amenities included a high-frequency horn, an improved 22-amp battery, and a sealed coil that enhanced the H-D reputation for having

waterproof electrical systems. The saddle-type tank held four gallons of gasoline and a gallon of oil.

The finish remained olive green but was highlighted by a vermilion stripe. By 1932, the olive caterpillar would become a multicolored, Art Deco butterfly. List price was $340 for each of four models: The standard V, the higher-compression VL, the sidecar-geared VS, and the VC, which featured nickel iron rather than Dow metal pistons and was designed for used with the Package Truck.

It has been said that the best bikes also have the most complete tool kits. The VL may be the exception that proves the rule. Here are the tool kit contents, typical of H-D models throughout this period. Unfortunately, VL owners got to know their tools on a regular basis.

1. Registration card.
2. Rider's handbook.
3. Wrench for valve spring covers, valve tappets, and various small nuts.
4. Socket wrench for cylinder head clamp screws.
5. Wrench for axle nuts and rear brake hub nut.
6. Spark plug wrench.
7. Tire patches.
8. Chain tool.
9. Screwdriver.
10. Wrench for transmission clamp nuts and transmission oil filler plug.
11. Wrench for valve tappets; also fits various small nuts.
12. Wrench for rear axle adjusting screw and lock nuts, cylinder base nuts, gas pipe nuts, and clutch pull rod lock nut.
13. Wrench for footboard support rod nuts, front fork rocker plate stud nuts, oil pipe nuts, and various other nuts.
14. Pliers.
15. Monkey wrench.
16. Steering head lock keys.
17. Ignition and lighting switch keys.
18. Tool box key.
19. Wrench for switch box terminal nuts, also feel gauge for adjusting circuit breaker point gap.
20. Rear chain repair links.
21. Front chain repair links.
22. Pump fastening clips.
23. Alemite grease gun.
24. Tire pump.

Another late 1950s 165-cc two-stroke; this one is configured for short-track racing. (David K. Wright)

Specifications (1930)

Number of cylinders: Two.
Bore: 3-7/16 inches (87.31 mm).
Stroke: 4 inches (101.66 mm).
Displacement: 73.73 ci (1208.19 cc).
Horsepower (N.A.C.C. rating): 9.45.
Wheelbase: 60 inches.
Gear ratios
Motor sprocket: 23.
Clutch sprocket: 51.
Countershaft sprocket: 28.
Rear wheel sprocket: 51.
High gear ratio: 4.04:1.
Tire data
Size: 4.00 inches.
Inflation (solo rider): 16 pounds front, 18 pounds, rear.
Motor or serial number: Stamped on left crankcase.

Servi-Car, 1932–1974

The Servi-Car, introduced in 1932, made a lot of sense. It enabled someone relatively unfamiliar with two-wheelers to take advantage of the fuel economy offered by the standard 45-ci R motor and the compact size of a motorcycle. Previewed to dealers in their November 9, 1931, news bulletin, the three-wheeler was "intended primarily for use by garages and service stations in the pickup and delivery of customers' cars." Unlike other tricycle-type vehicles of the time, there seems to have been quite a bit of engineering in the Servi-Car. The frame was a complete unit; there had been no ill-planned attempt to graft a motorcycle onto a pair of wheels. A double roller, enclosing a chain leading to the three-speed transmission, provided primary drive. A single chain transmitted power to a sprocket on the rear axle. Final drive was by means of a modified automobile differential, completely enclosed.

In addition to a hand-controlled, internal expanding brake up front, a foot pedal activated a drum brake on a larger internal expanding brake attached to the rear axle. Origin of the rear brake was no puzzle: shoes and linings were interchangeable with the rear unit on 74-ci H-Ds. An important consideration was the distance between the rear wheels: 42 inches. This allowed riders to follow the paths forged by car tires in mud and snow.

The wheelbase measured 61 inches. The body of the machines, immediately behind the rider, looked like a large soft-drink cooler. It was 29 inches wide, 23 inches long, a foot high, first metal and then fiberglass, and was supported on a subframe. The subframe was hinged to a tie bar fastened on the Servi-Car frame and supported in the rear by a pair of coil springs. Rear mudguards and a rear apron were attached to the body, which was hinged at the top by two latches (one of which could be locked). The flat rear end was "perfectly adapted to advertising signs and lettering," an early bulletin pointed out. The standard color initially was turquoise blue for the tanks, rear fenders, and body, with the frame, chainguards, front forks, tow bar, battery box, and running gear in black. Price in 1932, with tow bar, was $450 fob Milwaukee.

Options offered initially included a passenger seat and a carrier for an automobile tire (should a service station specialize in fixing flats). Never advertised as a machine designed for the highway, the three-wheeler instead offered a way for one individual to drive to a parked car, hook up the Servi-Car with a standard tow bar and drive the car to a service station or garage, the tricycle in tow. As sound as this seems to be, the Servi-Car was most commonly used by traffic and parking authorities through 1974.

Changes throughout its years of production included making the tow bar an option in 1963 (no service station in its right mind would come to you by then), installing electric starting the following year, and using fiberglass for bodies in 1966. Despite its ability to poke along at in-town speeds all day, the Servi-Car had a few quirks. A 1969 owner's handbook admonishes to "put shift lever in neutral before stopping engine while parking. If left in gear when engine is stopped, rock Servi-Car to shift out of gear to neutral." Neutral-only starting was a minor annoyance, but that was not what killed the machine. Instead, it was done in by various Cushmans and stripped-down Jeeps, which offered meter maids, postal employees, and such weather protection, and, usually, a heater. In its final year, only 70 Servi-Cars were sold, primarily to municipalities. A new, 74-ci Servi-Car never got past the prototype stage.

I can remember one or more Servi-Cars operated by police in my hometown of Richmond, Indiana, when I was a kid. Initially, the three-wheelers were silver and black, then black and white when H-D went to a fiberglass body, and were used to enforce parking regulations. They looked somewhat dated, what with their automotive-type tires and stubby wire wheels, also painted black. Except for tipping over once in a while, they provided quiet, faithful service from as early as 1946 to at least 1960.

Specifications

Model G (1963 and earlier): with tow bar.
Model GA (1963 and earlier): less tow bar.
Model GE (1964 and later): electric start (less tow bar.)
Wheelbase: 61 inches.
Overall length: 100 inches.
Overall width: 48 inches.
Fuel tank: 3.4 U.S. gallons.
Oil tank: 3-1/2 quarts.
Transmission: 3/4 pint.
Engine: See specifications for DS 45 engine.
Battery: 12-volt, 60 amp/hr. capacity.
Circuit breaker points: .022 inch.
Spark plugs, type: Harley-Davidson No. 3.

Size: 14 mm.
Gap: .025 to .030 inch.
Spark timing: Retard 0 degrees (front piston top center); automatic advance 30 degrees (5/16 inch before piston top center).
Transmission type: Constant mesh.
Speeds: Three forward, one reverse.
First gear: 14.4:1.
Second gear: 9.7:1.
Third gear: 5.85:1.
Reverse: 12.45:1.
Tire size (1966 and earlier): 5.00 x 16 inches; 1969 and later, 5.10 x 16 inches.

80-ci Side Valve Twin, 1936–1945

The 80-ci side valve twin, designated ULH and produced from 1937 through 1941, featured the Y-type intake manifold found on the more popular 45- and 74-ci models, plus deeply finned heads and a new combustion chamber design shared with the smaller models. The factory especially recommended the ULH for sidecar work. In 1937, the giant twin shared

A 1961 250-cc Sprint motor. Not comparable to the full-size Harleys, the Aermacchis nevertheless introduced cycling to a number of beginning riders. (David K. Wright)

the circulating oil pump and dry sump lubrication with the 45 and 74. This was an entirely satisfactory bike in virtually every respect; the original four-speed transmission caused minor problems only the first year of production. The decision not to continue the 80-ci side valver following World War II probably was due to materials shortages and to the on-going popularity of the Knucklehead.

Former H-D dealer Conrad Schlemmer points out that "considerable confusion" surrounds Harley-Davidson's V-series and U-series engines. The V-series began in 1930, ceased with the end of the 1936 model year, and included the VL, VLD, VLH, and others. The U-series, with the circulating oil system, began with the 1937 model year and includes the U, UL, ULH, and so on. Harley-Davidson advertised the bore on the 1930–1936 74s and 80s as 3-7/16 inches but in reality, it was a bit less than that. The standard bore on the V series was 3.422 inches and this was also the bore on the 1937 and later 80-ci models.

Specifications (From a 1936 dealer brochure)

Motor: Air-cooled four-stroke cycle, side by side valves, Ricardo cylinder heads. Lynite, cam-ground pistons. Cylinders straight honed, mirror finish. Bore, 3.422 inches; stroke, 4-1/4 inches.

Muffler: Burgess straight-through with gas-deflecting end.

Carburetor: Linkert.

Transmission: Three-speed standard. Reverse gear available. Fourth speed available.

Lubrication: Throttle-controlled oil pump for motor with automatic front chain oiling. Transmission lubricated separately. All other bearings Alemite fitted.

Ignition: Harley-Davidson generator-battery.

Electric equipment: Large, 7-inch headlight with pre-focused double filament bulb. Dual beam control from handlebar. High output generator with automatic increase when headlight is in use. 22 amp/-hour battery. Disc-type horn.

Handlebars: One piece, with double-acting twist grip controls fully enclosed.

Frame: Extra low, strongly reinforced, seamless steel tubing, with drop forged fittings. Entire frame heat-treated. Theft-proof lock.

Clutch: Multiple dry disc, foot-operated.

Front forks: Combination rigid and spring fork construction. Rigid fork dropforged. Spring fork seamless steel tubing and dropforging fitted with two sets helical cushion bumper and recoil springs.

Drive: Duplex extra heavy roller chain for front. Rear chain, extra heavy single roller.

Tires: Full balloon, 19 x 4.00 inch standard, 18 x 4.00 inch optional.

Wheels: Front and rear quickly demountable and interchangeable. Both wheels wire with drop-center rims.

Wheelbase: 60 inches.

Overall length: 94 inches.

Saddle height: 29-1/2 inches.

Tank: Saddle type, large capacity. Main gas tank, 21-3/4 pints (approximately 3 gallons); reserve tank 8-1/2 pints (approximately 1 gallon). Oil tank, 8-3/4 pints.

61-, 74-ci Overhead Valve Models 1936–1947

As nice a guy as President Walter Davidson may have been, he had run out of patience. The National Recovery Administration, a product of the Depression, prevented his engineers from working overtime in 1934. The government body encouraged hiring more people rather than over-working people already on the payroll, and that was one of the reasons why the 61-ci overhead valve model failed to make its debut until 1936 (and why just six variations on two models were offered in 1935). Despite the delay, the Knucklehead, as it came to be known, had a few initial problems. There seemed to be no way to regulate oil flow to the valves. Other parts received either too much or too little lubrication, so a crash lube improvement program began almost immediately, and the new and usually reliable recirculating oil system of 1937 was the result.

The 74-ci overhead valve model introduced for the 1941 model year was identical to the highly popular 61-ci overhead valve model. According to the factory, the 74 was created by "a demand from a small number of riders for a model of this type of larger cubic inch capacity—a model that would handle a sidecar with ease and speed, and a solo motorcycle with performance far beyond ordinary requirements." Nice as that sounds, the 74 was instead an insurance policy to prevent speed oriented H-D enthusiasts from being passed by an Indian. The biggest mechanical news within was a centrifugally controlled oil pump that at last solved the 61's problem of too much oil in some parts of the engine and not enough in others. A bypass valve, regulated by RPM, closed at high speed for maximum lubrication of the motor. At low speed, the valve opened to bypass the gear case and return to the supply tank. Vane-type pumps were installed in 1937 on the 45-, 74-, and 80-ci side valve motors, with gear-driven pumps on the 61- and 74-ci overhead valvers.

The other major improvement on all models involved the clutch. Three steel discs, three friction (fiber) discs, and a spring disc meant seven friction surfaces on all big twins, instead of the five used in 1940. A total surface increase of 65 percent over the previous models made for smoother shifting, as did the new and larger clutch hub. Many niceties found on the new overhead valve bike were shared with other models. These included a larger and more effective air cleaner; larger rear brake on the 1937 and later models; better feel to the front brake lever, which was made of die-cast aluminum; a quieter muffler; a "new airplane-style speedometer dial" featuring silver numerals on a black face with a white needle; and sturdier gearshift and foot clutch lever mechanisms. Unfortunately, all models also shared stainless steel styling strips on the gas tanks. These hunks of metal, viewed today, just don't come off as well as the decals on the mid-1930s Harley-Davidsons.

The 74 overhead valve was produced in extremely limited quantities during World War II and in only slightly larger batches in 1946 and 1947. Henry Koster, a longtime mechanic employed at Harley-Davidson of Rochelle Park, in Bergen County, New Jersey, says the 1941 and 1942 74s were the most efficient motors ever to come out of Milwaukee. James Lang, a former New England dealer who is familiar with every model H-D since 1924, shares his view. And Michael Lange, a top restorer, says his 1941 74 runs with and stays cooler than the hydraulic-lifter 74-ci models that superseded the overhead valve machines in 1948.

Specifications (61-ci model, from a 1936 brochure)

Motor: V-twin, overhead valve configuration, bore 3-5/16 inches, stroke 3-1/2 inches, displacement 60.32 inches, horsepower rating (N.A.C.C.) 8.77.

Fiberglass saddlebags were an option on this 1967 Sportster. (David K. Wright)

Compression: EL (high compression, created by high piston), 7:1 without cylinder shims, 6.5:1 with cylinder shims. EL (low compression, created by low piston), 6:1 without cylinder shims, 5.6:1 with cylinder shims.

Horsepower: 40 at 4800 rpm.

Gear ratios

Motor sprocket: 23.

Clutch sprocket: 37.

Countershaft sprocket: 22.

Rear sprocket: 51.

Third-gear ratio: 4.57:1.

Fourth-gear ratio: 3.73:1.

Battery: Six volts.

Dry weight: 565 pounds.

Model S-125, 1947–1952

The first new model after World War II was only new to these shores. The design was the work of prewar German DKW engineers, who had two strikes against them. First, losing the war meant losing all patent rights. Second, the DKW factory, like most of Germany, had been reduced to rubble.

Therefore, BSA in England and Harley-Davidson in America produced the two-stroke, single-cylinder machine. Returning soldiers were cycle hungry, but they wanted more than this. William H. Davidson told directors that 10,000 were built and sold in the first seven months of 1947. However, the little bike never fulfilled the lightweight craving of H-D dealers, who have never welcomed a two-stroke cycle.

Specifications (From a 1947 collateral piece)

Serial number: The engine (serial) number is stamped on the front end of the engine crankcase, on the left-hand side.
Wheelbase: 50 inches.
Model designation: S.
Type of engine: Two-cycle.
Number of cylinders: One.
Bore: 2-1/16 inches (52.39 mm).
Stroke: 2-9/32 inches (57.94 mm).
Displacement: 7.6 ci (124.87 cc).
Compression ratio: 6.6:1.

Horsepower (N.A.C.C. rating): 1.7.
Brake horsepower (approximate): 3.
Tire size: 3.25 x 19 inches.
Gasoline tank, total: 1-3/4 gallons.
Main supply: 1-1/2 gallons.
Reserve: 1 quart.
Transmission case: 1-1/4 pints.
Low gear: 29.3:1.
Second gear: 15.4:1.
High gear: 8.45:1.

Model K, 45- and 55-ci V-Twin 1952–1956

The Harley-Davidson Model K, introduced in 1952, looked more like a contemporary cycle than anything produced by the company prior to that year. It featured rear suspension consisting of a swingarm and a pair of sturdy shocks, a revamped 45-ci side valve motor, and a combination foot shift and hand clutch. Unfortunately, problems plagued the sleek machine from its inception.

Most worrisome from the corporation's point of view were some serious mechanical and performance maladies, among them the breaking of gear teeth in the 1954 and 1955 KH models. Art Kauper, in the H-D experimental department, noticed that there was a pattern to teeth breakage, but he could not initially tell why. On a visit to a steel supplier, however, he watched an ingot being rolled into flat stock and saw the corner outlines of the ingot in the finished steel. These corners correlated with the teeth that were breaking. By going immediately to a forged gear, the problem was solved. But performance remained dismal, both in leaving a stoplight and attempting to reach a speed in excess of 80 mph. Boosting the motor to 55 ci in 1954 helped some, but not enough.

The first joint effort between Harley-Davidson and Aeronautica Macchi was this 250-cc (15-ci), single-cylinder Sprint road bike. Introduced in 1961, it was well finished and sold briskly. Riders of full-size Harleys expressed amazement at the size of the fuel tank, which was much larger than the cylinder. (David K. Wright)

Nevertheless, there was such a thing as a desirable K bike. Tom Lyman, now retired from a career as a chiropractor, remembers getting a ride on a new K and trading his 1951 Hydra-Glide immediately for a KK model, in 1953. The KK featured hotter cams, less chrome, and flatter bars, and gave Lyman perfect service. He said: "Where the KK was really great was out on the road, blasting through a canyon. It cruised very nicely at 70 to 75 mph and had a top speed of 90 to 95 with the shorter gearing I had put on. All I can say is, it was smooth, leaned well into the twisties, and was easy to take care of." Searching hard for a flaw, Lyman concedes that the ride might have been "mushy" by today's standards. Nevertheless, the bike was no lemon.

The K was a stopgap model, according to William H. Davidson, who reported that development time ran out on a radical, 60-degree V-twin called the KL. Unlike other H-Ds at the time, the KL featured connecting rods offset in side-by-side fashion. (In other models, the big end of one connecting rod fit within the big end of the other.) The aluminum high-cam motor was created with dual carburetors and probably was the performance equal of the 1954 Golden Anniversary KH, with its 55-ci motor and engine-transmission unit construction, a first for H-D.

The MX-250, produced only for the 1977 and 1978 model years, may be among the more competitive single-cylinder motocross racers ever constructed. (David K. Wright)

Specifications *(From a 1951 brochure)*

45-ci side valve motor: Air-cooled four-stroke, V-type, twin cylinder. Removable aluminum alloy cylinder heads. Enclosed valve gear. Low-expansion, aluminum alloy, cam-ground, double slot pistons. Cylinder bores honed and parkerized. Deep cylinder fins extend around intake and exhaust ports for proper cooling. All main bearings retained roller type; double tapered Timken bearings on the sprocket side. Linkert carburetor. Motor develops approximately 30 horsepower. Bore, 2-3/4 inches. Stroke, 3-13/16 inches.

Transmission: Harley-Davidson four speed. Incorporated as an integral part of crankcase casting. Sliding dog clutches. Large, rugged gears for durability. Constant-mesh design. Foot shift, hand clutch.

Lubrication: Circulating lubrication system with gear-type pressure pump and gear-type scavenger pump with pressure feed direct to cylinder walls. Transmission and front chain lubricated by oil supply separate from engine. All other bearings Alemite-Zerk fitted.

Ignition: Two-brush shunt, voltage controlled generator, storage battery, spark coil, circuit breaker. Easy starting and waterproof.

Electrical equipment: Large, sealed ray headlight with prefocused 32-32 candlepower, double filament bulb. Generator and oil pressure warning lights incorporated in the headlights. Electric, trumpet-type blast horn.

Clutch: Harley-Davidson multiple dry disc with bonded-on clutch facings. Left hand operated.

Drive: Motor to transmission by 3/8-inch pitch triple chain running in oil bath and adjusted by Stellite-faced sliding shoe. 5/8-inch pitch single-row roller chain to rear wheel. Engine has compensating sprocket.

Frame: Double loop, silver brazed tubular steel. Heat-treated steel head, seat post cluster, rear support arms, and axle clips.

Rear suspension: Swingarm type sprung by means of two helical coil springs and controlled by means of two hydraulic, automotive type shock absorbers, all encased in royalite covers. Pivot point of swingarm is supported by pre-loaded Timken bearings.

Front fork: Easy riding hydraulic fork. Load is transmitted by long helical springs supported and contained in main tubes, hydraulically dampened by oil of high viscosity index. Hydraulic stops are provided in both recoil and cushion positions.

Muffler: Designed to reduce backpressure and has resonating chamber to produce low note. Inner tube and end bells of heavy gauge steel. Chrome-plated finish.

Handlebars: Seamless steel tubing. Rubber mounted Buckhorn type. Neoprene twist-grip controls for throttle and spark, fully enclosed.

Wheels: Drop center rims. Cadmium plated spokes. Knockout type axles. Ball bearing mounted.

Tires: Goodyear or Firestone, 3.25 x 19 inches, four ply.

Brakes: Fully enclosed, front and rear brakes with molded anti-score lining. Cast iron rear brake drum. Front drum of steel. Front and rear brakes 8 inches in diameter and 1 inch wide.

Tanks: Extra large, welded heavy gauge steel gas tank with center filling cap. Capacity: 4-1/2 gallons, with reserve in addition. Reserve controlled by two-way gas tank. Capacity: 3 quarts, with provision for filter. Oil tank has screw-down provision in cap.

Instrument panel: 120-mph speedometer, ignition and light switch incorporated in the top part of the front fork cowling. Each switch incorporates a tumbler type lock.

Saddle: Suspended on two seat posts. Each part incorporating a helical coil spring. Form fitting, bucket type with foam-rubber padding, covered with soft, genuine leather.

Finish: All surfaces to be painted are treated to resist rust and corrosion. Available in Persian Red, Rio Blue, and Brilliant Black. Available at extra cost, Metallic Bronco Bronze. Chrome and stainless steel trim. Frame in black enamel.

61- and 74-ci Models, 1948–1965

The Panhead motor began life in a hardtail frame, became the Hydra-Glide a year later, showed up as the Duo-Glide in 1958, and ended up as the Electra Glide in 1965. Its 18 years of dependable existence allowed the company to perfect non-motor aspects of the bikes.

The new overhead valve 61- and 74-ci engines previewed in 1948 featured aluminum cylinder heads and used pushrod-type hydraulic lifters in the valve train. The rocker arms and cylinder heads were redesigned, with the latter the source of the eventual Panhead nickname. The new heads dissipated heat more rapidly than did the Knuckleheads, while the new lifters eliminated tappet noise. To accommodate the change in the length of the rocker arm fingers, a new camshaft was designed. Also new were the exhaust ports and pipes; the new intake manifold was fabricated from brazed tubing. Extensive work was done with oil flow and pressure. A new and larger pump delivered a reported 25 percent more oil to the overhead mechanism at 15 pounds of pressure per square inch. The motor had no external oil pipes.

The cylinder heads were made of aluminum alloy, having aluminum-bronze valve seat inserts and steel valve guides. The lower portion of the rocker arm support was cast iron and the upper portion, or cap, of the rocker arm support was bronze. The cylinder heads were provided with steel inserts for the cylinder bolts and the spark plugs. The plugs had a broader heat range, providing better performance at low speeds. The 74-ci Panhead engine weighed 8 pounds less than its Knucklehead predecessor, though horsepower was about the same.

Improvements outside the motor in 1948 included a steering head lock, a safety guard mounting plate on the frame, and a more comfy latex-filled saddle. Two forms of corrosion protection were applied to all body parts, including tanks. Nineteen forty-eight also was the first year for what may have been H-D's most startling color so far: Azure Blue.

In 1949, the year following the Panhead's premiere, the company installed hydraulic front forks. These were an immense improvement over the rigid-spring forks known previously. Riders reported crossing railroad tracks—even railroad ties—with ease. The forks were the biggest single improvement to date in terms of ride and handling and contributed to the touring reputation the 74 has passed down to the FLHT. The 1949's low-speed handling might put off today's touring rider: the uncanny balance of the big bikes was still several years down the road. Also on the 1949 was a front brake with a 34 percent larger drum. The Panhead transmission would be familiar to today's rider, since the harder it was shifted, the better it changed gears. The hand shift and foot clutch, by the way, had showed a pattern change in 1947. From the rider's view, first gear was closest to him or her and fourth closest to the steering head. Prior to 1947, riders pulled rather than pushed when upshifting.

Porting work produced ten more horses for 1950, while 1951 models boasted 55 horsepower and combined the ugly flexible exhaust headers (seen through 1973) with a chromed lower exhaust system. With an eye on traditional riders, Harley-Davidson continued to offer hand shift after 1952, the year of the first foot-shift Panhead. Competing for sales with such long-gone makes as Delfino, James, Panther, and Sunbeam, the 1952's were the final year for the 61-ci motor. The 1952s sported wide tanks and 5.00 x 16-inch tires, whereas 1953 models are most easily identified by the speedometer, which reads 1, 2, 3 rather than 10, 20, 30.

There was no mistaking the 1953 models, since all H-Ds that year displayed a 2-1/2-inch gold medallion on the front fender. A "trumpet blast" Jubilee air horn was standard, and plastic saddlebags were optional. A chrome medallion with "V" device replaced gold the following year, together with a streamlined front chain guard and rubber-mounted, horizontal tail lamps. Not until 1956 did the trusty Panhead motor need attention; high-lift cams and a freer air cleaner produced a reported 12 percent power hike. A lower seating position combined with the ever-plush saddle for an adequate ride, even with the solid rear. That was about to change.

Ever hear of a fit too perfect on a motorcycle? That was the only initial problem with the Duo-Glide, offered from 1958 through 1961 and still seen in some numbers. A series of prototypes was built, some nearly a decade before production. All of the prototypes were afflicted with a fork-damping problem, according to the late Art Kauper, who worked at the time with engineers assigned to the project. "We went into production at the absolute 11th hour," he said. "The problem was solved when it was discovered during the first few months that the rubber seals on the fork legs rubbed the legs to a mirror finish, creating a perfect fit. This left no room for oil, which was forced past the seals as the forks worked up and down. The solution proved to be a new seal with slightly looser tolerance and a slightly rougher finish on the fork legs.

The only other malady surfaced following delivery of a sizeable Duo-Glide order to the California Highway Patrol. Officers experienced instability at or above the legal limit. The late John Nowak, service school dean and a troubleshooter for years with the company, was sent to the West Coast to solve the problem. "The police took a ride and wanted the solid rear ends back," said Nowak, who tried a number of fixes before discovering that the head bearing was too tight. "Service Bulletin 510 tells dealers how to set the bearing. All the other stuff suggested is baloney." Proof that H-D could solve suspension problems was made evident a year or so later when airplane manufacturers consulted the factory before developing their landing gear.

The FLs and FLHs in 1958 also showed a gold, silver, and black tank insignia and enjoyed larger cylinder head fins for improved cooling. The insignia took on an arrow shape the following year, and there was now a neutral indicator light. The Duo-Glide by 1960 featured the same style headlight nacelle seen on the Sportster. Other early 1960s modifications included a larger rear chain, a new chain oiler, and external oil lines to the overhead valve gear in 1963; and full-width, finned, aluminum front brake drums in 1964. The stage was set for an idea that fostered a new name for the FL and FLH.

The Electra Glide was one of three new Harley-Davidson models for 1965, yet its 12-volt electrics, push-button start, sealed and enclosed primary chain, and 5-gallon "turnpike" tank made riders forget the Sprint Scrambler or the M-50. H-D had for years preached that the 74-ci bike was the ultimate highway cycle, and the Electra Glide certainly

A crowd surrounds a new V-Rod. (David K. Wright)

backed that claim. Instant starting proved to be the final tribute to the Panhead motor, a V-twin that began life as a postwar improvement on the Knuckler and ended with a reliability record roughly equivalent to the path of the sun. "H" stood for highway and was an indication that the model carried extras for touring; but any of the 74s would roll all day down any road to anywhere.

Specifications (From a 1949 magazine road test)

Motor: V-type, two-cylinder, four-stroke engine, 3-7/16-inch bore, 3-31/32-inch stroke, 74-ci displacement (also offered with 61-ci motor). Dry sump lubrication, battery ignition, Schebler 1-5/16-inch carburetor, 50 horsepower (estimated) at 4800 rpm.
Transmission: Four speeds, hand gear change, foot clutch, oil capacity 1 quart, primary chain drive, secondary chain drive.
Frame, running gear: Double loop seamless steel frame, Hydra-Glide forks, rigid rear suspension, 59-1/2-inch wheelbase. Oil tank capacity, 4 quarts; gasoline tank capacity 3-3/4 gallons. Brakes, 8-inch front, 8-inch rear. Tire size, front and rear, 5.00 x 16 inches. Dry weight, 560 pounds.

XL Models, 1957 to Present

If the Model K was disappointing, the Sportster, introduced in 1957, was successful beyond the wildest dreams of even the most optimistic engineer or designer. Larger by 10 ci than the original K, the 55-ci machine boasted overhead valves that helped produce 12 more horsepower, a claim no unsuspecting Triumph rider would contest. Now in their 46th year of production, the X models have proliferated into as many as 1200 cc of corner straightening that retains heaps of torque and the deep thuds that bring joy to the ears of V-twin owners to this day.

The motor initially measured 53.9 ci (883 cc), producing 40 horsepower at 5500 rpm. Introduced with a 7.5:1 compression ratio, the musclebike shared all of the assets and none of the liabilities associated with its predecessor. The engine and transmission were one unit, with service to the transmission accomplished via an easily removed cover. Automotive-style shocks (one of several shock types used from then to now) nestled beneath the seat, providing sufficient buffer for the bike to be touted originally as either an on- or off-road model. In only its second year of production, the fast got faster, thanks to higher compression through domed pistons, cleaner ports, larger valves, and aluminum tappets. The stage was set for the awesome XLCH.

High pipes, a magneto-generator ignition, peanut gas tank, and semi-knobby tires warned the timid away from the lightweight XLCH. Here was a case where Harley-Davidson slightly misjudged the market—and reaped the rewards. Riders everywhere passed up enduros for the highway with the XLCH (CH stood for "Competition Hot). They quickly ran off or removed the knobbies to become the favorites in any asphalt game being played. Both XLs in 1959 received a horsepower hike with the addition

Daytona Beach visitors admire the Evolution engine and final belt drive, displayed in a cutaway frame. (David K. Wright)

of a high-lift intake cam and redesigned exhaust cams. Owners found ways to use that power.

John Heidt, formerly a top drag racer and the H-D dealer in Fond du Lac, Wisconsin, believes the 1962 Sportster was the fastest of all early models. "There were more fast 1962s than any other year, though any 1959 to 1965 Sportster with a stock Linkert carburetor would reach 115 miles an hour in the quarter mile," he says. "I ran a 13.4-second quarter with a 1959 Sportster without the muffler, which actually made the bike slower due to insufficient back pressure. I ran 105–107 mile-an-hour quarters Sunday after Sunday with a 1962. The denser the air, the better it ran." With an eye on reliability, Heidt says he frequently drag-raced two hours steady at the Union Grove, Wisconsin, strip without shutting the motor down. Not until a decade later was there a stock motorcycle that could stay with the Sportster.

Style became as important as speed. The staggered, shorty dual exhausts, first seen in 1962, have become classic Sportster equipment. A year earlier, H-D announced that all of the new Hi-Fi colors were available for either model, plus any color combination the prospective owner could conceive. That option lasted through 1971, when Sportster production reached such numbers under AMF that standardized hues were made mandatory. Nacelled headlights in various configurations appeared beginning in 1959 and lasted for more than a decade.

As the look changed, so too did the iron. The 1959 model started with a single-switch ignition, while in 1962, the speed-conscious engineers on Juneau Avenue converted such items as fork brackets and motor mounts to weight-saving aluminum. Full-width aluminum front wheel hubs, light but tough, were standard from 1964, as riders of all ages and sizes were stuffing H-D stroker kits into the machines for even better drag strip hole shots. The following year, the electricals were upgraded to a full 12-volt system, in anticipation of the 1967 electric starter. The XLH lost its kick-starter in 1968, the year before the magneto ignition finale for the XLCH. Starting a magneto-equipped Sportster, by the way, taught a whole generation of riders how to used manual spark advance—and profanity. The battery system still in use employs a centrifugal advance with automatic retard. Riders who kick (no pun

intended) about the lack of a manual starter never attempted to turn over a magneto-equipped XLCH.

The chassis continued to evolve, with a new front fork in 1968. The motor, a wonder in 1957, got better each year. Not even a "California" muffler, to control emissions, could prevent the V-twin in 1968 from producing 58 horsepower at 6800 rpm. Small wonder the following year Michael Parks chose such a machine for *Then Came Bronson*, the prime-time television show about a large-hearted drifter. For 1971, the timer was integrated into the cam cover, providing easier timing adjustment. A more important alteration was the switch that same year from a dry to a wet clutch. The engineers were preparing the bike for the full 1000-cc treatment in 1972.

The megamotor combined with the reintroduction of the classic peanut tank and a low-profile seat to take advantage of the increasing interest in cruising bikes. Throughout the 1970s, in fact, the Sportster became increasingly stylized as the feds descended upon H-D with a number of regulations. The pleasant late 1960s "bread box" air cleaner evolved into the infernal "ham can" in 1979. Side reflectors became mandatory in 1971, though Willie G. and the stylists were able to work these shiny bits into elements already present on the bikes. About the only federal edict that made sense was the switch to a spring return and an external throttle cable in 1975.

Aware that a sound engine can look good with a number of chassis, the company began to broaden the appeal of the XLs in 1977. Enter the XLCR Café Racer, a black-on-black single-seat machine that proved Willie G.'s styling versatility and became an instant classic despite its two-year lifespan. The bikini-fairinged bike displayed siamesed exhausts and dual discs up front, the latter showing up on the XLH and XLCH from 1978 onward. The XLCR is so highly regarded that Willie G. and his two sons each own one. Finally, with an eye on the calendar, the Sportster has appeared in 75th anniversary and 25th Sportster anniversary models, limited-production versions of everybody's favorite sports bike.

Other variations on the Sportster theme in 1979 were the Hugger, with its short shocks and low seating position, and the XLS Roadster, with Low Rider styling and 16-inch rear tire. Two additions for 1983 were the no-frills XLX, initially priced at $3,995, and the limited-production XR-1000. This bike's heritage is evident in the dual Dell'Orto carbs and XR750-style pipes and aluminum heads and pistons from the racing bike. Horsepower, something H-D recently has downplayed, was 70.

All of these configurations operate on the cutting edge of almost any rider's ability, thanks, at last, to the 1982 introduction of a frame combining stamped and welded tubular construction. If you are unaware of the reception given those fresh-framed Sportsters by the press, you have been out of touch—which is something no one will ever accuse the Sportster of being.

As late as the 1985 model year, the company was offering three variations on the Sportster theme: The XR-1000, the bargain-priced XLX, and the Sportster itself, all with the same 1000-cc motor. Things changed in 1986, when the 883-cc Evolution XLH replaced the XLX, and the Sportster 1100 XLH superseded its 1000-cc brethren. (Sadly, the XR-1000 was dropped from the model line.) Both of these motors showed the Evolution top end, complete with hydraulic lifters; new camshaft gear drivetrain; high-strength heads with new, oval combustion chambers; computer-designed camshafts; new rocker covers for easier servicing; three-piece flywheels; and revised intake and exhaust systems. Both machines run cooler than their elders, due mostly to superior oil flow.

By the 1993 model year, the company had expanded the Sportster line to five models: The basic XLH 883; the XLH 883 Hugger; the XLH 883 Deluxe; the XLH 1200; and XLH 1200 90th Anniversary edition! Sportsters acquired a number of upgrades from 1988 to 1993, including belt final drive, improved oil pumps, better generators, stronger top ends, and short-throw, five-speed transmissions (standard with the 1991 model year). All 1993s displayed redesigned, low profile clutch and brake levers and a sight glass on the master brake cylinder so owners could quickly check the fluid level. The 90th Anniversary Edition gleamed in 1993 with a cloisonné tank emblem and serialized nameplates.

The XL 1200S Sportster arrived in 1996. This distinguished bike included adjustable forks and shocks, floating disc brakes, and Dunlop Sport Elite tires. Laced wheels and low bars characterized the basic XLH 883 that same year, while more expensive models offered cast wheels. The first Sportster constructed in Kansas City was early in 1998, and the machines that year featured either the 883-cc or 1200 Evolution motor, coupled to five-speed transmissions. One model, the Sportster Sport, had a tachometer to keep the speedometer company. Most recently, engine noise has been reduced, the oil pump has been redesigned, and a high-tech cylinder liner borrowed from the Twin Cam 88 program is now employed.

Because Sportsters have evolved so completely, here are specs on the very first and very latest bikes. No list of parts and dimensions can convince a rider that the Sportster isn't the same hard starting, filament-busting, frame-humming beast it once was. But a test ride most assuredly will.

Specifications: Sportster H *(From a 1957 brochure)*

Engine: 55-ci air-cooled four-stroke, V-twin cylinder overhead valve engine. The size of the bore is 3 inches. The length of the stroke is 3-13/16 inches. Enclosed valve gear. Low expansion aluminum alloy cam-ground pistons. Cylinder bores honed and parkerized. Deep cylinder fins extend around exhaust ports for proper cooling. All main bearings retained roller type; double tapered Timken bearings on the sprocket side; straight retained roller bearings on the gear side. Linkert carburetor. Includes cylinder heads with enlarged intake port openings, increased-size intake valves, lightweight racing-type tappets, special 9:1 high dome pistons.

Transmission: Harley-Davidson four-speed. Incorporated as an integral part of crankcase casting. Sliding dog clutches. Large, rugged gears for durability. Constant-mesh design. Foot shift, hand clutch.

Lubrication: Circulating lubrication system with gear-type pressure pump and gear-type scavenger pump. Transmission and front chain lubricated by oil supply separate from engine. All other bearings Alemite-Zerk fitted or prepacked.

Ignition: Two-brush shunt, voltage controlled generator, storage battery, spark coil, circuit breaker. Easy starting and waterproof.

Clutch: Harley-Davidson multiple disc. One-piece clutch discs. Left hand operated.

Drive: Motor to transmission by 3/8-inch pitch triple chain running in oil bath and sliding shoe tension control. 5/8-inch pitch single-row roller chain to rear wheel.

Rear suspension: Swingarm-type sprung by means of two helical coil springs and controlled by means of two hydraulic, automotive-type shocks absorbers, all enclosed in chrome covers. Pivotal point of swingarm is supported by preloaded Timken bearings.

Front fork: Easy riding hydraulic fork. Load is transmitted by long helical springs supported and contained in main tubes, hydraulically dampened by oil of high viscosity index. Hydraulic stops are provided in both recoil and cushion position.

Tires: Goodyear or Firestone, 3.50 x 18 inches.

Brakes: Fully enclosed, front and rear brake with molded anti-score lining. Front and rear brake 8 inches in diameter and 1 inch wide.

Tanks: Extra large welded heavy gauge steel tank and center filling cap. Capacity: 4.4 gallons including reserve in addition. Reserve controlled by two-way gas valve with fuel strainer. Welded heavy gauge steel oil tank. Capacity: 3 quarts with provision for filter. Oil tank has secure, screwdown provision.

Special equipmen: This model available with the Deluxe Group.

Finish: Harmonizing two-tone color styling: Black, Calypso Red, Skyline Blue, or Sabre-Grey Metallic with Birch White tank panel. (Other colors and combinations available on special orders through dealers.) Chrome and stainless steel trim.

Specifications: XL 1200S Sportster 1200 Sport (From a 2001 brochure)

Length: 88.5 inches.
Seat height: 28 inches.
Ground clearance: 6.7 inches.
Rake/trail: 29.6/4.6
Wheelbase: 60.2 inches.
Dry weight: 501 pounds.
Engine: Overhead valve V2 Evolution
Bore x stroke: 3.498 inches x 3.812 inches.
Displacement: 73.2 ci, 1200 cc.
Compression ratio: 10.0: 1.
Fuel system: Carburetor.
Oil capacity: 3 quarts.
Fuel capacity: 3.3 gallons.

A prospective owner tries on the V-Rod in the Ocean Center at Daytona Beach. (David K. Wright)

Exhaust system: Black staggered shorty duals.
Primary drive: Triple-row chain.
Gear ratios (overall): 1st, 9.047; 2nd, 6.210; 3rd, 4.823; 4th, 3.973; 5th, 3.366
Torque: 78 ft-lbs at 4000 rpm.
Brakes (front/rear): 11.5 x 20-inch dual disc/11.5 x 23-inch.
Braking (maximum loaded vehicle): 143 feet at 60 mph.
Tire size (front/rear): 100/90-19SIV; 130/90-1664V
Wheels: 13-spoke silver cast aluminum alloy.
Miles per gallon: 52 hwy/45 city.
Lean angle (degrees, left/right): 37.5/37.
Instruments: electronic speedometer with odometer and resettable trip meter; tachometer; oil pressure indicator lamp.
Color options: Vivid black, diamond ice pearl, jade sunglo pearl, white pearl, luxury rich red pearl, chrome yellow pearl.

Model B, Hummer, 1959–1960

A glance at the specs will reveal that the Hummer evolved from the 125-cc DKW copy. Bore, stroke, and dimensions were either the same or too close to call. The motorbike-like conveyance lasted only two years, due to the importation of the small Aermacchi/Harley-Davidsons from Italy.

Specifications

Serial number: the engine (serial) number is stamped on the front end of the engine crankcase, on the left-hand side.
Wheelbase: 51-1/2 inches.
Model designation: Hummer.
Type of engine: Two-cycle.
Number of cylinders: One.
Bore: 2-16 inches (52.39 mm).
Stroke: 2-9/32 inches (57.94 mm).
Displacement: 7.6 ci (124.87 cc).

Compression ratio: 6.6:1.
Horsepower: 1.7.
Brake horsepower (approximate): 3.
Tire size: 3.50 x 18 inches.
Gasoline tank, total: 1-7/8 gallons.
Main supply: 1-1/2 gallons.
Reserve: 1-1/2 quarts.
Transmission case: 1-1/4 pints.
Low gear: 26.5:1.
Second gear: 15.4:1.

A group of V-Rods used for demonstration riding awaits customers at Daytona Beach. (David K. Wright)

Topper Scooter, 1960-1965

How many Harley-Davidsons can you name that had a parking brake? Or a starting system that involved neither kicking nor any kind of electrics? Or a buddy seat wherein there was room for a six-pack? Sound like your kind of bike? Sorry to report that is was no one's kind of bike but rather was the 165-cc Topper scooter. Sold for six years, the Topper was H-D's answer to the brief popularity of domestic Cushmans and Italian Vespa and Lambretta scooters. Among its features was a front brake lever on the left handlebar that could, via locking a cam, also serve to brake the bike when parked. The cam slid into the gap created when the front brake was squeezed; it wedged itself between the brake lever and the bracket that held the lever to the bar. Nothing tricky, but it worked. Anyone who ever started a lawnmower or a snowblower will be familiar with the Topper's hand recoil method. It worked, too. While the factory recommended carrying two-stroke oil beneath the buddy seat for mixing at fuel stops, the space frequently was devoted to schoolbooks or worse.

The scooter fad peaked about the time the Topper was introduced, which was unfortunate because the Topper seems to have used its original engine design to good advantage. The only complaint voiced by more than an occasional owner concerned the transmission. The unit automatically changed the driving ratio by varying the diameter of front and rear flanges on which the belt drive ran. Engine speeds caused balls operating on cams to move together, altering the diameter of the flanges. Negligent owners or those who ran the machines in muck quickly learned that the belt slipped on and off the flanges. Final drive was by a conventional chain. Both the 5- and 9-horsepower models sold for $445 in 1962. The smaller model could be driven in some states without an operator's license.

Specifications

Serial number: The engine (serial) number is stamped on the engine crankcase.
Wheelbase: 51.5 inches.
Model designation letter: A or AU.
Type of engine: Two-cycle.
Number of cylinders: One, horizontal.

Bore: 2.375 inches (60.325 mm).
Stroke: 2.281 inches (57.937 mm).
Piston displacement: 10 ci (165 cc).
Compression ratio: 6.6:1.
Fuel tank: 1.7 U.S. gallons, with .5 U.S. pint reserve.
Horsepower: 2.26.
Spark plug type: Harley-Davidson No. 4.
Size: 14 mm.
Gap: .025 to .030 inches.
Circuit breaker point gap: .018 inches.
Ignition timing: 5/64 inch (.078 mm) to 7/64 inch (110 mm) before piston top center.
Number of sprocket teeth: Transmission drive, 14; rear wheel, 63.
Overall ratio: Maximum, 18.0; minimum, 5.9.
Tire size: 4.00 x 12 inches.

Bobcat, Ranger, Pacer, Scat, 175 cc, 1962-1966

These U.S -designed and constructed bikes were aimed at riders not yet ready for the 250-cc Sprint or Sprint H Aermacchi/Harley-Davidsons being imported at the time. They sold well in one form or another for five years. The 175-cc two-stroke "would go just fast enough to get you hurt," according to one veteran dealer, who said he preferred selling kids the larger though less peaky four strokes. Others contend these bikes were quite easy to ride, though with three-speed transmissions it took skill to keep the machines in their power bands.

The only sort of problem involved the electrical system. Off-road riders frequently experienced shorts of various kinds, while roadrunners found flickering headlights the norm more than the exception. Full-size H-D riders also could not get used to some of the most unyielding upholstery known to man. No wonder the off-road guys stayed up on the footpegs.

The machines were introduced with solid rear ends. The Ranger, a trail bike without lights, was sold only in 1962, while the surviving (street) Pacer and (on- or off-road) Scat received swingarm and shocks in 1963. The Bobcat, offered either as a road or trail model, displayed an attractive one-piece body in 1966, its only year of production.

Specifications (From a 1966 Bobcat owner's manual)

Wheelbase: 52 inches.
Overall length: 79 inches.
Overall width: 30.5 inches.
Model designation: BTH
Type: Two-cycle.
Number of cylinders: One.
Bore: 2.375 inches.
Stroke: 2.406 inches.
Displacement: 10.7 ci (175 cc).
Compression ratio: 7.5:1.
Fuel tank: 1.87 U.S. gallons.
Ignition timing: 7/32 inch before piston top center.
Circuit breaker point gap: .018 inch.
Spark plug type: H-D No. 4.
Size: 14 mm.
Gap: .040 to .045 inch.
Transmission type: Constant mesh.
Speeds: Three forward.
Transmission: 1.25 U.S. pints.
Engine sprocket teeth: 15 standard, 15 trail model.
Clutch sprocket teeth: 31 standard, 31 trail model.
Countershaft sprocket teeth: 15 standard, 12 trail model.
Rear wheel sprocket teeth: 49 standard, 84 trail model.
Tire size: 3.50 x 18 inches.

250-cc, 350-cc Sprint Four-Stroke Singles, 1961–1974

The first Aermacchi/Harley-Davidson effort was single-cylinder machines that sold almost as well as Hondas during the first few years of importation into the U.S. However, the superior Italian-American styling could not overcome an inferior electrical system and a price tag that seemed to climb as the Japanese competition, such as the 305-cc Honda Super Hawk and Scrambler, stayed cheap and were fast.

A Sprint H could compete on a regional racing level with most other machines; accomplished scrambles riders such as Alabama's Phil Scarborough made their presence known. Then along came the two-strokes and that blew the four-strokes, Italian and Japanese, off the off-road courses. Part of the Aermacchi problem was that it made hardly

anything except the engine, which was reliable. H-D supervisors on the scene fought constant quality battles with suppliers. Often, they lost. Still, the Sprint would, with dry points, give reliable service.

The motor was hung from a single-strut frame, substantial enough for the H model, introduced in 1962. More popular than its street counterpart, the H scrambler ran bobbed fenders, high exhausts, and semi-knobby tires, yet had a street-legal lighting system. By 1963, both bikes more closely resembled their big brethren cosmetically, while the H glistened with a new and large chrome air cleaner, together with the largest air-hose cartridge ever seen on a non-racing H-D. Dubbed the Scrambler the following year, power was boosted with a 27-mm Dell'Orto carburetor, 9.5:1 compression ratio, and a megaphone to 25 horses at 8700 rpm.

The capacity stayed the same but the iron cylinder and aluminum head took on a shorter stroke and a larger bore in 1966. Little else changed until the 1969 model year, when the street models, now called the SS, showed up with a 350-cc motor and dual exhausts. The Scrambler received the new motor and a new designation, the SX, in 1972.

*Specifications: **Sprint** (From a 1961 owner's manual)*

Serial numbers: The engine (serial) number is stamped on a pad on the engine crankcase, below the cylinder. The frame serial number is located on the right side of the steering head.
Wheelbase: 52 inches (Sprint); 53.3 inches (Sprint H).
Overall length: 78.5 inches (Sprint); 81 inches (Sprint H).
Overall width: 28.5 inches (Sprint); 28.8 inches (Sprint H).
Model designation letter: C (Sprint); H (Sprint H).
Type: Four-cycle, single cylinder.
Number of cylinders: One.
Bore: 2.598 inches (66 mm).
Stroke: 2.835 inches (72 mm).
Piston displacement: 15 ci (246.2 cc).
Compression ratio: 8.5:1 (Sprint); 9.2:1 (Sprint H).
Torque: 18 ft-lbs at 7500 rpm (Sprint); 19.5 ft-lbs at 6700 rpm (Sprint H).
Horsepower: 2.7.
Fuel tank (total capacity): 4 U.S. gallons (Sprint); 2.64 U.S. gallons (Sprint H).

Reserve: 2 quarts (Sprint); 0.62 quarts (Sprint H).
Crankcase oil: 2 quarts.
Valve tappet clearance (cold): .004 inch (Sprint); intake .003 inch, exhaust .005 inch (Sprint H).
Ignition timing: Retard 21 degrees (7/64 inch) before top dead center, automatic advance 41 degrees (13/32 inch) before top dead center (Sprint); retard 1 degree before top dead center, automatic advance 41 degrees (13/32 inch) before top dead center (Sprint H).
Circuit breaker points, gap: .018 inch.
Spark plug type: Harley-Davidson No. 7.
Size: 14 mm.
Gap: .020 inch.
Transmission type: Constant mesh.
Speeds: Four forward.
Drive pinion gear teeth: 26.
Clutch ring gear teeth: 65.
Transmission internal ratios: 1st, 2.91; 2nd, 1.76; 3rd, 1.27; 4th, 1.00.
Transmission sprocket: 16 (Sprint); 15 (Sprint H).
Rear wheel sprocket: 38.
First gear: 17.28:1 (Sprint); 18.44:1 (Sprint H). Second gear: 10.45:1 (Sprint); 11.15:1 (Sprint H). Third gear: 7.54:1 (Sprint); 8.09:1 (Sprint H).
Fourth gear: 6.33:1 (Sprint); 5.94:1 (Sprint H).
Tire, front: 3.00 x 17 inches (Sprint); 3.00 x 18 inches (Sprint H).
Tire, rear: 3.00 x 17 inches (Sprint); 3.50 x 18 inches (Sprint H).

M-50, M-50 Sport, M-65, M-65 Sport, Shortster, 1965–1968

"A menace."

That is how a retired Harley-Davidson engineer described the M-50 and M-50 Sport motor-driven cycles, constructed in Italy by Aermacchi/Harley-Davidson, and offered in the U.S. in 1965 and 1966. The 50-cc two-stroke bikes were handsomely finished in Holiday Red with White panels. The M-50 displayed in ads with females aboard followed traditional motorbike lines and was available both years. The Sport model featured a racing-style gas tank and a flat, competition-look seat to entice riders of both genders. It was offered only in 1966. All of this was of little consola-

tion to riders who found themselves short of acceleration as a Freightliner bore down on them.

Essentially the same machines, enlarged to 65-cc, were offered beginning in 1967. "Sudden disinterest" in 1966 resulted in 4,000 M-50s in inventory. They were sold well below the $225 suggested retail price. (The Sport model was offered in 1966 for $275.) The M-65 and M-65 Sport went for $230 and $265, respectively. Such tiny transportation in the form of Japanese bikes is still around.

Specifications

Wheelbase: 44.1 inches.
Overall length: 71.4 inches (M), 67.8 inches (MS).
Overall width: 25.6 inches (M), 24.0 inches (MS).

This V-Rod displays an accessory windshield. (David K. Wright)

Ground clearance: 4.3 inches.
Model designation letter: M, MS.
Type: Two-cycle
Number of cylinders: One.
Bore: 1.527 inches (38.8 mm).
Stroke: 1.654 inches (42.0 mm).
Piston displacement: 3.03 ci (49.66 cc).
Taxable horsepower: .93
Fuel tank: 1.6 U.S. gallons (M), 2.5 U.S. gallons (MS).
Transmission: 1 pint.
Compression ratio: 10:1.
Circuit breaker point gap: .018 inch.
Spark plug type: Harley-Davidson No. 7.
Size: 14 mm.
Gap: .025 to .030 inch.
Ignition timing: 27 degrees (0.115 inch) before top dead center.
Transmission type: constant mesh.
Speeds: 3 forward.
Drive pinion gear teeth: 13.

Racing orange is the color of choice for this 2002 883 cc Sportster. (David K. Wright)

Clutch ring gear teeth: 59.
Transmission internal ratios: 1st, 3.18; 2nd, 1.78; 3rd, 1.17.
Transmission sprocket: 13.
Rear wheel sprocket: 27.
Low (first) gear: 29.85:1.
Second gear: 16.76:1.
Third gear: 11.06:1.
Tire size: 2.00 x 17 inches front, 2.00 x 17 inches rear.

Rapido Model 1968–1977

The Rapido and its successors, the TX (1973), the SX (1974), and the SXT (1975) were offered to the public during Aermacchi/Harley-Davidson's final decade. While price competitive with the Japanese, they suffered in dealerships not used to catering to off-road riders, even young ones. All of the assets and liabilities associated with the Italian line were present here, though a four-speed transmission made the engine more flexible than previous play racers.

Specifications (From a 1970 Rapido owner's manual)

Overall length: 76.6 inches.
Overall width: 32.7 inches.
Wheelbase: 48.9 inches.
Ground clearance: 6.7 inches.
Model designation: MLS.
Type: Two cycle
Number of cylinders: One.
Bore: 2.21 inches.
Stroke: 1.97 inches.
Displacement: 7.53 ci (123.5 cc).
Taxable horsepower: 1.95.
Fuel tank: 2.4 U.S. gallons (1 quart reserve).
Transmission: 1 pint.
Compression ratio: 7.65:1.
Circuit breaker point gap: .016 inch.
Spark plug type: H-D No. 6 or 5-6.
Size: 14 mm.
Gap: .025 to .030 inch.
Ignition timing: 20 degrees (0.073 inch) before top dead center.
Transmission type: Constant mesh.
Speeds: Four forward.

Drive pinion gear teeth: 19.
Clutch ring gear teeth: 61.
Transmission internal ratios: 1st, 2.50; 2nd, 1.40; 3rd, .92; 4th, .72.
Transmission sprocket: 14.
Rear wheel sprocket (standard): 50.
Rear wheel sprocket (trail): 62.
First gear: 28.7:1 standard, 35.5:1 trail.
Second gear: 16.1:1 standard, 19.9:1 trail.
Third gear: 10.6:1 standard, 13.1:1 trail.
Fourth gear: 8.3:1 standard, 10.3:1 trail.
Tire size: 3.00 x 18 inches front, 3.50 x 18 inches rear.

Baja, SR 100 1970–1974

Bike magazines lavished high praise on the Baja after a class win in the Greenhorn Enduro. However, over its five-year lifespan under two names, it failed to improve as the Japanese off-road bikes made major advances. Not even a lighting option in 1972 or automatic oil-gas mix, available in 1973, could keep it in the fore of race-minded youngsters.

Specifications *(From a 1970 owner's manual)*

Wheelbase: 52 inches.
Overall length: 78.5 inches.
Overall width: 34 inches.
Ground clearance: 10.8 inches.
Model designation: MSR.
Type: 2-cycle.
Number of cylinders: One.
Bore: 1.97 inches.
Stroke: 1.97 inches.
Displacement: 5.98 ci (98.1 cc).
Taxable horsepower: 1.55.
Compression ratio: 9.5:1.
Fuel tank: 2.5 U.S. gallons (1 quart reserve).
Transmission: 1.3 pints.
Circuit breaker point gap: .016 inch.
Spark plug type: H-D No. 7.
Size: 14 mm.
Gap: .025 to .030 inch.
Ignition timing: 20 degrees (0.073 inch) before top dead center.

Transmission type: Constant mesh.
Speeds: Five forward.
Drive pinion gear teeth: 19.
Clutch ring gear teeth: 61.
Transmission internal ratios: 1st, 2.06; 2nd, 1.33; 3rd, .92; 4th, .75; 5th, .58.
Transmission sprocket teeth: 12, 13, 14, 15.
Rear wheel sprocket: 72.
Tire size: 3.00 x 21 inches front, 3.50 x 18 inches rear.

SS/SX-175, SS/SX-250 Singles, 1974–1978

The off-road SX-175 was introduced in 1974, the streetgoing SS- and off-road SX-250 in 1975, and the street SS-175 in 1976. Timing could not have been worse, since the federal Environmental Protection Agency and the Department of Transportation were looking askance at two-cycle engines, and public acceptance of the ring-a-ding sound was not great.

These motors were copies of the Yamaha DT-1, the force in motocross in the 1970s. Although the two-strokes were as trouble-free as their four-cycle Aermacchi counterparts, they contributed to the demise of the Italian lightweights. Folks just didn't like the sound. The 250 enjoyed some off-road competition success, notably in the hands of Californian Don Ogilvie.

Specifications *(From a 1976 dealer brochure)*

Wheelbase: 56 inches.
Overall length: 86 inches.
Overall width: 31 inches (SS), 35 inches (SX).
Ground clearance: 7 inches.
Type: Two-cycle.
Number of cylinders: One.
Model designation: SS/SX-175, SS/SX-250.
Bore: 175, 2.40 inches (61 mm); 250, 2.84 inches (72 mm).
Stroke: 2.35 inches (59.6 mm).
Displacement: 175, 10.63 ci (174.1 cc); 250, 14.80 ci (242.6 cc).
Taxable horsepower: 175, 2.3; 250, 3.22.
Compression ratio: 175, 10.6:1; 250, 10.3:1.
Fuel tank: 2.8 gallons.
Reserve: 1.2 quarts.

Transmission: 2.5 pints.

Oil tank: 3.3 pints.

Spark plug type: 175, Harley-Davidson No. 7-8; 250, Harley-Davidson No. 7.

Size: 14 mm.

Gap: .025 in.

Ignition timing: 21 degrees (.100 inch) before top dead center.

Ignition timing pickup tap: .012 to .016 inch.

Transmission type: Constant mesh.

Speeds: Five forward.

Drive pinion gear teeth: 20.

Clutch ring gear teeth: 56.

Transmission internal ratios: 1st, 2.53; 2nd, 1.79; 3rd, 1.30; 4th, 1.0; 5th, .80.

Transmission sprocket teeth: SX-175, 13; SS-175, 14; SS/SX-250, 15.

Rear wheel sprocket teeth: SX-175, 49; SS-175, 50; SX-250, 50; SS-250, 49.

The V-Rod motor is marked by 60 degrees of separation and the inclination to wind. (David K. Wright)

74-, 80-ci V-Twin, 1966–1983

The name disappeared from the front fender in 1983, but the effect the Electra Glide had on contemporary Harley-Davidson motorcycles lingers on.

Electric starting was introduced in 1965, with the motor now known as the Shovelhead making its debut in 1966. A Tillotson diaphragm carburetor combined with a new "power pac" head design to produce five more horses than the Panhead offered. That extra power came in handy as a higher percentage of riders were going the "Dresser" route—thanks to the company's numerous touring accessories. The motor itself evidenced less vibration than earlier V-twins, emitting only a slight rhumba beat when decelerating. The FLH, with higher compression, made 60 horses, versus 54 for the FL. Soft, oversize handgrips, by this time an H-D trademark, neutralized most other commotion.

Contemporary road tests indicated that the FLs and FLHs remained the touring machines by which other bikes were judged. The H-Ds were faulted only for inadequate brakes and the external presence of oil. The latter may have been a cheap shot, since those unfamiliar with the big V-twin frequently mistook the drip of the rear chain oiler for a lack of close tolerances.

Immediately following its introduction, evolutionary improvements began. In 1967, the bikes received a push-pull choke that allowed for infinite adjustment. Also added to the line was a pleated seat that made the already plush H-D bench even more so. A new oil pump and warning lights for oil, generator, and ignition were added in 1968, followed by the unveiling in 1969 of the classic, bar-mounted, FLH fairing. This piece, produced by H-D in the Tomahawk fiberglass plant, was offered initially only in white, as were matching fiberglass saddlebags. The most noticeable change for 1970 was the disappearance of flexible headers. The Shovelhead spat out its exhaust via chrome headers that looked infinitely better and worked as well as the parts they replaced.

Meanwhile, customers were casting admiring glances at the Shovelhead motor in the FL frame, in part because 150,000 riders in 1970 were left with money in hand but no bikes—demand created by the Vietnam War-era economy was strong. Formerly content with modifying Sportsters, the would-be cruisers were cutting off the formidable Electra Glide forks and installing wild aftermarket front ends. These bits and pieces varied from dainty to dangerous, as West Coast extension forks kept pushing the front wheel farther from the motor. Fortunately, Willie G. was able to head the trend off with a design that has become a true watershed in U.S. riding: the Super Glide.

"Is the American motorcyclist ready to ride around on someone else's expression of personal, radical taste?" *Cycle* magazine asked before testing the new 1971 Super Glide. The publication put the bike through its paces and concluded that the machine "will succeed in this country like no machine Harley-Davidson has ever made or dreamed of making."

Davidson is characteristically modest about his first major design under the auspices of AMF. The conglomerate, he said, never knew what to make of the styling department, so they just let it alone. Consequently, Willie G. grafted the Sportster's handsome and stable aluminum front forks onto the massive frame, compensating for the stock fork appearance by making the Super Glide graphically exciting. The boat-tail Sportster seat worked surprisingly well on the initial batch of Super Glides, which still carried the FLH designation on the timing cover.

The FX, as the Super Glide was designated, was significant for the following reasons:

- It was the first factory custom. Before 1971, no company had ever listened so closely to owners of its products. Until then, riders bought what was offered and set about individualizing as best they could.
- It combined traditional parts of one motorcycle with traditional parts of another for an entirely new look. This alone endeared it to the Electra Glide and Sportster faithful, which could identify with the FX even if they did not intend to buy it.
- It was the first cruiser, the first bike to make so personal a statement about a whole new kind of rider who had never before had an acceptable, showroom-stock cycle offered him. Harley-Davidson dealers were talking to a new kind of customer about a new kind of machine.
- It was the seed that sprouted everything from the Fat Bob to the Wide Glide to today's Softail Deuce. Thanks to this machine, no Harley owner has any excuse for riding a bike exactly like anyone else's.

Moreover, it was a good bike. It kick-started easily, the transmission was traditionally unbreakable, the clutch action was "the best in motorcycling," said a magazine, and it handled much better than anyone imagined. Slimmer by 70 pounds than an FL, the FX rocketed away from stoplights, yet would chug willingly around town all day. Drum brakes front and rear prevented the Super Glide from state-of-the-art stops, but that would be remedied soon. With an optional red, white, and blue color scheme, the Super Glide was the perfect bike at the perfect time. Somehow, Willie G. had created something that, in a single stroke, was both outrageous and conservative.

At this time, the feds descended upon manufacturers of transportation; their well-intentioned regulations were designed to make all vehicles safer. Harley-Davidson, thanks to AMF and healthy sales, had more development dollars than ever before. Because of the federal edicts, however, most of those bucks went into safety or emissions work rather than higher performance or newer products.

For example, left-hand shift became mandatory in 1972 and turn signals were the rule in 1973. Besides jacking up consumer prices, the regs meant that H-D had to divert time, money, and manpower to find new suppliers, conduct safety testing, and so on. Except for development of the "King of the Road" tour package in 1973, no significant modifications were made to the FLs through 1975. One employee noted that the company wanted magazines to conduct road tests at a time when the company had nothing new to show them.

Nevertheless, H-D soldiered on. Disc brakes showed up in 1973, silencing the major complaint voiced about the company's products in postwar years. The Super Glide received optional electric starting to become the FXE in 1974. In 1976, the company displayed a stylized eagle and five "Liberty Edition" versions of the V-twin, to coincide with the U.S. bicentennial.

In cruised the FXS Low Rider in 1977, a contrast to another new model, the Sportster-inspired XLCR Café Racer. The FXS deposited the rider just 27 inches above the ground, featured highway pegs as standard equipment, and displayed a split or Fat Bob gas tank. It also bore, in its second year of production, the "ham can" air box, a unit shared with all other V-twins in hopes of appeasing Uncle Sam's noise and emissions savants.

The 1978 Electra Glide received the optional, enlarged 80-ci motor, just in time for the company's diamond (75th) anniversary. The less ornate FL was dropped in 1979 as the FLH was offered with more standard equipment than any motorcycle ever: fairing/windshield, saddle bags with safety guards, luggage rack, passing lights, safety bars, and running boards. At this time, owners of virtually all heavyweight cycles began to notice that their bikes did not run worth a damn on the lower-octane gasoline that, in leaded or unleaded form, was crowding premium fuel off the pumps. The vintage flywheel medallion on the handsome FLH tank reminded riders that the old bikes dieseled less because there were fewer federal impediments. Dealers leaned out the carburetion under the direction of a factory service bulletin, sold lots of octane additive, and hoped for the best.

Harley-Davidson introduced four new models in 1980, the most significant being the FLT Tour Glide. Most evident was the dual headlight, frame-mounted fairing, a slick answer to the aftermarket wind slicers. Less noticeable was Harley-Davidson's first five-speed gearbox. The unit made two-up riding with the standard TourPak especially effortless, while a new frame and the patented positioning of the steering head in front of the fork crowns created excellent low-speed stability.

The FLT's vibration-isolated motor, which used elastomer mounts to intercept vibes transmitted to the drivetrain, swingarm, or frame, received high marks from heavyweight riders. So did the V-Fire (1980) and V-Fire II (1981) ignitions, both of which created a hotter spark without points. An enclosed secondary chain, 5-gallon fuel tank, triple disc brakes, styled wheels, and every conceivable touring amenity standard made the Tour Glide complete.

If the FLT was the ultimate tourer, the new Sturgis was the ultimate cruiser. One of the three new-for-1980 offspring of the Super Glide, the FXB (for belt) was a study in black trimmed lightly in orange. Technically, the bike broke new ground with its 1-1/8-inch primary and 1-1/2-inch secondary drives, accomplished with Aramid fibers from the Gates Rubber Company. Nevertheless, the machine was so stylish that few owners cared if the driveline was quieter, lasted twice the life of a chain, and required neither lubrication nor adjustment. They had to notice, however, a compensating sprocket on the primary drive that all but eliminated lash characteristics of chain-driven bikes. Drag bars with risers, a Fat Bob tank, a seat only 27 inches high, the Bar and Shield adorning the tank—the Willie G.-designed cycle is among the most handsome Harley-Davidsons in the company's 100 years.

Joining the Sturgis were the FXWG Wide Glide and the FXEF Fat Bob (the latter and one 1980 FLH being final evidence of the 74-ci motor). The Wide Glide sported a 21-inch tire up front, a 26-1/4-inch high seat, the pullback bars that had become common on H-Ds, and spoke wheels. The Fat Bob was so named because of its bobbed rear fender and 5-gallon fuel tank. (Speaking of gasoline, the 1982 bikes ran just fine on regular. That was due to lower compression.)

The pinnacle of Harley-Davidson achievement for 1983, final year for the Shovelhead, was the FXR/FXRS, both termed Super Glide II. Recipients in 1982 of the five-speed transmission and a new frame that used FLT-type mounts to isolate the motor, *Cycle World* judged these models "H-D's Great Leap Forward." Besides cosmetic differences, the FXR ran traditional spoke wheels, while the FXRS possessed mag-style wheels. There was even an economy model Super Glide, the FXE, offered without the five-speed or the elastomer-mount frame.

And what of the Shovelhead engine itself, which delivered dependable power for 18 years? It was replaced first in the Softail in 1984, then throughout the line the following year. It was the victim of excessive oil consumption, too much iron, and not enough weight-saving aluminum. Yet retirement is a relative term, as any H-D fan can see. There are still lots and lots of Shovelhead-powered bikes on the open road.

Specifications: FL, FLH *(From a 1965 owner's manual)*

The engine (serial) number is stamped on the left side of the engine crankcase.
Wheelbase: 60 inches.
Overall length: 92 inches.
Overall width: 35 inches.
Model designation: FL, FLH.
Type: 45-degree V-twin.
Number of cylinders: Two.
Horsepower: FLH, 60 at 5400 rpm; FL, 55 at 5400 rpm.
Taxable horsepower: 9.44.

Bore: 3-7/16 inches (87.3 mm).

Stroke: 3-31/32 inches (100.8 mm).

Displacement: 73.66 ci (1207 cc).

Torque: FL, 62 ft-lbs at 3200 rpm; FLH, 65 ft-lbs at 3200 rpm.

Compression ratio: FL, 7.25:1; FLH, 8.0:1.

Fuel tank total: 5 or 3-3/4 gallons.

Reserve: 1 or 1-1/4 gallons.

Oil tank: 4 quarts.

Transmission: 1-1/2 pints.

Circuit breaker point gap: .022 inch.

Spark plugs size: 14 mm.

Gap: .025 to .030 inch.

Heat range for average use: No. 3-4.

Spark timing: Retard 5 degrees before top dead center.

Automatic advance: 35 degrees before top dead center.

Transmission type: Constant mesh.

Speeds: Four forward (foot shift or hand shift), three forward and one reverse optional.

Clutch sprocket teeth: 37.

Transmission sprocket teeth: 22.

Rear wheel sprocket teeth: 51.

Engine sprocket teeth (four-speed transmission): FL, 23; FLH, 24.

Engine sprocket teeth (three-speed transmission): FL, 23, FLH, 24.

High gear ratio (four-speed transmission): FL, 3.73; FLH, 3.57.

High gear ratio (three-speed transmission): FL, 3.73, FLH: 3.57.

Tire size: 4.00 x 18 inches, 4.50 x 18 inches, 5.00 x 16 inches.

Overhead Valve Evolution V-Twin, 1984–1997

The Evolution engine represented a summary of what the buyback members had learned about the needs of Harley-Davidson customers. The motor went into the Softail after some production delays, and then into the entire line.

That included the FXRT Sport Glide, introduced in 1986, which showed a wind tunnel-tested fairing and a look that successfully linked touring and sports riding. In 1988 came the FXSTS or 85th Anniversary Springer Softail, a bike with more than 4 inches of front suspension travel. The Springer looked positively retro, though H-D engineers had subjected the front end to all sorts of computer input and road testing. The Ultra Classic rolled up in 1989

A 2002 FXSTS Springer Softail awaits its rider at Daytona Beach. (David K. Wright)

with electronically mounted cruise control, a new intercom, and a sound system packing 80 watts of power. The 1990 Low Rider Convertible displayed nylon saddlebags cunningly designed to look leathery soft while they kept their shape at speed. All the 1991s featured the self-canceling turn signals, and 1992 witnessed the introduction of the Dyna Glide chassis, which mixed the appearance of the original Low Rider cycles of the late 1970s with the handling and rubber-isolated ride of today's Low Riders. Meanwhile, the Dressers were being fine tuned with amenities such as a better 40 mm carburetor for cold-morning starts, continuously vented gas tanks, and surer brakes.

The Electra Glide was refined further, with well-thought-out amenities for luxury long-distance cruising. Those included saddlebags that closed on reliable gaskets. Equally practical, 1992 FLs featured easier access to the oil filter and better brake feel and action. For 1993, much attention was paid to the company's 90th anniversary. Many of that model year's bikes show cloisonné emblems on their tanks as best evidence of their heritage. What was left to do?

Not a great deal, but for the fact that the Evolution engine occasionally leaked oil and, despite the elastomer, still sent waves of vibration through bike and rider. More powerful than its predecessor mostly because of freer flowing intake and exhaust, the Evolution returned to primary chain drive. The Evo Sportster was physically smaller, had fewer parts, and went to cylinder and heads of plain aluminum. The motors in the Sportsters were installed rigidly, without benefit of elastomer. Ride a Softail and a Sportster from that same era and you will quickly feel the difference.

Specifications: 1993 FLSTN Heritage Softail Nostalgia

Length: 93.8 inches (238.8 cm).
Wheelbase: 64.2 inches (158.75 cm).
Seat height: 27.25 inches (67.31 cm).
Dry weight: 710 pounds (359.9 kg).
Engine: Overhead valve V2 Evolution.
Bore: 3.498 inches (88.8 mm).
Stroke: 4.250 inches (108 mm).
Displacement: 80 ci (1340 cc).
Carburetion: 40 mm constant velocity with enricher and accelerator pump.
Ignition: Inductive, battery-powered V Fire III electronic breakerless with solid-state dual stage advance.
Transmission: Five-speed, constant mesh.
Torque: 77 ft-lbs at 3600 rpm.
Mileage: 42 mpg city, 51 mpg country.
Instruments: Speedometer with odometer and resettable tripmeter.

Twin Cam 88, 88B, 1998–

This is the engine that proves Harley-Davidson riders, at least those thought of as traditional H-D fans, are a cantankerous bunch. When the 88B (for "Beta," but more accurately, for "Balanced") came out, riders bitched because it was *too smooth*. Imagine, if you will, a universe in which a Harley-Davidson hums like a battery-powered watch. What accounts for this smoothness?

The yin and yang of counterbalance is responsible for a new-generation H-D engine that simply has no vibration to transmit to the front end, the handlebars, the seat, or anywhere else. Harley-Davidson created a new-in-2000 engine with twin counterbalancers that cancel out vibrations without losing the "potato-potato" exhaust note of the familiar air-cooled V-twin. (It should be noted here that not all Twin Cam 88s are counterbalanced; as of 2002, some still offered elastomer-mounted 88s without the "B" designation.)

The Beta engine was conceived in order to insert it into the Softail line. That was not as easy as it may seem, since the Softail was used to a rigidly mounted engine—there simply was no room for the elastomer baubles. More important, H-D engineers have known for years that the vibration transmitted from engine to everywhere shortened the lives of all the components it shook. Now, at all legal speeds, vibration is very minor. However, it builds as the speedometer passes 70 mph. Experienced 88B riders probably have a very good idea of how fast they are going by how the motorcycle feels. That has not always been the case.

At the moment, the 88B is one of five engines produced by Harley-Davidson (the other four are the 883- or the 1200-cc Evolution Sportster; the touring series vibration isolation-mounted Twin Cam 88; and the 60-degree, eight-valve, V-Rod wonder). All Dyna Glides are available with either carburetion or fuel injection.

Specifications: 2002 FXSTD/FXSTDI Softail Deuce (From the Harley-Davidson, Inc., Internet site.)

Length: 95.4 inches.
Seat height: 26 inches.
Ground clearance: 5.6 inches.
Engine: Twin Cam 88B (balanced)
Bore: 3.75 inches.
Stroke: 4 inches.
Displacement: 88 ci.
Compression ratio: 8.9:1.
Fuel system: Carburetor or electronic sequential port fuel injection.
Fuel capacity: 4.9 gallons.
Fuel capacity reserve: .5 gallons.
Oil capacity: 3.5 quarts.
Miles per gallon: Carburetor: 50 hwy, 42 city; fuel injection: 50 hwy, 44 city.
Exhaust: Over/under shotgun duals.
Lean angles: right, 36.7 degrees; left, 33.2 degrees.
Rake/trail: 34 degrees (5 inches).
Wheelbase: 66.6 in.
Dry weight: 644 pounds.

VRSCA V-Rod, 2002–

The most important line in the *Enthusiast's* introduction of the V-Rod may have been a subhead running along the bottom of the Summer, 2001, issue. It read: "The first member of a new family of liquid-cooled performance customs." Shades of BMW! Like the German firm a decade or more ago, H-D is introducing an entirely new kind of engine that, many realize, will eventually power some or most of the American motorcycle company's entire lineup. Once you learn about the 60-degree V-twin, it seems a worthy successor to a near-century of 45-degree V-twin performance.

"Have you ridden a V-Rod yet?" A dealer asked of a media friend he had not seen in a while. Before the friend could answer, the dealer gushed, "It just pulls and pulls and pulls and pulls . . ."

Harley-Davidsons have always been known for their ability to accelerate without playing gearshift tunes. The V-Rod, with 115 horsepower and a 9000-rpm redline, will make the torquey Harleys of old pale by comparison. It has a number of features never seen before on a Milwaukee product. They include:

- The 60-degree V-twin, which has liquid cooling. Yes, the configuration was perfected on the late VR 1000 Superbike.
- A lanky 67.5-inch wheelbase, achieved in part via a 34-degree rake and a 38-degree fork angle.
- A fuel tank hidden beneath the seat.
- Hydroformed perimeter chassis.
- Anodized aluminum body panels and a silver powder-painted frame.

The V-Rod is a blend, with an engine derived from the road racer encased in a street-legal drag bike. Early road testers have noted that it lopes a bit lackadaisically through a turn; the machine more than makes up for this leisurely approach by easily smoking its 180-mm Dunlop/H-D rear tire when leaving a starting line or a stop light. The bike is long and low, connoting straight-line stability that is at least the equal of any other mass-produced bike and may well be superior.

The reception given the new design, which was created in collaboration with Porsche engineers, was stupendous. Dealers, allotted only a finite number of V-Rods, told customers to head for the official H-D website and attempt to order from some other dealer. As early as September 2001, somebody was selling a full retail-plus V-Rod on E-Bay! Harley-Davidson/Buell of Reno had 24 V-Rod orders as of early December 2001, with no delivery dates promised.

The new, silver, 2002 cycle looked to be a sellout by the end of 2001. If, as one grumpy old H-D fan said, "It looks like a Kawasaki," it may attract a whole new market. The look and the sound are just different enough from any other Harley-Davidson that it will be noticed wherever a rider chooses to cruise.

Specifications: 2002 VRSCA *(from the Summer, 2001, issue of the* Enthusiast*)*

Dimensions
Length: 93.6 inches.
Seat height: 26.0 inches.
Seat height TUV: 27.1 inches.
Ground clearance: 5.6 inches.
Rake (steering head): 34.0 degrees.

Sportsters were unchanged for '03, with the exception of the anniversary badging and paint options. (Dain Gingerelli)

Fork angle: 38.0 degrees.

Trail: 3.9 inches.

Wheelbase: 67.5 inches.

Tires: Radial D207.

Front: 120/70ZR-19.

Rear: 180/55ZR-18.

Fuel capacity: 3.7 gallons.

Reserve Fuel Capacity: No reserve due to fuel injection.

Oil capacity: 4.0 quarts.

Dry weight: 595.7 pounds.

Vehicle weight in running order: 615.5 pounds.

Gross vehicle weight rating: 1,022.4 pounds.

Engine Dynamics

Engine type: Four-stroke, four valve per cylinder, 60-degree liquid-cooled V-twin.

Displacement: 69 ci (1130 cc).

Bore x stroke: 3.94 x 2.83 inches.

Compression ratio: 11.3:1 nominal.

Max sustained engine speed: 9000 rpm.

Idle RPM: 1200 rpm, auto idle speed and cold start speed control.

Crankcase: Aluminum, horizontal split, low-pressure permanent mold.

Cylinders: Integral cylinders, cast iron drop-in wet liners, double O-ring seat.

Cylinder head: Aluminum, permanent mold, four valves per cylinder, single 12 mm spark plug.

Crankshaft construction: Single piece forged steel, single throw.

Connecting rod type: Side by side, forged steel, cracked cap.

Balancing system: Forged steel, single counter weight, crank driven at engine speed.

Fuel system: Sequential port electronic fuel injection.

Ignition system: Sequential, single fire non-waste spark plug, coil on plug.

Lubrication system: Gerotor, wet sump, 4-quart capacity.

Oil type, change interval: HD360, 20W-50.

Engine controls/throttle: Twin, 53 mm throttle bores.

Engine controls-sensors: Manifold absolute pressure (MAP),

A 2002 FLSTF Fat Boy.
(David K. Wright)

crank position (CKP), Charge Air temp (CAT), Throttle position (TPS), Engine coolant temperature.

Engine controls-Spark knock control: ION sense spark knock control.

Combustion chamber volume: 54.89 cc nominal.

Alternator type/output: Permanent rare earth magnet, 18 amp at 1000 rpm, 38 amp at 3600 rpm (70 F degrees ambient).

Water pump: Impeller type, thermostat-controlled bypass.

Main and con rod bearings: Plain hydrodynamic con rod and main bearings.

Drivetrain

Primary drive: High contact ratio spur gear, 64/117.

Final drive ratio: 28/72.

Clutch: Nine-plate wet pressure fed with integral compensation.

Transmission: Five-speed dog and pocket, spur type first and fifth gears, second through fourth helical gears.

Gear ratio, 1st: 11.749:1.

2nd: 7.897:1.

3rd: 6.321:1.

4th: 5.456:1.

5th: 4.889:1.

Performance

Nominal peak horsepower at crankshaft: 115 at 8500 rpm.

Nominal peak torque at crank: 74 ft-lbs at 7000 rpm.

Lean angle (per SAE J1168): 32 degrees right, 32 degrees left.

Chassis

Frame: Steel perimeter upper frame with Hydroformed main rails and bolt on lower frame rails.

Swingarm: Cast aluminum polished.

Front Fork: Wide 49-mm custom fork.

Wheels: 9-inch (48.26 cm) x 3.0-inch (7.62 cm) cast disc front wheel; 18-inch (45.72 cm) x 5.5-inch (13.97 cm) wide cast disc rear wheel.

Wheel bearings: Dual-sealed, automotive-style, ball-type.

Brakes: Caliper type, four-piston front and rear.

Rotor type (diameter x width): Patented, one-piece floating rotor (front), uniform expansion rotor (rear). Front (dual), 11.5 inch x .20 inch (292.1 mm x 5.08 mm). Rear 11.5 inch x .23 inch (292.1 mm x 5.84 mm).

Suspension travel: Front wheel, 3.94 inch (100 mm) (Travel along the length of the suspension; not vertical wheel travel). Rear wheel, 2.36 inch (60 mm) (Travel along the length of the suspension; not vertical wheel travel).

Electric

Battery: Sealed, maintenance-free, 12-volt, 12 amp/hour, 200 cca (per Battery Council International rating).

Charging: 38-amp permanent rare earth magnet alternator with solid-state, three-phase regulator.

Starting: 0.9 KW with direct drive engagement and slip clutch.

Lights: Headlamp, Reflector optics 55-watt low beam, 60-watt high beam. Tail/stop lights, 8w/28w reflector optics (5w/21w). Turn signal lights, 28w self-canceling (21w). Running lights, front turn signals (except where prohibited by law). Indicator lamps: High beam, neutral, oil, turn signals, engine diagnostics, security systems (optional), cooling temperature, low fuel.

Styling/Convenience

Engine trim: Powdercoated platinum silver crankcase, silver cylinder heads and chrome-plated covers.

Exhaust system: Highly stylized two into one into two.

Seat: Two-piece textured vinyl with flip-up fuel-fill access.

Passenger backrest: Available genuine motor accessories.

Handlebars: One piece welded with integrated risers.

Brake and shift lever: Forward foot controls.

Rear fender supports: Internal to rear fender with included saddlebag mounting points.

Instruments: Electronic speedometer with odometer and resettable tripmeter with diagnostic capabilities and solid-state telltale indicator module; tachometer; fuel gauge.

Hazard warning: Integrated into turn signal controls.

Fork lock: Common with ignition key.

Colors

Anodized aluminum body panels, silver powder painted frame.

Warranty

Warranty: 12 months (unlimited mileage).

Service Interval: First 1,000 miles (1,600 km); every 5,000 miles (8,000 km) thereafter. (Inspections of certain systems and components required at 2,500 mile (4,000 km) intervals.)

Chapter 4

Uniforms

No one on a Harley-Davidson ever caught up with Pancho Villa. But neither did any of the National Guard members on horseback, in cars, or on foot during the "punitive expedition" in northern Mexico in the spring of 1916. From the military point of view, the foray south of the border to nab Villa and fellow banditos was a bust. For H-D fans, however, the raid stands out as the first use of the product in a combat situation.

The Army's First Aero Squadron owned the Harleys ridden south. They were equipped with sidecar-mounted machine guns and were sufficiently impressive to warrant two additional orders for motorcycles, on March 16 and March 27. Credit for mating machine gun and bike was given jointly to the New Mexico Military Institute, the Springfield (Massachusetts) Armory, and H-D engineers, according to a 1916 copy of *The Enthusiast*.

"When machine guns were carried on mules in the old way, from two to four minutes were required to set up and begin firing.

The California Highway Patrol's first batch of Harley-Davidsons, 1930 VL models, delivered at Frank Murray's Sacramento dealership. (Armando Magri collection)

The motorcycle machine gun permits of (sic) instant firing from the sidecar and when it is desired to set up separately, firing can be started within 50 seconds from the command to halt when the rate of fire is 480 shots per minute," *The Enthusiast* enthused. At least 22 such machines saw service.

Other folks in uniform were experimenting with cycles and sidecars. In Spain at about the same time, the militia raided the homes of alleged revolutionaries, confiscating "a lot of seditious papers" and hauling them off in an H-D sidecar outfit. The same issue of the *Enthusiast* reported the McKeesport (Pennsylvania) Police Department's conversion to Harleys from another make, indicating that motorcycles were becoming accepted transportation for the law.

Even earlier, in 1909, Pittsburgh's first motorized police vehicle turned out to be a Harley-Davidson. From the mid-1910s through the 1960s, *The Enthusiast* dutifully reported every city, county, and state police department astride H-Ds. While there were few service problems associated with the use of the cycles by police, that futile pursuit of the bandits in Mexico pointed out the need for in-field maintenance. Yes, Harley riders have Pancho Villa to thank for inception of the company's service school.

Beginning in July 1917, however, H-D dealer personnel were no longer admitted to the school. Instead, groups of 30 enlisted men spent three weeks in Milwaukee learning how to maintain the thousands of Harleys seeing service in France and, to a greater extent, at Army camps throughout the U.S. More than 300 enlisted repairmen were put through the service school in the 16 months before the World War I armistice was signed in November 1918. Most of the newly trained mechanics never made it to France, primarily because the U.S. was not fully mobilized when peace came.

The first glimpse of Harley-Davidsons by World War I soldiers may have been the line of bikes that gave rides to the wounded at various hospitals in England before U.S. entry into the war. This country was strongly supportive of the English and French months before American involvement. Once war was declared, the cycles were shipped with all other vehicles, though they were used primarily for messenger service rather than in actual combat. It is reasonable to assume that as many as 7,000 Harley-Davidsons found their way to France. War Department records show that 26,486 H-Ds were ordered through November 1, 1918, and that 20,007 Indians and Harley-Davidsons were shipped

Seventeen new 1930 VLs delivered to Buffalo, New York, police. William H. Davidson, second from left in the far group, was sent to Buffalo to remedy matters after the police reported disappointment with speed. The first one serviced by Davidson reached a speed of 90 miles per hour, he stated. (William H. Davidson collection)

The late Trooper W. J. Lally on his 1936 H-D 74-ci police bike. "The red lights and the mirror were mine," Lally said. "The saddlebags I borrowed from my horse—no foolin'." (W. J. Lally collection)

Sgt. Carmen R. Sicilia works on a New York State Police cycle in the mid-1930s. Many municipalities now rely on the selling dealer for service. (W. J. Lally collection)

overseas. The most noteworthy was a sidecar rig ridden boldly, inadvertently, and prematurely into Germany.

A Unit of One

"The first Yank to enter Germany" is a photo showing a lone soldier riding a Harley-Davidson with sidecar and heading west, *out* of Germany, as the Kaiser's forces solemnly retreat. A resident of a town near the Rhine River took the picture and it was reproduced worldwide. The date was November 11, 1918, the very day Germany surrendered. But who was the Allied soldier? What were the circumstances? More than 25 years would elapse before the rider's identity became known.

In 1944, toward the end of the next world war, an electrical contractor named Roy Holtz, from Chippewa Falls, Wisconsin, showed up at company headquarters on Juneau Avenue in Milwaukee to obtain a copy of his photo. Puzzled, the editors of *The Enthusiast* learned that Holtz was the unidentified soldier in the famous World War I picture. "I didn't even remember when the picture was taken," Holtz said. "It appeared first in American newspapers and magazines . . . But there's nothing exciting about the incident."

Under questioning, Holtz gave this account: On the night of November 8, 1918, Holtz left a forward position in northern Belgium with his captain in the sidecar. A heavy rain disoriented the officer, who insisted that Holtz steer his H-D east, into Germany. When the two stopped at a farmhouse to ask directions, they were taken prisoner by German officers from a Bavarian division. Holtz, a corporal who spoke fluent German, was treated to shots of potent potato whiskey while his inept superior sat soaking in his uniform. The two were imprisoned until the morning of the armistice, November 11, then freed to return to Allied lines.

Because both were in unfamiliar territory, they rode farther into Germany, and then became separated. At one time as much as 60 miles east of his unit, Holtz rode westward, through retreating Germans, to meet the Allied advance. Not only was he the first Yank into Germany, he was there nearly 72 hours ahead of his comrades.

At war's end, the company did not need to convert to peacetime production—the cycles it had furnished the military were no different than the H-Ds available in approximately 1,000 dealerships throughout the U.S. The most visible indication that Harley-Davidson had been to war was the olive paint job, which lasted with minor variations into the 1930s.

Since, in 1919, Henry Ford's assembly line was only beginning to make a low-priced car a reality, municipalities bought motorcycles in sizeable numbers. Many of the bikes found their way into the hands of the police, who could use the machines in metropolitan areas to ease their way through traffic. Briefly, before the Great War, Harley-Davidsons even offered a sidecar unit with fire extinguishers and first-aid equipment. They and at least a small number of public officials reasoned that two firefighters on a cycle could reach a blaze and haul out victims while a cumbersome fire truck was stuck in what was becoming a familiar phenomenon—the traffic jam.

An extremely rare bike—a shaft-drive Knucklehead Servi-Car. The Army designated these Motor-Tricycles and ordered 16 of the prototypes constructed. The Jeep made military three-wheelers obsolete. (David K. Wright)

A close-up of the same three-wheeler shows a universal joint just below and to the right of the hinge that is visible in the upper left portion of the photo. (David K. Wright)

By 1925, more than 2,500 city and county police units used Harley-Davidsons. As American salaries rose and the prices of cars created by mass production fell, more and more four-wheelers were on the roads. The 1920s may have been roaring in part because there were few speed limits outside towns and any rural limits were hardly ever enforced. Consequently, highway fatalities rose at an alarming rate and states responded with troopers, highway patrols, and police. "Harley-Davidson will curb this tragic traffic slaughter," trumpeted a 1926 company publication, and a special office for fleet sales to law enforcement agencies was established. With each large order, *The Enthusiast* would report that another state was covering its major highways with H-Ds. By the mid-1930s, the cartoon showing a motorcycle cop hiding behind a billboard had become a cliché.

In other countries, law enforcement, frequently indistinguishable from the military, was employing the Harley-Davidson. Movietone newsreels, *LIFE* magazine, and daily newspapers commonly showed at least half a dozen Guatemalans forming a human pyramid atop a police-style H-D that is somehow still in motion. Such stunts made Americans forget that Latin lawmen probably were using the bikes to deprive fellow citizens of their rights. In

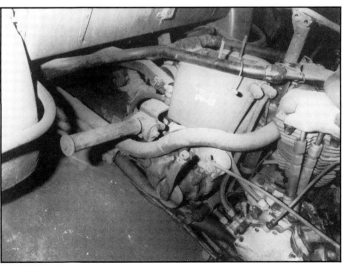

The XA featured a BMW-type horizontally opposed twin-cylinder engine and shaft drive. Just 1,000 were constructed in the early years of World War II. (David K. Wright)

fact, police in the U.S. had their own drill teams. Such cities as Detroit and Washington, D. C. turned out dozens of precision police riders. They did much to maintain interest in law enforcement by performing close-order drill on wheels in parades and in competition. The Miami Beach Police Department, for example, won a national drill team competition in 1955, sponsored by the American Legion. Police drill teams exist today. Among the most accomplished is the 12-man Louisville H-D force.

One-Way Radios

By 1930, police models differed from street Harleys in several ways. The most evident to the populace was the one-way radio, with volume turned up to be heard above the exhaust. The radio was the motorcycle cop's only link with headquarters. In 1948, H-D introduced the two-way radio. The first two-way, delivered on a Servi-Car to Oshkosh, Wisconsin, dealer Joe Robl's shop, was a Motorola FM unit. It featured a 152,000-kilocycle frequency that eliminated most of the "dead spots" found on earlier rolling radios. Installed

just to the rear of the driver's left hip, the unit was cushion-mounted and proved successful virtually from the start. State police, using even higher frequencies, reported a range of 75 miles with their Motorolas.

What was being a motorized police officer like in the 1930s? The late William J. Lally, who retired in 1962 from the New York State Police, reported that the H-Ds were ridden each year from about May 1 through October 15, enforcing speed limits that changed several times during Lally's years in the saddle. In 1937, New York laws stated, "A speed of over 50 miles an hour for a distance of over a quarter of a mile is considered operating a vehicle in a manner not careful and prudent." (The heavily populated Northeast has always observed slower speeds than other parts of the U.S. Nevada, for example, posted speed limits only within city limits until 1974.) Happily for the officers, the Harleys were more than a match for passenger cars of that era. "In the years I rode (1937–1941 and 1946–1948), I never had anyone with any make of automobile get away from me," Lally said.

Working out of the Oneida barracks in central New York, Officer Lally and fellow troopers were provided with bikes devoid of the paraphernalia usually associated with law enforcement. "They were taken out of the crates 'bare' and assigned to the troopers," Lally recalled. "Any red lights, sirens, mirrors, or windshields had to be purchased by the troopers. It was not until 1938 or 1939 that sirens and radios were installed (by the State Police) . . . If you didn't have some sort of makeshift arrangements, you carried all your reports and papers in your pockets. And as far as rain protection was concerned, you simply strapped a plain, everyday black raincoat over the back fender. If you got caught in a bad storm, you would drive in some farmer's barn and call the station. They would send a car out to pick you up—or tell you to ride back to the station."

Lally said a New York cycle trooper not only enforced speed limits but performed all tasks normally associated with police work: homicide investigations, aid at the scene of an accident, directing dragging operations in connection with a drowning, and so on. In contrast, states such as Wisconsin limited state officers to traffic control or to involvement in an investigation only if the crime actually took place on a state highway.

Prelude to War

While mounted officers patrolled Depression-era highways, war clouds were gathering again over Europe. Fascists and Communists used Spain from 1936 to 1939 as a location for testing the weapons they were to fire in Poland, France, and elsewhere. It was from the conflict in Spain that one of the classic stories about Harley-Davidsons turned up.

Some 500 soldiers and civilians took refuge during fighting in Toledo inside the Alcazar, the fortress-like Spanish military academy. As the foe laid siege to the structure, food supplies dwindled. At night, the defenders stole out to nearby fields and gathered whatever grain they could find. Returning, they hooked one of two Harley-Davidsons via a belt to a small hammer mill. The mill ground the grain into coarse flour, used in bread that fed the inhabitants of the old stone fortress. The H-D, despite being run in a stationary position for two months, did not falter. The Alcazar did not fall.

This Harley-Davidson WLA, which belongs to the factory, has nine miles on the odometer. Note the shift pattern, which was turned around after World War II. The twin almond shapes just below the speedometer housed warning lights on the civilian bikes but were virtually invisible on military models. (David K. Wright)

Other garrisons, towns, even countries were falling beginning in August 1939, more than two years before Pearl Harbor. U.S. industry, including Harley-Davidson, was put on a war footing. "That war was planned," The late John Nowak, former dean of the service school, believed. "The Army came in 1937 to look over the civilian service school and equipment, making sure everything was ready." Nowak was ready too, traveling to every Army encampment east of the Mississippi to ensure that the 50 service school mechanics turned out in Milwaukee every four weeks were doing things by the books. In four years, he logged an incredible 200,000 miles on a 61-ci EL with sidecar.

A total of 88,000 motorcycles (plus spare parts for an additional 30,000) reportedly were produced during World War II. The cycles were put through some unique tests at Fort Knox, Kentucky, and in Louisiana by Nowak, under the direction of founder Bill Harley. "We were told our cycles had to ford a stream 16 inches deep," Nowak remembered. "So we stuck the oil breather tube up toward the gas tank. If we hadn't done that, the circulating oil system would have sucked water into the crankcase through the breather. The spark plugs were above the water, but any speed over 3 miles an hour would splash them and drown out the bike."

A World War II WLA, as displayed at Daytona Beach. (David K. Wright)

The 42XA-Solo

The Model 42XA-Solo motorcycle built by Harley-Davidson for the U.S. Army from late 1941 into 1943 probably looked more familiar to German prisoners of war than it did to GIs. The twin-cylinder, L-head bike with a carburetor for each cylinder and shaft drive was copied from BMWs used by the Axis early in the war. H-D engineers converted the various measurements from centimeters to inches and began to tool up for production. Just 1,000 of the XAs were built, because the Germans had, by 1942, been chased successfully across the Sahara Desert in North Africa.

"Somebody in the Army—who should have been shot—got the idea for a shaft drive. Why have two completely different sets of parts (the 45-ci WLA and the XA)? That should have been the question from the beginning." So states the late Wilbur Petri, a mechanical engineer whose assignments included everything from plant layout to postwar liaison with the Aermacchi factory. He confirmed William H. Davidson's belief that the XAs cost the Army slightly less than $1 million, or $1,000 per machine. Those figures include design, tooling, development, and so on. "We practically gave it to them," Davidson once remarked.

This World War II WLA features genuine leather saddlebags. (David K. Wright)

The consumer got no closer to the XA (which featured a four-speed transmission, hand clutch, and both hand and foot shift) than isolated photos of cyclists in training at Fort Knox. *The Enthusiast* pointed out as early as mid-1942 that this bike was experimental and that H-D riders would be told when—and if—it was offered to the public. Plans to produce the XA in civilian form were explored to the point that a prototype with an overhead valve engine and hydraulic forks was created and ridden extensively in 1946.

The view from atop a World War II WLA was unencumbered. (David K. Wright)

Petri rode the XA and said it was smoother than the V-twin, since the vibration in opposed-engine cylinders tends to be self-canceling. The usual shaft drive quirks, including the feeling of levitation when the throttle was cracked open, were present, too.

Specifications *(issued February 1, 1942)*

Type of engine: Twin cylinder, opposed, L-head.
Bore: 3-1/16 inches.
Stroke: 3-1/16 inches.
Displacement: 45.038 ci.
Compression ratio: 5.7:1.
Horsepower: 7.5.
Wheelbase: 59-1/2 inches.
High gear ratio: 4.70:1.
Tire size: 4.00 x 18 inches.
Crankcase capacity: 2 quarts.
Transmission capacity: 2 quarts.
Rear drive housing: 4-1/2 ounces.
Left gasoline tank: (Slightly more than) 2 gallons.
Right gasoline tank: (Slightly more than) 2 gallons. Includes 1/2-gallon reserve supply.

The WLA

If the Army should indeed have shot the officials who gave the nod for the XA, it should have staged a parade for the honchos on the WLA project. Instead of drawing up specs on a clean sheet of paper, the bureaucrats wisely looked at the proven H-D WL, added some military adornments, and went off to war. Although the WLA varied minutely from one defense contract to another, it generally differed from the civilian machine in only these ways:

- A more substantial luggage rack was installed.
- A scabbard for a Thompson machine gun or a rifle ran parallel to the right front fork.
- Blackout lights front and rear were standard.
- Oil, spark plug, and speed recommendations were listed on a metal plate attached to the gasoline tank, between the instruments and the seat.
- A skid plate was attached to the crankcase.

Francis Blake, sidecar restoration specialist, in his U model with sidecar. "SP" stands for Shore Patrol, the Navy's military police.

Anyone who ever rode or serviced a WLA reported staggering abuse without any sort of non-repairable breakdown. Standard procedure for riders included throwing the bikes down whenever the enemy was nearby. The WLAs slid, without complaint, on their tanks on several continents, since every armored division listed 540 cycles in it complement of vehicles. Nor were U.S. armored divisions the only units lucky enough to have the trusty 45s. Approximately 20,000 WLCs, the Canadian version of the 45 and almost one-quarter of wartime production, were shipped north.

The Canadian bikes featured the clutch on the right, brake on the left, right foot shift, and the horn atop the headlight rather than beneath it. The metal luggage rack, mounted on the rear fender of the WLA only, was designed to carry a 40-pound radio the Army never quite managed to affix to the bike in any quantity. The Canadians did have an "auxiliary box" atop the front fender and must have been less concerned about being followed: The WLC was shipped without a rearview mirror.

W. T. Basore, who now lives in Tulsa, recalls his introduction to the WLA on a remote island off Burma in the Bay of Bengal. Stationed there as a private first class in late 1944, Basore used the motorcycle to take him to his assignment on

the other side of the island. "I generally made the return trip each night about midnight, traveling 20 to 30 mph with the lights off." Unlike the highly publicized riders trained at Fort Knox and elsewhere, Basore had never ridden a cycle.

"Due to a severe shortage of fuel (all air-lifted in), two or three Harleys had been brought in to make best possible use of the fuel we had," he reports. Basore learned the rudiments of riding, failing to encounter anything more hostile than an occasional jackal or cow on his midnight rides. "I found that blipping the ignition switch would cause a racket not unlike a high-powered rifle," he says, adding that the 45 never let him down.

Specifications (Training manual No. TM 9-879, no issue date listed)

Engine (serial) number left side engine base, below front cylinder.
Type of engine: Two-cylinder, V-type, L-head, air-cooled.
Cylinder bore: 2-3/4 inches.
Stroke: 3-13/16 inches.
Wheelbase: 59-1.2 inches.
Length, overall: 88 inches.
Width, overall (handle bars): 41 inches.
Wheel size: 18 inches.
Tire size: 4.00 x 18 inches.
Tire type: Drop center.
Weight, without rider or armament: 540 pounds.
Ground clearance (skid plate): 4 inches.
Fuel: 72 octane or higher gasoline.
High gear ratio: 4.59:1.
Engine sprocket: 31-tooth.
Counterweight sprocket: 17-tooth.

Oshkosh, Wisconsin, dealer Joe Robl, seated, and William H. Davidson check out the two-way radio on the first Servi-Car so equipped.
(William H. Davidson collection)

Rear wheel sprocket: 31-tooth.
Maximum allowable speed: 65 mph.
Miles per gallon (hard surface): 35.
Cruising range: 100 miles.
Fording depth (carburetor): 18 inches.
Fuel capacity (left tank): 3-3/8 gallons.
Oil capacity (right tank): 1-1/8 gallons.
Transmission capacity: 3/4 pint.

Wartime Projects

While the WLA and the XA were addressing armed forces needs, the H-D factory chased several wild geese in an effort to win the war. In 1941, sidecar-equipped Indians wound up in Louisiana for a series of tests in swampy, tropical conditions. The inability of these machines to function hastened development of another all-terrain vehicle, the Jeep. Shortly after the Willys Jeep entered production,

Harley-Davidson provided Willys with XA-type, opposed-twin motors intended for airborne mini-Jeeps. However, the Toledo, Ohio, firm was so busy cranking out full-size models that the junior version never got past the Willys experimental experts. Some 5,000 motor generators, based on the XA engine, were ordered, but the war ended before these units could be produced. In addition, H-D's most closely held wartime secret—mating two V-twin engines for installation in a Canadian mini-tank—also failed to materialize. By war's end, H-D was building such things as telescope equipment under subcontract to Bell & Howell and Argus.

The fortunate few who received new Harley-Davidsons during the war years included civilian police, of course, and those who could demonstrate a legitimate need. Mounted, armed guards patrolled the sprawling munitions plant operated by the Olin Company outside Baraboo, Wisconsin, keeping it safe from saboteurs. Of even less importance were such quasi-police units as the Dayton (Ohio) Funeral Escort

Montgomery County, Maryland, police show a sizeable Harley-Davidson fleet.

Service, which led processions through the city on H-Ds bearing the only civilian paint job then available—gray. Cyclists who, for one reason or another, were not drafted kept their 1930s machines together as best they could, riding on rationed rubber and gasoline.

John Nowak, the former H-D service school dean, pinpointed the justification for rationing: "We had plenty of gasoline throughout the war, but we didn't have much rubber. I guess the government figured that the best way to preserve tires was to keep people off the roads. They did that by restricting the sale of fuel."

Harley-Davidson's fortunes with the military may have diminished since World War II, but police worldwide are riding the bikes as never before. The U.S. Army and

Deputy Jerry Lawrence of the Ventura (California) County Sheriff's Department.

The United States Park Police are based in Washington, D. C. Their duties include escorting the president.

The Harley-Davidson Motor Company

Trooper Robert Benefiel of the Colorado State Patrol sharpens his skills aboard his Harley-Davidson.

Navy use a few motorcycles for military police and shore patrols, whereas more than 1,000 state, provincial, county, and local law-enforcement departments ride Harley-Davidsons here, in Canada, Mexico, and worldwide. It's safe to say that H-D is the overwhelming favorite of law enforcement throughout the U.S.

Police sales are no foregone conclusion, however. Recently, for example, the California Highway Patrol chose BMWs over every other make. It is difficult to see how this makes economic sense when the factory gives such great deals on police bikes. Madison, Wisconsin, has leased a tricked-up police cruiser, for the sum of $1 per year, so that officers could take it to elementary schools and impress the kids. The company also offers service training and, in cooperation with Northwestern University, course work on proper police cycle operation.

In 2002, Harley-Davidson offered half a dozen different police model bikes as well as a sidecar. They include the FXDP Dyna Defender, the FLHPI Road King, the FLHTPI Electra Glide, the Police Officer Special Edition, the Firefighter Special Edition, the XL Sportster 883, and the TLE sidecar (compatible with the Road King or the Electra Glide). The Police Officer Special Edition and the Firefighter Special Edition are intended for private ownership. The Firefighter version is bright red with gold stripes, while the Police counterpart is either two-tone blue or "Dark Police Officer Blue." Fire and police professionals can order their special deals for the Road King, Electra Glide Ultra Classic, or Electra Glide models.

Specifications: 2002 FXDP Dyna Defender

Dimensions

Ground clearance: 5.6 inches.
Wheelbase: 63.5 inches.
Weight: 697.4 pounds.
Overall length: 91.6 inches.
Overall width: 33.5 inches.
Overall height: 47.5 inches.
Saddle height: Solo sprung, 31 inches, frame mounted, 28 inches.

Engine

Engine: 1450-cc overhead valve Twin Cam 88 vibration isolated V-twin.
Bore and stroke: 3.75 x 4.00 inches.
Compression ratio: 9:1.
Exhaust: Staggered 3.25-inch diameter (oversize) shorty chrome duals with low interconnect.
Powertrain: New powertrain black powder-coated engine; wrinkle black and texture black component covers.

Officers Mary Ann Thurber and Carl Leiterman of the Madison, Wisconsin, Police Department pose with their Harley police bike and a German tourist. The bike was leased to the department by H-D for $1 per year. (David K. Wright)

Lubrication system: 3 quarts.
Fuel system: Carbureted.
Improved oil system venting.

Drivetrain

Primary drive: Double-row chain.
Clutch: Requires clutch disengaged for starter motor operation. Latest multiple plate clutch design.
Transmission: Five-speed.
• Gear ratios: 1st, 10.110; 2nd, 6.958; 3rd, 4.953; 4th, 3.862; 5th, 3.150.

Brakes

Caliper type: Four-piston calipers.
Rotor type: Flat expanding rotors.
Front (dual disc): 11.5 x 0.20 inches.
Rear (single disc): 11.5 x 0.23 inches.

Suspension

• Heavy-duty shocks and forks designed for demanding police duty cycle.
• Rear suspension with swingarms having bearings that require no lubrication for the life of the motorcycle.
Suspension travel: 6.9 inches, front, 3.1 inches, rear.

Electric

Battery: Sealed, maintenance-free, heavy duty, 12-volt, rated capacity 19-ampere hours, 275 cold-cranking amps.
Charging: Providing 45-amp high output alternator and solid-state regulator.
Starting: 12-volt starter with solenoid operated engagement and relay required.
Ignition: Non-waste spark, MAP-N control.
Hand controls: Water-resistant switches.
Horn: Emits a sound level adequate to be heard above motorcycle and traffic generated noise.
Connectors: Industrial grade throughout.
Lights: Quartz halogen headlight, tail/stop lights, four-way flashers integrated into turn signal switches.
Pursuit lamps: Front mounted PAR-36 lamps, one red, one blue, incandescent.
Indicator lamps: Including pursuit lamp indicator.
Optional electronic siren: Designed for a Whelen 100-watt elec-

tronic siren system, amplifier and speaker; waterproof amplifier (two tones: wail and yelp) airhorn; microphone jack.

Performance
Engine torque: 84.8 ft-lbs at 3500 rpm.
Lean angles: right, 30 degrees; left, 35 degrees.
Fuel: 5.2 U.S. gallons.

Wheels/Tires
Front tire: MM90B19 PT
Rear tire: MM90B16 (D402 PT tires).
• Cast wheels.
• Tubeless type tires have non-skid tread.
• Bead retention extended mobility tires designed to remain on wheel during sudden loss of pressure.
• Sealed automotive style wheel bearings requiring no endplay adjustment; service interval of 100,000 miles.

Color options
Birch white, black, black/white, police color palette special paint (must be approved by H-D paint facility).

Styling/Convenience
Engine trim: Black and polished.
Exhaust system: 3-1/4-inch diameter mufflers for increased horsepower and torque.
Front fenders: Sport-style.
Handlebars: Narrow to enhance rider comfort.
Seat: Latest deluxe solo sprung saddle, special police type, covered with breathable material; optional frame mounted seat for riders of differing stature available.
Side stand: Jiffy type steel stand, locking type when engaged.
Footboards: Hinged/pivoting footboards.
Engine guards: Front engine guard, rear saddlebag guards.
Saddlebags: Factory installed, water resistant law enforcement type saddlebags. Easy open and close, lockable, with push-button latch.
Drive: final belt drive, Gates Aramid fiber reinforced Poly Chain.
Mirrors: Two true image mirrors.
Windshield: Frame mounted; breakaway and adjustable.
Instruments: Analog speedometer indicates 0–120 mph or kph equivalent; calibrated, cumulative odometer.

Daytona Beach police Harley-Davidson. (David K. Wright)

Chapter 5

Dealing

The last time I saw Jim Dricken was when I brought my bike in to be serviced in 1984 or so. He had been my hometown Harley-Davidson dealer, but I switched hometowns. So when I called him for this centennial edition, I was aware things might have changed. After all, dealers as well as the corporation have benefited from H-D sales of 300,000 or more bikes a year, right?

Veteran dealer Jim Dricken of West Bend, Wisconsin, in front of his new dealership.
(David K. Wright)

Boy, have they! Dricken's dealership formerly occupied part of a defunct brewery on the main street in West Bend, Wisconsin. These days, he has a palatial, 20,000-square foot place on the main east-west highway leading out of town, and a satellite dealership in nearby Hartford that's nearly as big at 15,000 square feet. He sells H-Ds exclusively these days, with 300 new bikes passing through his stores for each model year. The old dealership had 6 employees; today, there are 19 in the two locations.

Dricken is about half as old as the corporation. He signed on as a mechanic with Irv Van Beek right out of high school in 1968, and he's been here ever since. He's an old-time dealer in the sense that he has grown and prospered as Harley-Davidson, Inc., has grown and prospered. At present, he's as apt to talk about market share or demographics as he is about baloney-slicer exhausts or dual-spark ignitions. From 1998 to 2000, he served as a member of the company's Dealer Advisory Council.

If Harley-Davidson has done and continues to do something right, it is that they listen to what their 740 U.S. dealers have to say. And why not? Dealers, after all, find out what the public thinks of the product every time a potential customer walks in the door. With that in mind, here are some of Dricken's thoughts on the eve of H-D's big anniversary.

He believes, among other things, that the female market has not reached anywhere near its potential. He may be right. At the moment, fewer than 10 percent of H-Ds are bought by women. As their income more nearly matches the income of any given male, they should be prime prospects. Jim also thinks the average buyer "used to be more of a gearhead." Perhaps the reason his shops do a tremendous amount of performance work ("everything but paint and chrome," he says, pointing to a dynamometer) is that the average buyer wants a machine that is neither stock nor sluggish. Dricken sees a rosy future for a computer-savvy, high-performance technician in every dealership.

Al and Pat Doerman, Columbus, Ohio, run the world's oldest H-D dealership. (David K. Wright)

Early Deals

Arthur Davidson was quick to realize the potential of the motorcycle. Immediately following 1907 incorporation, he set off on a dealer recruiting odyssey that began in New England and spread south and west. Ten years later, on the eve of America's entry into World War I, Arthur had almost single-handedly signed up Harley-Davidson dealers in every one of the 48 states—more than 800 total. Records are scarce on who these cycling pioneers were, but it is safe to guess that they were already in-

Dudley Perkins Company, San Francisco, is among the world's oldest Harley-Davidson dealerships. Begun in 1914 as Maggini and Perkins, the facility remains in the hands of the Perkins family. (David K. Wright)

Dudley Perkins, Sr. (James Perkins collection)

Dudley Perkins, Sr., tilts his hill-climber skyward for a publicity shot. (James Perkins collection)

the Depression. The pioneering dealer attributed the leveling off of sales in the 1920s to the failure of city fathers to maintain roads and to the harebrained drivers of automobiles. Lang himself had earlier been "run down by a flivver driver and crippled in one leg ever since."

Meanwhile, fellow H-D dealers were doing well elsewhere. In 1907, a 14-year-old Californian named Dudley Perkins first straddled a Reading Standard cycle and became not only an enthusiast but a racer as well. A mechanic by trade, he worked for Excelsior, Merkel, and Indian dealers in the Bay Area before joining Al Maggini to open a Jefferson and Deluxe dealership in 1913. Perkins realized that racing was one way to promote his dealership and parlayed his flat-track successes into floor traffic and sales. Arthur Davidson was recruiting West Coast dealers at the time and convinced Perkins of the superiority of the H-D twins and singles. In January 1914, Maggini and Perkins opened their Harley-Davidson dealership at 626 Market St. in San Francisco.

volved in transportation (car or bicycle dealerships), or a manual trade (blacksmiths, mechanics), or were riders who saw a way to mix business and pleasure. Wisely, Arthur shied away from offering his cycles to competing dealers.

The very first Harley-Davidson dealer sought out the tiny shed on Milwaukee's west side to find out if the Davidsons and William Harley were serious about producing motorcycles. C. H. Lang of Chicago sold all of the H-Ds produced in 1904; depending on whom you talk to, that may have been one or three machines. He set up an office on the fifth floor of a Windy City building and by 1912 was selling 800 machines a year without a showroom or even a demonstrator model. Lang, a successful businessman, was the nation's leading motorcycle dealer by 1916. He told a cycle magazine at the time that his brisk trade was due to constant distribution of "direct literature" via a 3,000-name mailing list and to a time payment plan of his own making.

Lang moved his business into showroom quarters after World War I, where 300–400 cycles were sold each year until

A Hillclimbin' Man

A booming business and a new bride who considered racing dangerous ended Perkins' racing career in 1915—more or less. The soft-spoken fellow turned to hillclimbs, winning hundreds of "slant meets" up and down the coast through 1936. His reputation established, Perkins bought out Maggini and moved into larger quarters. Throughout the 1920s, he sold not only hundreds of road bikes, but commercial vehicles as well. By 1928, Perkins' knowledge of municipal and private business had made him the largest Package Truck dealer in the country.

There are two dealerships older than Perkins' still in existence. They are Farrow's Harley-Davidson in Columbus, Ohio, and Kegel's Motorcycle Company in Rockford, Illinois. There would be more but for the Great Depression, which left cyclists penniless from 1929 until after 1940. Since most enthusiasts were young and able-bodied, they were drafted before they could purchase a machine. Riders who remained behind during World War II had a ravenous appetite for new bikes that only an extremely enterprising dealer like Dudley Perkins could feed. By 1944, Perkins realized that the Allies would emerge victorious and that many of the 80,000-plus machines produced by H-D for the military were still in crates. Therefore, the San Francisco dealer located the bikes, purchased them from the government, repainted them, and peddled hundreds of new 45-ci WLAs to civilians. It is no coincidence that parts for 45s are still plentiful in northern California.

Dealers without such resources often found World War II to be more of a hardship than the Depression. Overnight, they went from down-at-the-heels idleness to manic activity. The late Harry Molenaar, a dealer in Hammond, Indiana, for more than 50 years, said he stayed in business by selling nothing and servicing everything. Molenaar held service contracts with a dozen police departments and was on call to keep running a number of Harley-Davidson two- and three-wheelers in use in the Gary-Hammond-East Chicago steel mills.

Another dealer, Alabama's Rathbun Chambliss, recalled his wartime activities to *American Motorcyclist* magazine in 1949:

"When the war came along, the picture was not too bright. No new motorcycles, no parts, practically no help … We (Chambliss and two mechanics) worked on motorcycles during the day, making what parts we couldn't buy. From five in the afternoon till midnight or later, we ran three lathes, making axle spindles for (Army) tanks—a subcontract. About the middle of the war, my next-to-last mechanic was drafted. We (two) made it through the war by working 18 hours a day."

A dealer who was an enthusiast and a good businessman could count on recognition. Dudley Perkins was named to the AMA competition committee in 1932 and served the AMA until his retirement. A fixture at dirt-track national races on the West Coast until his death in 1978, Perkins also sponsored a number of great riders, including 1969 AMA national champ Mert Lawwill. The Perkins organization still does a brisk business in San Francisco.

The Oldest Dealership

Farrow's Harley-Davidson in Columbus was mentioned a bit earlier. If Perkins was a star on the West Coast, this sprawling shop on West Broad Street in Ohio's capital city has for years been a heartland rendezvous. The dealership came to life in 1912 in tiny Nelsonville, southeast of Columbus on the northern edge of Appalachia. Mr. Farrow moved the business to the state capital in the 1910s. He died in 1927 and his widow became one of the first female H-D dealers. The establishment relocated to its present site a few blocks west of downtown in 1941; Al and Pat Doerman, long-time enthusiasts, bought the dealership from the Farrows' son in 1983.

"We knew all along it was the oldest continuously operating dealership," Al said, though he was a bit nervous until official confirmation came from the factory. Al had worked at other Ohio dealerships for about 10 years when the Farrow opportunity arose. He points out that the dealership's antique storefront is in the new AMA museum in Pickering,

North Dakotans Louis (left) and Arnold Hoffman with their 1939 61-ci overhead valve demonstrator. The Hoffmans ran the dealership out of their farmstead and, at the time, were typical of rural dealers. (Arnold Hoffman collection)

He attributes part of the success of the enterprise to the city of Columbus, which has a reputation for being able to survive the ups and downs of the economy. Husband and wife both have a real sense of Harley history and their place in it. As for success since the buyback, he asks with a smile, "How crazy do you want it to be?"

More than 200 dealerships were up and running by the time Farrow opened the doors in 1912. This prosperity allowed Arthur Davidson to pay attention to the related chores of advertising and sales promotion. He retained a Milwaukee advertising agency and created a barrage of

Ohio; that AMA national champion Jimmy Chann was a frequent visitor; and that this may be the only H-D enterprise on earth with its own ice cream parlor! Farrow Harley-Davidson celebrated its 90th anniversary in 2002.

The Doermans sell about 800 bikes (500 new and 300 used) a year. The facility takes up 21,000 square feet, has 35 employees now, and will soon offer a new service center in a nearby building that once was a shoe factory. Among a number of firsts, Al hawked the first Buell ever sold by a dealer and has been a Buell retailer since 1989.

printed matter to combat Indian, Thor, Excelsior, and other brands either established early or with strong followings in a particular state or region. By 1919, just 16 years after the first H-D was constructed, the world's largest manufacturer was providing dealers with:

- Service bulletins, issued whenever a problem surfaced. Those who wonder how things got done before product recalls have only to look at these fliers.
- Motorcycle manuals, now called owners' manuals, issued with each machine. Dealers were advised to keep additional copies on hand, since they were "particularly complete and comprehensive."
- Engine and transmission blueprints "suitable for framing" but intended primarily for reference.
- "Standards of Practice" manuals, designed to be used by the dealer when he held seminars for his buyers on operation and maintenance. Such a piece contained 410 questions and answers and was developed initially to train World War I soldiers.

Other items included electrical repair manuals, lubrication charts, a hint-filled flier on service topics, actual cutaway motors, and tables of standard bearing sizes and clearances. The in-shop guides were supplemented by *The Enthusiast*, which in 1919, was about to be published monthly; posters that boasted of H-D accomplishments on the race track; even letters that taught mechanics how to bill their customers.

Look-alikes

All of the above contributed to uniformity, making Harley-Davidson dealerships in Oregon resemble H-D dealerships in New Jersey. At that time there were too many Mom 'n' Pop storefronts or even sheds where the motorcycle was peddled. Today, except for size and location, dealerships look prosperous and pretty much alike. Nevertheless, there are exceptions, frequently made to accommodate the local market. In Littleton, Colorado, for example, a rider will find an authorized shop with its own tattoo facility and a distinct skull-and-crossbones look. Vinnie, the proprietor, says he gets no heat from the factory because he is a top dealer and "I pay my bills on time."

Murray's shop. Lack of doors indicates this may have been on the second floor. (Armando Magri collection)

Maybe Vinnie really knows his market, and maybe a little individuality is a good thing. A continuing challenge is to turn enthusiasts, whether individualists or conformists, into good businesspeople.

Murray's original showroom in his Sacramento storefront. (Armando Magri collection)

"Harley-Davidson is successful because of its dealers. And remember, that's the opinion of someone who was a factory engineer." So said the late Wilbur Petri, who shared responsibility for some of H-D's better designs over the years and the man who helped the lightweight factory in Italy turn a profit during the period 1969–1976.

In the beginning, Harley-Davidson demanded and received total brand loyalty. In return, a dealer could count on a finely tuned marketing force that could lead the inexperienced or greatly assist the established. The company today has expanded its dealer-

The resplendent showroom of Rossiter's Harley-Davidson in Sarasota, Florida.

ship base to nearly 750 in the U.S. alone (an increase of almost one-third in the last 20 years). A pair of dealers who have expanded their own businesses recently are worth a visit. They symbolize the success enjoyed by most H-D sellers in the last two decades.

Dealers Old and New

Wayne Wiebler and his brother grew up in Illinois. His brother bought a motorcycle and Wayne became addicted to bikes. In 1951 at the age of 14 and still in school, Wayne started work as a mechanic at Walters Harley-Davidson in Peoria. Among other things, he figured out how someone his size, weighing only 130 pounds at the time, could kick over a huge V-twin. He also learned to ride: in 1959, he placed fourth in the 100-mile National at Daytona in the final race run on the old beach course. When he wasn't wrenching he spent long days riding off-road with friends including former Daytona winner Roger Reiman, from nearby Kewanee, Illinois.

Eric Rossiter and his wife with Eric's personal machine. "The pipes," he says, "are almost legal." (David K. Wright)

Wiebler had good teachers with the Walters brothers, who opened their first dealership up the road in Galesburg in 1921. Bob Walters stayed in Galesburg, while Bruce and Gladys Walters opened the Peoria store in 1931, hiring Wayne 20 years later. By 1971, Wayne was the manager and by 1980, he was the owner of the downtown dealership. To this day, he admires the perseverance of the Walters family through some very lean years. "I've seen the early books," Wiebler says. "There was one amazing year when they made only $3,200."

The newer owner has done better, moving from gross annual sales of $500,000 when he took over to $2 million per annum during the lean years of the 1970s and 1980s. Obviously, he does much, much better today. He has been able to help a son and a nephew open Wiebler Harley-Davidson in Bettendorf, Iowa, and his shop has earned a reputation that is at least statewide. Much of this success has been due to his longtime involvement in all sorts of motorcycling activities, from the Peoria TT to the Springfield Mile races and beyond.

Wiebler has been a consistent H-D supporter, noting that the big difference between the old days and now is that dealers worked more often with individuals at the factory back then. When the company urged him to modernize, Wayne first remodeled and enlarged his in-town dealership and then, in 1998, moved into a new place that is state of the art. Like fellow dealer Jim Dricken, he now has the wherewithal to cheerfully support racing. That money comes from sales of more and better accessories and peddling all of the bikes Wiebler is allotted in Harley-loyal Peoria each year.

A contrast to Dricken and Wiebler is Eric Rossiter: "I'm a businessperson, not a mechanic. I was national vice president of sales and marketing for a Cleveland company that made mattresses. I'd been there 15 years, so I was vested. I dreamed of relocating to Florida, retiring from the business I was in, and opening up a Harley-Davidson dealership. There were 100 applications for this (Sarasota) dealership. I think Harley-Davidson is looking for people with business backgrounds, because what I'm really doing is running a retail store."

Rossiter opened in 1990, having made a "tremendous investment" in a designer showroom. He sold 53 bikes the first year, 87 the second, and has not looked back since. Now, he also owns a H-D dealership in Bradenton, Florida.

Rossiter has been able to expand because the Sarasota market was more than twice as lucrative as he and the company had projected.

"Buyers are a real cross section," Rossiter observed a few years back. "There's a good income level here and a number of bike buyers are white-collar people. The average dealership is supposed to net 4 percent of gross sales. Right now, my net is 12 percent. I'm beginning to realize there is the economy and there is the 'Harley economy.' If a person wants a Harley bad enough, the unemployment rate or rate of inflation or cost to borrow just won't matter."

Want to Deal?

Do you have what it takes to be a dealer? Where there might have been 50 dealerships for sale some years back, only a few dealerships come up for sale now and then. That number has dwindled as Harley success has continued to climb. The first hurdle a prospect must cross is the fat-wallet rule: H-D notes on its website that a dealer wannabe should

Harley-Davidsons were always popular raffle prizes, even in the 1930s, as this photo from Walters Brothers Harley-Davidson in Peoria, Illinois, attests. (Wayne Wiebler collection)

Two riders in front of the Walters Brothers dealership in Peoria sometime in the 1950s. (Wayne Wiebler collection)

Davidson dealer meeting is held at a different spot each year. Moved into July recently, the confab introduces dealers to the models they will begin receiving during the last three months of the current year. In other words, the 2003 models began to arrive in showrooms in October of 2002. In addition to turning dealers on to new bikes, accessories, and plans for the company's future, the July meeting gives the corporation a venue to publicize its quarterly earnings and lots of lead time to introduce its products. The V-Rod, for example, was first shown to dealers, press, and public in connection with the 2001 dealers' meeting, held at the Los Angeles Convention Center. One sign of H-D prosperity is that 6,300 folks showed up for the 2001 event.

Dealer Versus Company

No company with the worldwide sprawl of today's Harley-Davidson is problem free. From time to time, H-D has had differences of opinion with a lone dealer or groups of dealers. At the time of the buyback, the legal department stayed busy ferreting products with unauthorized trade and service marks out of dealerships. The company also took a West Coast dealer to court to prevent him from selling bikes on his own out of the country.

Perhaps because the corporation feared a rider backlash, it joined several other companies in 1997 in an unresolved attempt to set maximum retail prices for its machines. In other words, Harley-Davidson, Inc., did not want dealers charging more than the company considered full retail for a product. This practice came about because there were more riders with money than available bikes.

Obviously, the petition to the U.S. Supreme Court annoyed those dealers who were bumping up the price of a new bike. Harley-Davidson did not want the federal trust laws thrown out in their entirety; rather, they wanted pricing policies considered on a case-by-case basis. Not too many years earlier, a dealer with more customers than new bikes could call around the country and find a dealership with a surplus bike waiting. That has not been the case in the last decade or so. It remains legal for a dealer to charge a customer whatever the traffic will bear.

Another bone of contention is non-Harley aftermarket products. Because H-D has plans for every square foot of

have at least $900,000 of his or her own cash in hand and a good line of credit. Here is how the company breaks that sum down for a new dealer with 160 motorcycles:

- Operating cash: $200,000.
- Parts, accessories, MotorClothes order: $400,000.
- Special tools and service equipment: $100,000.
- Dealer management system: $50,000.
- Interior fixtures, plans, permits: $145,000.
- Exterior signage: $5,000.

With Harley-Davidson's newfound wealth has come a numbing number of touchy-feely services provided to dealers. In addition to software that shows, tells, and records how to run it all, there are visits by the district manager, various factory folks who drop by for company-conceived chats, seminars called Harley-Davidson University, cooperative direct-mail programs, plus optional administration of the local Harley Owners Group (H.O.G.) chapter. Perhaps because of increased complexity, some owners have hired general managers for their dealerships. The annual Harley-

every dealership, the corporation feels that devoting space to, say, Arlen Ness footpegs or Jardine shotgun exhausts means fewer official parts, accessories, and MotorClothes will be on display. Today's dealer will order any aftermarket item a customer wants. However, if that dealer stocks much non-Harley stuff, he may not receive as many new bikes to sell as he is used to. The corporation would deny this pressure, but dealers say it is implied, and not with subtlety.

Another problematic area involves financing. Harley-Davidson not only finances the purchase of individual bikes, it underwrites the remodeling and expanding of dealerships. Consequently, many dealers with big new showrooms and high-fashion layouts repay the company a huge sum each month, much like an individual might repay a home-improvement loan. Dealers are afraid of getting too uppity with a corporation that holds their note. Happily, interest rates have strongly encouraged dealership expansion in the last decade, sometimes with bank financing.

The strongest dealerships tend to be where Harley-Davidson is most popular, and vice-versa. California, Texas, and the Snowbelt, from Massachusetts to Minnesota, show especially numerous registrations. California and Texas lead because of their large population. They are followed by Michigan, Ohio, Pennsylvania, and, of course Wisconsin.

A contemporary H-D dealership, this one in Maitland, Florida. (David K. Wright)

Chapter 6

Restoration

Harley-Davidson fans owe it to themselves to attend an antique motorcycle weekend. There they will find devotion at least as intense as an XR750 is loud. Sure, vintage Indian or Matchless or BMW fans exist, but most of the crowd is Harley-crazed. They are quite a bunch, being a mix of survivalists, iconoclasts, ex-gang members, and everyday Joes, with a nice sprinkling of intellectual dudes who are immersed in the history and aesthetic of Harley-Davidsons down through the years. Maybe antique bike weekends take place at fairgrounds because they are the best shows in town.

Here is what's great: All restorers have fascinating stories about how they found the bikes of their dreams. There are lessons to be learned for those who long to discover and restore Harley-Davidsons of their own. None of the stories are alike, yet each is utterly absorbing.

A Two-cam Racer

Michael Lange, who lives outside of Milwaukee, attributes the finding of his two-cam racer to the guy who stole his car. Lange was driving down an alley on the way to test-drive a car to replace the one taken from in front of his home some years ago. "I saw those Castle springs sticking out from under a blanket in a garage, so I stopped," he recalls. Lange offered the owner $2,000 cash on the spot for what

turned out to be a 1924, but the owner decided to make things somewhat difficult. He insisted that he would trade the grotty old bike for a new 350-cc four-cylinder Honda.

Vintage Harley-Davidsons on display at the Ocean Center in Daytona Beach. (David K. Wright)

Banker Greg Duray shows one of two XR750s he has restored. One member of his race-bike registry owns "16 or 17" of the legendary XRs! (David K. Wright)

Lange ordered the Honda—and the JD owner reneged. Finally, the deal was consummated for $1,500.

"I bought the two-cam because I needed valve springs for the JD," he says. Said valve springs were located in Louisiana, along with a two-cam motor the owner offered for sale but refused to ship. So Lange drove to Louisiana, picking up the valve springs, the two-cam motor, the front end, and a keystone frame, all for $750. Lange ran the research and development department of a large job shop and so had skill and access to all the right machinery. He began to restore both bikes simultaneously. The results speak for themselves, though he did dismantle the JD at least once to fix a couple of things that annoyed him. Except for a crack in the lower rear portion of the frame (which Lange fixed in the shop), the two-cam is as tidy as it was eight decades ago,

when the serial number, 24FHAC577 was manually hammered into the engine case.

"I made a chopper before I came to my senses," says Lange, who also has restored a 1941 74-ci Knucklehead with sidecar, plus a WLDR racer. Unlike many restorers, he has ridden the two-cam at high speed. One such trip almost cost him damage to the bike and himself. "There's no transmission and it's geared for a mile track," he says. "It doesn't even start to breathe till 70 to 90 miles an hour, and I'm guessing the top speed is 140." On a seldom-traveled portion of road, Lange opened 'er up, running at least 80 mph. The rear Universal tire, never intended for anything much past idle, flew off the rim, wrapping itself around the axle. Somehow, the brakeless machine and rider managed to stop without incident.

Michael Lange's 1950 WR. He painted the bike yellow before discovering that the color was offered in 1950, but not on this model. He repainted the WR an authentic Ruby Red. (David K. Wright)

Michael Lange's 1941 Knucklehead. (David K. Wright)

(Lange and his wife, Linda, now run their own restoration-related business, as we will see later in this chapter.)

A One-part Start

Glenn Harding's 1941 restored 61-ci EL had been reduced to just one part—the rear cylinder head—when he got hold of it in 1962. The former Harley-Davidson dealer, who also taught at Patrick Henry Community College in Martinsville, Virginia, spent the following 19 years acquiring parts here and there for what may be the nicest Knucklehead in existence. The son of an engineer/machinist, Harding began working in a cycle shop at the age of 12 and from 1939 to 1962 ran a combination Harley-Davidson–lawn mower and small engine dealership. Only after he sold the business did he begin to long intensely for an EL. The cylinder head was discovered inside a fenced area filled with junk parts at his former dealership.

"As luck would have it, I began to pick up old parts and was given others—first the engine, then a transmission, then a frame," he said. The frame itself was created from parts of three choppers. Harding paid heed to old books and manuals for proper dimensions. "Every part I managed to find was worn out or discarded. If someone has a valuable part these days, money won't work—you have to trade him something he wants more than that part." The motor on the bike carries serial number 41EL2394 and is entirely stock except for minor internal refinements. Harding modified the valve gear for quiet, more endurable running. The paint, he admits, is a compromise. The black is authentic DuPont enamel, whereas the red is DuPont lacquer. "Originally, it was all enamel, but the more you rub lacquer, the better it looks."

The saddlebags aren't stock, but they can be considered authentic, since Harding sold similar units out of his business. "I went to Daytona right after the war and saw these great looking square leather saddlebags. So I came home and designed them to sell in my shop." The bags were made by hand-carving wood to the proper shape, then applying a thin layer of foam rubber and stretching the leather over the wooden mold. The hand-tooled bags and seat skirt were sold in quantity at the dealership, and Harding was able to recall how he created them. The original bags, incidentally, continued to sell well until 1957, when swingarms and plastic conspired to make rigid bags more practical and capable of matching the color of the bike.

"I was forced to use a non-authentic seat rail," he admits, pointing out that the small rim of bright metal did not come out until the 1950s. Since no one he knew performed cadmium plating, Harding found a shop in another part of the state that imparts a cadmium look to the plating process. It is, he said, a different appearance than chrome.

No attempt was made to run the bike until it was entirely together. On June 15, 1981, the EL started on the first kick. Only a toolbox and Eagle fender tips have been added since these photos were taken. The machine, says its proud owner, is a joy to operate. "It's very easy to handle, since it has a low center of gravity. It honestly feels like a 150- or 200-pound minibike. The ride is harsh by today's standards, but vibration is negligible. If you had significant vibrations, you had a problem with these bikes. It was my experience that Harley-Davidson was never as critical as they should have been with engine balancing. The bike just doesn't have any brakes compared to the new ones. Moreover, the front spring has just 1-1/2 inches of travel. The model had ride control, which consisted of two plates and a friction disc. The disc, mounted on the rigid fork, tightened steering."

Harding does not ride the bike excessively or at high speeds, and he is not set up for parades, which require more cooling than the

This 45-ci model, from 1929, is being restored by Norwegian Ola Jonassen.

This restored 1937 45-ci V-twin belongs to Norwegian restorer Ola Jonassen. Parts for the 45 turn up in the U.S. and throughout Europe.

motor gets at long periods near idle. The EL is more to be admired than anything else, as was the owner's next project. He restored a 1934 Seafoam Blue VLD, which he says has "bushels of power."

Still Rollin'

The paint is wrong, the shift arm is missing, the head was borrowed from an Excelsior, and many small items are elsewhere. So, what is Bill McMahon's 1914 magneto single doing in a chapter on restoration? First, his bike is in running order, something many antique H-D owners may never achieve due to missing parts. Second, the Wisconsin Rapids, Wisconsin, owner rides the darned thing at regular intervals. In 1972, McMahon, an antique Ford buff, noticed in a newspaper that a "1915 motorcycle fram (sic)" was among the contents of an old farmstead coming up for auction. "My partner in old car parts and I bought the contents of five sheds at that auction," he says. "I bought the frame for $15."

Attached to the frame were a front wheel, dangling from broken front forks, plus rusted tanks, both fenders, and bent

This 30.50-ci cinder-track or speedway machine from early 1934 belongs to restorer Dan Pugens of Milwaukee. No more than a dozen of the overhead valve machines, which feature direct drive and weigh 265 pounds, were made. Most such bikes were sold on the East Coast or in California. This example may have been run by East Coast star Goldy Restall. (David K. Wright)

Dan Pugens of Milwaukee restored this 1931 500-cc (28.4-ci) speedway racer, a twin-port single with lower end modified to accept a Bosch magneto. Stock 1926–1931 H-D singles frames were modified at the factory for these bikes, which were assembled by hand. Handmade items include push rods, cylinders, J.A.P. -style forks, handlebars, and steering damper. Bore is 3-1/2 inches and stroke is 4 inches. (David K. Wright)

handlebars. In one of the sheds McMahon uncovered a motor, extra handlebars, fenders, running boards, linkage, another gas tank, and miscellaneous parts that appeared to be from the magneto, fuel lines, etc. He then purchased those pieces from his partner for $35 and had "what I thought was a fairly complete pile of parts. Little did I know …"

Once in his basement, McMahon discovered that he had purchased a 1914 Model 10C, serial number D7807. The bike appeared rust colored, but underneath showed faint flecks of gray paint. He spent seven years following parts leads, shopping swap meets, and contacting the factory. Failing to receive any company information, McMahon snooped around the headquarters in Milwaukee, met a man on a loading dock who identified himself only as "a Harley friend," and eventually provided him with photos and a copy of a 1914 owner's manual.

Glenn Harding's 1941 61-ci overhead valve model. His restoration project began with only a rear cylinder. The saddlebags and skirt are similar to ones offered by Harding when he was a H-D dealer. The seat rail resembles those found on postwar models. (Luther Oehlbeck)

Purchasing the only new parts available—tires, tubes, decals, and rubber mats—McMahon brought the motor to life for the first time in 1979. "As soon as I got it running, everybody wanted to buy it," he said, despite the fact that running condition was more important to him than 100 percent faithful restoration or checks for $3,000 or more. In addition to the parts already mentioned, the bike is missing a shift crank, which prevents the rider from using top gear in the two-speed, hub-mounted transmission. Also missing are the primary chain guard, the muffler cutout, and the original nickel plating. A manual H-D klaxon horn is affixed, while the carbide lamp and kerosene tail lamp were borrowed from a long-forgotten motorcycle or bicycle.

"It isn't restored perfect. That's why I let a lot of people ride it and why I ride it a lot," says McMahon. The 1914 mod-

Harding says he has eliminated much of the motor's inherent vibration by balancing the original parts. (Luther Oehlbeck)

els were the first year for the step starter; starting, he says, is easy. "You start the oil to drip to the motor at about 30 drops a minute, then fill the carb with gasoline using the tickle valve," he reports. "Bring it up to compression and step down hard with either pedal. One or two kicks are all it needs. It idles like a new Harley. You know—thumpa, thumpa."

McMahon allows the bike to warm up for about two minutes before jumping aboard, easing out the clutch, and riding off. "I locked it in low gear and that's fast enough," he says. "I can go between 35 and 40 miles an hour. If I could shift it, it should go 60 to 70 miles an hour. That's too fast for 2-1/2-inch tires and an old machine." Nevertheless, you will see McMahon—and other folks he trusts—aboard the milky gray machine in local parades, at a big antique car show in Iola, Wis., each summer, and at an occasional antique meet. "It has chipped paint, but it's a runner. I like to drive my antique vehicles, not look at them."

Viewing Vintage Bikes

Now that your appetite is whetted, where can you see old-time Harley-Davidsons? The company's traveling "A Highway Through Time" display is the best bet since the old museum in York closed and the new museum in Milwaukee has yet to open. If you and the display cannot connect, there is at least one historic H-D being shown within a long day's drive of virtually every American rider. Rather than speeding to find out if that is true, note the location and stop in the next time you tour.

Harley-Davidson of Sacramento, Inc.
1000 Arden Way
Sacramento, CA 95815
Tel. 916-929-4680
www.hdsac.com

Yes, this is a dealership, but it is no ordinary dealership. Once owned by the late Armando Magri, H-D of Sacramento proudly displays his collection of vintage Harleys in a newly remodeled showroom. In addition to being good people, the folks here like the old bikes as well as the new ones. And there is never a charge to visit. Many other dealerships have at least one restored machine on display, which is as good a reason as any to stop in.

Restorer Francis Blake was given this pre-World War II 45 with sidecar—if he would renovate a similar model. Both were recovered by an American visiting Egypt. (Francis Blake)

American Police Hall of Fame and Museum
3801 Biscayne Blvd.
Miami, FL 33137
Tel. 305-573-0070
http://www.aphf.org/

A 1960 Duo-Glide police solo stands tall in a museum that has taken on added meaning since the September 11 tragedy. Admission is $12 for adults. Open 10 AM–5:30 PM every day.

Henry Ford Museum and Greenfield Village
20900 Oakwood Blvd.
Dearborn, MI 48124
Tel. 313-982-6100

Willie G. noted the absence of any worthwhile motorcycles in 1956 while styling for Ford's Lincoln division. A year later, he and Walter C. Davidson remedied the situation by presenting the museum with an authentically restored 1907 single. The machine was found in mediocre shape in Milwaukee and redone by the factory. The museum also now has a 1941 Fleet Red 74-ci Knucklehead with sidecar, restored by Don Montgomery. Open 9 AM–5 PM, admission charged.

Salvatore LaFerrera of San Francisco rides this 1928 V-twin daily. He says the bike's performance is entirely adequate—except for the brakes. Front brakes were introduced on H-Ds in 1928.
(David K. Wright)

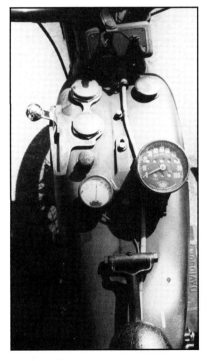

Here's a rider's view of La Ferrera's machine. The speedometer was an option in 1928.
(David K. Wright)

Indianapolis Motor Speedway Hall of Fame Museum

4790 W. 16th St.
Speedway, IN 46201
Tel. 317-920-2660
www.Indy500.org/museum/

There are more than 25 Indy 500-winning cars on display, but that is not why we are here. A fairly authentic reproduction of Joe Petrali's 1935 "Peashooter," restored with the help of the late H-D dealer Harry Molenaar, and presented by the company, was admitted to the museum several years ago. Admission charged.

Kersting's Cycle Center and Museum

Indiana Hwy. 39 South
North Judson, IN 46366
Tel. 219-896-2974
http://kerstingscycle.com

This Harley-Davidson dealer shows more than 100 vintage cycles in a part of the country charitably described as the middle of nowhere. Open Tuesday through Saturday, there is no charge to see H-Ds as old as 90 years.

Motorcycle Hall of Fame Museum

13515 Yarmouth Drive
Pickerington, OH 43147
Tel. 614-856-2222
www.ama-cycle.org/museum/

In a new and stylish building in a suburb of Columbus, the American Motorcyclist Association's museum shows the handiwork of Antique Motorcycle Club of America members and other vintage machine owners. There are old racing bikes, lots of memorabilia, themed exhibits that change from time to time, and more. AMA headquarters is here, too. Admission is charged for the chance to see at least 75 great rides, a number of them Harley-Davidsons.

Museum of Science and Industry

57th Street and Lake Shore Drive
Chicago, IL 60607
Tel. 773-684-1414
www.msichicago.org/

This place is huge, but it is so interesting that you may not mind searching in coalmines and Gay Nineties streets for the lone H-D on exhibit. The bike is a 1922 horizontally opposed 37-ci Sport Twin. The nearby blurb says the company "was a leading manufacturer of early motorcycles," but makes up for the past tense by pointing out that a similar machine once set the cross-country speed record.

This immaculate 1926 JD showed up at Sturgis a while back with California restorer John Campbell aboard. Much of the bike appears to be original, though the cloth oil-line braiding is an old aftermarket item. (Richard Creed)

National Motorcycle Museum and Hall of Fame
P.O. Box 602
Sturgis, SD 57785
Tel. 605-347-2001
www.e-blackhills.com/museum/

There is no shortage of Harley-Davidsons here! We recently counted nine, and other machines and cool memorabilia surround them. Created in 1990 and now housed in the old post office, the museum is open Monday through Saturday from Memorial Day to Labor Day and Monday through Friday the rest of the year. Admission charged.

National Motorcycle Museum and Hall of Fame
200 E. Main St.
Anamosa, IA 52205
Tel. 319-462-3925
www.nationalmcmuseum.org

Some 60 vintage and antique bikes are shown at this newish, 8,000-square foot museum located between Cedar Rapids and Dubuque. The walls are lined with memorabilia and there is a nice gift shop. Open every day except national holidays, this version of a national museum seeks $4 for admission.

The National Museum of American History
Smithsonian Institution
1000 Jefferson Drive S.W.
Washington, D.C. 20560
Tel. 202-357-2700
www.si.edu/

A pair of Harley-Davidsons graces the Smithsonian. In and out of display are a 1913 Model 9-B single and a 1942 74-ci overhead valve model. Both are in decent shape and worth visiting. Hours are 10 AM–5:30 PM.

Rocky Mountain Motorcycle Museum
308 E. Arvada St.
Colorado Springs, CO 80906
Tel. 719-633-6329
www.travelassist.com

Affiliated with the Antique Riders Club of America ("Ride 'em, don't hide 'em"), this museum is free and open Monday through Saturday. It has more than 50 bikes and includes an entire section devoted to Harley-Davidson.

San Diego Hall of Champions

1649 El Prado, Balboa Park
San Diego, CA 92101
Tel. 619-234-2544
www.sandiegosports.com

The late Brad Andres, who rode a 750-cc side valve to a Daytona win and a national championship, is feted here. The bike is on display amid all the stick-and-ball sports. Donation requested.

Trev Deeley Motorcycle Collection

13500 Verdun Place
Richmond, BC, Canada
Tel. 604-273-5421
http://canadianbiker.com/deeley1.html

The late Trevor Deeley may be Canada's most well known motorcyclist, having been a rider, dealer, and distributor for many years. His collection totals some 250 machines, including a great many Harleys.

(A couple notes of caution: museums come and go, change hands and move. Small museums keep erratic hours and big museums constantly rotate displays in and out of storage. A telephone call could save aggravation.)

Restoration Resources

Restoration, like museum visitation, can be shot through with disappointment. You may find the original cylinder head for your 1926 Single, only to learn that money won't buy it. The person who owns the head will insist on your providing, say, a gas tank from a 1920 Sport model in trade. In other words, some parts can be worth more than money, and bartering is the rule. Virtually all of the folks on the following list accept money for the precious parts they peddle. Some have catalogs, while others report that their parts come and go too quickly to put anything on paper. Frequently, they are so busy searching for and salvaging parts that they can't write down a lot. Please accept the descriptions for what they are—groundwork you may not have to cover in bringing that VL or ULH back to showroom shape. Happy hunting!

Antique Cycle Supply

P.O. Box 600
Rockford, MI 49341
Tel. 888-636-8208

Now in its 28th year, Antiques has a sumptuous, hefty, 208-page catalog with many authentic and remanufactured parts, accessories, and literature. The strength of the catalog lies in the number of large, easy-to-understand, exploded drawings of carburetors, generators, cases, covers, motors, tanks, and more. Happily, this endeavor now holds the copyright to many old, official, previ-

Bill McMahon adjusts the gravity oil feed on his restored 1914 single. (David K. Wright)

More than 100 bikes are stored in a barn to the east of the York assembly facility. (David K. Wright)

Joe Petrali's dirt-track bike is in the foreground; in the back is the Cal Rayborn Bonneville record breaker. Harley-Davidson donated the former to the Indianapolis Motor Speedway Museum. (Indianapolis Motor Speedway)

ously unobtainable Harley-Davidson photos. Terms include MasterCard, Visa, COD, or prepaid.

Antique Harley Works
P.O. Box 2063
Seffner, FL 33584
Tel. 813-689-2957

Bruce Palmer is among the country's leading experts on old Harleys. Need we say more?

Bill's Custom Cycles
7145 New Berwick Highway
Bloomsburg, PA 17815
Tel. 717-759-9613

Bill's shop is just off Int. Hwy. 80, two hours north of York. It overflows with old bikes, old parts, and memorabilia. Open Tuesday through Saturday, Bill has a free catalog and an adjacent museum, "Bill's Old Bike Barn," that he built after Harley-Davidson, Inc., leaned on him over all that company stuff on display in his shop.

Charleston Custom Cycle
211 Washington Ave.
Charleston, IL 61920
Tel. 217-345-2577

New old stock parts for American- and Italian-made H-D lightweights, 1948–1978, are the specialties. The fellows accept MasterCard or Visa and they will ship via UPS.

Coker Tire Co.
1317 Chestnut St.
Chattanooga, TN 37402
Tel. 800-251-6336
www.coker.com

A large number of vintage bike tires exist here, bearing the Coker brand name. If they seem especially willing to work with restorers, it is because Corky Coker owns a 1947 Knuckle-head. The color catalog shows tires, tubes, flaps, valves, and more—and is free. Coker takes all major credit cards, too.

Custom Cycle, Inc.
1895 New Bridge Rd.
Bellmore, NY 11710

Tel. 516-826-8720

www.footpeg.com

These fellows run specials on parts that look to have been on bikes made since about 1970. Their website recently showed a Fat Boy front end and a Shovelhead primary drive, both at bargain prices. A deposit of $60 is required on special orders.

"45" Restoration Company

P.O. Box 12843

Albany, NY 12212

Tel. 800-445-1945

www.45restoration.com

You may remember this enterprise as the H. D. 45 Restoration Company. That was before lawyers for Mother Harley got after Warren and Tammy Bennett, forcing them to modify the name. Luckily, for owners of Flatheads, 45s, and Servi-Cars, they are still at it, with a 64-page catalog that is a mere $2. They have been in business virtually since that last Flathead rolled off the assembly line, and they are proud of their ability to quickly fill orders from this mail order-only endeavor.

In 1977, Conrad Schlemmer restored this 1930 21-ci hill-climber. He has owned the machine, believed to have been ridden by racer Herb Rieber, since 1943.

This 30.50-ci single was constructed from parts by Conrad Schlemmer of Council Bluffs, Iowa. When Schlemmer could not find originals, he built the exhaust and fenders by hand.

Conrad Schlemmer astride his 1932 45-ci model. The paint is original delft blue and turquoise.

The late Armando Magri, the Harley-Davidson dealer in Sacramento, showed restored bikes on his showroom floor. (Armando Magri collection)

Harbor Vintage Motor Company
Box 248, Route 2
Jonesville, VT 05466
Tel. 802-434-4040

In business for nearly a quarter century, these guys buy out old dealerships and restore antique American bikes. Among the bikes they have set right are a 1934 VL and a 1936 Knucklehead. Since parts turn over quickly, you should call about your needs.

Harley Hummer Club
4517 Chase Ave.
Bethesda, MD 20814
Tel. 301-652-1569
www.harleyhummerclub.org

Introduced as a 125-cc machine in 1955, the Hummer lightweight has a following, as this non-profit club with 700 members indicates. The organization puts out a nice newsletter every other month and is represented at the major Antique Motorcycle Club of America events. These machines are handsome enough to line up alongside the singles of the 1920s and early 1930s. By the way, the last domestic lightweight was the 1966 Bobcat. Dues are $15 per year. The website is a treat, too.

Chris Haynes
9716 Lemona Ave., Unit 36
North Hills, CA 91343-2422
Tel. 818-894-2113
Fax 818-895-3063
E-mail hd36knuckl@aol.com

This Panhead sidecar outfit graced Magri's showroom window. (David K. Wright)

The Harley-Davidson Motor Company

These days, former H-D dealer Chris is immersed in restoring Knuckleheads and Panheads. "Original parts are getting tough to find," he says, "but many quality reproduction parts are on the market." He offers lots of Knuckle and Pan parts, plus large collections of memorabilia from within and outside Harley-Davidson. He also has a complete block of H-D accessory catalogs 1929–2002.

J & P Cycles
13225 Circle Dr., P. O. Box 138
Anamosa, IA 52205
Tel. 800-397-4844
www.jpcycles.com

These folks offer a catalog of more than 150 pages for just $2. The piece contains vintage and restoration parts for 1936–1977 Big Twins, 45s, Flatheads, and Sportsters. In business since 1979, J & P has approximately 100 employees, a retail store, and an easy way to receive a 10 percent discount off everything they sell. The website shows their very latest offerings, plus a state-by-state listing of vintage and other cycling events.

Michael T. Lange
6W22935 River Ave.
Big Bend, WI 53103
Tel. 262-662-4432

We talked about Mike earlier. Since 1994, he and his wife, Linda, have gone into the parts and restoration business full time. Something of a perfectionist, Mike does partial and full restorations, manufactures parts, and gives advice, primarily on pre-1930 H-Ds. His handiwork is displayed at Antique Motorcycle Club of America meets.

Seven of the dozens of original motorcycles owned by the late Harry Molenaar, former Hammond, Indiana, H-D dealer. The bike in the foreground is an Aermacchi/H-D road racer equipped with a front disk brake. (David K. Wright)

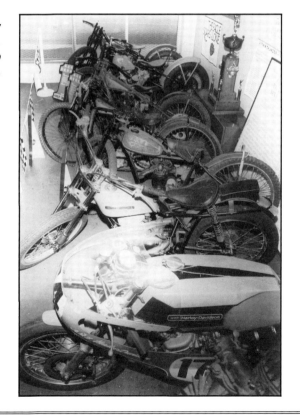

This 1928 single, an overhead valve 350-cc BA model, proves that overseas restorers are active. The owner is Ollie Ridelius, a Swede. Scandinavian sales of H-Ds before the Great Depression were high.

A restored 80-ci flathead from 1936. (David K. Wright)

Coker Tire offers rubber for antique bikes. (David K. Wright)

The Shop: American Motorcycle Specialists
6541 Ventura Blvd.
Ventura, CA 93003
Tel. 805-650-6777

Service manuals are a specialty here. Go to the website for a rundown of what is available. There were also at least four neat rides on premises the last time we looked: a 1913 Silent Gray Fellow, a 1939 Knucklehead, a 1977 XLCR, and a 1977 XR750.

Universal Tire Company
987 Stone Battery Rd.
Lancaster, PA 17601
Tel. 800-233-3827; Canada: 800-321-1934

In the next big town east of York, Universal specializes in motorcycle tires for the period 1903–1930. "We also carry an extensive line of tubes," says an employee, "which means we can accommodate the short, 1-1/4-inch motorcycle brass stem, which was original and authentic for many restorations of early motorcycles." Their color catalog is free and they accept American Express, MasterCard, and Visa.

Walneck's Classic Cycle Trader
P.O. Box 420
Mount Morris, IL 61054-8388
Tel. 800-877-6141

The best thing about this thick monthly is that it will let a would-be restorer know how much a fully redone bike may be worth. The worst thing about it is that founder Buzz Walneck now works only as a consultant for the magazine—he recently became an author and he advises the upscale auction house, Sotheby's, when they have a bike to move. A single issue is $4.95; a subscription is $24. Available at many newsstands.

A 1940 74 or 80-ci model with sidecar. This rig was seen at a recent Antique Motorcycle Club of America meet. (David K. Wright)

The AMA's new Motorcycle Hall of Fame Museum in Pickerington, Ohio, a suburb of Columbus. (David K. Wright)

Engines, transmissions, and more for sale at an antique bike meet. (David K. Wright)

An immaculate XR750, displayed in the infield at the Springfield Mile in 2001. (David K. Wright)

The $4,500 price tag on this 1937 Knucklehead motor indicates how expensive restoration can be. (David K. Wright)

Chapter 7

Adornments

Jerry Wilke, formerly vice president for motorcycle parts and accessories marketing, had no trouble recalling the low point in his three decades with Harley-Davidson. It was 1983 or so, shortly after a two-year salary freeze had gone into effect following a 9 percent salary reduction. A friend who had been among the 40 percent of employees terminated called. He offered to secure Wilke a job at the friend's new workplace. The friend warned Wilke that he had better move quickly—Harley was about to fold. Staying with the company was one of the tough personal decisions a lot of key employees had to make at the time.

If staying on was tough, it also proved to be astute. The demand for the cycles is high and ongoing, and so is the demand for clothing, collectibles, parts, and accessories. That's because, Wilke said, the company has a different marketing philosophy. The sale of the product is just the beginning of the relationship. Harley-Davidson spends more marketing dollars to reach people after the sale than before. That makes H-D different from the other cycle companies and from Detroit. One result is that one-third of H-D's gross income is realized from parts and accessories.

Not one buyback member realized the importance of parts and accessories on that auspicious ride from York back to Milwaukee in 1981, the one that symbolized H-D departing the conglomerate world. During the desperate early 1980s, however, someone became aware that there was untapped

Safety guards, an aftermarket item, were first made available in 1935, as this company-owned 45-ci model shows.
(David K. Wright)

"BROWN LEADER" IS FINEST JACKET

The "Brown Leader" jacket is made up to our own specifications, and is everything that we think a motorcycle jacket should be. It is designed to take care of all sorts of conditions under which you would wear it, and when you get one you will agree that it is the ideal jacket.

This extra fine jacket is made from rich, brown horsehide leather, that will not scuff or scar in the hardest kind of service. It is lined throughout with a good brown moleskin cloth that has excellent wearing qualities. The collar is leather, and so are the cuffs and waist band. Cuffs can be buttoned tight to keep the wind out, and two take-up straps at the waist band assure a good fit. The two pocket flaps button down. Has a genuine Talon zipper.

This jacket, being full grain horsehide, is shower proof and absolutely windproof. It is soft and flexible and can be doubled up and stowed away in a saddle bag without damage. Fully guaranteed. Sizes 34 to 46 are standard.

Code

11067-34—Brown Leader Jacket.....................$11.85 bytuj

FINE LOOKING RIDING BREECHES

This 1934 line of riding breeches is an even better assortment to choose from than we have shown in previous years. Careful purchasing in large quantities has enabled us to maintain prices at very low figures. Every number has been carefully selected as the best available at anywhere near the price.

Good riding breeches are a very good investment, as they are comfortable, very good looking, and wear for a long time. They are particularly well adapted to motorcycle riding.

The sizes available from our stock are as follows:

11093-34 In standard lengths only—28, 30, 32, 34, 36, 38 waist measures.

Other numbers—
Sizes 28, 30, 32, 34, 36, 38, 40 in standard lengths
Sizes 30, 32, 34, 36, 38 in extra longs
Sizes 28, 30, 32 in extra shorts

These sizes should fit nearly everyone. Where special sizes are needed, they can be supplied at an extra charge.

Cavalry Style Tan Breeches

Full peg top as shown, with double knees and seat. A very good looking tan mixture, of great wearing quality. Five roomy, turned and stitched pockets. No special sizes.

Code

11093-34—Tan whipcord breeches ....$2.95 byize

Polo Style Dark Oxford Breeches

Extra wide peg top, with safety pockets, double knees and seat. Very dressy. Extra good grade of Oxford Whipcord. A really excellent breech for any service—many worn by Police.

Code

11097-34—Oxford Whipcord Breeches ....$3.95 bakah

Polo Style Tan Whipcord Breeches

These are the same style as described above, with button top safety pockets, leather knee facings, double seat, and full peg. The material in these breeches is made from a double twisted yarn that insures extra long wear. Color is a light brown or tan mixture that will not soil easily. Very smart appearing.

Code

11098-X ....$4.75 bakfo

English Military Style Breeches

These are very high grade, part wool breeches, that anyone would be proud to wear. The English Military Style is very attractive, as you can see from the picture. Full grain leather facings are used on the knees. Button top safety pockets are fitted. These breeches will please the most particular.

Code

11099-X ....$7.75 bajox

Cavalry Style Breeches

Polo Style Breeches

English Military Style Breeches

"Styles may change, but motorcycle clothing either keeps you warm or it doesn't," said the late William H. Davidson. This is a page from the 1934 accessories catalog.

Here's how Harley-Davidson riders took a friend along before twin seating became standard equipment. This is from the 1934 catalog; the first accessories catalog came out in 1915.

Details of the New Buddy Seat

TAKE YOUR FRIEND ALONG ON THE "BUDDY SEAT"

The Buddy Seat provides the safest, most comfortable, and most practical means of carrying an extra passenger on a solo motorcycle. It has been received most enthusiastically by motorcycle riders everywhere. Thousands are in service.

With a Buddy Seat you will find it just as easy to handle your motorcycle with an extra passenger as without. Over good roads or bad, at high speeds or slow, you will find a Buddy Seat the most satisfactory passenger carrying accessory.

This seat is well cushioned with sponge rubber, covered with full grain leather that is well waterproofed. You will find it the softest seat you have ever used, and it is almost impossible to wear it out.

It is made in our own plant and guaranteed by us.

Showing the Buddy Seat in Service

potential in aftermarket items. Not only is the money there, the potential continues to expand. H-D now markets several kinds of parts: Genuine, which, as the name implies, are factory replacements for current bikes; Eagle Iron, reasonably priced parts for non-current models; and Screamin' Eagle, high-performance parts for today's bikes.

The bolt-ons, kits, shims, and other stuff compete very capably at the dealership with Arlen Ness, Drag Specialties, Storz, and many others. That is because the playing field is not level. A dealer will happily order a non-Harley aftermarket item, but he or she fears keeping lots of Brand X parts in stock. With new motorcycles in short supply, dealers are afraid that the company will not give them the benefit of the allotment if they sell lots of other folks' parts and accessories.

Aftermarket Parts

Competing parts were a problem very early, and Arthur Davidson warned dealers that the company would not tolerate affixing aftermarket parts to H-D bikes. He knew he was addressing many people who had attended the Baling Wire School of Motorcycle Maintenance and that insisting on genuine parts and accessories to carry the H-D trademark would maintain the company's reputation. The first parts and accessories to show the bar and shield were aimed at the rider rather than the bike. The initial issue of *The Enthusiast* in 1916 shows several wool-lined leather gloves and mittens, designed for operating the bikes in cold weather (it should be remembered that cycles were competing for sales with automobiles at that time, and that bikes were about as warm as cars in the winter). William H. Davidson, the late former H-D president, fondly recalled those trusty mittens, which retailed for up to $2.50. "The styles may change, but cold weather gear either keeps you warm or it doesn't."

A separate parts and accessories department was actually formed in 1912, indicating how early Harley and the Davidsons realized the importance of these items. Down through the years, the company has tried to accommodate an incredible variety of interests, from the highly successful molded plastic saddlebags introduced for the 1954 model K

(text continued on page 131)

This Model U, from 1941, could be a 74- or an 80-ci model. It is still ridden. (David K. Wright)

Author Steven Wright owns this very early twin. (David K. Wright)

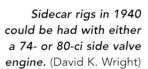

Sidecar rigs in 1940 could be had with either a 74- or 80-ci side valve engine. (David K. Wright)

This 2001 FXDWG II Wide Glide belongs to an H-D employee. (David K. Wright)

A 1998 Sportster in 95th Anniversary configuration. (David K. Wright)

A 1947 Knucklehead. The 74-ci machine was designated the FL. (David K. Wright)

The Wide Glide for 2003 maintains a classic formula: Big Twin power combined with street-cruiser style.
(Dain Gingerelli)

Mechanically unchanged for '03, the Super Glide T-Sport looks sharp in black with the anniversary logos and striping.
(Dain Gingerelli)

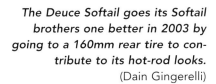

The Deuce Softail goes its Softail brothers one better in 2003 by going to a 160mm rear tire to contribute to its hot-rod looks.
(Dain Gingerelli)

A *restored 80-ci flathead from 1936.* (David K. Wright)

The V-Rod's curvaceous lines should do a good job of showing off the Sterling Silver paint – 2003 models will have the anniversary tank badging as well. The V-Rod's Revolution engine is Harley's first water-cooled powerplant, and develops 115 horsepower for 2003. (Dain Gingerelli)

Is this a Harley? While it looks like a Milwaukee product, the bike is assembled from Drag Specialties parts. (David K. Wright)

Here is an early 61-ci racer, restored and shown at an antique bike meet. (David K. Wright)

This World War II WLA features genuine leather saddlebags. (David K. Wright)

Aermacchi/Harley-Davidson road racers came in two- and four-stroke versions. (David K. Wright)

Michael Lange of Big Bend, Wisconsin, restored this 1929 Class A racer with sidecar. (David K. Wright)

A 30.50-ci single racer from 1926 or 1927. (David K. Wright)

Sportsters in a support event at the Springfield Mile, 2001. (David K. Wright)

A close-up of contemporary Springer front suspension. (David K. Wright)

This 2003 Road Glide wears one of the special Anniversary two-tone paint job – Sterling Silver over Vivid Black. The '03-only silver paint is unique; it consists of a black base coat, a 0.2 mils thick (regular paint is up to 1.2 mils thick) silver coat that actually contains metallic silver, and a clear coat to protect it. (Dain Gingerelli)

The Springer Heritage Softail is the only 2003 Softail to retain the smaller 140mm rear tire – it provides a more proportional look to the bike's wide-whitewall tires. (Dain Gingerelli)

The Heritage Softail also got a 150mm rear tire. This shot also shows the special anniversary derby cover and timing covers. (Dain Gingerelli)

The 2003 Fat Boy beefs up its attitude with a bigger 150mm rear tire – this is another model that will wear the Sterling Silver paint well. (Dain Gingerelli)

A Road King was featured on the 2001 Street Vibrations promotional literature. (Roadshows, Inc.)

(text continued from page 122)

to the hunting-fishing (trail riding) kit for the 1963 Aermacchi H-D Scat. While the majority of accessories ideas came from within (the first safety bars were an option beginning with 1935 models), occasional aftermarket firms preceded H-D thinking (such as the B&H foot-shift conversion, shortly after World War II, and the Softail idea in the 1970s).

The First Customs

It can be argued that custom bikes originated the moment the first rider pried off a fender or replaced the first factory part with an aftermarket trinket. However, consistent custom evidence surfaced initially in California in the 1930s. Destitute riders, aching for new bikes but unable to afford them, took to bobbing fenders and repainting their machines to make the Harleys and other rides look new and different. It is a credit to H-D that owners were largely content to leave the engines and transmissions alone before World War II. After that, riders found themselves in exactly the opposite situation: they oozed money but were able to buy only designs that were several years old. Therefore, they began to toy with performance.

Numerous Harley-Davidson dealers have been sources of performance parts, since they fielded Class C AMA racers as early as the mid-1930s. The most successful was Tom Sifton, owner of the dealership in San Jose, California. Before World War II, Sifton earned his reputation for the porting work he performed on his own racers. As GIs returned to civilian life, Sifton sold them cams and related hardware that propelled Milwaukee iron to unheard-of speeds on the California dry lakes, at Bonneville, on drag strips, and on flat tracks. Both the factory and independent speed shops responded.

The introduction of the overhead valve

FOR THAT EXTRA LAMP, Etc.

One of these handlebar crossbars provides the ideal mounting for that spotlight and other items. It is made from steel tubing with four rounded grooves formed in the steel. Each groove is lacquered in a bright color and the rest of the crossbar is a highly polished chromium plate. This combination makes a beautiful job that is light but very strong.

11359-XB—Handlebar Crossbar .... $3.50 bendu

DON'T LOOK BACK

This big new mirror can be clamped to your handlebars in just the right position to give you a clear, uninterrupted view of the road behind you. No need to take a chance on turning your head to see oncoming traffic.
Very substantially made with black enameled steel frame and bracket, and 4" mirror glass. A ball and socket joint gives adjustment to any desired angle.

11350-X—Mirror Complete .... $2.00 bemap

WRITE IT DOWN

The handy memo pad and holder is a very handy accessory for the commercial driver to use for his list of calls, for the Mounted Officer to list stolen car numbers, etc., or for route lists on an endurance run or a long trip. Mounts nearly anywhere on the handlebar so it can be seen easily when you drive along.

11795-X —Memo Pad Complete .... $0.50 boayl
11795-XA—Paper Refill .... .05 blofe

MADE FOR YOU

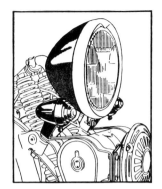

These sturdy parking lights match up well with the headlight and make a fine looking combination. They are fitted with beehive lenses so they can be seen from the side as well as the front.
Parking lamps are obtainable in different finishes to suit the individual taste. They fit 1931 and later models.

11400-X—Pr. Black and Chrome with white lenses .... $2.75 bervo
11402-X—Pr. All Chrome with white lenses .... 3.75 bipyv
(Either of the above can be supplied with red or green lenses at $0.50 extra.)

VERY EASILY HANDLED

The simple Harley-Davidson tandem was designed particularly to give easier riding comfort for the passenger and easier handling for the driver. The seat centers over the rear axle and is adjustable up or down to suit the load.

11235-34 —To fit 1934—74" twins .... $12.50 byhot
11235-34A—To fit 1934—45" twins .... 12.50 byhpu
11235-30 —To fit 1930 to 1933 74" twins .... 12.50 belth
11235-30A—To fit 1926 to 1934 singles, 1929 to 1933—45" twins .... 12.50 belui
11235-30B—To fit 1925 to 1929 —74" twins .... 12.50 belym

Mirrors were an option in 1934, as this page from that year's catalog shows. The notepad indicates that numerous Harley-Davidsons continued to be used for deliveries.

Sportster in 1957 appeased most performance buffs, so riders took a page from the 1930s and began modifying the way their bikes looked. The factory declined to find out who could produce the most outrageously extended front forks, but bikes designed by Californians Ed "Big Daddy" Roth, Von Dutch, and others became less and less transportation and more and more artistic statements. In the last few years, customizers have retreated from the radical chopper look. The bikes don't always pass state inspections and they are pure hell on long rides.

Among several pioneers was a Minnesotan named Tom Rudd. Rudd opened a retail store in 1968, selling custom parts for Harleys. Demand was constant and the business grew. At first in retail, Rudd and his wife, Penny, changed Drag Specialties to a wholesaler offering their own concepts and the best of everyone else's. There was no wholesale aftermarket at the time, and the firm prospered. Drag Specialties was the leader in H-D items for a while, before it got into financial trouble and was sold to the LeMans Corporation. Rudd now runs a smaller business, KüryAkin, in western Wisconsin.

This candy-apple custom is the work of Hall's Harley-Davidson in Chico, California. In addition to being an important source of income, custom work allows dealers to show their design talents.

Arlen Ness

Also from Minnesota, and even more well known, is Arlen Ness, the godfather of the Harley-Davidson aftermarket. Ness has a great website (http://www.arlenness.com), a fat catalogue, examples of his bikes all across the country, and a record of having consulted for H-D, Victory motorcycles, Kawasaki, and Yamaha. Ness moved to California as a youngster and turned a wonderful ability to look at a bike and make it unique into a thriving business. The company celebrated its 31st year in 2002 and recently moved from cramped headquarters in San Leandro to spacious facilities in Dublin, California.

"I never had a bike as a kid," Ness confesses. "I married young, and neither my dad, my mother, nor my wife wanted me to have a motorcycle."

This sumptuous fiberglass trailer shows what "Boss Hawg" used when his Dresser became overloaded. The bike and trailer were seen at Daytona.
(David K. Wright)

Audrey Xydas of Hyattsville, Maryland, created this Knucklehead-powered three-wheeler.
(David K. Wright)

Arlen acquired his first motorcycle at the ripe old age of 27. To get the money, he had to save winnings earned as a professional bowler. His "half-trick" used Knucklehead pleased him, but not so much that he was content to leave it alone. The ideas he incorporated on that used bike turned up on bikes belonging to friends. They saw his machine and wanted him to work the fabricating and molding magic on their H-Ds so they'd look as exotic as his old Knucklehead. A truck driver at the time, Ness switched to carpentry; the four and one-half day workweek for San Leandro carpenters gave him a bit more time to work out of his home. "My house became a place to hang out," he says.

Ness rented a storefront, set it up for painting, then began to design the dramatic parts that have become his signature. He created ram horn bars, welded frames, and more. Along the way, he began to farm out the work to those he could trust: racing car builders who knew materials and

Best's bike throbs with chrome and detail. (David K. Wright)

Gary Best is a tool and die maker at the Capitol Drive plant and the exacting creator of the custom 1992 Sportster.
(David K. Wright)

A popular modification—Panhead cylinders and heads atop a Sportster bottom end. This example, dubbed a Panster, was seen at Daytona in 1982.
(David K. Wright)

Best's modified Sportster includes leather trim.
(David K. Wright)

how to form those materials into finished products from Ness drawings. "Long front ends looked unsafe to me, so I lowered the bike all around, like a drag bike. The look worked well. After that, I designed a series of sleek tanks, then clamps, brackets, etc." Like Drag Specialties, which carries his products, the Ness catalogue goes to his hundreds of dealers. He has many, many imitators, and unlike some of the aftermarket wheeler-dealers, he is scrupulous about not using the H-D trademark. His products sell well without it.

Son Cory, who has his father's eye for bike design, now runs the company. Arlen and Cory have time to turn out new designs, several of which debut in Sturgis each year. The elder Ness also holds still for newspaper, magazine, and television interviews, as pleasant to deal with, as he is capable. Recently, he has tracked down and purchased some of his early designs, which are parked in his new facility. Modestly, he says: "I'm lucky. I can look at something and it will fall into place. Somehow I can foresee good lines on a bike."

Here's a well-turned-out FLH Classic. The owner is Ken Smance of Manchester, New Hampshire. The sidecar features a convertible top and a television set.

Factory Customs

Riders who are interested in custom bikes really should talk to someone like Doug Scritchfield. Doug sells Thunder Mountain custom cycles and Harley-Davidsons out of Ft. Collins, Colorado. Unlike many other custom bikes, the one-of-a-kind machines are being offered along with brand new (balanced) Twin Cam 88B motors. The bikes offered by Scritchfield in the Rockies and in a second store in Daytona Beach carry warranties—something that is hard to come by among other competitors. Because it is hard to distinguish between a bike with a Harley engine and a bike with, say, an S&S Evolution-style engine, Doug says, "Harley-Davidson would like to see those other bikes disappear."

The primary reason is that the non-Harley bikes deprive the company of income and they are markedly less reliable than the Milwaukee versions. In 2001, the Discovery Channel did a piece on Jesse James, the California bike builder. He was shown with two friends, all bound from Los Angeles to Sturgis on wild-looking bikes. During the 14-hour trip, all three machines suffered mechanical problems; something the factory feels would be much less likely on a customized Dyna Glide, for example.

One of the problems with most customs is that, for all the money, time, and technology, many are hardtails. Between the lack of rear suspension and the installation of a too-big motor in a rigid frame, the vibes make the bikes unreliable. Even Arlen Ness cheerfully admits that customs are nowhere near as reliable as an assembly line product. "Sure, they're like hot-rod

A Ness-equipped Sportster, owned by Andrew Oberle of New York. (David K. Wright)

Chevys or Fords," he said a while back. "You have to work on them all the time."

Thunder Mountain sold approximately 600 custom bikes in 2002. Scritchfield points out that a typical bike of theirs sells for $21,900 to $23,900. "Compare that to a guy customizing his own Fat Boy piece by piece," he says. "That fellow would spend about $28,000. We can do it for less because we buy the parts in bulk. And they are genuine Harley-Davidson parts."

Dealers with designs in their veins can be found all over. Several are carving out regional reputations for good lookin' unique bikes. Among the leaders in this sort of work is Santa Cruz Harley-Davidson in the California seaside town. For a mere $39,500, these folks will lay a silvery, minimalist-style Fat Boy on you that is a limited edition. The gas tank shows the kind of art painted on the noses of World War II Army Air Corps bombers. Custom though they may be, the Bomber Bikes, as they are called, show a very finished and professional look.

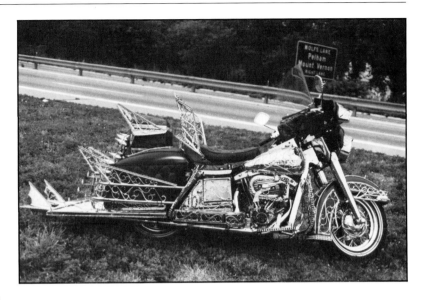

This six-gun encrusted Dresser was created for a Texan (who else?) by the Modern Cycle Works in Mount Vernon, New York. (Joseph Espada)

Do It Yourself

We have said it before and we will say it again: With all of the great parts, accessories, and ideas out there, a rider has no excuse for saddling up anything that looks the same as any other bike. Should you desire to start a custom project, the place to begin would be the latest Motor Accessories and Motor Parts annual catalogue from the Company. Toward the back of the book is the color shop, where an owner can pick any conceivable combination of hues for his or her tank and have it delivered in clear, pearl, or candy finish. After that, performance enhancers and dazzling hunks of chrome accessories are no further away than the next paycheck.

Customizing costs time and money, but it was worth it for the three bike owners we are about to meet. Gary Best of Hartland, Wisconsin, took several routes toward individuality in modifying his black 1992 Sportster with the 2.2-gallon peanut tank. He opted for a Low Rider custom tank, sending it and the fenders off to the factory custom paint program.

While tank and fenders were receiving a black and golden-orange finish, the tool and die maker went to work individualizing every nut, bolt, bracket, and gusset.

"I strive for perfection and settle for excellence," Best says. Immediately after purchasing the bike, he began to machine and fabricate parts. The engine remains stock internally, but since Best has a very understanding employer, he had access to million-dollar machines, computers, and software to design his vision. A nut made by hand replaced almost every nut. The oil tank ribs are silver soldered. The exhaust heat shields, which work well, were made with a die. The rocker boxes read "Born in the USA" and "Simply the Best" and were machined so that the letters on them stand out. Then Best saw that the air cleaner was .030-inch thick so he machined everything down around a portrait of the American flag. The flag stands about .015 inch above the new surface.

"The better you know a Sportster, the better you can appreciate this bike," he says. He estimates that he has 700 hours in the custom, or about 100 days of staying at his job an extra seven hours. The Screamin' Eagle exhaust system he

A custom bike prepared in the 1980s by Hall's Harley-Davidson in Chico, California for former drag racer and Bonneville runner Les Waterman. This machine began as a 1977 XLH Sportster. In addition to a high-performance motor, the creation has a handling package and is capable of high 10-second quarter miles. Fabrication and paint were by Ron Hall.

chose for the renovated Sportster is, in his words, "street illegal but not as loud as you might think."

Speaking of the street, Best rides the leather-trimmed cycle all over the place. He gets 51.7 miles per gallon on an Evolution motor that took some time to feel broken in. "I try not to ride in the rain," he says, adding that he plans to enter the creation in a show or two. We may as well reveal that Best is a Harley-Davidson employee, by day creating engines similar to his Sportster. This project, he says, was undertaken because, as a young man, he did not have the time to ride or to customize his own bike. He is amazed at the civility of the 1990s Sportsters. As for this particular bike, the project "was meant to be a relief, but it didn't turn out that way."

Best got his bike together much quicker than did Audrey Xydas of Hyattsville, Maryland. She bought the motor for her 1946 Knucklehead three-wheeler as a basket case, then spent time now and then tearing it down and rebuilding it, chroming as she progressed. A fellow with a wooden

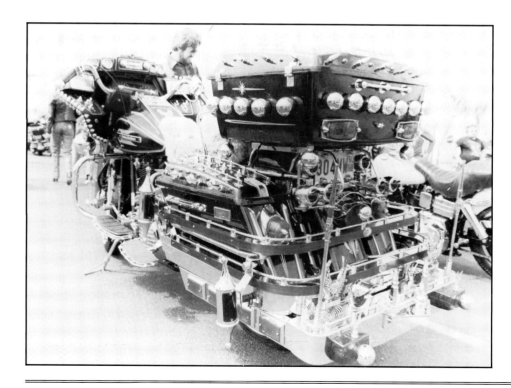

Ornately yours, from Daytona Beach.
(David K. Wright)

The annual H-D parts and accessories catalog is hundreds of pages thick. (David K. Wright)

leg who said he wanted to try two-wheel cycling once again sold the frame and the transmission to her.

"I got my ideas by going to different shows and looking around," she says. She attributes the trike's stubby appearance to the Springer front end. A bit later, she acquired a handsome set of pipes that has only one failing—they hit the pavement when she rides over large bumps. A friend who is a carpenter created the little seat in the back. The deep blue bike with Freebird on the tank was completed to Audrey's satisfaction, with her own money, back in 1988.

So far, she has entered four shows, two in the Baltimore area and two in Daytona Beach, and has four trophies to display. "There are two trike classes," she says, "one for auto engines and one for cycle engines. I didn't do anything really outrageous to the bike, but I change a few things from one year to the next."

Audrey rides on an irregular basis for one good reason. The Knucklehead is tough to kick over, so if she stalls in traffic there is not much she can do. A large male friend in Florida who is an expert in such matters can consistently kick over her V-twin with one stomp. Nevertheless, the owner is content to show more than ride the three-wheeler, which has been featured in a magazine in France. "An American magazine wanted to do a story on it, but they backed out when I refused to show my tits in a photo. I don't need that."

Those who customize cruisers and those who customize dressers should communicate more. While their tastes differ, the amount of labor and degree of devotion to the machines are the same. A case in point is the well dressed Dresser of Joseph and Alice Espada of Mount Vernon, New York. The Espadas took their Electra Glide to Modern Cycle Works in their hometown. The results speak ornately for themselves. Here, courtesy of the builder, is a list of adornments on what may be the ultimate attention getter:

- Scrolled and chained front bumper, front fender, rear crash bars, bag guards, transmission cover, battery cover, oil tank cover, front crash bars, gas tank, and hooded "peace" light.
- Front fender with built-in running light.
- Chained axle stars.
- Custom turn signals built into fairing.
- Air scoop-mounted "six gun."
- Air cleaner-mounted "six gun."
- Chrome engine, chrome Mikuni carburetors.
- Chained floorboards with fore and after air vents.
- Passenger pegs replaced with illuminated, stained glass, scroll-paneled running boards.
- Stock seat rail replaced with highback scrolled and chained "Bird of Paradise" rail.
- Padded dashboard features built-in television set, quartz LED clock, cylinder head temperature gauge, battery-generator gauge, map light, cigarette lighter, accessory switches, indicator lights.
- TourPak is lined with white mink fur.
- Within the padded and chrome-plated TourPak is an electric clock, FM quad stereo with concealed antenna, and eight-track cassette.
- Padded saddlebags feature scroll and rhinestone trim and carry stereo quad speakers.
- Custom light mount carries nine chained and hooded lights.
- The custom rear pan is topped with a staggered-step rear bumper.
- "Star-tipped" Hollywood mufflers.
- Fairing and front and rear fenders painted royal blue metal flake with 24 coats of clear lacquer.
- All else except tires and upholstery is chrome plated.

One look at the Espadas' cycle indicates that anything added to this chapter would be anti-climactic.

Is this a Harley? While it looks like a Milwaukee product, the bike is assembled from Drag Specialties parts. (David K. Wright)

Drag Specialties showed these Harley-inspired creations at the Mile in Springfield, Illinois, in 2001. (David K. Wright)

Yet another Drag Specialties special, assembled from the many parts in the firm's catalog. (David K. Wright)

With the factory and other special paint deals available, no two Harley-Davidsons should look alike. (David K. Wright)

These days, H-D has lots of competition in the cruiser and custom markets. (David K. Wright)

Here is a Harley-Davidson display, complete with bikes, clothing, and accessories. (David K. Wright)

Cruisers cost a lot and look great. (David K. Wright)

Cory and Arlen on bikes they designed. (Mike Chase)

Cory and Arlen Ness with their creations. (David K. Wright)

This 2002 Sportster displays such aftermarket items as a Softail rear fender.
(David K. Wright)

Chapter 8

Racing

The late Charlie Thompson, a former Harley-Davidson president, saw his first motorcycle race in 1966 at the Springfield, Illinois, mile. Two kids died that weekend and he

Harley-Davidsons were raced everywhere, as this 1925 postcard attests. Exact date and location are unknown, but the gentlemen are Orlandi and Gantarini.

thought if that was what happened at every race, Springfield would be his first and last event. Former football coach Thompson understood the analogy between racing and the belief that, when you throw a forward pass, three things can happen and two are bad. In racing, that's also true. A rider can race and be maimed or killed, he can race and end up broke, or he can race and finish without a completely empty wallet or permanent disability.

Since the early 1910s, when H-D began fielding racing bikes, not much has changed. The riders still flirt with death, they live from payoff to payoff and frequently have day jobs, most labor in relative obscurity—and they will be racing as long as there are vehicles with which to compete. Those vehicles will include Harley-Davidsons as long as several dealers and key employees continue to enjoy it or to believe that racing benefits the company.

Harley-Davidson has played a part in five kinds of racing over the years. They include:

- **Flat-track racing.** This is the familiar half-mile or mile horse track, where riders stay on the gas and off the brakes, if any, pitching the bikes sideways to scrub off enough speed so as to make it around two level, 180-degree bends. There has never been a national dirt-track event without a Harley-Davidson in the field, which indicates the part the machines have played in U.S. racing. This kind of competition evolved from racing on dirt roads and oval tracks constructed of 2 x 4s laid on their sides in the 1910s and 1920s. Variations today include TT courses, which are ovals punctuated by one or more jumps and a couple of right turns, and short (a quarter mile or so) track for smaller-displacement bikes.

- **Off-road racing.** This can be anything from a neighborhood scrambles track to stadium motocross to runs down the Baja Peninsula to the Jack Pine Enduro. Before bikes became excessively specialized, H-Ds capable of operation on the highway proved their versatility by slogging through swamps and pounding across deserts. These forms of racing have spawned not only top dirt-track competitors, such as former national champion Scott Parker, but great road racers, too.
- **Road racing.** Left turns, right turns, elevation changes, blind corners—in short, all the situations except oncoming traffic that a rider is likely to encounter on a twisting stretch of blacktop. The amazing thing about road racing is the number of talented riders this country has produced, given that road racing was not very popular here until the mid-1970s, when Superbikes came along. Harley-Davidson was especially competitive into the early 1970s. Today there are H-D products at a few road racing weekends.
- **Drag racing.** Road riders were cracking the throttle open long before California drag bikes took to the dry lakes following World War II. Harley-Davidsons starred at the beginning and continue to be popular mounts in running down a quarter mile from a standing start. Of all forms of racing, this is the most grass-roots type: For every double-engine fueler there are dozens of street Harleys at drag strips every weekend.
- **Hillclimbs.** This is what ski hills do to look busy in the summer. It's also a very social scene, as spectators line the hill to watch various classes of bikes attempt to climb. Less popular due to environmental concerns, hillclimbs nevertheless refuse to die because they're a great deal of fun.

The mechanical stars of these events down through the years were, most often, Harley-Davidsons. What follows are brief descriptions of H-D racing bikes from almost a century of competition. If details are lacking, it's because the company has not always been eager to share specifications on what propelled its machines into the winner's circle. If your personal favorite is missing, see Chapter 3. Many race bikes were little more than street models with the lights pried off.

The Eight-Valve, the Two-Cam, 1915–1921

Harley-Davidson's first model built exclusively for competition was the 61-ci (999-cc), eight-valve V-twin, created just prior to World War I for the group of racers that came to be known as the Wrecking Crew—Hepburn, Parkhust, Davis, Weishaar, and others. The first of the three-speed bikes was constructed in 1916 in three versions, one lubricated by a manual

Gordon (left) and William H. Davidson after two days on Michigan's Jack Pine trail in 1931. Harley-Davidsons captured 10 consecutive Jack Pine Enduros. (William H. Davidson collection)

plunger, one with an oil pump, and one that featured both a plunger and a mechanical pump. To prevent dilettantes from dabbling with their eight-valves, Harley-Davidson priced the machines at $1,500 apiece (compared to $350 for a new Indian racer). Unfortunately, verifiable specifications on these neat bikes no longer exist. That's true, too, for the two-cam racing models, which at 65 ci had a top speed approaching 120 mph. Both machines had wheelbases of about 50 inches; 28 x 2-1/2-inch tires; 40-spoke, soldered wheels, a magneto cutout switch on the handlebars that served as the only means of braking for a turn; and direct drive. The shortened exhausts carried absolutely no muffling. With their very high compression, the bikes frequently needed to be pushed by two or three men or pulled by an automobile in order to start.

JH, JDH "Two-Cam," 1928–1929

Harley-Davidson billed the two-cam as "The Fastest Model Ever Offered by Harley-Davidson," and it was in-

Who says you can't drag race a Duo-Glide? Jeff Mowry, Patterson, New Jersey, took top stock eliminator honors at Atco Dragway in 1968 on this A/Stock Harley-Davidson. His elapsed time was 14.96 seconds with a speed of 82.56 miles per hour. (National Hot Rod Association)

deed that. Independent cam action was provided for each valve by two big, broadfaced cams on the gears. The results were better timing, higher compression, and more RPM. The appearance was striking, too, since the tall engine protruded into the lower edge of the gas tank to accommodate valve stems, valve springs, and pushrods. The JDH 74-ci model was "particularly recommended by our engineers for greatest speed and maximum performance," a brochure noted. It cost $370 fob Milwaukee. The JH 61-ci cost $360, certainly a strong temptation to spend $10 more.

Harley-Davidson enthusiasts at the time were quite familiar with the two-cam, since it had been winning races for several years before its public offering. On July 4, 1925, Joe Petrali became the first two-cam rider to exceed 100 mph on a racetrack when he averaged 100.36 mph in winning at the Altoona, Pennsylvania, speedway. The machine, with its increased horsepower, retained a broad power band. Hill-climbers, particularly in the East and Midwest, hauled home lots of silver courtesy of these bikes.

Joe Smith on his double-engine Harley smokes off the line during a 1976 meet. Smith broke the 9-second quarter-mile barrier on this bike. (National Hot Rod Association)

Why, then, were the classic motorcycles offered for just two years? As attractive as the prices appear today, they were considered excessive in the late 1920s. Americans were buying automobiles by the hundreds of thousands, but they were unwilling to purchase more than 19,911 H-Ds in the prosperous year of 1927. These were Superbikes in the contemporary sense of the word; racing-type adornments (special tank and handlebars, solo seat) were standard rather than optional. The 1930 VL models could at least be called new and inexpensive, even if they offered less power.

Specifications (From a 1928 brochure. The following figures are for the road bikes, since specs on the racing bikes are much less complete.)

The mighty XR750, as formerly displayed in York. (David K. Wright)

Motor: Two-cam, twin-cylinder, V-type, air-cooled, four-stroke cycle. Fitted with Dow metal pistons. 74-ci model: bore 3-7/16 inches, stroke 4 inches, piston displacement 7- ci. 61-ci model: bore 3-5/16 inches, stroke 3-1/2 inches, piston displacement 60.34-ci.

Carburetor: Schebler DeLuxe with air cleaner.

Transmission: Harley-Davidson three-speed progressive sliding gear with positive gear shifter locking device.

Lubrication: Harley-Davidson throttle controlled motor oiler provides proper lubrication at all motor speeds. Transmission lubricated separately. 20 Alemite fittings.

Ignition: Harley-Davidson generator-battery.

Electric equipment: Harley-Davidson generator, weather and waterproof coil, timer, 22-amp/hr storage battery, motor driven horn, two-bulb headlight, standard tail light, switch panel. Relay cutout in generator-battery circuit.

Starter: Harley-Davidson rear stroke on right side.

Clutch: Harley-Davidson multiple dry disc, foot operated.

Handlebars: Roadster type, one piece, 1-inch tubular, double stem with closed end grips. Regular style handlebars optional.

Frame: Strongly reinforced heavy gauge high carbon, seamless tubular steel with wide trussed loop. Drop forged steel head.

Controls: Grip, double-acting wire controls enclosed in handlebars and cables. Toe operated compression relief.

Brakes: Harley-Davidson foot controlled contracting rear brake and built-in hand controlled expanding front wheel brake.

Driving chains: Roller, 5/8-inch pitch, and 3/8-inch width.

Saddle: Large, roomy form-fitting Mesinger. Harley-Davidson adjustable spring seat post.

Tires: Full balloon, 25 x 3.85 inches. Standard 27 x 3.85-inch size optional.

Wheelbase: 60 inches.

Tanks: Narrow saddle type. Gasoline capacity 2-1/2 gallons. Reserve gasoline tank, 1-1/4 gallons. Lubricating oil tank, 1 gallon. Wide, standard capacity tank optional.

Footboards: Harley-Davidson folding.

Tool equipment: Complete tool and tire repair kit.

Finish: Harley-Davidson Olive Green with maroon stripe with gold center and edged in black.

WR, WR-TT, 1940–1951

As ungainly as they look today, the rigid-tail WRs gave a good account of themselves in the controversial years when the AMA allowed 750-cc capacity for side valve machines, but just 500 cc for overhead valve (i.e., foreign) bikes. The WR was characterized by a low compression ratio, another criterion used by the Harley-Davidson-dominated sanctioning body to keep the English vertical twins out of the winner's circle. The WR put out about 40 horsepower, quite modest by today's standards, but when combined with the sheer number of Harleys on the track, quite enough. Hot shoes Paul Goldsmith and Jimmy Chann gave the WR a good ride, while youngsters including Joe Leonard and Everett Brashear cut their racing teeth on these bikes. The WRs were the overwhelming favorites of TT riders, who found the frames as reliable as the motors.

Specifications (From a 1951 brochure.)

Engine: 45-ci side valve; bore, 2-3/4 inches; stroke, 3-13/16 inches; Dow metal or aluminum pistons. Wico vertical magneto, mounted on side of engine; optional Wico Horizontal magneto, mounted in front.

Frame: Special light frame, chrome molybdenum tubing (WR); Standard WL (WR-TT).

Tanks: Narrow, rubber mounted. Capacity, 1-3/4 gallons of gasoline and 1-3/4 gallons of oil (WR); large, rubber mounted tanks for long distance racing. Each side holds 2-1/2 gallons of gasoline, can only be used with aluminum oil tank, part No. R 3501-41. Narrow rubber mounted tanks; hold 1-3/4 gallons of gasoline and 1-3/4 gallons of oil (tank choice on WR-TT).

Handlebars: Speedster bars; solid or rubber mounted.

Wheels: Special ball bearing hubs, no brake, 18 inches or 19-inch rims optional, Firestone tires, 4.00 x 18 inches or 3.25 x 19 inches (WR). Standard WL with brakes; 18 inches or 19-inch rims optional, Firestone tires, 4.00 x 18 inches or 3.25 x 19 inches.

Transmission: 3/8-inch pitch clutch sprocket, standard or close ratio gears (WR). 3/8-inch or 1/2-inch pitch clutch sprocket, standard or close ratio gears; 1/2-inch pitch recommended for long-distance racing only (WRTT).

Petrali goes up . . . and over the Hornell, New York, hill during a 1938 climb. (William H. Davidson collection)

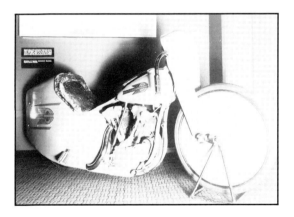

Joe Petrali's 1936 Knucklehead record breaker, as once displayed in the Rodney C. Gott Museum in York. The fairing was constructed from a gasoline tank. The machine is painted light blue. (David K. Wright)

Front mudguard: Not supplied on track models (WR). Special front mudguard (WR-TT).

Rear mudguard: Special WR, special WR-TT.

Footpegs: Footpegs and Servi-Car-type clutch (WR). Footboards and side bars, standard WL (WR-TT).

Saddle: Special, no seat bar or seat post (WR). Special WR with standard WL seat bar and post (WR-TT).

Front chain guard: 1940 type outer, standard WL inner.

Tank pad: Furnished with large tanks only (WR-TT).

Gear ratio: 3/8-inch pitch front chain; 22, engine; 59, clutch; 17, countershaft; 39 rear wheel equals 6.15:1 (WR). 3/8-inch pitch front chain; 30, engine; 59, clutch; 17, countershaft; 41, rear wheel, equals 4.74:1 (WR-TT). 36, 37, and 38 tooth rear wheel sprockets furnished with WR. Other sprockets available as follows: 17 to 33 tooth 3/8-inch pitch engine sprockets and 15 to 16 tooth countershaft sprockets (WR). 1/2-in. pitch front chain; 24, engine; 45, clutch; 17, countershaft; 41, rear wheel, equals 4.52:1 (WR-TT). Other sprockets for WR-TT available as follows: 17 to 33 tooth 3/8-inch pitch engine sprockets; 14 to 25 tooth 1/2-inch pitch engine sprockets; 15 and 16 tooth countershaft sprockets; 42 tooth rear wheel sprocket and brake shell assembly.

Colors: Brilliant black, ruby red and riviera blue at no extra cost. Available at extra cost: metallic green, flight red, azure blue, white.

Leo Payne ran a 9.71-second quarter mile, turning 152.38 miles per hour in 1967 at Connecticut Dragway. (Brian King)

Drag racer Ron Fringer poses with wife, kids, trophy girl, trophy, and Top Gas Eliminator H-D. Fringer, seen at Beech Bend (Kentucky) International Raceway, had just posted a 10.09-second time and a 133.72-miles per hour speed during a 1971 meet. The Woodstock, Illinois, racer was one of numerous Midwesterners who did especially well in the 1960s and early 1970s using Sportster motors. (National Hot Rod Association)

The company has been known to advertise its victories.

Harley Owners Group (H.O.G.) has sponsored factory teams, as this flyer indicates.

KR, KR-TT, 1952–1969

The KR is the bike that no one considered very good. In fact, it was just good enough to win. Riders Carroll Resweber, Bart Markel, Mert Lawwill, George Roeder, and others won on these supposedly outmoded side valves. Specifications show that the KRs were 750-cc machines. That was not the case. As delivered to the customer ($1,320 for the dirt tracker, $1,425 for the road racer in 1966), the motors measured 744 cc. Following 200 miles of break-in, however, the cylinder barrels distorted and had to be rebored. The AMA permitted racers to be 0.045 in. oversize, so the eventual size of the engines was 767 cc.

The AMA also was responsible for the demise of the bike, since it ruled in 1969 that European cycles no longer would have either a compression or displacement limita-

tion. Before 1970, the KR 750 side valve competed against 500-cc overhead valve racers from Triumph, BSA, Norton, and Matchless, as had its predecessor, the WR. In addition to producing almost twice as much horsepower per cubic inch, the English bikes handled better, particularly on TT courses and on asphalt.

The difference between Harley-Davidson's KR-TT-designated road racer and the flat track KR bike were few but significant. The road racer ran inert gas shocks, as opposed to a solid rear end; it showed up with a 6-gallon gas tank; and its pavement wheels and tires were daintier than those of the broadsliding TT. Top speed of the bike in its peak years exceeded 150 mph, as clocked on the high banks of Daytona International Speedway. That held up until about 1967, when the British bikes ran with and then away from the H-D team on the straights. The riders of English ma-

An 883-cc Sportster awaits its rider in the Daytona Beach infield.
(David K. Wright)

Cal Rayborn in 1973.
(Cycle News, Inc.)

chines had an even greater advantage on the several tight road courses—Laconia, New Hampshire; Marlboro, Maryland; and Nelson Ledges, Ohio—where Nationals were held. No one ever merely flicked a KR-TT from side to side in an S-turn. The large, heavy machine was a chore to ride. After breaking in on KRs, Cal Rayborn was able to pitch the new XR into a corner with ease. Still, this bike won national championships for the factory 12 of its 17 years. Not bad for an "obsolete" race bike.

Specifications

Motor: 744-cc side valve V-twin, bore 2.747 inches, stroke 3.8125 inches, compression ratio 9:1, horsepower 48 at 7000 rpm. Torque, 50 ft-lbs at 5000 rpm. Linkert carburetor with 1.312-inch bore.
Frame: Chrome moly seamless steel tubing, 1 inch.
Wheelbase: 56 inches.

Suspension: Telescopic front forks; inert gas shock absorbers (KR-TT only).
Ignition: Fairbanks-Morse magneto.
Brakes: 8 x 1-1/2-inch front and rear, 50.3-square inch braking surface (no brakes on KR).
Weight: 385 pounds (KR-TT), 377 pounds (KR).

XR750, 1970 –

The year 2003 marks the 33rd year that riders, independent as well as factory-sponsored, have chosen the very narrow bike with the destroked 883-cc Sportster engine to do battle on Grand National dirt tracks. With each event, the XR750 cements its reputation more firmly as the most successful two-wheel racing device of all time.

Introduced in 1970 with iron barrels, the XR suffered through that season and the next before aluminum cylinders and cylinder heads were perfected and installed. Since then, except for brief periods when Yamaha, then Honda, spent big bucks to run out front, the XR has been the over-dog on everything but pavement. In the hands of Cal Rayborn and, later on, Jay Springsteen, the machine even chalked up significant road victories, notably at Daytona and Loudon, New Hampshire, before being edged out by multi-cylinder Japanese machines.

The aluminum version of the XR differed from the iron head and from today's lighter, sleeker, and more powerful XR. The iron version featured straight pipes, painted silver, which exited on the right. The 1972 bike, and today's racer, display flat-black megaphone exhausts that run high and on the left side.

Both early versions carried Ceriani forks, Girling shocks, and were delivered with either Goodyear tires on both ends or a Goodyear on the back and a Pirelli up front. Nowadays, look for Goodyears, Continentals, and Pirellis, depending on the bike and the rider. Other common fea-

tures of the iron-barrel and the initial aluminum-barrel include frames of 4130 mild, tubular steel, aluminum rims, and wire wheels. The first 100 frames were made under the direction of the Harley-Davidson dealer in St. Louis. Internally, both early machines used valves, pistons, and cams that were polished and valve stems that were chrome plated. The aluminum version's flywheel was enlarged to handle the hike in horsepower from 70 to 90.

A company employee who served as the product designer for the racing department noted that another major difference between the two older bikes was the compression ratio. "We had to run very low compression—about 8:1—for the (iron) head to stay together. The motor had a shorter stroke and larger valves than the aluminum motor. It was fast but not reliable." Compression for the aluminum head was 10.5:1.

What's riding an XR750 like? The first clue after straddling the machine is provided by the bike's size, or rather

Dealer Don Tilley noted in the early 1990s that a rider could make an 883-cc Sportster race worthy for $7,000, which included the cost of a new bike. That's about the same price as the VR 1000's crankshaft. (David K. Wright)

lack of it. The XR750 is by far the leanest Harley-Davidson currently in production. The second hint is the utter lack of any sort of starting mechanism. Run-and-bump is the order of the day. Once the engine thumps to life, the rider realizes his right hand is much more lethal than usual. That is because the throttle goes from nothing to everything in a quarter-turn. There is a rear disc brake, which ex-motocrossers use to advantage on some flat tracks, whereas most riders rely on compression and a good broadslide to grind away speed as they head into a corner. The power band is as wide as any bike on earth, with the XR pulling forcefully from 2000 rpm. Since the cycle produces 100

Scott Zampach rode the rapid Tilley H-D Buell in the Pro Twins event at Daytona in 1991. (David K. Wright)

squirming horsepower flat-out on dirt, you will have to ask a racer what it's like out there.

Specifications

Engine type: Overhead valve V-twin.
Carburetion: Dual 36-mm Mikuni carburetors.
Exhaust system: Tuned dual exhausts with reverse-cone megaphones.
Bore and stroke: 3.125 x 2.983 inches.
Displacement: 45 ci (750 cc).
Clutch type: Multi-plate, dry.
Primary drive: 25-tooth motor sprocket, 59-tooth clutch, triple row roller chain.
Rear drive: 16-tooth transmission sprocket, 40-tooth rear wheel sprocket.
Drive ratio, overall: 5.90:1.
Transmission: Constant mesh, four-speed.
Transmission ratio: 1st, 2.091:1; 2nd, 1.51:1; 3rd, 1.14:1; 4th, 1.00:1.
Weight: 290 pounds.
Tire size, front and rear: 4.00 x 19 inches.
Gas capacity: 2-1/2 gallons.
Oil capacity: 3 quarts.
Electrical equipment: Fairbanks-Morse magneto.
Color: Jet Fire Orange.

Aermacchi/H-D RR-250, RR-350 1971–1976

The Aermacchi/Harley-Davidson RR-250 and RR-350, in the hands of the late Walter Villa, proved to be world-beaters. Like most front-running Italian bikes, they featured bits and pieces from all over—Dunlop tires and Girling forks from England, Mikuni carburetors from Japan, and Ceriani forks, Borrani rims, and Dansi ignitions from around the block (in Italy). The bikes' only drawback, in air- or water-cooled configuration, proved to be the brakes. Initially, the drums were very good, but drums nonetheless, at a time when discs were seen on most competing machines. Like many things associated with Italian machinery, there was a reason for the drums: The maker paid A/H-D to use them.

Villa overcame early braking points to win three 250-world championships, in 1974, 1975, and 1976, onboard the two-stroke version of the machine. The following year, he snagged the 350-world title. All that is quite a feat for a company that built its first-ever two-cycle engine in 1967. The bike enjoyed some success stateside, ridden by Cal Rayborn, Gary Scott, and others. However, U.S. racers and fans preferred bigger-bore equipment, despite 58 horsepower at 12,000 rpm for the 250 and 70 horses at 11,400 rpm for the 350. Since these bikes were constructed by hand, specs differed from one machine to the next. The switch to disc brakes up front took place prior to the 1976 season.

Specifications: 250 cc (dated 1972)

Engine type: Two-cycle, liquid cooled twin.
Bore: 2.213 inches.
Stroke: 1.968 inches.
Displacement: 15 ci (248.06 cc).
Compression ratio: 11.33:1.
Clutch type: Multi plate, dry.
Primary drive: Helical gear, 2.438:1.
Final drive: Chain.
Transmission gear: 16 teeth.
Rear wheel gear: 46 teeth.
Drive ratio: 6.427:1.
Transmission: Six-speed, constant mesh.
Transmission ratio: 1st, 2.00:1; 2nd, 1.527:1; 3rd, 1.286:1; 4th, 1.087:1; 5th, 0.958:1; 6th, 0.917:1.
Front suspension: Ceriani forks.

Rear suspension: Girling 3-position shock absorbers.
Front brake: Twin double leading shoe.
Rear brake: Double leading shoe.
Carburetor: Twin 34 mm Mikuni.
Tire size, front: 3.00/18-inch Dunlop.
Tire size, rear: 3.00/3.25/18-inch Dunlop.
Dry weight: 230 pounds.
Fuel capacity: 6 gallons (pre-mix),
Oil capacity: 2 quarts.
Ignition: Dansi or CDI.
Color: Jet fire orange and black w/ white number plaques.

Aermacchi/H-D MX-250 1977–1978

This Aermacchi/Harley-Davidson, made for only two years, was a potent motocross or dirt-track machine in the hands of a good rider. Jay Springsteen showed how good he and a bike with an MX-based motor were in 1982 when he won the short-track event to kick off the season's AMA/Winston Pro Series in the Houston Astrodome. It should be remembered that, for every MX bike raced, there were many more of the four-stroke Sprints on local short tracks and in scrambles, proving once again how prone street-stock H-Ds—even foreign models—were to racing.

Dave Feazell leaves the line during the AMRA Harley Homecoming National in Union Grove, Wisconsin, in 1988. Feazell won the pro stock class, setting two national records. Later, he turned 8.99 seconds for the quarter mile, the fastest time ever recorded for an Evolution-engine Sportster. (Jerry Cummings)

Dave Feazell churns up an Anamosa, Iowa, hill during a meet on his 750KR several years ago. In addition to climbing hills and drag racing, Feazell holds a Bonneville Salt Flats record, set in 1991. (Jerry Cummings)

Specifications: MX-250, MX-250 Dirt Tracker

Overall length: 83.6 inches (212.5 cm).
Handlebar width: 34.2 inches (87 cm).
Ground clearance: 12 inches (30.5 cm).
Wheelbase: 57.3 inches (145.5 cm).
Dry weight: 233 pounds (105 kg).
Steering angle: 45 degrees.
Rake: 30 degrees.
Trail: 5.5 inches (140 mm).
Front suspension: Telescopic oil dampened, 8.9 inches (225 mm) of travel.
Rear suspension: Swingarm, coil spring, oil dampened.
Front wheel tire: 3.00 x 21 inches.
Rear wheel tire: 4.50 x 18 inches.
Front brake: Internal expanding, single leading shoe type, inside diameter 140 mm.
Rear brake: Internal expanding, single leading shoe type, inside diameter 140 mm.
Rims: Akront, shoulderless light alloy.

Spokes: 36 per wheel, 4 mm diameter.
Transmission: 2-1/8 pints (1000 cc).
Fuel tank: 2.2 gallons (8.5 liters).
Front forks: 7 ounces (wet) each side (210 cc).
Model designation: MX.
Type: Two-cycle, single cylinder.
Bore: 2.835 inches (72 mm).
Stroke: 2.346 inches (59.6 mm).
Displacement: 14.81 inches (242.6 cc).
Compression ratio: 11.8:1.
Lubrication system: Fuel and oil mixture, 20:1.
Starter system: Primary kick-starter.
Type: Capacitor discharge Dansi or CDI Motoplat.
Ignition timing: .080 inch (18 degrees, 2 mm) before top dead center.
Trigger air gap: (Dansi) .012-.016 in. (.30-.40 mm).
Spark plug: Champion N59G.
Plug gap: .020 inch (.5 mm).
Dell'Orto carburetor (not included) type: PHB E 38.
Venturi diameter: 1.496 inches (38 mm).

Main jet: 170.
Low speed jet: 70.
Mikuni carburetor (not included) type: Vm-38.
Venturi diameter: 1.496 inches (38 mm).
Main jet: 320.
Needle (middle position): 6CTI.
Needle jet: Q0.
Slide: 2.0
Needle valve: 3.3.
Air jet: 1.0.
Pilot jet: No. 45.
Clutch: Wet, multi-plate.
Primary drive pinion gear: 22 teeth.
Primary drive clutch gear: 60 teeth.
Primary ratio: 2.73.
Gear ratios: 1st, 14/27; 2nd, 18/28; 3rd, 21/26; 4th, 21/21; 5th,
23/19.
Gearshift pattern: One down, four up.
Transmission sprocket: 13-, 14-, 15-, 16-tooth supplied.
Chain type: 5/8 x 3/8 inches.
Fuel-oil recommendation: SAE 30 viscosity racing oil mixed 1
part oil to 20 parts high-octane leaded gasoline.

XR1000 1983–1984

Whenever race fans believe they have seen all of the tricks in the Juneau Avenue bag, along comes a machine like the XR1000. The XR750-inspired, XL-based street bike and AMA Battle of the Twins road racer was developed in just 60 days in the fall of 1982, allowing H-D to meet AMA rules by producing 200 such bikes in time for the 1983 racing season.

The $6,800 H-D cranked out 70.6 horsepower at 5600 rpm (compared to 56 for the stock XL). With high-performance kit parts from the factory, 90 horses became a reality. Power emanated from XR aluminum heads and rocker boxes, high-compression (9:1) aluminum XR pistons, Branch Flowmetrics heads, a redesigned combustion chamber and port area, plus dual Dell'Orto slide carburetors, and XR-style megaphone exhausts.

The frame was 100 percent XL, though a number of performance adornments were added. Dunlop K291 Sport Elite tires, dual front 11-1/2-inch disc brakes up front, an 11-1/2-inch single disc in the rear, flat-track bars, and a 2.5-gallon

fuel tank added up to a dry weight of 480 pounds. Performance options included higher compression ratio pistons, special cams, and special exhausts.

Dick O'Brien, former racing director, oversaw the quick, quality work. In the hands of Jay Springsteen, the bike handily won the Battle of the Twins contest at Daytona in 1983. In-

A 45-ci flathead racer, well preserved and for sale. (David K. Wright)

The XR750 looks fast even when standing still. (David K. Wright)

The K Model preceded the XR750. It ran the 45-ci flathead motor. (David K. Wright)

terestingly, 20 of the 1,777 XR1000s produced were imported to Italy, apparently in racing trim. There's no telling what happened to the bikes, though it's fun to imagine the familiar "potato-potato-potato" idle turning the heads of a few Ducati and Cagiva owners.

Specifications

Wheelbase: 60.0 inches.
Seat height: 29.0 inches.
Tire size, front: MM90V-19 (100/90V-1).
Tire size, rear: MT90V-16 (130/90V-1).
Rake: 29.7 degrees.
Trail: 4.5 inches.
Overall length: 87.7 inches.
Ground clearance: 6.8 inches.
Engine type: Overhead valve V-Twin.
Bore & stroke: 3.189 x 3.812 inches.

VR 1000 superbikes await a practice session at Road America in 2001, the final year of their participation in the popular AMA roadracing series. (David K. Wright)

Oil capacity: 2.5 quarts.

Carburetion: Dual 36 mm slide Dell'Orto.

Ignition: V-Fire III electronic breakerless.

Clutch: Multiplate oil bath.

Primary drive: Triple chain.

Gear ratios, overall: 1st, 10.02:1; 2nd, 7.25:1; 3rd, 5.49:1; 4th, 3.97:1.

Brake, front: 11.5 x 20 inches (diameter x width) (x 2).

Front brake swept area: 99.5 square inches.

Braking distance from 60 mph: 145 feet.

Suspension travel, front: 6.9 inches; rear, 3.25 inches.

Dry weight: 480 pounds.

Wheels: 9-spoke cast aluminum.

Headlamp: Quartz halogen, 50-watt high beam.

Color options: Slate gray/silver striping.

Electrical system: 12-volt; battery, 19 amp-hour; generator, 13 amp; coil, regulator, headlight, tail light, turn signals, stoplight, horn; entire system meets or exceeds all state and federal regulations for lighting, electric start.

Displacement: 61 ci (1000 cc).

Compression ratio: 9.0:1.

Fuel capacity: 2.25 gallons; reserve, .25 gallons.

Exhaust system: Left side, high-megaphone dual.

Cam: Q cam.

Factory mechanics work on a VR 1000 before a 2001 race. (David K. Wright)

Transmission: 4-speed, constant mesh.

Final drive: Single chain.

Primary drive ratio: 1.74.

Final drive ratio: 2.29.

Torque: 71.4 ft-lbs at 5600 rpm.

Brake, rear diameter x width: 11.5 x 23 inches.

Total brake swept area: 198.5 square inches.

Lean angles: (SAE J1168) Right, 37 degrees; left, 36 degrees.

Optional equipment: 18-inch mag rear wheel; 3.3-gallon gas tank.

Gross vehicle weight rating: 900 pounds.

VR 1000, 1994–2001

This is all about the VR 1000—or is it? The company was very hush-hush about specifications for the AMA Superbike, perhaps because they were in cahoots with Cosworth, Ford, Gemini Technologies, Showa, Porsche, their own Buell organization, and others in trying to make the 60-degree V-twin run up front. That was no small project, since Ducati and all four Japanese companies have put major efforts into U.S. and world Superbike technology.

For Harley-Davidson, it was an uphill battle. The VR appeared almost capable of a win in 1999, finishing twice on

Pascal Picotte at speed on the VR 1000 in 1999. (Werner Fritz)

Pascal Picotte. (David K. Wright)

the podium in the hands of Pascal Picotte. But the Italians and Japanese came back with a vengeance, and at the end of the 2001 season there were 10 to 12 bike-rider combinations that usually qualified and finished ahead of the black-and-orange machines. Most were four-cylinder 750-cc cycles, though Honda and Ducati ran high-revving 900–1000-cc V-engines, often far forward.

It took courage and confidence to go up against half a dozen race-hardened manufacturers, and H-D is to be commended for even making the attempt. John Baker, who became H-D's director of racing prior to the 2001 season, believed the company had recruited the best technology the world had to offer. Besides, customers expect a H-D racing presence, even though the company's bread and butter these days is the cruiser market.

Watching the VR 1000 perform, beneath either Picotte or Mike Smith, it was obvious that the machines entered and exited a corner as fast as anything on the track. It was equally obvious that the V-twins ran out of revs, and therefore horsepower and speed, on the straightaways. A race fan pointed all this out to Picotte, who, with a mix of good humor and exasperation, said, "Is that what you think? Well . . . you're right!" Front-running Superbikes were at least a dozen miles faster at top end than the Harley. The search for

more horsepower from an engine already capable of 150 horses at 10,000 rpm, ended in September 2001, when the bikes were retired.

Specifications

Engine: 60-degree, water-cooled, dual overhead cam V-twin.
Capacity: 61 ci (1000 cc).
Horsepower: 150 at 10,000 rpm.
Torque: 100 ft-lbs at 9000 rpm.
Transmission: 6-speed.
Front suspension: Showa.
Rear suspension: Aluminum rectangular swingarm with adjustable pivot.
Front brake: Dual rotors with six-piston calipers.
Rear brake: N/A
Tires: Dunlop.
Weight: N/A.
Fairing: Carbon fiber.

Buell Firebolt XB9R

Who says Harley-Davidson is not still in road racing? The Buell Firebolt XB9R, which debuted as part of the 2002 model year, has an all-new, fuel-injected 984-cc, 45-degree, fan-cooled V-twin with a short stroke/light flywheel configuration. The Erik Buell design displays a 52-inch wheelbase and weighs just 385 pounds. Riders who competed with it at Daytona in 2002 said the XB9R whistled through corners faster than nearby Ducatis—not a bad credential. A Firebolt-only eight-race series is scheduled to take place in England in the summer of 2002. Several rounds are being run in conjunction with the Superbike events. Stay tuned.

The Riders

What kinds of people race motorcycles? Few have ever done it for the money; the dollars simply are not there. Fewer still have any conscious need for fame or glory, though fame and glory are the assets and liabilities of winning. Not one racer in anyone's memory ever believed he would end up in the ambulance, so death wishes can be ruled out. What's left is the rush racers receive from competition, from playing a game made fast far beyond human power by means of an internal combustion engine.

The first group of riders to race Harley-Davidsons with major success was called The Wrecking Crew. That included, at various times, Eddie Brinck, Jim Davis, Walter Higley, Ralph Hepburn, Irving Jahnke, Maldwyn Jones, Fred Ludlow, "Red" Parkhurst, Otto Walker, and Ray Weishaar. Created following a poor showing by H-D in the 1914 Dodge City, Kansas, road race, the Wrecking Crew all but owned the dusty road courses until 1921, when the company opted out of racing for economic reasons.

Far from being scooter trash, these riders frequently possessed an advanced degree of mechanical knowledge and held full-time jobs off the track. Typical was Eddie Brinck, the Dayton, Ohio, native who raced for 15 years while a foreman with the U.S. government-testing department at McCook Aviation Field. Brinck applied what he learned on the job (internal combustion engines were still relatively new) to his cycles. In addition to scoring significant victories here, he took the single-cylinder H-D Peashooter to Australia in 1926 and recorded several wins. A family man, Brinck died on August 13, 1927, when his tire blew on the first lap of a Springfield, Massachusetts, event.

Brinck was one of several brilliant riders discovered by Bill Ottoway, an engineer recruited by Harley-Davidson from the Thor Motorcycle Company in 1913. Ottoway was a capable engineer, a shrewd assessor of talent, and, according to his contemporaries, as trusting as he was honest. On one occasion, after Gene Walker's Indian ran suspiciously fast to sweep a series of events, Ottoway was asked by race officials if he wanted the competing motor torn down. "If Indian says the motor is okay, it's okay," he replied. One indication of Harley-Davidson stability is that just three men—Ottoway, Hank Syvertson, and Dick O'Brien—ran the racing department from 1913 through the buyback.

Ottoway watched a number of his riders come and go, including Otto Walker and Ralph Hepburn. Both Wrecking Crew members, the pair ran board and horse tracks as factory riders and as independents. Walker capped a stunning career in 1921 by winning a 50-mile race at the San Joaquin, California, speedway in 29 minutes, 34.6 seconds (101.43 mph), posting one lap in excess of 109 mph. All this was accomplished on a 61-ci machine. In contrast to Walker, who re-

Jay Springsteen. (David K. Wright)

tired to a charter fishing boat, Hepburn competed until 1948, when, at the age of 51, he died at the wheel of the infamous, supercharged Novi V-8 at the Indianapolis Motor Speedway.

Chris Carr checks the time with a crewmember prior to the Springfield Mile in 2001. (David K. Wright)

Racers await their chance to take on the dirt. (David K. Wright)

Sadly, death was common in the early years, as riders donned cloth caps at worst and gauze-and-airplane dope helmets at best for 100-plus mile-per-hour competitions. In addition to Brinck, racing has claimed H-D riders Walter Stoddard, Tommy Hayes, Billy Huber, Dick Ince, Cal Rayborn, Renzo Pasolini, Walter Villa, and, more recently, Willie Crabbe, Ted Boody, and Will Davis. Automobiles, through the years, have also take a toll, off the track (Fred Nix) and on (Hepburn and David "Swede" Savage). Joe Leonard, first of the modern national champions, was disabled after a successful career on four wheels. Still, racing seems almost natural.

Harley-Davidson recorded victories all over the world in the 1920s, in the hands of U.S. and foreign riders alike. In England, D. H. Davidson (not related to the company) exceeded 100 mph as early as 1920 in a speed run, and Fred Dixon won numerous solo and sidecar races. Grass tracks were popular in Australia and New Zealand, and H-D scored well there. Another surface, ice, was favored in Scandinavia by little-known but highly talented Erik Westerberg. He averaged an incredible 87.561 mph in winning a 1923 ice race aboard his eight-valve machine. In 1930, Olle Virgin captured a dirt-track series run in Sweden and Denmark by posting average speeds as high as 111.78 mph on an overhead valve 45-ci machine. Clearly, the world's largest manufacturer was well represented at the world's start-finish lines.

While Harley-Davidsons were winning speed contests, they were faring equally well in various endurance runs. Less than a decade after Walter Davidson's Long Island endurance win, Alan Bedel ran 1,000 miles nonstop at Ascot Park, California. He averaged 48.3 mph for nearly 21 hours, a creditable speed for 1917. History failed to record the kind of H-D beneath Bedel, but noted that he also set a 24-hour mark (48.1 mph), a 500-mile world record (50.1 mph), and a record for 12 hours (49.5 mph). Almost simultaneously, C. F. Bruschi and Walter House set a 1,000-mile record for sidecars, pushing their H-D to an average speed of 48.42 mph in less than 20 hours.

As U.S. roads improved, riders began to challenge each other from one point to another. Walter Hadfield repeatedly lowered the elapsed time from Vancouver to Tijuana in what became known as the Three Flags Run. Hap Sherer, aboard a Sport Twin, rode from Denver to Chicago in 1920 in about 48 hours (averaging 26.4 mph). While racer Otto Walker was establishing flying-mile world records in excess of 112 mph, Canadian H-D distributor Fred Deeley and friends were setting a world economy record; they rode from Vancouver to Tijuana in 1926 averaging 104.67 miles per gallon of fuel and 1,234.7 miles per gallon of oil. However, the king and queen of the endurance riders were Earl and Dot Robinson.

The Michigan Harley-Davidson dealer twice lowered the time and upped the speed needed to run between Los Angeles and New York City. Earl toured the 3,000 or so miles solo in 77 hours, 53 minutes in 1935, then teamed with his wife to cover the same wide-open space in a sidecar in 86 hours, 55 minutes.

13 Races, 13 Wins

That same, Depression year, a young man named Joe Petrali entered every AMA national race and won all 13, riding a 45-ci Harley-Davidson. No one else in motorcycling history has come close to the numbers he put together in 1935. Born in San Francisco in 1904 two years before the great earthquake, Petrali grew up in Sacramento. By the age of 13, he owned a beater bike, and three years later, he was winning events at local tracks. A mechanic as well as a rider, Petrali's work took him to Kansas City, where for several years he raced and wrenched for Indian.

Alliances were rather loose in those days, so when Joe showed up at the Altoona, Pennsylvania, board track in 1925 without a ride, Ralph Hepburn noticed. Hepburn had broken his hand in a practice spill and offered the youngster his Harley-Davidson factory mount. Joe rode around the track a few times, experimented with a new substance known as tetraethyl, and then left the field in a cloud of additive. The 100-mile race ended just 59 minutes, 47.2 seconds later; that's right, Petrali had averaged more than 100 mph on the 61-ci H-D.

The motor company bowed out of racing between 1926 and 1930, so Petrali successfully entered the new 350 cc class on an Excelsior. He returned to Harley-Davidson to ride the Milwaukee version of the 350 cc class, an overhead valve single dubbed the Peashooter. From then until his voluntary retirement in 1938, Petrali mowed down every other professional racer on every other kind of bike. During his all-conquering 1935 season, he won five national races in a single day in Syracuse, New York. Two years later, he set a record speed of 136.183 mph on a new 61-ci overhead valve Knucklehead on the beach at Daytona.

Some will blame the demise of AMA Class A (350 cc) professional racing after 1937 on the economy. Others will pin it on Petrali, who dominated a series as no one has before or since. When the rules changed for the 1938 season to 750-cc Class C road bikes, Petrali opted to enter a few hillclimbs, another area in which he excelled. For all of his ex-

J. R. Schnabel. (David K. Wright)

Now retired, still-young Scott Parker obliges a fan with an autograph. Parker won an incredible 94 national events on dirt. (David K. Wright)

Riders get the green in a qualifying race. (David K. Wright)

perience, he hardly ever crashed. He once cracked ribs at a hillclimb and fell hard on the dirt avoiding another competitor's fallen bike. "He was tough," said the late William H. Davidson. "He was a nice guy, but he wouldn't give an inch on the track." Modern racers who come upon the spindly racing bikes of the 1920s wonder how any man could muster the courage to climb on the gearless, brakeless machines. Petrali got on and stayed on for 20 years.

Hillclimbing

There were of course other stars at the time. Another Californian, Windy Lindstrom, won more than 300 hillclimbs between 1925 and 1950. While less successful "slant artists" played games with elongated frames, Lindstrom stuck with the standard 45- or 74-ci H-D hillclimbers with special gearing, a rear-wheel chain, and a kill button. He attributed his success to using the same throttle opening all the way up the hill, tapping the kill button for a split second whenever the front end of his machine threatened to head where it had come from.

Movietone newsreels showed Lindstrom and others astride their bucking bikes, a strip of leather running from the right wrist to the spark plug contact points in the electrical circuit. Lindstrom rarely departed his bike anywhere but

at the end of his run; but when he did, the leather strip was yanked from between the points, grounding out the motor. Such a precaution prevented a riderless bike from veering into the crowd that lined the hill.

There were good riders aplenty in the 1930s, though the economy and lack of national news coverage might have indicated otherwise. East Coast honors were upheld by Arthur "Babe" Tancrede and Ben Campanele, who were superb on road courses such as Laconia and Daytona Beach, and Goldie Restall, who did battle on cinder-track speedways. Out west, Lindstrom, Sam Arena, "Sprouts" Elder, Jack Cottrell, Joe Herb, and Milt Iverson starred in hillclimbs, TTs, and flat tracks, with Arena winning from 1934 until after 1950 in one of the most versatile careers of all time. Midwesterners Herb Rieber and Paul Goldsmith were joined after World War II by Roger Soderstrom and Leo Anthony, while down south such racers as June McCall, Herman Dahlke, and Buck Brigance were to be reckoned with. These and others seldom made the sports sections but were seen regular in racing coverage by *The Enthusiast*.

Not even the H-D owners' magazine covered the so-called outlaw races in the 1930s, though Harley-Davidson was the most common machine on the track. Bob Holder, now retired and living in Lincoln, California, reports that "You could ride whatever you wanted at outlaw tracks, so long as the size of the engine was legal—45 ci for side valves and 30.5 ci for overhead valves . . . We used to take a 1929 Harley 61-ci bike and remove one cylinder and rebalance the rest. We had a 30.5-ci in. bike with one overhead valve. I was riding one of these at Santa Ana one Sunday and just before I crossed the finish line the crankpin broke, causing parts of the engine to fly up between my legs. When I got the checkered flag I didn't have an engine in the frame."

Low-buck Racing

Things were more orderly, and not much more expensive, under AMA sanctioning. Ed Rusk, who competed throughout the South in the 1940s and 1950s, was a good racer and a meticulous record keeper. In 1947, for example, he ran 27 TT and flat-track races from Jacksonville to as far north as Peoria. He picked up six trophies and more than $2,100 in prize money, paying out just $335 for expenses and only $260 to his 45- and 80-ci motors. After doling out $12 (!) to a Columbus, Georgia, hospital following a spill, he still had enough cash ($600) for a new motor at season's end. Purses have failed to match the cost of tires, repairs, motels, or gasoline since then, though better sponsors certainly ease the financial pain.

The invasion of the U.S. by English manufacturers following World War II meant more registrations. As those registrations increased, so did the number of top-flight racers; many were able to give H-D some competition at last. Although Indian was on its last legs, ageless Ed Kretz and Bobby Hill won just often enough to make things interesting. Throughout the 1950s and 1960s, Triumphs and BSAs tormented Milwaukee bikes on dirt and pavement, all but going broke in the process.

Meanwhile, hundreds of talented riders who would never see a No. 1 plate were competing regionally and nationally on Harley-Davidsons. They included Paul Albrecht, Rex Beauchamp, Ernie Beckman, Everett Brashear, Scott Brelsford, Duane Buchanan, Charles Carey, Babe DeMay, Darrel Dovel, Chet Dykgraaf, Harry Fearey, Walt Fulton, John Gibson, Dick Hammer, Bill Huber, Corky Keener, Troy Lee, Bill Miller, Tony Murguia, Ronnie Rall, Roger Reiman, George Roeder, Greg Sassaman, Larry Schafer, Dave Sehl, Bob Tindall, Joe Weatherly, Ralph White, and many, many others.

Drag racing and motocross gained popularity as hillclimbs and the inclination to try for a land speed record at Bonneville declined. The Utah site saw H-Ds run with great frequency, from Jack Dale's Class C record of 123.52 mph on a 45-ci side valve in 1951 through Les Waterman's 164.89-mph effort with a pair of 80-ci motors in 1962 to factory-backed efforts. George Roeder, a fast and versatile racer, drove a missile-shaped bike with a Sprint engine to a speed of 177.255 mph in 1965, while Cal Rayborn posted a speed of 265.492 inside an 89-ci, fuel-burning Sportster streamliner five years later. In 1990, Joe Campos ran an *Easyriders*-sponsored H-D streamliner to a two-wheeled record of 322.15 mph.

Motocross was forced on H-D by its acquisition of Aermacchi and by the herd of Japanese two-strokes that first gained popularity on the West Coast. The Aermacchi riders, despite factory support in the late 1970s, found themselves victim of an old Harley stunt: They were beaten simply by being greatly outnumbered. The money saved when Aerma-

cchi was sold went, albeit belatedly, into drag racing. Marion Owens and others campaigned against megabuck Japanese multicylinder machines, with varying degrees of success in 1979 and 1980.

Dealers including Bartel's, Harley-Davidson of Sacramento, West Bend Harley-Davidson, Lancaster Harley-Davidson, Widman Harley-Davidson, and many others have contributed disproportionately over the years to H-D's racing success. Willing to experiment with competition motors, they are part of the reason the non-factory Harley riders can count on running with or near current factory rider Rich King if they possess the talent. Another source of speed is the independent tuner. Working on bikes after long days at their full-time jobs, these guys have propelled riders such as Rickey Graham (1982) and others to the podium, if not to the AMA Progressive Insurance U.S. Flat Track Championship.

Money and Results

In the last twenty years, racers have had it tougher than their predecessors, and that hardship has nothing to do with speed. Money is the all-important ingredient, whether from parents who are willing to sacrifice, a sponsor with deep pockets, or a dealer who is able to write off lots of time, parts, and travel so that a young man can run up front. Buell roadracer Brian Henning, from Florida, worked 16-hour

Harley-Davidson tuner Bill Werner and factory rider Rich King. (David K. Wright)

days (with no days off) on an Alaskan fishing boat to earn enough money to buy a bike and make it fast. His story is no more grueling than many other up-and-coming riders. Who are these guys, anyway?

After 100 Harley years, the competitors vying for the AMA national flat-track title are a mix of veterans and kids:

- **Chris Carr.** Now that five-time national champ Scott Parker has retired, Chris Carr is the man to beat at half-mile, mile, and TT events. A Californian by birth, Chris moved to Pennsylvania for racing reasons; he turned 36 in 2002. At that age, lots of riders lose their edge. Chris, on the other hand, just seems to get better and better, with more than 50 national wins and three championships. A factory rider in the early AMA years, Carr now races for H-D of Sacramento.
- **Rich King.** Iowa's contribution to going fast is another oldster (he was 37 in 2002) who runs at the front of the pack. His mount the last couple of years has been a factory XR750, tuned by wizard Bill Werner. He finished in flat track's runner-up position three different years.
- **Joe Kopp.** The state of Washington is not best known for its racers, but maybe it should be. Kopp, who turned 33 in

The best hope now for a roadracing victory is the new 2002 Buell Firebolt. (David K. Wright)

2002, has one national title to his credit and was in the hunt in 2001 before being sidelined by an injury. He and Rich King are especially competitive running against each other.

- **Nicky Hayden.** Hayden turned pro in 1997 at the age of 16, one indication of just how good he really is. Primarily a road racer, he returns to flat-track competition as time permits. Anyone who saw him challenge Chris Carr for TT honors at Springfield in 2001 can recognize his ability. From a racing family, Hayden has been plagued with mechanical problems on the half-mile and mile tracks, but when everything is hooked up, the Owensboro, Kentucky, native runs fast.
- **Kenny Coolbeth.** What is a skinny kid from Connecticut doing on a big dirt-track bike? Running among the leaders if he is Kenny Coolbeth. Despite busting up his hands in an accident late in the 2001 season, he looks to be a favorite for several seasons to come. Right now, he is the best rider never to have won a national race.
- **J. R. Schnabel.** Another young dude, the West Bend, Wisconsin, resident has only a single national victory, at the Houston half-mile, to his credit. Yet, it is obvious watching him that any deficiencies are mechanical rather than human. Among his credits are numerous flat-track wins in support events.
- **Mike Hacker.** Hacker was 25 in 2002 and poised to win his first national. The Virginian has been competing in AMA nationals since 1995 and seems able on any given day to run with anyone on the circuit.

There are others, of course. Racing is the kind of sport where fast kids are constantly coming out of nowhere. One who won't return anytime soon is Jennifer Snyder. The teenage Texan, who became the first woman ever to win a major flat-track event in 2001 when she took the Formula USA Pro Singles event at Colonial Downs in Virginia, is on the mend. She suffered major injuries in Seattle in the autumn of 2001 while riding a factory-backed Harley. Whether she can and will compete again remains to be seen.

The Best Rider Ever?

Two soldiers, one from Indiana and one from Wisconsin, were sharing a bunker in 1967 at the Ninth Infantry Division base camp in Vietnam. The Hoosier, who had attended Charity Newsies events in Columbus, Ohio, said he thought Dick

Mann was the best rider he had ever seen. "That's because," the Wisconsin native said, "you never saw Carroll Resweber."

Resweber caused that kind of comment from the time he first climbed on his old Knucklehead in Port Arthur, Texas, challenging his friends to race on Gulf Coast area roads. Everett Brashear, an expert rider from nearby Beaumont, was sufficiently impressed with Resweber to take the novice rider north on the dirt-track circuit. Carroll had been promised a ride on a Paul Goldsmith machine, arriving in Illinois only to find that Goldsmith had bent the bike in a crash. Resweber rode what he could find in three junior events in Wisconsin, winning all three and impressing independent tuner Ralph Berndt. Berndt worked for H-D but put together his own bikes since there were no true factory riders in those days. By 1956, Resweber was an expert; by 1957, he finished ahead of Brashear in the point standings, and by 1958, he displayed the No. 1 plate.

Resweber won 16 nationals in his four-consecutive-year reign as the national racing champion. Moreover, he did it while working full time for Mercury Marine in Cedarburg, Wisconsin; this was the only village ever to fete a cycle champ by holding a "Carroll Resweber Day." The slim Texas native would no doubt have earned a fifth consecutive title in 1962, but for a tragic evening in Lincoln, Illinois. The half-mile track was so dusty, legend has it, that Resweber ran into fallen Jack Gholson and Dick Klamfoth because his eyes were closed. The champ suffered a broken neck in the spill, an incident he cannot recall. "I remember looking over to Ralph (Berndt), who was timing other riders, and I remember leaving the pits. That's all," he said recently. "I'm told I wasn't breathing when they picked me off the track in a sheet—they'd run out of stretchers. But an ambulance attendant gave me mouth-to-mouth."

Ironically, 1962 was to have been Carroll's last year on two wheels. He had an offer to race stock cars. He lay unconscious for nine days, then spent two years being told by medical experts that his left arm was useless. He eventually regained 80 percent use of the arm, which was enough to climb on and ride the stylized street bike he designed while working as a fabricator and machinist in Dick O'Brien's company race shop.

"I loved to win," Resweber said a few years ago. "On equal equipment, I believed I could beat the other guys. That's

The XR750 that belonged to the late Will Davis was auctioned for $22,000 and the proceeds given to his family. (David K. Wright)

the way I felt inside." Known for running a precise groove lap after lap, Resweber was said to have psyched Bart Markel, the high road, low road, anywhere in-between competitor. "If Bart would have slowed down, he would have beaten me," Resweber said with a smile. His records on 50-horsepower bikes withstood the onslaught of today's 90-horsepower machines until about 1990—that shows how fast he was. At the Springfield Mile in 1962, Resweber lapped the entire field in the 50-mile main event before running out of fuel.

Black Bart

The old guys, the ones who have been around racetracks for years, smile slyly when Bart Markel is mentioned. His name causes them to flash on something they saw at a race Bart ran during his professional career, which stretched from 1957 through 1979. In those 22 grueling years, the stubby AC Delco tool-and-die machinist from Flint, Michigan, bounced off hay bales, guardrails, and other competitors in winning 28 dirt-track nationals and three No. 1 plates, in 1962, 1965, and 1966.

Harley-Davidson and Vance & Hines are collaborating on this Pro Stock V-Rod drag bike. (Vance & Hines)

A high-cushion rider, Markel was best on the half-mile tracks, where the bikes and the action were the thickest. As one of his admirers once said, he would win every race run through a room full of coat hangers. He was once suspended, accused by the AMA of rough riding and thereby earning him the nickname "Black Bart." Few who know him believe he ever intentionally ran anybody into the fence (except maybe Sammy Tanner, who did it to Bart several weeks before Bart did it to him). Rather, Markel is probably the most extreme example of a rider who violated all of the laws of gravity and still won. He raced as if he were allergic to the groove, in contrast to his old nemesis, Resweber.

Former head of H-D racing Dick O'Brien knew why Bart was a less-than-successful road racer. He refused to slow down for the turns, O'Brien recalled. While other asphalt competitors rode with clip-on bars and fairings, Markel's machine sported wide, dirt-style bars; he sat bolt upright, waiting impatiently for the opportunity to pitch the bike into a slide, an opportunity that usually came along in the worst possible way. Photos in company archives show him in every turn, foot in the outrigger position, waiting for the cushion to propel him out in front of the pack.

Markel never suffered any lasting injury, though he might show up for a national race with his left leg supported by a bungee cord looped around his waist. The fact that he kept himself in superb physical condition, even as age caught up with him, probably helped Bart overcome aches and pains that would have sidelined lesser riders. He is still seen occasionally at a half-mile or mile race, a quiet man wearing glasses. Markel's legacy is still on the track in the form of almost every Michigan rider competing for national points. The fact that Michigan seems to produce as many flat-trackers as cars is a tribute to the rider they called "Black Bart." However, they don't call him that to his face.

Cal Rayborn

"Cal Rayborn never played out his string," says one veteran dealer, who turned his shop over to the H-D factory and independents alike each year when the big national show came to town. Indeed, Rayborn's star seemed to be ascending when he reluctantly left Harley-Davidson at the end of the 1973 season. The XR750 had at last been eclipsed by the Japanese two-strokes on pavement, and the lanky resident of Spring Valley, near San Diego, signed with Suzuki. Rayborn had acquired a Chevy-engined racing car and decided to take the machine to Australia to sell it—at a handsome profit. Dick O'Brien warned Rayborn not to ride any junk while there, but the temptation to climb on an Aussie dealer's bike was too much. The machine locked up, throwing Rayborn violently into a trackside steel barrier. He died shortly afterward.

Cal's career began with a severe injury, a broken back suffered in a road race on the Riverside, California, course in 1958. The 18-year-old recovered, began to ride scrambles, and then was taken under the wing of dealer Leonard Andres. Andres' son, Brad, had won one national title, and was a superior road racer himself. Andres senior knew what to look for. Fighting perennially weak brakes, Rayborn emerged almost overnight in front of a pack of very, very talented road racers: Dick Mann, Gary Nixon, Dick Hammer, and Brad Andres. Rayborn won Daytona with ease, he once won six straight pavement races, and he passed Roger Reiman in an Indianapolis Raceway Park turn by sliding his bike sideways for nearly 100 feet. Yet, Rayborn never mastered the dirt, which prevented him from affixing the No. 1 plate to the fairing of his XR. A loner and a constant complainer, Cal scuffed the cases, the pegs, the fairings, and more, no matter how far up and in the mechanics moved things. Dick O'Brien believes that the ultimate one-on-one race would have been Rayborn against the late, legendary Mike Hailwood of Great Britain.

Jay Springsteen

Jay Springsteen has been luckier than either Carroll Resweber or Cal Rayborn. The Michigan resident has won on every kind of dirt: short track, TT, half mile, and mile. Springer also is an able road racer. As an example, he finished sixth in the 1978 250-cc 100-miler at Daytona on a vastly underpowered machine. The wiry dude who loves to race but dislikes the hoopla attached to racing is an avid hunter and fisher. He lives in the small town of Lapeer, Michigan, where he has to do little more than walk out his back door to be in an ideal setting. Only a chronic stomach problem that defied control for years kept Springer from rolling up more than his 43 wins and 4 AMA Grand National titles.

The illness surfaced repeatedly throughout the 1980s. Jay would show up with the factory team, watch tuner Bill Werner set up his bike, turn qualifying laps, and then, before or during the heats, he would find himself in great pain. Dieting helped. He stayed away from the deplorable food some racers live on. Medication helped. He was diagnosed as having a rare form of diabetes and was dosed accordingly. Nevertheless, the shy fellow with the No. 1 plate had to sit frequently and watch others run for his title. "I think it may all be in my head," he has said, though tests show his stomach produces 2-1/2 times the normal amount of digestive acids. With the problem now behind him, the elder statesman of the dirt has no reason to keep going, especially since he continues to finish ahead of most competitors. Springer was 43 and in good condition in 2002.

In other racing matters, the company has enlisted Vance & Hines, the respected aftermarket firm in Trinidad, Colorado, to develop the Screamin' Eagle Pro Stock Harley-Davidson. Perhaps because the V-Rod has a distinctive dragster look, H-D joined the National Hot Rod Association series in 2002. At the Gatornationals in March at his first meet on this bike, Gary Tonglet dialed off a time of 7.704 seconds and a speed of 162.47 mph for the quarter mile. The winner, Matt Hines, ran 7.156 seconds and 193.85 mph, which indicates that Byron Hines and the rest of the fellows at Vance & Hines still have some development work to perform. Other prominent drag racers include Houston H-D dealer John Mancuso and Doug Vancil, who races a V-twin Harley under Vance & Hines auspices.

Doug Vancil has turned a time of 6:45 seconds and a speed of 224.21 miles per hour on this Vance & Hines, 160-ci, nitromethane-powered Harley-Davidson.
(Vance & Hines)

Chapter 9

Scenes

There are at least two huge annual Harley-Davidson events in this country, Sturgis and Daytona. With the explosive popularity of Harley-Davidsons since the buyback, there also are a number of Sturgis and Daytona wannabes. So far, the big parties in South Dakota and in Florida have no real competition.

Daytona Beach, downtown. (David K. Wright)

Visiting Sturgis

"You know what makes Sturgis better than Daytona?"

Wait a minute—is this a trick question? The guy doing the asking is on the outskirts of the South Dakota town perched on his Low Rider with a Florida plate.

"I'll tell you," the Floridian volunteers. "At Daytona, you walk around or sit in traffic all day. Out here," he says, sucking in several cubic inches of high-plains air, "you can really *ride*!"

The Black Hills rally and races began in 1938 under AMA sanction. The Jackpine Gypsies Motorcycle Club got things started by posting a race purse of $300 and the event grew, despite the Depression economy and the thunder in the distance that became World War II. Bikers who showed up in Sturgis each year demanded even more riding, in the form of tours that featured the small farming and ranching town as a jumping-off point. There are now several full days of organized tours during the week in early August set aside each year for the event.

The late J. C. "Pappy" Hoel formed the Jackpine Gypsies Motorcycle Club in 1936. The perseverance of Pappy and fellow club members put Sturgis on motorcycling's map, despite gaining and then losing national sanction of their racing event (it's still an AMA regional). "We have never had any serious problems with the 'outlaw' group," the founder said several years back. "We have their cooperation as long as we do not hassle them. We have a few motorcycles stolen, but that is normal when you consider that we have an estimated 15,000 motorcycles in a town of 5,000 people. There is nothing quite like it anywhere in the world and reservations, even months early, are hard to get."

Things have changed a bit since Pappy uttered those words. The crowd has swollen (650,000 in 2000, 400,000 in 2001), the riders are older and more typically middle-class guys and gals misbehaving than gang members, and the Sturgis Chamber of Commerce actively works to promote the get-together. Proof of that can be had by giving them a call at 605-347-2556. Once the mechanical operator answers, the caller has a choice: Chamber business or the Black Hills bike rally. Cycling really has become mainstream.

The first day of the event is devoted to signing in, being seen, and checking out the iron and the riders. They have rolled in from the east and west (Interstate Highway 90) and

Visitors look over a Buell a few years ago at the Harley-Davidson show in Daytona Beach. (David K. Wright)

the north and south (U.S. Highway 85). Sturgis is more or less in the middle of the continent (1,700 miles west of New York City, 1,500 miles east of San Francisco), and the weather in August in South Dakota is as good as it gets. The rally-races are a nationwide meeting of the East Coast cruisers and baggers, the Heartland Harleys, and the West Coast wonderbikes.

Campgrounds fill up early with the mirthful. Here is where you are likely to get your first look at a female chest unencumbered by bra or T-shirt, where you will get the first of several whiffs of marijuana, and where beards are so common it looks like a tree farm. The authorities in Sturgis assume you are on the up-and-up unless and until you do something illegal, obscene, or stupid.

The road tours, like the event itself, feature Harley-Davidsons and their riders almost exclusively. Except for the Milwaukee H-D homecomings, this has to be the most all-American bike event on earth. Some well-to-do riders and metal benders have been known to get a custom bike ready primarily for the ride to, from, and around Sturgis. Those who tire of touring the rugged and beautiful Black Hills can attend motorcycling-aftermarket shows in the armory or go to four nights and an afternoon of flat-track

Harley-Davidson's Cuban dealer, Del Campo (center, with camera) brought family members and race fans to Daytona in the late 1940s. That's William H. Davidson in the plain shirt, beneath the banner. (William H. Davidson collection)

A passenger goes for a dangling, mustard-dipped hot dog in one of several contests in the Harley Heaven section of the Daytona International Motor Speedway. (David K. Wright)

Because Daytona Bike Week is in March, some northern riders arrive like this: in a Cadillac with a Dresser attached. (David K. Wright)

competition. Leather goods, ersatz accessories, T-shirts, and more are peddled by the thousands to visitors.

The locals also make a lot of money off the bikers. The United Presbyterian Women turn out great hotcakes each morning, while the gals at Grace Lutheran Church offer lunch all day long. The Bear Butter Café sells enough Grain Belt beer to irrigate the wheat crop, while Mr. Al's Main Street concession stands just keeps the hot dogs coming. Those who take a pass on any of the tours can test their bravery on the highway leading to Deadwood. There are several days of swap meets and two nights of sanctioned dragbike racing.

Speaking of racing, an illuminated Lucite memorial devoted to White Plate Flat Trackers, the select group of racers who ran the AMA professional expert class at one time or another, acts as a beacon. After hours, or perhaps days, in the saddle, it's nice to pay your respects to the fellows who attracted the very first crowds. As for Sturgis today, if Willie G. attends on a regular basis, and if the com-

pany chose Sturgis as the site to first announce its 2003 celebration plans, it can't be all bad.

Regarding relative importance, think about this: If Daytona, like Sturgis, attracted more riders than there are state residents, Daytona would have to play host to 16 million people.

Bike Week at Daytona

Daytona is an even larger event than Sturgis—or is it? Currently, more than 500,000 people show up in this Atlantic Coast Florida town for racing, shopping, drinking, and profiling. The event, says the Daytona Beach/Holly Hill Chamber of Commerce, is growing. It used to take guts, gristle, and a good rainsuit to show up each year in early March. Now all it takes is money.

That's why corporate Harley-Davidson is here. That, and an excuse for employees from Milwaukee, Kansas City, and

Former H-D Chairman Vaughn Beals holds a news conference in Daytona in the early 1980s to talk about newer and better bikes. (David K. Wright)

Main Street, Sturgis, South Dakota. Virtually every bike in the photo is a Harley-Davidson. (Richard Creed)

York to depart the dismal northern late winter. It is less of an all-Harley event than Sturgis, but only marginally so; Daytona is proof that overpopulation concerns are real. The two most popular rendezvous are the Ocean Center on North Atlantic Avenue, where the company shows its wares, and Main Street, where Harley riders like to check each other out.

The disc brake up front betrays this V-twin's authenticity. Other giveaways include the headlight, turn signals, tires, and mirror. The motor is from the J series. Hundreds of "blend" bikes are ridden to Sturgis each year. (Richard Creed)

A Knucklehead and a tent are all you need to fit in at the Sturgis campground. (Richard Creed)

Harley-Davidson, Inc., puts on quite a show at the Ocean Center, starting as early as the Tuesday before Sunday race day. There are indoor demonstrations, a traveling museum, poker run signups, fashion shows, service seminars, ride-in shows, a Dresser light show, and more. Harley-Davidson's orchestrated presentations overshadow the Rat's Hole Chopper Show on the boardwalk, the Saturday bike auction and concours in Deland, cavorting at the Boot Hill Saloon on Main Street, and other events.

Being a member of the Harley Owners Group (H.O.G.) helps, as there are special events for members. The company will have forewarned members about everything from places to score free food to private shindigs. The big speedway on the west side of town was deprived of Harley sounds for a while after 1973, when the XR750s retired from competition. With the demise of the Superbike team at the end of the 2001 season, Harley race fans must nourish themselves during vintage and support races, but the folks who show up here don't seem to mind.

Daytona International Speedway wasn't really constructed with motorcycles in mind. The track is dangerous, spectators seem to be miles from the race bikes, and the heat, even in March, can make attending an ordeal. The closest many riders get to the oval are the opportunities outside the bowl to take motorcycle demo rides. In 2002, H-D and Buell joined many other manufacturers in offering free putts to adults with proper gear and licensing. Nothing can sell a new model like a test drive, even in the hideous traffic of Daytona Beach.

A rider works out on the Harley-Davidson pinball machine, introduced at Daytona in 1991. (David K. Wright)

A California priest offers a prayer before a club ride in the 1950s. Note the saddlebag purse carried by the lady nearest the camera. (James Perkins collection)

Milwaukee and Elsewhere

The popularity of Daytona and Sturgis has not gone unnoticed. Nowadays, people with promotional blood in their veins are staging all sorts of ride-in reunions. While the factory plans epic parties for the centennial, Milwaukee-area H-D dealers will be staging their own shows. The early June date coincides with the AMA Superbike races at Road America and the Formula USA short-track date in Plymouth, Wisconsin. Sure, this is a fledgling event, but how do you think Daytona and Sturgis got started? Or Ruidoso or any other H-D hoedown?

A H.O.G. member searches the club's Daytona message board for familiar names. (David K. Wright)

Colors, unless they say Harley Owners Group, have lost favor with most riders these days. (David K. Wright)

A typically growing annual event is Street Vibrations, which goes down in Reno each September. This part of the country may be the ultimate place to ride, and Northern California Harley-Davidson dealers know how to put on a good show. How good? An estimated 50,000 riders showed up for the event in 2001, which took place only eight days after the World Trade Center tragedy.

Reno is a gracious host to the riders, who, by the looks of things, are about 95 percent Harley-mounted. For approximately $50 participants can enter parades, graze at buffets, hear pretty good music, check out aftermarket accessories, ride in multiple poker runs and parades, watch showgirls wash bikes, attend a tattoo expo, compete in a bike giveaway, visit the H-D Factory Store, and gamble. Accommodations are inexpensive, booze is cheap, the high desert country and Tahoe areas are dazzling, and everyone appears laid back. Look for more of such up-and-coming events during Harley's second century.

Clubs and Organizations

The easiest way to stay abreast of various events is to join one or more clubs. The following organizations have either a strong H-D orientation or welcome Harley-Davidson owners. They gather regularly at Sturgis, Daytona, Reno, and at functions of their own.

American Motorcyclist Association
13575 Yarmouth Drive
Pickerington, OH 43147
Tel. 614-856-1900
http://www.ama-cycle.org

This is the oldest and second largest (270,000 dues payers) motorcycling organization in the country. The association has evolved from being a shill for manufacturers in the 1920s to today's diverse group of tourers, competitors, dealers, and promoters. In addition to sanctioning racing activity, AMA personnel lobby in Washington. The association puts out American Motorcyclist, *a nice national monthly magazine, operates a snazzy new museum, and conducts a variety of racing and nonracing events. Annual membership is $39, which gives the member voting rights on club issues, a break on insurance, discounts on everything from eyewear to RV rentals, and more. Discover, MasterCard or Visa work here.*

Antique Motorcycle Club of America
c/o Dick Winger
P.O. Box 333
Sweetser, IN 46987
http://www.antiquemotorcycle.org

America's largest cycle restoration club has chapters in 25 states and a couple of Canadian provinces. It holds meets across the country where members buy and sell parts, display their machines, go on rides, etc. Any bike 35 or more years old is considered an antique with these experts, who produce an informative quarterly magazine and show a real spirit of camaraderie.

Harley Owners Group (H.O.G.)
Harley-Davidson, Inc.
P.O. Box 653
Milwaukee, WI 53201
Tel. 800-Club-HOG
http://www.hog.com/

Perhaps because every buyer of a new Harley is automatically enrolled for a year, Harley Owners Group is the largest bike club on earth. There are chapters everywhere, from wherever you happen to be to Kuala Lumpur and back. The 650,000 folks in 1,157 chapters participate in all sorts of rides, events, feeds, and parties, though not every

Bikes and people crowd downtown Reno for Street Vibrations each September. (David K. Wright)

Like most U.S. bike rendezvous, Street Vibrations is largely a Harley affair. (David K. Wright)

Folks queue for a look inside Daytona's Boot Hill Saloon, which is across the street from a cemetery. (David K. Wright)

dealer has the HOG calling. Conceived shortly after the buyback, this organization has played a huge part in keeping H-D enthusiasts connected. Dues are $40/year.

This is the scene at Daytona Beach each March. (David K. Wright)

Motor Maids, Inc.
P.O. Box 1664
Engle wood, FL 34295
www.motormaids.org

Founded in 1940, this female-only club is made up of women who own and ride any kind and any size of cycle. The organization goes way back with Harley-Davidson, since the first president was Dot Robinson, co-owner of an H-D dealership and a record-setting cyclist. The club has an annual, nationwide convention in July, and state districts hold meets throughout the year. It is against club rules to tow a bike to a Motor Maid event. Dues are $20 per annum.

Women in the Wind
P.O. Box 8392
Toledo, OH 43605
http://www.womeninthewind.org

Founded in 1985, this women-only organization has 44 U.S. chapters and several in Canada. The club is open to any female rider with any kind of bike; founder Becky Brown says H-Ds are the most popular machines. Dues are $15 for full membership and $10 for associate. Activities include twice-yearly get-togethers. In 2002, Women met in Florida and in Oregon. There is a semi-monthly newsletter, too.

The Fringe

The list does not include organizations that are not much into mainstream membership, or have initiation or membership requirements they would rather not discuss. Such a bunch is the Hell's Angels, once the subject of much toadying by the news media and a group that has been unfortunately associated with Harley-Davidson.

The Angels were one of many California bike gangs until immortalized on film and in print in *LIFE* magazine photos and in a Hunter Thompson book that, from a cycling enthusiast's point of view, was heavy on entertainment but weak on mechanicals. Somewhere along the line, the Angels began to believe their press clippings and performed some genuinely outrageous, antisocial acts. It all seemed bearable—runs into the California outback to suck wine and smoke dope, volunteering to take their bikes to Vietnam to root out the Viet Cong, showing what they thought of peace and civil rights in nearby Berkeley—until they became entwined in the drug trade. Local, state, and federal authorities began to take them seriously once guns and drugs were being moved in earnest by the Oakland, California, based group. While other gangs nationwide were dealing in (relatively) harmless stolen cycle parts, the Angels were snuffing and being snuffed on a regular basis. Even their leader at the time, Sonny Barger, had to park his Harley for a stretch while in prison.

The Oakland Police Department reported recently that the gang remains active, though there have not been many problems on the West Coast in several years. In contrast, a Hell's Angels chapter on Long Island threw a party in late winter of 2002 that was invaded by a bunch known as the Pagans. When the smoke cleared, one Pagan was dead and some 75 fellows described as "beefy" by *The New York Times*, were under arrest. The Angels evidently had chosen to party on Pagan turf, an imprudent move.

Long Island Pagans reportedly lived by extorting money from the owners of area topless bars. That ended in a wave of arrests a few years back. Nowadays, Angels, Pagans, Bandidos, Outlaws, and other meanies often make their money underwriting drug labs and making the distribution, once the labs have produced their poison.

H-D Victimized

There is absolutely no evidence to indicate that Harley-Davidson ever had any dealing with or condoned the actions of local or national motorcycle gangs. In fact, an incident in 1973 shows that at least one gang treats the company as badly as it treats everyone else. The first hint of a problem came from an authorized—and very reputable—dealer in California. The dealer had been approached by a Milwaukee-area biker, who offered to sell 10,000 Harley-Davidson spark plugs at 50 percent of the cost of manufacture. Shrugging off the easy profit, the dealer notified Juneau Avenue. Employees discovered 29,000 spark plugs missing, and then notified the FBI.

Agents obtained a court order and placed a tap on the phone of John Buschman, who had been an H-D employee for less than three months, in late 1965 and early 1966, before being dismissed for excessive absenteeism. Buschman lived in Mequon, an exclusive suburb north of Milwaukee, without evident means of support. The monitored telephone, the bureau reported, indicated "Buschman was a captain in a local chapter of a nationwide motorcycle gang called the 'Outlaws.'" His long-distance calls amounted to orders for parts. Conspiring with another former employee, a then-current employee, and one or more truck drivers, Buschman managed to steal hundreds of thousands of dollars in parts, selling them as far away as the West Coast and Florida. One United Parcel Service shipment from Buschman's home to California was valued at $24,609.

"Their primary income is their old ladies and stolen Harleys," reported a cycle mechanic in Florida who had been approached by an Outlaw peddling new factory parts. He, too, was suspicious; he was used to buying only *used* stolen parts from the gang! The FBI obtained more court paperwork and a raid was staged on Buschman's residence in 1974. The agents found hundreds of Harley parts and "an arsenal of weapons" in the home and in a rented barn. Trial testimony indicated that parts were moving out of the plant in quantity in trucks and vans, and piecemeal via a few dishonest employees. Buschman went to prison, but his caper left its mark on even the most casual plant visitor. Everyone leaving the premises is liable to inspection by guards.

Motor Maids convene in Tennessee in 1999.

Chapter 10

Image

The first edition of this book informally surveyed Harley-Davidson dealers to learn more about the kinds of people buying the bikes. That was almost 20 years ago, and a lot has changed. While there remain "riders between the ages of 20 and 30, blue-collar workers of macho status," there are more and more well-educated, aging, affluent, baby-boomers, people less obsessed with the cult of motorcycling but who always wanted to throw a leg over and motor down the road. Approximately 9 percent of today's riders are female, a significant number. The average age of H-D owners is 45.6, and household income totals $77,700 a year. Some 45 percent owned H-Ds previously, 30 percent moved to a Harley from a competing bike, and 25 percent are either new to cycling or have not owned a bike for at least five years. The company has successfully managed to reach a mature, middle-class, worldwide audience, and "a whole new, middle-age breed of rider," according to *USA Today*.

Advertising History

The first advertisement to appear in any sort of non-company publication may have been a simple piece extolling the virtues of the 1914 models. That half-page example appeared in *Western Bicyclists & Motorcyclist*, a monthly magazine aimed as much at dealers as riders. A third audience, business-government, attracted the majority of Harley-Davidson advertising well into the 1920s. In fact, the company expended a large sum of ad money in 1915 to obtain approval for the use of motorcycles in the then-new U.S. Post Office Rural Free Delivery (RFD) system. Once cycles were given federal approval, Harley-Davidson not only used them in print ads, but also based an entire campaign on the high number of miles and low cents-per-mile rates recorded by rural postal service workers. One ad, produced

Direct mail, 1939. Penny postcards such as these were provided to dealers to announce new models.

Each September issue of The Enthusiast *during the 1930s and 1940s was devoted to new models. Here is the 1940 customer's first look at the newest Knucklehead.*

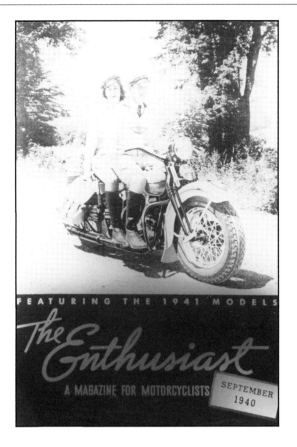

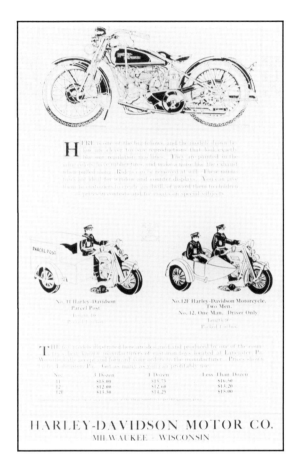

Harley-Davidson toys have been around a long time, as this 1929 ad in The Enthusiast *shows. Either a sidecar or a parcel car was available; both made "a noise like the exhaust when pulled along." The metal models featured authentic paint, rubber tires, and removable drivers.*

shortly after World War I, "proved" that a Harley-Davidson was less expensive than shoe leather!

Meanwhile, consumers were reached primarily through dealers, with a direct-mail campaign outlining innumerable advantages for the young factory worker, who could depart the gloomy city and head for the countryside with or without a female acquaintance in a sidecar. Since most H-Ds were sold with sidehacks well into the 1920s, hauling a friend was a snap. Harley-Davidson's incredible racing results during

this period were not used much to attract first-time buyers but were instead reported regularly in *The Enthusiast* and in a few trade magazines. Marketing experts then and marketing experts now see no direct link between success on the track and luring the new rider. While the 1930s were hub-deep in wonderful H-D models, sales were so weak that the company had to strain to produce *The Enthusiast* each month.

Following World War II, Harley-Davidson continued with Milwaukee's Klau-Van Pietersom-Dunlap, the only ad agency used until the 1960s. Print ads were inserted in such national magazines as *Mechanics Illustrated* and *Popular Science*; monthlies, including *Boy's Life,* were used to advance the Topper scooter and other small machines. Throughout the 1950s, the company continued to devote more than half its national print budget to motorcycling magazines. Those ads alternated between street model previews and racing results. Naturally, when something as stupendous as H-Ds 1960 sweep of the first 14 places in the annual Daytona race occurred, more advertising money was spent.

The cycling boom that began in the mid-1960s and has waxed hot and cold ever since pretty much terminated racing ads, as the company sought the thousands of would-be riders who identified with street machines. These days, Harley-Davidson conveys the feeling a rider gets on a Harley, a feeling, the ads say, can't be had on any other kind

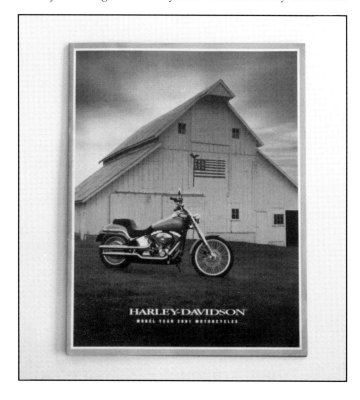

New models are featured each year in a full-color catalog.
(David K. Wright)

of machine. Such TV spots show up most Tuesday nights on "American Thunder," the weekly, 30-minute television show on cable's Speed Channel.

Serving Dealers

There are approximately 750 U.S. Harley-Davidson dealers (up from about 550 just 20 years ago), and no two serve exactly the same kind of rider. With that in mind, the advertising department is expected to entice *every* kind of customer. That used to be a big-league problem, according to Bill Dutcher, former AMF motorcycle products group public relations director.

Way back in 1977, a study commissioned by Harley-Davidson noted that there were three types of H-D riders: custom/performance (now termed cruiser), touring, and sport. "H-D has a sizeable share of the custom market, is strong in the touring market, and is absolutely nowhere with the sport rider. ... They're on opposite sides on virtually every issue. Therefore, if you run an ad that appeals to one, you're automatically turning off the others. Ruidoso (New Mexico, site of a touring rally) doesn't mean anything to a guy on a chopper, and seeing guys with bandanas in H-D ads won't win you any touring riders. And without any models that stay with the current crop of Japanese superbikes, H-D isn't likely to corner the sport market," Dutcher said.

The company evidently viewed the market in a similar way until 1982. In addition to offering the usual custom (FXRS, Sturgis, Low Rider, Wide Glide) and touring (Electra Glide, Tour Glide, FXR) bikes, Harley produced a pair of sport bikes (Sportster, Roadster). These met with critical acclaim from cycle magazines and from riders who get off on being able to flick a cycle through a series of sharp turns, and then come to a safe, sure stop. Harley-Davidson still makes performance motorcycles. The challenge was to spread the world.

It was more difficult then than it is now; in 2003, H-D and its riders see themselves as one big, non-judgmental family. Twenty-one years ago, the company segregated its products among three brochures. A dealer, the thinking went, could size up a customer after a brief conversation. Said dealer then presented a brochure tailored to the type of rider. No bandanas with Electra Glides, no choppers amid the fiberglass, no sport bikes ridden by members of the Booze Fighters M. C. This sounds simpler than it really was, since the enthusiast publications were not about to give H-D high marks just to benefit a marketing plan. Were the bikes better, or were such credible magazines as *Cycle World* succumbing to Harley-Davidson propaganda? The products *were* greatly improved, which sure made advertising easier.

Advertising has never been easy for H-D, particularly since the company labored throughout the 1910s, 1920s, and early 1930s under a delusion. "We tried for a long time to convince the people that motorcycles had some utility value," said William H. Davidson, the late former president. "Motorcycles have never been anything but pleasure." His assessment coincided with a styling change made for 1933, wherein the bikes dropped the delivery look in favor of a rainbow of colors and ads with models who looked more like cycle club members and less like parking-lot attendants. Today, the last thing you will find in a Harley ad is a bike made for carrying pizzas or dry cleaning.

Harley-Davidson attempts to reach stock-car fans by partially sponsoring this NASCAR Ford. (David K. Wright)

Early Ad Men

The role of those involved with advertising also has changed. The first person concerned with spreading the word was Lacy Crolius, whose photo turns up frequently in the racing archives. Crolius and Walter Davidson took time off from their duties as ad manager and president, respectively, to enter endurance runs in the very early years. Later came W. E. Klemenhagen, a more polished chap but one who could argue the relative merits of the Crocker motorcycle with a dealer as readily as any rider. During Klemenhagen's 30-year tenure, there was almost an exact correlation between how attractive the ads were and how well the cycles were being received by the public. The early-1930s and early-1950s print materials have a listless appearance, while the later-1930s and later-1950s ads, brochures, and posters carry a snap that portrays the company as knowing what it was about. In fact, H-D had a better understanding of its role than did AMF.

American Machine & Foundry hired Benton & Bowles, a prestigious Chicago agency, to create advertising for all of the conglomerate's recreational lines. Harley-Davidson was given a rigid set of guidelines as to format and appearance of all advertising and collateral (dealer) material. AMF be-

lieved, with some validity, that the polished advertising firm would bring needed marketing expertise to its big subsidiary. Thus began a battle that did not end until just before the buyback. The Chicago agency was staffed by non-riders trying to communicate with riders. It did not work well.

Other problems upset Harley-Davidson personnel. Since Benton & Bowles had been retained by AMF, the feeling was that the agency was most interested in satisfying the Connecticut parent rather than the Milwaukee child. Since AMF saw itself as highly visible and therefore vulnerable to attacks from all sides, an individual ad had to pass through five levels of corporate approval.

Harley-Davidson remained in charge of its own sales promotion and hired another agency to create brochures, literature, point-of-purchase displays, and related collateral. Since Benton & Bowles was responsible only for national, mostly print, advertising, H-D marketers hired a third agency to create radio and television spots. H-D paid for production and the dealers then had an opportunity to run the radio and TV spots locally, splitting the costs with Harley on a cooperative basis. As time went on, H-D spent more on those segments of advertising under its control and less on national print. The tail was wagging the hog, so to speak, even though Harley was obeying AMF advertising edicts.

Juneau Avenue continued to run this devious pattern until the spring of 1978. Responding to numerous dealer requests, H-D saw to it that a full-page ad was placed in *Easyriders*, the largest circulation outlaw-type sex/bike monthly. AMF was mortified that one of its subsidiaries was a part of the "Swastika" set and ordered Harley not to run future ads in such a prurient publication. Lou (Spider) Kimzey, the force behind *Easyriders* at the time, filled the page meant for the H-D ad with a Surgeon General's-type warning stating that the motorcycle manufacturer had determined *Easyriders* was injurious to its image. The black page with the small, rectangular block of type was a stroke of genius. Letters displaying varying degrees of literacy poured in to the magazine, the motor company, and the conglomerate. The public was pacified by new Harley ads said to have been conceived and placed by the dealer network. The space was paid for with funds from the dealer co-op program.

The co-op program grew from $200,000 in 1976 to $2 million in 1978. Numerous heated meetings followed between AMFers and H-D personnel. The conglomerate had a deal with Benton & Bowles wherein the agency was paid a flat annual fee and all ad commissions were rebated to AMF. The large, independent sum spent by Harley-Davidson prevented AMF from getting any sort of rebate on H-D advertising. Like a parent who has run out of patience with a child, in the spring of 1980, AMF ordered Harley-Davidson to run the cooperative ad program through Benton & Bowles.

The economy was beginning to sour, so H-D abandoned the more expensive advertising in favor of a direct-mail approach. The result was that no revenue was rebated to AMF, since a Minneapolis agency prepared the creative work and a Chicago agency was retained for other dealer co-op programs. The parent firm capitulated in January 1981, stating that all recreational subsidiaries could select their own agencies. The point was moot, since both sides were aware that the motorcycle company would be on its own very soon.

Today's Ads

Carmichael Lynch Spong was the Minneapolis agency that got its creative foot in H-D's door with direct mail campaigns more than 20 years ago. To some degree, agency and company personnel grew rather chummy, which may be why ads from 1979 and ads from 2002 don't look all that different. In fact, all makes of bikes run similar ads: the dirt-bike ads all look alike, as do all of the cruiser, touring, and sport ads. With demand continuing to exceed supply, why does H-D bother with any kind of advertising?

First, and maybe most important, the company has money to burn. Advertising does remind a prospective buyer that there is a large number of H-Ds from which to choose. It also provides H-D with a forum to talk about the products in ways that no bike editor would. Second, if the company ceased to advertise, do you really believe the bikes would be so regularly and favorably tested by writers and editors? It never hurts to pony up a little money to the trade. Third, since H-D buyers are like the rest of us, they like to be told how smart they were for buying a Sportster or Road King or Dyna Glide. Fourth, advertising lures riders to the dealership for parts and accessories. Fifth, an ad can convey that there is something called the Harley experience and that it is unique.

Savvy marketing is good, but having a mystique about its products is even better. Companies larger than H-D have spent millions trying to create similar devotion, only to fail. How do Apple computers, Porsche cars, and Harley-Davidson bikes do it? They may not be sure themselves. (Why do you think it's called mystique?) A few years back, an H-D executive sized it up this way: He said the attraction was like a fire. A person can pull and use a color from the fire, but if he or she tries to grab the whole thing, that person will be burned. The analogy cuts several ways. On a personal level, a Harley-Davidson president during the AMF years got so caught up in the mystique that he is said to have bitten the ass of a biker's old lady in full view of guests at the Daytona Beach Hilton. On a marketing level, it appears that Japanese manufactures grab the fire but not the colors.

The company is not at all elitist about it. In fact, they share the mystique with folks like the Ford Motor Company, working with the automaker to offer a truck with bar-and-shield logos and a two-wheeler posed in print ads. H-D also spends money in areas such as stock car racing, as a partial sponsor of a NASCAR competitor. In non-transportation areas, the company promotes itself by giving money and equipment to war veterans, to victims of the September 11 tragedy, and to such causes as the continuing search for a cure for muscular dystrophy.

Chapter 11

Celebrities

For a while, mostly in the 1970s, it was difficult to find a photo of a Harley-Davidson without a famous person attached. The more the hardcore enthusiasts thought about it, the more they may have realized a truism: When things are not going all that well, cloud the issue with well-known people. That's what the AMF public relations machine did at a time when labor, management, and quality problems threatened the loyalty of even the most dedicated H-D rider. Now that the personnel and the assembly problems have been solved, perhaps it is time to look inside the company for folks who are either widely known or should be. A good place to begin is with Willie G. Davidson.

Willie G. Davidson

What are the odds of the boss's son being in the right place at the right time? That was the case on February 18, 1963, when then President William H. Davidson invited his son to sign on as the company's styling director. Willie G. said he would pack his crayons and be right down, because he had been preparing for the position for much of his life. In addition to spending more than five years working for Brooks Stevens (designer of the Excalibur sports car), Davidson had styled for Ford Motor Company's Continental Division. According to his proud father, Willie G. owed much of his success to a magazine known as *The Saturday Evening Post*.

"It was Christmas and Bill was home from the University of Wisconsin," William recalled. "He was in his junior

Robert (Evel) Knievel.

One of Knievel's XRs. The bike, along with a car, and Evel paraphernalia, is on display in a suburban Chicago auto museum.

year majoring in art and complained that he wasn't looking forward to a career teaching unwilling school kids how to draw in rural Wisconsin. He read about a kid who was doing well at the Art Center College of Design in Los Angeles and showed me the *Post* article. I checked with an ad agency artist who gave the place high marks. Two weeks later, Bill was enrolled and on his way to California."

It is easy to conclude that the lush designs created by Willie G. have been influenced by his Los Angeles stay. Yet, there is no comparison between the custom motorcycles in California in the mid-1950s and the V-Rod, for example. A lifetime of being in and around every department at the Juneau Avenue plant, plus the Art Center training, were much more likely to have left their marks on the former president's elder son. Willie says he realized early that he was part of something unique. His dad rode a bike to work every day, unlike any other neighborhood father. Willie also hung around the experimental shop and went to the races. He got the bug at an early age.

If California played only a small part in his designs, it has influenced his lifestyle. Long before the corporation went to casual dress for all employees, Willie G. shucked

suits for leather vests, jeans, and the kinds of opulent personal accessories popular with many past and present H-D owners. Since he puts lots of miles on bikes year round, the gear serves its purpose. While he is all business in the design center, he is affable and laid back on the boardwalk at Daytona or on the main street of Sturgis.

He really likes being with Harley people, he says, since it's his hobby as well as theirs. He considers them a fun-loving group of people. The motorcycles attract devotion, a dedication that he admires.

Willie G.'s own dedication shows through, at work or during long hours spent enjoyably in the saddle. A few years back, returning from the annual rally in Sturgis, he stopped at a Minnesota wayside with an idea. Rummaging in a trash receptacle for the cleanest piece of paper he could find, he set to work frantically with a pencil, recalling what he had seen and liked at the bike event. He worked to design a look that was possible for stylists and engineers to create. That brief stop to sketch at a picnic table resulted in the Sturgis model. Not a bad day's work for a guy who showed up with his crayons and has chosen to stay.

The motorcycle company heir has been recognized for his abilities both inside the company and out. The Harley-Davidson product development center, which opened for business in 1997, was named after the vice president. The $25 million facility is filled with laboratories and testing facilities, boasting such equipment as a one-of-a-kind vehicle simulator. At the end of 1997, *Motor Cycle News*, an English publication, named Willie G. the winner of its lifetime achievement award. He was chosen, they said, "because he has been a marvelous ambassador for the sport throughout his lifetime and is one of the motorcycle industry's greatest assets."

Back in 1982, when smart money was steering clear of America's only remaining motorcycle maker, someone asked a laid-off employee if Willie G. was good or bad for Harley-Davidson. The more the company progresses, the dumber that question becomes. Willie G. is the soul of a huge, hugely successful corporation. Yet he is human: He has been fighting a potentially fatal illness for some time. When he retires, which could happen any time during or after the 2003 shindig, his talented and magnetic presence will be an indescribable loss.

Cycles and Stars

Harley-Davidson has always been associated with an incredible number of celebrities who either proved they had made it by buying one or more Harleys, or were conned into posing for some kind of publicity stunt. Sylvester Stallone, an H-D owner, may have said it all in *Rocky II*. Heavyweight boxing hopeful Rocky Balboa is asked by the press why he wants a return match after the beating administered by the champ. Rocky's only audible reason is that the money won in the fight will enable him to buy a motorcycle. Muhammad Ali once warned Joe Frazier, "Motorcycles is for crazy people." Later, Ali bought a Harley-Davidson.

Perhaps ownership among the stars provides the same kind of rush it gives everyone who has ever owned or ridden a Harley. It is also one of the only ways the most famous actors, singers, and athletes can assume a little welcome anonymity. Pulling on a full-face helmet, they can ride among their adoring public without fear of being recognized. A few years ago, however, a fellow from Montana inverted the equation. He used a motorcycle to escape anonymity, becoming the most famous celebrity rider of all time. His name: Evel Knievel.

Evel Knievel

Robert Knievel grew up like a lot of us. He played a good game of high school football and hockey, tried his hand at rodeo, held an AMA amateur competition license, chased a lot of women and caught a few, sold insurance, even worked as a private detective. But success seemed beyond his grasp until he hit on the idea of jumping objects—cars, trucks, fountains, canyons, you name it—on a motorcycle. Evel, as he came to be known, worked the West Coast in the beginning, accruing cash in direct proportion to the size or number of objects a track promoter or county fair director wanted him to leap. By 1968 he had cleared most possible obstacles and, despite many broken bones, may have thought himself indestructible. He announced that he would leap the Grand Canyon. An Indian tribe and the federal government prevented Evel from performing this one and one-half mile jump (or plunge), so he continued to thrill crowds while he waited for another ultimate trick to come along.

The public paid millions of dollars to watch Evel clear 21 cars at the defunct Ontario (California) Speedway, sail over another large number of vehicles before crashing into a wall in the Astrodome, and fly above the Caesar's Palace fountain. The Las Vegas stunt, next to the assassination of President John F. Kennedy, may be the most widely seen strip of film in history. It shows Evel taking off, landing badly, and going end-over-end, seemingly forever, across a parking lot. Bones snap and poke his leathers and skin singes on the asphalt as speed rips at man and riderless machine. Following numerous stays in the hospital, Evel emerged, believing more strongly in his invincibility and in the righteousness of his cause (whatever that may have been).

Harley-Davidson entered the picture in 1970, providing Evel with a modest fee, technical expertise, and, what he wanted most, an All-American machine. It is more than coin-

Chicago's Medinah Temple Shrine features this 13-man team.

Tony Hulman (right), the late owner of the Indianapolis Motor Speedway, accepted this restored Peashooter racer from William H. Davidson and Willie G. in 1964. Hulman rode a Harley while a student at Yale. (Indianapolis Motor Speedway)

Two-wheeled Stunts

Knievel is not the only fellow out there who has ridden motorcycles to fame, if not fortune. Back in the 1920s and 1930s, a brief and nutty fad involved running one's bike into and—the rider hoped—through a wall of wood. These daredevils performed at county fairs and were regarded much the same as the contemporary barnstormers in their rickety airplanes. The first documented board bash on a Harley-Davidson was performed in Texas in 1932 by a Texas Tech student named Daisy May Hendrich. He proved life could be hard for a boy named Daisy May by slamming his H-D repeatedly through inch-thick boards constructed in a 6 x 6-foot wall. Another H-D rider, Adam Beyer of Fond du Lac, Wisconsin, entertained folks up north in a similar vein.

J. R. Bruce of Wooster, Ohio, outdid both Hendrich and Beyer by setting the wooden wall aflame before he rammed successfully through it. While Putt Mossman was running up and down a ladder mounted to his H-D as it traveled at 40 mph, a resident of Valparaiso, Chile, *really* upped the ante. Juan Maliu climbed aboard his Milwaukee marvel and pleased a crowd by roaring intentionally through a wall of plate glass. Prudently, most U.S. stunt riders settled for flaming wood.

Among them was the late Harry Molenaar, for more than 50 years a Harley dealer in Hammond, Indiana, south of Chicago. Molenaar and a friend performed flaming wall crashes in the 1930s as part of a thrill show featured throughout northern Indiana. On one particular evening, following a day of rain, the grandstand was packed as Harry and his pal lined up to do their promised simultaneous side-by-side crash through a pair of flaming walls. The friend noticed that 2 x 4s were being used and that the boards were so rain-soaked they were not turning into ashes, which had been the key to their success so far. He told Harry that he felt ill and that the show must go on without him. Molenaar promised the throng that he would eliminate both burning walls, kicked over his bike, and aimed for wall No. 1. "I hit it and it knocked me cold. But I stayed on the bike and woke up half way around the track," he recalled. He got the bike

cidence that Evel and the entire H-D lineup took on the stars-and-stripes motif simultaneously and in earnest. The deal garnered reams of publicity for the company, since everybody from silk screeners to toymakers was reproducing Evel's likeness and his bike. The company even made sure that the AMF logo was on board Knievel's jet-powered bike as it sailed off for a test run in 1973 and fizzled during the real Snake River Canyon jump attempt in 1974. Harley-Davidson and Evel diplomatically parted company after the stunt man was convicted of beating a former business associate, Sheldon Saltman, with a baseball bat. Saltman had co-written a book that poked holes in the Knievel legend. Saltman suffered a broken left arm and right wrist—small change for a daredevil but enough for Saltman to sue successfully.

Today, Evel Knievel lives modestly, dividing his time between painting—he's a decent artist—and his son Robby's stunt-riding career. The late H-D President Charlie Thompson pointed out that, despite his reputation, Evel abided by every agreement he made with the company.

aligned once again and roared down the muddy straight-away toward wall No. 2. That collision gave him a concussion but he said, the crowd loved it.

Not all tricks with a motorcycle are so dangerous. People who have seen a cadre of Shriners perform on their Hogs know that speed is not necessary for a good show. "The Masons do the work and the Shriners have the fun," says Freddy Ephrem of Jacksonville, Florida, a Shriner who has been involved for years with Harleys. Ephrem says the southeastern U.S. is the most active area in the country for motorized Shrine drill teams, adding that the most impressive unit may come out of Nashville.

Shrine On

Nashville's Al Menah Shrine has 16 members aboard H-D Shrine bikes (similar in appearance to police bikes, minus sirens, red lights, and radios). Two years after its creation in 1960, the Al Menah Motor Corps began winning awards and hasn't stopped. Temple member Jim Hester relates that Al Menah has won one or more first, second, or third place trophies in every regional, national, or international competition each year. The "finals" for such competition includes rigid inspection for cleanliness and uniformity by no less than the U.S. Marines. Routines are worked out in long, arduous hours on a drill field. Any organization that can pass military muster must find the numerous parades and other civic functions easy by comparison.

If thousands have seen the Shriners, millions have watched Harley-Davidsons as they were put through their paces in the movies. It's no coincidence that the naughty biker image was spread by overly dramatic films and television, eager to show a fringe element of motorcycling that may never have existed in the numbers Hollywood believed. Harley-Davidson's first recorded appearance on the silver screen was in 1926, when Christy comedy star Bill Dooley cantered along on a JD in a silent, slapstick film with a long forgotten title.

California's Highway Patrol acquired motorcycles in 1930, and Columbia pictures responded in 1933 with a movie entitled *State Trooper*. A less-than-memorable production starring Bob Artman, thousands nevertheless viewed the film, since the movies were the primary entertainment of the Depression. A bit later, Movietone newsreels delivered brief, well-edited news capsules, among them "selected short subjects" that accompanied the feature. The Movietoners knew that a strip of film was worth a thousand words; all of them contained, between views of Franklin Roosevelt or Hitler or Churchill, sports action scenes. These seemed to be either some poor soul jumping barrels on ice skates or jumping off a hillclimbing Harley-Davidson as the front wheel kicked skyward.

Going Hollywood

Movie actor Victor McLaglen formed a precision drill team in 1937 that performed for a number of years. At about the same time, an enterprising *Photoplay* magazine photographer named Hyman Fink began furnishing *The Enthusiast*

Not all drill teams are Shriners, as this photo proves. The Schuylkill County Pennsylvania MC Drill Team favors dissimilar H-Ds and similar white shirts with black vests.

with snapshots of movie stars and starlets on one or more H-Ds. Jimmy Durante, Ward Bond, Robert Taylor, Robert Young, Clark Gable, Tyrone Power, Preston Foster, Gene Tierney, Van Johnson, Keenan Wynn, Marlene Dietrich, Andy Devine. Riders and non-riders alike were snared by Fink's lens. Captions showing the actresses made no bones about the fact that the accompanying photos were publicity ploys. The actors were said to be doing things like saving World War II-rationed gasoline or memorizing lines for a movie as they rode. Many actors, such as Keenan Wynn, actually were avid cyclists. A Hollywood group, "the Three" began slowly but built momentum. Unfortunately, numerous Harley-Davidsons could be seen in Stanley Kubrick's *The Wild One*, starring Marlon

Country singer Tanya Tucker is one of numerous celebrity owners. (Ian Vaughan)

Former racecar driver Bob Bondurant gets around his California driving school on a Sportster. (Buzz Buzzelli)

Brando. Although the company was silent on this somewhat accurate portrayal of the sacking of Hollister, California, in 1947 by a motorcycle gang, dealers to this day blame the movie for cycling's lingering bad-boy image. Ironically, Brando rode a Triumph in the film. To the average American, however, a bike was a bike—something nice people avoided. An MGM movie at about the same time, *Code Two*, with Keenan Wynn, Ralph Meeker, and Robert Horton, failed to make a counterbalancing impression. The three portrayed cycle cops with less verve, apparently, than the superstar Brando in his role as the leader of the pack. Rank-and-file cyclists tried to change the negative image in several ways. The Lexington (Kentucky) Eagles Motorcycle Club put on a ride in 1957 for the March of Dimes and several clubs staged a "blessing of the motorcycles" before taking off on tour. Nevertheless, the damage had been done in front of millions of moviegoers.

Many of the Harley-Davidsons seen in the movies (such as the early twin ridden by the late Jimmy Stewart in the Lindbergh story, *The Spirit of St. Louis*) came from Bud Ekins. The former desert racer and friend of the late Steve McQueen has provided bikes for films and for such television series as *Nichols*, which starred James Garner astride an H-D single. Most of the cycles seen in 1960s films were straight from the factory. They included everything from Edd (Kooky) Byrnes's 1960 Topper scooter to Robert (*Baretta*) Blake's Electra Glide as late as 1973. The latter may be the only bike ever to have a movie named after it, since the story of the Arizona state patrolman was titled *Electra Glide in Blue*. Meanwhile, the success of *Easy Rider*, the 1969 Peter Fonda/Dennis Hopper/Jack Nicholson low-budget film that became a blockbuster, spawned several cheap imitations. American-International pumped out a slew of forgettable flicks, among them *The Wild Angels* and *Run, Angel, Run*. Drive-in screens across the country were filled with the thunder of choppers and the biker lifestyle.

Racer as Star

Fortunately, a pair of Hollywood productions made up for the American-International films. *On Any Sunday*, a documentary covering most aspects of motorcycle competition, featured a modest, swarthy, handsome young man new to the screen: Mert Lawwill. Harley-Davidson's top factory rider at the time (1970), Lawwill was highlighted throughout an entire AMA season, riding at Daytona, riding at San Jose, riding in his van from one track to the next. The production was a success because motorcyclists saw it numerous times, and the image it projected had nothing to do with outlaws. An effort with even more impact was *Then Came Bronson*, starring Michael Parks. Once a week in 1969 and 1970, the televised roar of a Sportster echoed in living rooms across the land. A sweet-tempered drifter coped with life on the road and the series was successful enough to survive the ratings war for 78 episodes. Cyclists were quick to point out that the lead character more closely resembled the average rider than did any previous effort from Tinseltown.

Even Evel Knievel got into the act, initially with George Hamilton playing the role of the infamous stunt man, then acting in his own production. Evel modestly titled his film *Viva Knievel*.

While the acting is mediocre, the picture, and Lauren Hutton, are visual treats to this day on late-night TV.

All of the films on earth have had less impact than television, which continues to shape the points of view of many Americans. Television, for a while, anyway, somehow saw a link between riding a motorcycle and outrageous and contemptible behavior. The portrayals were aired, riders complained to the networks, and not much happened. Fortunately, most Americans today know there is no correlation between riding a motorcycle and hunger for pre-teen children or road-killed game. With that in mind, here is a list of famous folks who, at one time or another, owned or rode a Harley-Davidson.

Michael Parks aboard his Sportster during filming of the 1969–1970 prime time television series, **Then Came Bronson.**

Kareem Abdul-Jabbar
Aerosmith
Muhammad Ali
Paul Anderson
Ann-Margret
Dan Aykroyd
The BoDeans
Bob Bondurant
Sonny Bono
Terry Bradshaw
James Caan
Earl Campbell
Sir Malcolm Campbell
Bobby Caradine
Kim Cantrell
Otis Chandler
Cheap Whiskey Band
Cher
Eric Clapton
Roy Clark
Wayne Cochran
David Allan Coe
David Copperfield
Dave Cowans
Loch David Crane
David Crosby
"Wild Bill" Cummings
Glenn Curtis
Charlie Daniels Band
Phil Delta
Jack Dempsey
Desert Rose Band
Andy Devine
Neil Diamond
Doobie Brothers
Buster Douglas
James Drury
Fred Dryer
Bob Dylan
Clint Eastwood
Foghat
Peter Fonda
Malcolm Forbes
Harrison Ford
Preston Foster
Russ Francis
Joe Frazier
Daniel Frohman

Clark Gable
John Gardner
Leif Garrett
Bobby Goldsboro
Barry Goldwater, Jr.
The Grateful Dead
Nick Halaris
Goldie Hawn
Isaac Hayes
Howard Hessman
Hulk Hogan
Larry Holmes
Tony Hulman
James Hylton
INXS
Billy Idol
Michael Jackson
Reggie Jackson
Lew Jenkins
Bruce Jenner
Billy Joel
Don Johnson
Alan Jones
Steve Jones
Jack Kelly
Lorenzo Lamas
Jay Leno
Charles Lindbergh
Howie Long
Victor McLaglen
Barbara McQueen
Al McGuire
John Mellencamp
George Michael
Billy Mitchell
Motley Crue
Willie Nelson
Olivia Newton-John
Ken Norton
Crown Prince Olaf
Roy Orbison
Michael Parks
Dan Pastorini
John Payne
David Pearson
Steve Perry
Kyle Petty
Joe Piscopo

Robert Plant
Poison
Tyrone Power
Elvis Presley
Priscilla Presley
Wade Preston
Peter Reckell
Lou Reed
Burt Reynolds
Roy Rogers
Mickey Rourke
Kurt Russell
Charles Russell
Neal Schon
Arnold Schwarzenegger
Brian Setzer
Charlie Sexton
Wilber Shaw
Roger Smith
Tommy Smothers
Bruce Springsteen
Ken Stabler
Robert Stafford
Sylvester Stallone
Starship
Steppenwolf
Andrew Stevens
Gil Stratton, Jr.
Stray Cats
Barbra Streisand
Elizabeth Taylor
Robert Taylor
The Fabulous Thunderbirds
Paul Tracy
Tanya Tucker
U2
Eddie Van Halen
Stevie Ray Vaughn
Visa
Hershel Walker
Mike Weaver
White Lion
Hank Williams, Jr.
Paul Winchell
Keenan Wynn
Robert Young
Robin Yount

Chapter 12

Present and Future

This is the golden age of the motorcycle. If you cannot find a bike you like, it is because you do not like bikes. All motorcycles are good, making cycling much less of a chore than in the old days. When the dozen or so employees who made up the buyback team took control of Harley-Davidson in the early 1980s, their products were among the least innovative, least reliable motorcycles. Their mission was to greatly improve the bikes while keeping the company's fiscal head above water.

The odds were not good, but buyback members had a few things going for them. First, customers were among the most loyal anywhere. H-D needed to improve before those customers tired of defending poor quality and either switched brands or found a new hobby. Second, the buy-backers had the courage to go deeply in debt in order to make a better machine. They put their hearts and everything they had, and then some, into reviving the company. Third, they knew what had to be done. Fourth, and maybe most important, the fellows took control of the company when a new mood was sweeping the land.

Ronald Reagan was elected president in 1980 and the manic drive for high-tech gizmos slowed. If Harley-Davidson was tied to the past, the Japanese were addicted to whatever lay just over the horizon. They copied H-D looks, but in strange ways that combined faux nostalgia with space-age engine mysteries. Japanese cruisers from the early 1980s remain tough to look at in detail. Their efforts failed to attract most Harley loyalists. Those retro folks went back to buying American with renewed vigor.

A Better Engine

Development had been under way on a new and better V-twin. The company borrowed heavily to bring the new motor to market in 1984. Despite production delays, the Evolution engine proved to be a more reliable, less seepy means of power than anything Harley-Davidson had previously offered. Other improvements ranged from the introduction of extended-life belt final drive to touring accessories that finally opened, closed, or locked, as they should. Riders who were sitting on the fence hopped back into the Harley-Davidson corral.

Vaughn L. Beals. (David K. Wright)

Willie G. discusses a detail with Louis Netz. (David K. Wright)

Willie G. Davidson, a buyback member, continued to style the bikes in innovative, old-becomes-new ways. New models were introduced, but not before they were better than whatever they replaced. Five-speed transmissions spread throughout the line as the decade progressed. In a brilliant marketing move, the company introduced the Harley Owners Group (H.O.G.) in 1983. Not only was this dealer-centered club a great way to keep customers coming back, it was the safest way yet to make white-collar riders believe they were bike gang members—cost accountants unchained! H.O.G. camaraderie also helped stifle complaints. Better, H-D realized, to have riders inside the garage pissing out than outside the garage pissing in.

Pared to the bone, the company made it through the recession of the early 1980s, only to be confronted by Citicorp. The financial behemoth did not like the numbers Harley-Davidson was showing and threatened to force the company into bankruptcy by calling a huge loan. That loan had been invested in expertise, materials, and machinery; there was no way to immediately pay it off. Was this the end?

A very early rendering by Willie G. Davidson on the back of his father's company letterhead. (William H. Davidson collection)

The late Charlie Thompson, left, former H-D president and Vaughn Beals, former chairman, aboard their 1982 Tour Glides. They rode the bikes from the Canadian Pacific to Florida to test the new oil-control package. (David K. Wright)

It could have been. Key buyback members including Richard Teerlink, then chief financial officer and treasurer, later president and chief executive officer, successfully returned the company to public ownership by offering two million shares of common stock and $70 million in high-yield notes in the summer of 1986. Led by then-Chairman Vaughn Beals, the buyback team suddenly had the money it lacked a few years earlier. The empty pockets had prevented further development, with Germany's Porsche, of a V-4 tentatively called the Nova. In the last 15 years, very little else has been canceled due to lack of money.

Mr. and Mrs. Willie G. lead the buyback team, plus wives and others, away from a fuel stop during the ride from York back to Milwaukee in July 1981. (People)

Millionaire Riders?

In searching for dramatic information for this final chapter, I ran across a statistic too good to buzz past. People who purchased $10,000 in Harley-Davidson, Inc. stock the day it was offered in 1986, and continuously reinvested it in H-D, are millionaires today. Ten grand was a lot back then—more than the price of most bikes—but it was not a prohibitive amount. What is more likely, the average Harley addict threw a few bucks at a couple of shares for sentimental reasons and now has stock worth about ten grand.

This great leap forward, which involved several two-for-one stock splits, plus dividends, may be more meaningful to those brave and loyal workers who stayed with Harley-Davidson in the early 1980s. These employees, regardless of whether they are buyback members or clerical workers, deserve every cent they have realized. Once Harley-Davidson, Inc. increased in value, it lured talented folks from respected colleges, universities, and other corporations.

As of mid-2002, only three of the dozen buyback members remained with the company. They were President Jeff Bleustein, Willie G. Davidson, and attorney Tim Hoelter.

Vaughn Beals, the head of the buyback operation and one-time chairman, is retired. So is Richard Teerlink, former chief financial officer and former president. Former president Charlie Thompson died of heart problems a few years back. Most of the others are finally enjoying the results of their labors. Willie G., styling vice president, probably will put his crayons in the drawer after the centennial. Tim Hoelter, head of legal, probably enjoys chasing down illegal use of Harley trademarks and service marks so much that he may remain in his spot for some time.

How fat have the buyback guys gotten off the new, highly successful, Harley-Davidson? In the fall of 2001, Chairman Jeff Bleustein sold 240,888 shares of the company's stock. The chunk of dough he received amounted to more than $12 million. The stock was peddled "to diversify his holdings," according to a corporate spokesperson. Before the sale, Bleustein owned 2.7 million shares, worth approximately $126.5 million. He was down to a mere $114 million in H-D stock after the sale. Yet, who among us begrudges any of the buyback members his success?

The Juneau Avenue facility in Milwaukee, headquarters of Harley-Davidson, Inc. (David K. Wright)

Looking down the road at Harley-Davidson's second century, it is difficult to perceive the future. Like the first 100 years, it may be fraught with peril one day and triumphant the next. Let's look at the problems first. That way, this book will have a happy ending.

Aftermarket firms including V-Twin Manufacturing offer frames and chassis parts with a Harley look to them. (David K. Wright)

Harley-Davidson's Dilemma

The most pressing problem is rider age. Loyal H-D riders tend to be older, and the oldest among them own touring bikes, known as baggers. Honda Gold Wings and other Japanese machines threaten H-D tourers, though reverence for H-D survives thick and thin. Look for the 60-degree V-Rod motor in bagger and cruiser models in the very near future. It won't show up in an introductory bike; the cost would make the machine anything but introductory.

The age thing and the source of new riders may be related to TV. Cable television coverage of AMA and international roadracing has created ongoing demand for sporty Japanese motorcycles, as well as Ducati and Aprilia. More than 50,000 fans showed up at Road America in Elkhart Lake, Wisconsin, in 2001 for roadracing, compared to maybe 20,000 at the famed AMA Springfield Mile event that same summer in Illinois. Right now, no Harley-Davidsons compete against the Superbikes.

Many young riders gravitate toward Supercross-type off-road machines and crotch rockets. Again, the Japanese have this market cornered. Perhaps the most encouraging numbers for H-D are those of the female persuasion. From 1990 to 2000, H-D female owners increased from 4 percent to 9 percent. Where this figure may top out is anyone's guess. A significant percentage of owners of the Buell Blast are women who ride with husbands or boyfriends. However, a dealer has to sell several Blasts to realize as much income as one cruiser.

Another dilemma facing Harley-Davidson is cost. Of 21 different Harley models identified in a magazine in late 2001, only the 4 Sportsters carried price tags of less than five figures. Among the bikes exceeding $10,000, 10 cost more than $15,000. In contrast, only 6 of 20 Honda models carry a five-figure tag. The costliest H-D, the Ultra Classic Electra Glide, at $18,980, is far less advanced than Honda's $17,499, six-cylinder Gold Wing. A related problem is that some dealers choose to bump the price of a new bike. Are you willing to pay $23,000 for a Dyna Glide or $26,000 for a V-Rod? These prices were seen at a dealership in the spring of 2002. Is the "pose factor" of a Harley that strong?

By the winter of 2001–2002, Harley-Davidson was aware that there was a recession out there. To quote George Fisher, an investment expert for Zacks.com, "Harley-Davidson is showing signs of a classic recession in its business. Prices and premiums over manufacturer's suggested retail price charged by dealers are dropping, waiting lists for new bikes are evaporating, and the gap between supply and demand is shrinking. Financing offered by H-D is also starting to take its toll as provisions for bad debt have doubled in the recent quarter … HDI (stock) seems overpriced based on a slowdown in its business and credit fundamentals." At the time, the stock was worth about $53 per share.

Any disruptive biker problem is a Harley-Davidson problem, and not just because the offenders almost always ride the Milwaukee brand. One of the more recent problems occurred in Laughlin, Nevada, in April 2002 at the 20th anniversary of a popular river run. Members of two gangs confronted each other in Harrah's casino. In the wake of gunshots and knife fights, three people died, a dozen were injured, and 100 were arrested. Lest anyone believe the Harley/gang connection is total coincidence, they should check out the big prize giveaways at the event: a V-Rod, a Road King, a Night Train, and a Fat Boy. The event was sponsored in part by Harley Davidson, unlike the Long Island Pagan/Hells Angels fight mentioned earlier.

Fascinated fans look over the new V-Rod at its introduction. (David K. Wright)

Here is a Victory, made by the same folks who created the Polaris snowmobile. Note that, like the Indian, the Victory is offered only with a V-twin. (David K. Wright)

The New York Times interpreted the East Coast event, which drew Pagans from as far away as Pennsylvania and New Hampshire, as the start of a war over turf. Long Island was Pagan territory until 1998, when authorities arrested 30 club members in connection with shaking down and threatening area owners of topless dance clubs. In addition to the Angels and the Pagans, other clubs with national reputa-

A **vibration-free motor, dazzling paint, and accessories that fit mark this 2002 Harley-Davidson.** (David K. Wright)

tions include the Bandidos and the Outlaws. A number of biker gangs across the country raise money through extortion or such dangerous endeavors as methamphetamine sales and distribution.

Such goings-on worry the company, but not as much as an incident closer to home. At a cycle rally in Milwaukee in the summer of 2001, as H-D President Jeff Bleustein was introduced to the throng, some dude went into a screaming, incomprehensible riff on motorcycles, Vietnam, and more. He was taken away, but his performance cast a pall over the crowd of riders and corporate folks. Is there an Altamont-type scene out there, waiting to take place during one of Harley-Davidson's worldwide 2003 parties?

Speaking of parties, the 2003 celebration may tell the company more than it wants to know about where the customer base is headed. By now, the Doobie Brothers, doobies, "Magic Carpet Ride," *Easy Rider*, "Easyriders," beer guzzling, Sturgis, Daytona Beach, old ladies, swiney leathers, and swiney people have become clichés. How does the company entertain geezer riders without making those in atten-

Bikes such as this Softail Springer are among today's best-selling Harley-Davidsons. (David K. Wright)

dance look and feel geezerish? In what may have been a telling form of entertainment, a large crowd gathered behind the H-D display in Daytona in 2002 to watch young guys hurtle high above the crowd on motocross bikes.

To summarize, Harley-Davidson would give much of what it owns (they're called development dollars) to produce a bike that would appeal to kids. Don't look for anything too radical—H-D will offer something non-motorcycle related at the same time McDonald's stops peddling food. Nevertheless, a new form of youth-oriented transportation, sold through a worldwide network of dealers, sure would be nice.

The Firebolt, along with the Blast, are said to be the two Buell models meeting sales expectations. Harley-Davidson, Inc., now owns Buell, which was begun by racing H-D engineer Erik Buell. (David K. Wright)

The Good News

While the company has made millions, Japan's economy has been underwhelming for the last several years. No one in Japan will adjust prices radically as long as production stagnates. The decision by Honda and Kawasaki to produce their bikes in the U.S. probably was a smart one. A generation from now, no one may know or care if a bike has Asian ancestry. If you doubt that, look at which cars are the best sellers in the U.S. each year. They ain't the winners on the NASCAR circuit, where brand allegiance is almost Harley-like.

Right now, there are two other domestically made motorcycles with traditional V-twin rumble, style, and price. Neither provides much competition. The Indian, assembled in California, offers an engine of its own design or an S&S engine that looks like the top and bottom of a Harley engine from two different eras. Polaris Industries' Victory, assembled in Iowa, also may be here to stay, since there are numerous dealers and the company is stable, but sales totaled only around 1,200 bikes a year recently. Noble yet futile experiments such as revival of the Excelsior Henderson nameplate apparently have fallen by the wayside. With no heritage (today's Indians are made in California, not Massachusetts), it is difficult to tell whether domestic bikes will ever pose a threat.

Which brings up another point: Why is Harley-Davidson so committed to exports? In 2000, for example, 45,775, or 22 percent, of the 204,592 H-Ds produced were sold offshore. The reason for this is as simple as it is effective. Recessions tend to hit countries differently and at different times. Should the U.S. economy go into the kind of tailspin seen during the early 1980s, Harley-Davidson can sell the bikes in places where no recession exists. Equally important, more and more of the world can afford a big ride. Italy, for example, now has an average per capita income of $21,500. With buying power like that, there are several million potential H-D owners in one country alone.

Harley-Davidson, in the last 20 years, has provided gainful employment for thousands of people all over the U.S. When aftermarket parts and positions are factored in, H-D has helped create thousands of jobs that either had gone

Two Daytona visitors take a Springer for a demo ride.
(David K. Wright)

away temporarily or were entirely new. Their suppliers are many and varied, which also results in jobs, prosperity, stability, and so forth. The facilities in Milwaukee, York, Kansas City, and elsewhere have become cornerstones of those communities. Small wonder H-D's labor unions are sufficiently content to sign long-term contracts.

The company spends lots of its cash for good causes. Thirty motorcycles and $1 million were provided to New York City and the American Red Cross, respectively, in the wake of the September 11 tragedy. Veterans' groups, muscular dystrophy victims, and similar organizations have benefited from H-D largesse. On a grass-roots level, many dealers run smaller but equally sincere versions of the Love Ride, designed to raise money for one good cause or another in their communities.

Speaking of dealers, they remain the company's best ambassadors. They and their employees are almost uniformly friendly, capable, decent people. Sure, some may mark up the price of their bikes excessively, but a number of the retail price-plus guys either suffered through some lean years in the 1970s or they have a monthly mortgage so big it's scary. H-D has helped dealers perfect websites, sales pitches, the look and feel and uniformity of dealerships, even the kinds of information a customer hears piped in as he enters the store. The success dealers have realized could not happen to a better bunch of people.

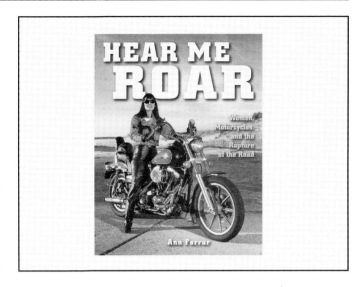

Denney Colt and her Low Rider on the cover of Hear Me Roar: Women, Motorcycles, and the Rapture of the Road. *Harley-Davidson believes that in the future more women will ride.* (Whitehorse Press)

The Electra Glide Classic is a classic highway tourer – new for 2003 is a 40-watt per channel CD player. Also for 2003, all of the FLH models, from Road King to Electra Glide Classic, benefit from larger and stronger swingarms, a wider-diameter rear axle, and a stiffer chassis for a more controlled ride.
(Dain Gingerelli)

Appendix A

H-D Models 1908-2003

This information was copied from Harley-Davidson factory archives with assistance from retired H-D dealer Conrad Schlemmer. Please note that no similar printed information exists concerning 1903–1907 models. Harley-Davidson, Inc., declined to provide model information for the years 1984–2002; a Harley-Davidson dealer provided these specs.

1908
Model 4: Single-cylinder, single-belt drive, 28-inch wheels, battery ignition, 3.9 horsepower, 3-1/8-inch bore, motor numbers under 2500.

1909
Model 5: Single-cylinder, single-belt drive, 28-inch wheels, battery ignition, 4.34 horsepower, 3-5/16-inch bore, 4-inch stroke, 35 ci, motor numbers 2500–4200.

Model 5A: Single-cylinder, single-belt drive, 28-inch wheels, magneto ignition, 4.34 horsepower, 3-5/16-inch bore, 4-inch stroke, 35 ci, motors numbers 2500–4200.

Model 5C: Single-cylinder, single-belt drive, 26-inch wheels, magneto ignition, 4.34 horsepower, 3-5/16-inch bore, 4-inch stroke, 35 ci, motors number 2500–4200.

Model 5D: Single-cylinder, single-belt drive, 28-inch wheels, magneto ignition, 6-1/2 horsepower, 3-inch bore, 3-1/2-inch stroke, 49.48 ci, motor numbers 2500–4200.

1910
Model 6: Single-cylinder, single-belt drive, 28-inch wheels, battery ignition, 4.34 horsepower, 3-5/16-inch bore, 4-inch stroke, 35 ci, motor numbers 4200–7600.

Model 6A: Single-cylinder, single-belt drive, 28-inch wheels, magneto ignition, 4.34 horsepower, 3-5/16-inch bore, 4-inch stroke, 35 ci, motor numbers 4200–7600.

Model 6B: Single-cylinder, single-belt drive, 26-inch wheels, battery ignition, 4.34 horsepower, 3-5/16-inch bore, 4-inch stroke, 35 ci, motor numbers 4200–7600.

Model 6C: Single-cylinder, single-belt drive, 26-inch wheels, magneto ignition, 4.34 horsepower, 3-5/16-inch bore, 4-inch stroke, 35 ci, motor numbers 4200–7600.

Model 6D: Twin cylinder, single-belt drive, 28-inch wheels, magneto ignition, 6-1/2 horsepower, 3-inch bore, 3-1/2 inch stroke, 49.48 ci, motor numbers 4200–7600.

1911
Model 7: Single-cylinder, single-belt drive, 28-inch wheels, battery ignition, 4.34 horsepower, 3-5/16-inch bore, 4-inch stroke, 35 ci, motor numbers 7600–10000, followed by letter A.

Model 7A: Single-cylinder, single-belt drive, 28-inch wheels, magneto ignition, 4.34 horsepower, 3-5/16-inch bore, 4-inch stroke, 35 ci, motor numbers 7600–10000, followed by letter A.

Model 7B: Single-cylinder, single-belt drive, 26-inch wheels, battery ignition, 4.34 horsepower, 3-5/16-inch bore, 4-inch stroke, 35 ci, motor numbers 7600–10000, followed by letter A.

Model 7C: Single-cylinder, single-belt drive, 26-inch wheels, magneto ignition, 4.34 horsepower, 3-5/16-inch bore, 4-inch stroke, 35 ci, motor numbers 7600–10000, followed by letter A.

Model 7D: Twin-cylinder, single-belt drive, 28-inch wheels, magneto ignition, 6-1/2 horsepower, 3-inch bore, 3-1/2-inch stroke, 49.48 ci, motor number 7600–10000, followed by letter A.

1912

Model 8: Single-cylinder, single-belt drive, 28-inch wheels, battery ignition, 4.34 horsepower, 3-5/16-inch bore, 4-inch stroke, 35 ci, motor numbers followed by letter AB, BA, or B.

Model X8: Single-cylinder, single-belt drive, 28-inch wheels, battery ignition, free-wheel control (clutch), 4.34 horsepower, 3-5/16-inch bore, 4-inch stroke, 35 ci motor, numbers followed by letters AB, BA, or B.

Model X8A: Single-cylinder, single-belt drive, 28-inch wheels, magneto ignition, free-wheel control (clutch), 4.34 horsepower, 3-5/16-inch bore, 4-inch stroke, 35 ci motor, numbers followed by letters AB, BA, or B.

Model 8D: Twin-cylinder, single-belt drive, 28-inch wheels, magneto ignition, 6-1/2 horsepower, 3-inch bore, 3-1/2-inch stroke, 49.48 ci, motor numbers followed by letter D.

Model X8D: Twin-cylinder, single-belt drive, 28 in wheels, magneto ignition, free-wheel control (clutch), 6-1/2 horsepower, 3-inch bore, 3-1/2-inch stroke, 49.48 ci, motor number followed by letter D.

Model X8E: Twin-cylinder, single-belt drive, 7 to 8 horsepower, 3-5/16-inch bore, 3-1/2-inch stroke, 60.34 ci, motor number followed by letter E.

1913

Model 9A: Single-cylinder, single-belt drive, 28-inch wheels, magneto ignition, 3-5/16-inch bore, 4-inch stroke, 35 ci, motor numbers followed by letter C.

Model 9B: Single-cylinder, single-chain drive, 28-inch wheels, magneto ignition, 4.34 horsepower, 3-5/16-inch bore, 4-inch stroke, 35 ci, motor numbers followed by letter D.

Model 9E: Twin-cylinder, single-belt drive, 28-inch wheels, magneto ignition, 8.68 horsepower, 3-inch bore, 3-1/2-inch stroke, 49.48 ci.

Model 9G: Twin-cylinder, single-belt drive, 28-inch wheels, magneto ignition, free-wheel control (clutch), 8.68 horsepower, 3-inch bore, 3-1/2-inch stroke, 49.48 ci.

1914

Model 10A: Single-cylinder, single-belt drive, 28-inch wheels, magneto ignition, 4.34 horsepower, 3-5/16-inch bore, 4-inch stroke, 35 ci, motor number followed by letters CF.

Model 10B: Single-cylinder, single-chain drive, 28-inch wheels, 4.34 horsepower, 3-5/16-inch bore, 4-inch stroke, 35 ci, motor number followed by letters DG or D, single-speed.

Model 10C: Single-cylinder, single-chain drive, 28-inch wheels, magneto ignition, 4.34 horsepower, 3-5/16-inch bore, 4-inch stroke, 35 ci, motor number followed by letters DG or D, two-speed.

Model 10E: Twin-cylinder, twin-chain drive, 28-inch wheels, magneto ignition, 8.68 horsepower, 3-inch bore, 3-1/2-inch stroke, 49.48 ci.

Model 10F: Twin-cylinder, twin-chain drive, 28-inch wheels, magneto ignition, 8.68 horsepower, 3-inch bore, 3-1/2-inch stroke, 49.48 ci.

Model 10G: Twin-cylinder, twin-chain drive, 8.68 horsepower, magneto ignition, 3-5/16-inch bore, 3-1/2-inch stroke, 60.34 ci.

1915

Model 11B: Single-cylinder, single-chain drive, 28-inch wheels, magneto ignition, 4.34 horsepower, 3-5/16-inch bore, 4-inch stroke, 35 ci, motor number followed by letter J, single-speed.

Model 11C: Single-cylinder, single-chain drive, 28-inch wheels, magneto ignition, 4.34 horsepower, 3-5/16-inch bore, 4-inch stroke, 35 ci, motor number followed by letter L, two-speed.

Model 11E: Twin-cylinder, twin-chain drive, 28-inch wheels, magneto ignition, 8.68 horsepower, 3-inch bore, 3-1/2-inch stroke, 49.48 ci.

Model 11F: Twin-cylinder, twin-chain drive, 28-inch wheels, magneto ignition, 8.68 horsepower, 3-inch bore, 3-1/2-inch stroke, 49.48 ci.

Model 11G: Twin-cylinder, twin-chain drive, 8.68 horsepower, magneto ignition, 3-5/16-inch bore, 3-1/2-inch stroke, 60.34 ci.

Model 11H: Twin-cylinder, twin-chain drive, 8.68 horsepower, generator, 3-5/16-inch bore, 3-1/2-inch stroke, 60.34 ci.

Model 11J: Twin-cylinder, twin-chain drive, 8.68 horsepower, generator, 3-5/16-inch bore, 3-1/2-inch stroke, 60.34 ci.

1916

Model 16B: Single-cylinder, single-chain drive, 28-inch wheels, magneto ignition, 4.34 horsepower, 3-5/16-inch bore, 4-inch stroke, 35 ci, motor number followed by letter L, single-speed.

Model 16C: Single-cylinder, single-chain drive, 28-inch wheels, magneto ignition, 4.34 horsepower, 3-5/16-inch bore, 4-inch stroke, 35 ci, motor number followed by letter L, three-speed.

Model 16E: Twin-cylinder, twin-chain drive, 28-inch wheels, magneto ignition, 6-1/2 horsepower, 3-inch bore, 3-1/2-inch stroke, 49.48 ci.

Model 16F: Twin-cylinder, twin-chain drive, 28-inch wheels, magneto ignition, 6-1/2 horsepower, 3-inch bore, 3-1/2-inch stroke, 49.48 ci.

Model 16J: Twin-cylinder, twin-chain drive, 7 to 8 horsepower, generator, 3-5/15-inch bore, 3-1/2-inch stroke, 60.34 ci.

1917

Model 17B: Single-cylinder, single-chain drive, 28-inch wheels, magneto ignition, 4.34 horsepower, 3-5/16-inch bore, 4-inch stroke, 35 ci, motor number preceded by 17S, single-speed.

Model 17C: Single-cylinder, single-chain drive, 28-inch wheels, magneto ignition, 4.34 horsepower, 3-5/16-inch bore, 4-inch stroke, 35 ci, motor number preceded by 17S, three-speed.

Model 17E: Twin-cylinder, twin-chain drive, 28-inch wheels, magneto ignition, 6-1/2 horsepower, 3-inch bore, 3-1/2-inch stroke, 49.48 ci.

Model 17F: Twin-cylinder, twin-chain drive, 28-inch wheels, magneto ignition, 6-1/2 horsepower, 3-inch bore, 3-1/2-inch stroke, 49.48 ci.

Model 17J: Twin-cylinder, twin-chain drive, 7 to 8 horsepower, generator, 3-5/16-inch bore, 3-1/2-inch stroke, 60.34 ci.

1918

Model 18B: Single-cylinder, single-chain drive, 28-inch wheels, magneto ignition, 4.34 horsepower, 3-5/16-inch bore, 4-inch stroke, 35 ci, number preceded by 18S, single-speed.

Model 18C: Single-cylinder, single-chain drive, 28-inch wheels, magneto ignition, 4.34 horsepower, 3-5/16-inch bore, 4-inch stroke, 35 cu. in, number preceded by 18S, three-speed.

Model 18E: Twin-cylinder, twin-chain drive, magneto ignition, 8.68 horsepower, 3-5/16-inch bore, 3-1/2-inch stroke, 60.34 ci, number preceded by 18T, single-speed.

Model 18F: Twin-cylinder, twin-chain drive, magneto ignition, 8.68 horsepower, 3-5/16-inch bore, 3-1/2-inch stroke, 60.34 ci, number preceded by 18T, three-speed.

Model 18J: Twin-cylinder, twin-chain drive, magneto ignition, 8.68 horsepower, 3-5/16-inch bore, 3-1/2-inch stroke, 60.34 ci, number preceded by L18T, three-speed.

1919

Model 19F: Twin-cylinder, twin-chain drive, magneto ignition, 8.68 horsepower, 3-5/16-inch bore, 3-1/2-inch stroke, 60.34 ci, number preceded by 19T or 19A, three-speed.

Model 19J: Twin-cylinder, twin-chain drive, magneto ignition, 8.68 horse-power, 3-5/16-inch bore, 3-1/2-inch stroke, 60.34 ci, number preceded by L19T or L19A, three-speed.

Model: Sport, front-to-back opposed twin, 2-3/4-inch bore, 3-inch stroke, 35.64 ci, three-speed transmission.

1920

Model 20F: Twin-cylinder, twin-chain drive, magneto ignition, 8.68 horse-power, 3-5/16-inch bore, 3-1/2-inch stroke, 60.34 ci, number preceded by 20T, three-speed.

Model 20J: Twin-cylinder, twin-chain drive, magneto ignition, 8.68 horse-power, 3-5/16-inch bore, 3-1/2-inch stroke, 60.34 ci, number preceded by L20T, three-speed.

Model: Sport, front-to-back opposed twin, 2-3/4-inch bore, 3-inch stroke, 35.64 ci, three-speed transmission.

1921

Model 21F: Twin-cylinder, twin-chain drive, magneto ignition, 8.68 horse-power, 3-5/16-inch bore, 3-1/2-inch stroke, 60.34 ci, number preceded by 21F, three-speed.

Model 21FD: Twin-cylinder, twin-chain drive, magneto ignition, 9.5 horse-power, 3-7/16-inch bore, 4-inch stroke, 74 ci, number preceded by 21FD, three-speed.

Model 21J: Twin-cylinder, twin chain drive, generator, 8.68 horsepower, 3-5/16-inch bore, 3-1/2-inch stroke, 60.34 ci, number preceded by 21J, three-speed.

Model 21 JD: Twin-cylinder, twin-chain drive, generator, 9.5 horsepower, 3-7/16-inch bore, 4-inch stroke, 74 ci, number preceded by 21 JD, three-speed.

Model: Sport, front-to-back opposed twin, 2-3/4-inch bore, 3-inch stroke, 35.64 ci, three-speed transmission.

1922

Model 22F: Twin-cylinder, twin-chain drive, magneto ignition, 8.68 horse-power, 3-5/16-inch bore, 3-1/2-inch stroke, 60.34 ci, number preceded by 22F, three-speed.

Model 22FD: Twin-cylinder, twin-chain drive, magneto ignition, 9.5 horse-power, 3-7/16-inch bore, 4-inch stroke, 74 ci, number preceded by 22FD, three-speed.

Model 22J: Twin-cylinder, twin-chain drive, generator, 8.68 horsepower, 3-5/16-inch bore, 3-1/2-inch stroke, 60.34 ci, number preceded by 22J, three-speed.

Model 22JD: Twin-cylinder, twin-chain drive, generator, 9.5 horsepower, 3-7/16-inch bore, 4-inch stroke, 74 ci, number preceded by 22JD, three-speed.

Model: sport, front-to-back opposed twin, 2-3/4-inch bore, 3-inch stroke, 35.64 ci, three-speed transmission.

1923

Model 23F: Twin-cylinder, twin-chain drive, magneto ignition, 8.68 horse-power, 3-5/16-inch bore, 3-1/2-inch stroke, 60.34 ci, number preceded by 23F, three-speed.

Model 23FD: Twin-cylinder, twin-chain drive, magneto ignition, 9.5 horse-power, 3-7/16-inch bore, 4-inch stroke, 74 ci, number preceded by 23FD, three-speed.

Model 23J: Twin-cylinder, twin-chain drive, generator, 8.68 horsepower, 3-5/16-inch bore, 3-1/2-inch stroke, 60.34 ci, number preceded by 23J, three-speed.

Model 23JD: Twin-cylinder, twin-chain drive, generator, 9.5 horsepower, 3-7/16-inch bore, 4-inch stroke, 74 ci, number preceded by 23JD, three-speed.

1924

Model 24FE: Twin-cylinder, twin-chain drive, magneto ignition, 8.68 horse-power, 3-5/16-inch bore, 3-1/2-inch stroke, 60.34 ci, number preceded by 24FE, three-speed, aluminum pistons.

Model 24 FD: Twin-cylinder, twin-chain drive, magneto ignition, 9.5 horse-power, 3-7/16-inch bore, 4-inch stroke, 74 ci, number preceded by 24FD, three-speed, cast iron pistons.

Model 24FDCA: Twin-cylinder, twin-chain drive, magneto ignition, 9.5 horsepower, 3-7/16-inch bore, 4-inch stroke, 74 ci, number preceded by 24FDCA, three-speed, aluminum pistons.

Model 24FDCB: Twin-cylinder, twin-chain drive, magneto ignition, 9.5 horsepower, 3-7/16-inch bore, 4-inch stroke, 74 ci, number preceded by 24FDCB, three-speed, iron alloy pistons.

Model 24JE: Twin-cylinder, twin-chain drive, generator, 8.68 horsepower, 3-5/16-inch bore, 3-1/2-inch stroke, 60.34 ci, number preceded by 24JE, three-speed, aluminum pistons.

Model 24JD: Twin-cylinder, twin-chain drive, generator, 9.5 horsepower, 3-7/16-inch bore, 4-inch stroke, 74 ci, number preceded by 24JD, three-speed, cast iron pistons.

Model 24JDCA: Twin-cylinder, twin-chain drive, generator, 9.5 horsepower, 3-7/16-inch bore, 4-inch stroke, 74 ci, number preceded by 24JDCA, three-speed, aluminum pistons.

Model 24JDCB: Twin-cylinder, twin-chain drive, generator, 9.5 horsepower, 3-7/16-inch bore, 4-inch stroke, 74 ci, number preceded by 24JDCB, three-speed, iron alloy pistons.

1925

Model 25FE: Twin-cylinder, twin-chain drive, magneto ignition, 8.68 horse-power, 3-5/16-inch bore, 3-1/2-inch stroke, 60.34 ci, number preceded by 25FE, three-speed, iron alloy pistons.

Model 25FDCB: Twin-cylinder, twin-chain drive, generator, 9.5 horsepower, 3-7/16-inch bore, 4-inch stroke, 74 ci, number preceded by 25FDCB, three-speed, iron alloy pistons.

Model 25JE: Twin-cylinder, twin-chain drive, magneto ignition, 8.68 horse-power, 3-5/16-inch bore, 3-1/2-inch stroke, 60.34 ci, number preceded by 25JE, three-speed, iron alloy pistons.

Model 25JDCB: Twin-cylinder, twin-chain drive, generator, 9.5 horsepower, 3-7/16-inch bore, 4-inch stroke, 74 ci, number preceded by 25JDCB, three-speed, iron alloy pistons.

1926

Model 26F: Twin-cylinder, twin-chain drive, magneto ignition, 8.68 horse-power, 3-5/16-inch bore, 3-1/2-inch stroke, 60.34 ci, number preceded by 26F, three-speed, iron alloy pistons.

Model 26FD: Twin-cylinder, twin-chain drive, generator, 9.5 horsepower, 3-7/16-inch bore, 4-inch stroke, 74 ci, number preceded by 26FD, three-speed, iron alloy pistons.

Model 26J: Twin-cylinder, twin-chain drive, magneto ignition, 8.68 horse-power, 3-5/16-inch bore, 3-1/2-inch stroke, 60.34 ci, number preceded by 26J, three-speed, iron alloy pistons.

Model 26JD: Twin-cylinder, twin-chain drive, generator, 9.5 horsepower, 3-7/16-inch bore, 4-inch stroke, 74 ci, number preceded by 26JD, three-speed, iron alloy pistons.

1926-7

Model A: Single-cylinder, single-chain drive, magneto ignition, 3.31 horse-power, 2-7/8-inch bore, 3-1/4-inch stroke, 21.098 ci, number preceded by A, side by side valves, iron alloy pistons.

Model AA: Single-cylinder, single-chain drive, magneto ignition, 3.31 horse-power, 2-7/8-inch bore, 3-1/4-inch stroke, 21.098 ci, number preceded by AA, overhead valves, aluminum pistons.

Model B: Single-cylinder, single-chain drive, generator ignition, 3.31 horse-power, 2-7/8-inch bore, 3-1/4-inch stroke, 21.098 ci, number preceded by B, side by side valves, iron alloy pistons.

Model BA: Single-cylinder, single-chain drive, generator ignition, 3.31 horsepower, 2-7/8-inch bore, 3-1/4-inch stroke, 21.098 ci, number preceded by BA, overhead valves, aluminum pistons.

1927

Model 27F: Twin-cylinder, twin-chain drive, magneto ignition, 8.68 horse-power, 3-5/16-inch bore, 3-1/2-inch stroke, 60.34 ci, number preceded by 27F, three-speed, iron alloy pistons.

Model 27FD: Twin-cylinder, twin-chain drive, generator, 9.5 horsepower, 3-7/16-inch bore, 4-inch stroke, 74 ci, number preceded by 27FD, three-speed, iron alloy pistons.

Model 27J: Twin-cylinder, twin-chain drive, magneto ignition, 8.68 horse-power, 3-5/16-inch bore, 3-1/2-inch stroke, 60.34 ci, number preceded by 27J, three-speed, iron alloy pistons.

Model 27JD: Twin-cylinder, twin-chain drive, generator, 9.5 horsepower, 3-7/16-inch bore, 4-inch stroke, 74 ci, number preceded by 27JD, three-speed, iron alloy pistons.

1928

Model 28A: Single-cylinder, single-chain drive, magneto ignition, 3.31 horsepower, 2-7/8-inch bore, 3-1/4-inch stroke, 21.098 ci, number preceded by 28A, side by side valves, Dow metal pistons.

Model 28AA: Single-cylinder, single-chain drive, magneto ignition, 3.31 horsepower, 2-7/8-inch bore, 3-1/4-inch stroke, 21.098 ci, number preceded by 28AA, overhead valves, Dow metal pistons.

Model 28B: Single-cylinder, single-chain drive, generator, 3.31 horsepower, 2-7/8-inch bore, 3-1/4-inch stroke, 21.098 ci, number preceded by 28B, side by side valves, Dow metal pistons.

Model 28BA: Single-cylinder, single-chain drive, generator, 3.31 horsepower, 2-7/8-inch bore, 3-1/4-inch stroke, 21.098 ci, number preceded by 28BA, overhead valves, Dow metal pistons.

Model 28F: Twin-cylinder, twin-chain drive, magneto ignition, 8.68 horse-power, 3-5/16-inch bore, 3-1/2-inch stroke, 60.34 ci, number preceded by 28F, three-speed, iron alloy pistons.

Model 28FD: Twin-cylinder, twin-chain drive, generator, 9.5 horsepower, 3-7/16-inch bore, 4-inch stroke, 74 ci, number preceded by 28FD, three-speed, iron alloy pistons.

Model 28J: Twin-cylinder, twin-chain drive, magneto ignition, 8.68 horse-power, 3-5/16-inch bore, 3-1/2-inch stroke, 60.34 ci, number preceded by 28J, three-speed, iron alloy pistons.

Model 28JD: Twin-cylinder, twin-chain drive, generator, 9.5 horsepower, 3-7/16-inch bore, 4-inch stroke, 74 ci, number preceded by 28JD, three-speed, iron alloy pistons.

Model 28JXL: Twin-cylinder, twin-chain drive, generator, 8.68 horsepower, 3-5/16-inch bore, 3-1/2-inch stroke, 60.34 ci, number preceded by 28JXL, three-speed, Dow metal pistons.

Model 28JDXL: Twin-cylinder, twin-chain drive, generator, 9.5 horsepower, 3-7/16-inch bore, 4-inch stroke, 74 ci, number preceded by 28JDXL, three-speed, Dow metal pistons.

Model 28JH: Twin-cylinder, twin-chain drive, two cams, generator, 8.68 horsepower, 3-5/16-inch stroke, 3-1/2-inch bore, 60.34 ci, number preceded by 28JH, three-speed, Dow metal pistons.

Model 28JDH: Twin-cylinder, twin-chain drive, two cams, generator, 9.5 horsepower, 3-7/16-inch bore, 4-inch stroke, 74 ci, number preceded by 28JDH, three-speed, Dow metal pistons.

(Note: All 61- and 74-ci models were offered with 25 x 3.85 tire size; the JD models were offered with these sizes standard and with 27 x 3.85 tires optional. Tire size for the singles was 26 x 3.30.)

1929

Model 29A: Single-cylinder, single-chain drive, magneto ignition, 3.31 horsepower, 2-7/8-inch bore, 3-1/4-inch stroke, 21.098 ci, number preceded by 29A, side by side valves, Dow metal pistons.

Model 29AA: Single-cylinder, single-chain drive, magneto ignition, 3.31 horsepower, 2-7/8-inch bore, 3-1/4-inch stroke, 21.098 ci, number preceded by 29AA, overhead valves, Dow metal pistons.

Model 29B: Single-cylinder, single-chain drive, generator, 3.31 horsepower, 2-7/8-inch bore, 3-1/4-inch stroke, 21.098 ci, number preceded by 29B, side by side valves, Dow metal pistons.

Model 29BA: Single-cylinder, single-chain drive, generator, 3.31 horsepower, 2-7/8-inch bore, 3-1/4-inch stroke, 21.098 ci, number preceded by 29BA, overhead valves, Dow metal pistons.

Model 29D: Twin-cylinder, twin-chain drive, generator, no horsepower given, 2-3/4-inch bore, 3-1/4-inch stroke, 45.32 ci, number preceded by 29D, three-speed, Dow metal pistons.

Model 29F: Twin-cylinder, twin-chain drive, magneto ignition, 8.68 horse-power, 3-5/16-inch bore, 3-1/2-inch stroke, 60.34 ci, number preceded by 29F, three-speed, iron alloy pistons.

Model 29FD: Twin-cylinder, twin-chain drive, magneto ignition, 9.5 horse-power, 3-7/16-inch bore, 4-inch stroke, 74 ci, number preceded by 29FD, three-speed, iron alloy pistons.

Model 29J: Twin-cylinder, twin-chain drive, magneto ignition, 8.68 horse-power, 3-5/16-inch bore, 3-1/2-inch stroke, 60.34 ci, number preceded by 29J, three-speed, iron alloy pistons.

Model 29JD: Twin-cylinder, twin-chain drive, generator, 9.5 horsepower, 3-7/16-inch bore, 4-inch stroke, 74 ci, number preceded by 29JD, three-speed, iron alloy pistons.

Model 29JXL: Twin-cylinder, twin-chain drive, generator, 8.68 horsepower, 3-5/16-inch stroke, 3-1/2-inch bore, 60.34 ci, number preceded by 29JXL, three-speed, Dow metal pistons.

Model 29JDXL: Twin-cylinder, twin-chain drive, generator, 9.5 horsepower, 3-7/16-inch bore, 4-inch stroke, 74 ci, number preceded by 29JDXL, three-speed, Dow metal pistons.

Model 29JH: Twin-cylinder, twin-chain drive, two cams, generator, 8.68 horsepower, 3-5/16-inch bore, 3-1/2-inch bore, 60.34 ci, number preceded by 29JH, three-speed, Dow metal pistons.

Model 29JDH: Twin-cylinder, twin-chain drive, two cams, generator, 9.5 horsepower, 3-7/16-inch bore, 4-inch stroke, 74 ci, number preceded by 29JDH, three-speed, Dow metal pistons.

(Note: 45 ci model offered with 25 x 3.85 tires standard; 61 and 74 ci models offered with 27 x 3.85 tires standard. No optional sizes listed.)

1930

Model 30-V: 74-ci Big Twin.
Model 30-VL: 74-ci Big Twin, high compression.
Model 30-D: 45-ci side valve V-twin.

Model 30-DL: 45-ci side-valve V-twin, high compression.
Model 30-DLD: 45-ci side valve Special Sport solo.
Model 30-C: 30.50-ci single.

1931
Model 31-V: 74-ci Big Twin.
Model 31-VL: 74-ci Big Twin, high compression.
Model 31-D: 45-ci side valve V-twin.
Model 31-DL: 45-ci side-valve V-twin, high compression.
Model 31-DLD: 45-ci side valve Special Sport solo.
Model 31-C: 30.50-ci single.
Model 31-VC: 74-ci Big Twin Commercial.

1932
Model 32-V: 74-ci Big Twin.
Model 32-VL: 74-ci Big Twin, high compression.
Model 32-R: 45-ci side valve V-twin.
Model 32-RL: 45-ci side-valve V-twin, high compression.
Model 32-RLR: 45-ci side valve Special Sport solo.
Model 32-C: 30.50-ci single.

1933
Model 33-V: 74-ci Big Twin.
Model 33-VL: 74-ci Big Twin, high compression.
Model 33-VLD: 74-ci Big Twin, Y manifold.
Model 33-R: 45-ci side valve V-twin.
Model 33-RL: 45-ci side-valve V-twin, high compression.
Model 33-RLR: 45-ci side valve Special Sport solo.
Model 33-C: 30.50-ci single.

1934
Model 34-B: 21-ci side valve single.
Model 34-C: 30.50-ci side valve single.
Model 34-CB: B model with the 30.50-ci motor.
Model 34-RL: 45-ci V-twin, high compression.
Model 34-R: 45-ci V-twin, low compression.
Model 34-RLD: 45-ci V-twin, Special Sport solo.
Model 34-VLD: 74-ci side valve twin, Special Sport solo, TNT motor.
Model 34-VD: 74-ci side valve twin, solo, low compression.
Model 34-VDS: 74-ci side valve twin, low compression, sidecar gears, TNT motor.
Model 34-VFDS: 74-ci side valve twin, heavy-duty commercial TNT motor.

1935
Model 35-RL: 45-ci V-twin, high compression.
Model 35-R: 45-ci V-twin, low compression.
Model 35-RS: 45-ci V-twin, low compression, sidecar gears.
Model 35-RLD: 45-ci V-twin, special Sport solo.
Model 35-VLD: 74-ci side valve twin, solo, low compression.

1936
Model 36-RL: 45-ci V-twin, Sport Solo, high compression, solo bars.
Model 36-RLD: 45-ci V-twin, Sport Solo, extra high compression, solo bars.
Model 36-RLDR: 45-ci V-twin, competition special.
Model 36-R: 45-ci V-twin, low compression, solo bars.
Model 36-RS: 45-ci V-twin, low compression, sidecar gears.
Model 36-VLD: 74-ci side valve twin, special Sport solo.
Model 36-VD: 74-ci side valve twin, low compression.

Model 36-VDS: 74-ci side valve twin, low compression, sidecar gears.
Model 36-VLH: 80-ci side valve twin, Sport solo.
Model 36-VHS: 80-ci side valve twin, low compression, sidecar gears.
Model 36-EL: 61-ci overhead valve twin, Special Sport solo.
Model 36-E: 61-ci overhead valve twin, medium compression.
Model 36-ES: 61-ci overhead valve twin, medium compression, sidecar gears.

1937
Model 37-WL: 45-ci twin, Sport solo.
Model 37-WLD: 45-ci Sport solo, extra high compression.
Model 37-WLDR: 45-ci twin, competition model.
Model 37-W: 45-ci twin, low compression.
Model 37-WS: 45- ci twin, sidecar gearing.
Model 37-UL: 74-ci twin, Special Sport solo.
Model 37-U: 74-ci twin, solo, medium compression.
Model 37-UHS: 80-ci twin, medium compression, sidecar gears.
Model 37-EL: 61-ci overhead valve twin, Special Sport solo.
Model 37-E: 61-ci overhead valve twin, medium compression.
Model 37-ES: 61-ci overhead valve twin, medium compression, sidecar gears.

1938
Model 38-WLD: 45-ci twin, Sport Solo, extra high compression.
Model 38-WL: 45-ci twin, Sport Solo, high compression.
Model 38-WLDR: 45-ci twin, competition model.
Model 38-UL: 74-ci twin, Special Sport solo.
Model 38-U: 74-ci twin, solo, medium compression.
Model 38-US: 74-ci twin, medium compression, sidecar gears.
Model 38-ULH: 80-ci twin, Special Sport solo.
Model 38-UH: 80-ci twin, solo, medium compression.
Model 38-UHS: 80-ci twin, medium compression, sidecar gears.
Model 38-EL: 61-ci overhead valve twin, Special Sport solo.
Model 38-ES: 61-ci overhead valve twin, sidecar gears.

1939
Model 39-WLD: 45-ci twin, Sport Solo, extra high compression.
Model 39-WL: 45-ci twin, Sport Solo, high compression.
Model 39-WLDR: 45-ci twin, competition model.
Model 39-UL: 74-ci twin, Special Sport solo.
Model 39-U: 74-ci twin, solo, medium compression.
Model 39-US: 74-ci twin, medium compression, sidecar gears.
Model 39-ULH: 80-ci twin, Special Sport solo.
Model 39-UH: 80-ci twin, solo, medium compression.
Model 39-UHS: 80-ci twin, medium compression, sidecar gears.
Model 39-EL: 61-ci overhead valve twin, Special Sport solo.
Model 39-ES: 61-ci overhead valve twin, sidecar gears.

1940
Model 40-WLD: 45-ci twin, Sport Solo.
Model 40-WL: 45-ci twin, Sport Solo, high compression.
Model 40-WLDR: 45-ci twin, competition model.
Model 40-UL: 74-ci twin, Special Sport solo.
Model 40-U: 74-ci twin, solo, medium compression.
Model 40-US: 74-ci twin, medium compression, sidecar gears.
(Aluminum head optional on all 74-ci V-twins.)
Model 40-ULH: 80-ci twin, Special Sport solo.
Model 40-UH: 80-ci twin, solo, medium compression.

Model 40-UHS: 80-ci twin, medium compression, sidecar gears. (Aluminum heads standard on all 80-ci V-twins.)
Model 40-EL: 61-ci overhead valve twin, Special Sport solo.
Model 40-ES: 61-ci overhead valve twin, sidecar gears.
(Four-speed transmission standard on all 61-, 74-, 80-ci V-twins.)

1941
Model 41-WL: 45-ci twin, high compression.
Model 41-WLD: 45-ci twin, Sport solo.
Model 41-WLDR: 45-ci twin, Special Sport solo.
Model 41-UL: 74-ci twin, Special Sport solo.
Model 41-U: 74-ci twin, medium compression.
Model 41-ULH: 80-ci twin, Special Sport solo.
Model 41-UH: 80-ci twin, medium compression.
Model 41-EL: 61-ci overhead valve twin, Special Sport solo.
Model 41-E: 61-ci overhead valve twin, medium compression.
Model 41-FL: 74-ci overhead valve twin, Special Sport solo.
Model 41-F: 74-ci overhead valve twin, medium compression.

1942
Model 42-WLD: 45-ci twin, Special Sport solo.
Model 42-WL: 45-ci twin, high compression.
Model 42-UL: 74-ci twin, Special Sport solo.
Model 42-U: 74-ci twin, medium compression.
Model 42-EL: 61-ci overhead valve twin, Special Sport solo.
Model 42-E: 61-ci overhead valve twin, medium compression.
Model 42-FL: 74-ci overhead valve twin, Special Sport solo.

1943
Model 43-UL: 74-ci twin, high compression solo.
Model 43-U: 74-ci twin, medium compression.
Model 43-EL: 61-ci overhead valve twin, Special Sport solo.
Model 43-E: 61-ci overhead valve twin, medium compression.
Model 43-FL: 74-ci overhead valve twin, Special Sport solo.
Model 43-F: 74-ci overhead valve twin, medium compression.

1944
Model 44-UL: 74-ci twin, high compression solo.
Model 44-U: 74-ci twin, medium compression.
Model 44-EL: 61-ci overhead valve twin, Special Sport solo.
Model 44-E: 61-ci overhead valve twin, medium compression.
Model 44-FL: 74-ci overhead valve twin, Special Sport solo.
Model 44-F: 74-ci overhead valve twin, medium compression.

1945
Model 45-WL: 45-ci twin.
Model 45-UL: 74-ci twin, high compression solo.
Model 45-U: 74-ci twin, medium compression.
Model 45-US: 74-ci twin, medium compression, sidecar gears.
(Aluminum heads a $7 option on all above models.)
Model 45-EL: 61-ci overhead valve twin, Special Sport solo.
Model 45-E: 61-ci overhead valve twin, medium compression.
Model 45-ES: 61-ci overhead valve twin, medium compression, sidecar gears.
Model 45-FL: 74-ci overhead valve twin, Special Sport solo.
Model 45-F: 74-ci overhead valve twin, medium compression.
Model 45-FS: 74-ci overhead valve twin, medium compression, sidecar gears.

1946
Model 46-WL: 45-ci twin.
Model 46-UL: 74-ci twin, high compression solo.
Model 46-U: 74-ci twin, medium compression.
Model 46-US: 74-ci twin, medium compression, sidecar gears.
(Aluminum heads a $7 option on all above models.)
Model 46-EL: 61-ci overhead valve twin, Special Sport solo.
Model 46-E: 61-ci overhead valve twin, medium compression.
Model 46-ES: 61-ci overhead valve twin, medium compression, sidecar gears.
Model 46-FL: 74-ci overhead valve twin, Special Sport solo.
Model 46-F: 74-ci overhead valve twin, medium compression.
Model 46-FS: 74-ci overhead valve twin, medium compression, sidecar gears.

1947
Model 47-WL: 45-ci twin.
Model 47-UL: 74-ci twin, high compression solo.
Model 47-U: 74-ci twin, medium compression.
Model 47-US: 74-ci twin, medium compression, sidecar gears.
(Aluminum heads a $7 option on all above models.)
Model 47-EL: 61-ci overhead valve twin, Special Sport solo.
Model 47-E: 61-ci overhead valve twin, medium compression.
Model 47-ES: 61-ci overhead valve twin, medium compression, sidecar gears.
Model 47-FL: 74-ci overhead valve twin, Special Sport solo.
Model 47-F: 74-ci overhead valve twin, medium compression.
Model 47-FS: 74-ci overhead valve twin, medium compression, sidecar gears.

1948
Model 48-S: 125-cc two-stroke single.
Model 48-WL: 45-ci twin.
Model 48-UL: 74-ci twin, high compression solo.
Model 48-U: 74-ci twin, medium compression.
Model 48-US: 74-ci twin, medium compression, sidecar gears.
(Aluminum heads an $8.35 option on all above twins.)
Model 48-EL: 61-ci overhead valve twin, Special Sport solo.
Model 48-E: 61-ci overhead valve twin, medium compression.
Model 48-ES: 61-ci overhead valve twin, medium compression, sidecar gears.
Model 48-FL: 74-ci overhead valve twin, Special Sport solo.
Model 48-F: 74-ci overhead valve twin, medium compression.
Model 48-FS: 74-ci overhead valve twin, medium compression, sidecar gears.

1949
Model 49-S: 125-cc two-stroke single (chrome rims, $7.50 option).
Model 49-WL: 45-ci twin (aluminum heads, $7.50 extra).
Model 49-EL: 61-ci overhead valve twin, Sport solo.
Model 49-ES: 61-ci overhead valve twin, sidecar gears.
Model 49-FL: 74-ci overhead valve twin, Sport solo.
Model 49-F: 74-ci overhead valve twin, medium compression.

1950
Model 50-S: 125-cc two-stroke single (chrome rims, $7.50 option).
Model 50-WL: 45-ci twin (aluminum heads, $7.50 extra).
Model 50-EL: 61-ci overhead valve twin, Sport solo.

Model 50-ES: 61-ci overhead valve twin, sidecar gears.
Model 50-FL: 74-ci overhead valve twin, Sport solo.
Model 50-F: 74-ci overhead valve twin, medium compression.
Model 50-FS: 74-ci overhead valve twin, medium compression, sidecar gears.

1951

Model 51-S: 125-cc two-stroke single (chrome rims, $8.50 option, chrome handlebars $3.75 option).
Model 51-WL: 45-ci twin (aluminum heads, $10 extra).
Model 51-EL: 61-ci overhead valve twin, Sport solo.
Model 51-ELS: 61-ci overhead valve twin, sidecar gears.
Model 51-FL: 74-ci overhead valve twin, Sport solo.
Model 51-FS: 74-ci overhead valve twin, medium compression, sidecar gears.

1952

Model 52-S: 125-cc two-stroke single.
Model 52-ELF: 61-ci overhead valve twin, Sport solo, foot shift.
Model 52-EL: 61-ci overhead valve twin, Sport solo, hand shift.
Model 52-ELS: 61-ci overhead valve twin, sidecar gears, hand shift.
Model 52-FLF: 74-ci overhead valve twin, Sport solo, foot shift.
Model 52-FL: 74-ci overhead valve twin, Sport solo, hand shift.
Model 52-FLS: 74-ci overhead valve twin, sidecar gears, hand shift.
Model 52-K: 45-ci twin, Sports model.

1953

Model 53-ST: 165-cc two-stroke single.
Model 53-K: 45-ci twin Sports model.
Model 53-FLF: 74-ci overhead valve twin, Sport solo, foot shift.
Model 53-FL: 74-ci overhead valve twin, Sport solo, hand shift.
Model 53-FLEF: 74-ci overhead valve twin, foot shift with traffic combination.
Model 53-FLE: 74-ci overhead valve twin, hand shift with traffic combination.

1954

Model 54-ST: 165-cc single cylinder, two-stroke.
Model 54-STU: 165-cc single cylinder, two-stroke, modified carburetor.
Model 54-KH: 55-ci twin, Sport model.
Model 54-FLF: 74-ci overhead valve, foot shift.
Model 54-FL: 74-ci overhead valve twin, hand shift.
Model 54-FLEF: 74-ci overhead valve twin, foot shift, traffic combination.
Model 54-FLE: 74-ci overhead valve twin, hand shift, traffic combination.

1955

Model 55-Hummer: 125-cc single-cylinder, two-stroke.
Model 55-ST: 165-cc single cylinder, two-stroke.
Model 55-STU: 165-cc single cylinder, two-stroke, modified carburetor.
Model 55-KH: 54-ci twin, Sport model.
Model 55-KHK: 55-ci twin, Sport model KH with special speed kit.
Model 55-FLF: 74-ci overhead valve, foot shift.
Model 55-FL: 74-ci overhead valve twin, hand shift.
Model 55-FLEF: 74-ci overhead valve twin, foot shift, traffic combination.
Model 55-FLE: 74-ci overhead valve twin, hand shift, traffic combination.
Model 55-FLHF: 74-ci overhead valve twin, Super Sport solo, foot shift.
Model 55-FLH: 74-ci overhead valve twin, Super Sport solo, hand shift.

1956

Model 56-Hummer: 125-cc single-cylinder, two-stroke.
Model 56-ST: 165-cc single cylinder, two-stroke.
Model 56-STU: 165-cc single cylinder, two-stroke, modified carburetor.
Model 56-KR: 45-ci side valve twin, four-speed transmission, magneto ignition, flat-track racing motorcycle.
Model 56-KRTT: 45-ci side-valve twin, four-speed transmission, magneto ignition.
Model 56-KHRTT: 45-ci twin-cylinder TT racing motorcycle.
Model 56-KH: 54-ci twin, Sport model.
Model 56-KHK: 55-ci twin, Sport model KH with special speed kit.
Model 56-FLHF: 74-ci overhead valve, Super Sport solo, foot shift.
Model 56-FLH: 74-ci overhead valve twin, Super Sport solo, hand shift.
Model 56-FLF: 74-ci overhead valve twin, Sport solo, foot shift.
Model 56-FL: 74-ci overhead valve twin, Sport solo, hand shift.
Model 56-FLEF: 74-ci overhead valve twin, foot shift, traffic combination.
Model 56-FLE: 74-ci overhead valve twin, hand shift, traffic combination.

1957

Model 57-Hummer: 125-cc single-cylinder, two-stroke.
Model 57-ST: 165-cc single cylinder, two-stroke.
Model 57-STU: 165-cc single cylinder, two-stroke, modified carburetor.
Model 57-KR: 45-ci side valve twin, four-speed transmission, magneto ignition, flat-track racing motorcycle.
Model 57-KRTT: 45-ci side-valve twin, four-speed transmission, magneto ignition, TT racing motorcycle.
Model 57-KHRTT: 45-ci twin-cylinder TT racing motorcycle.
Model 57-XL: 55-ci overhead valve twin, designated the Sportster.
Model 57-FLHF: 74-ci overhead valve twin, Super Sport, foot shift.
Model 57-FLH: 74-ci overhead valve twin, Super Sport, hand shift.
Model 57-FLF: 74-ci overhead valve twin, Sport solo, foot shift.
Model 57-FL: 74-ci overhead valve twin, Sport solo, hand shift.

1958

Model 58-XL: Sportster, 55-ci overhead valve twin, medium compression.
Model 58-XLH: Sportster, 55-ci overhead valve twin, 9:1 compression.
Model 58-XLC: Sportster, 55-ci overhead valve twin, 9:1 compression.
Model 58-XLCH: Sportster, 55-ci overhead valve twin, 9:1 compression, magneto ignition.
Model 58-FLHF: 74-ci overhead valve twin, Super Sport, foot shift.
Model 58-FLH: 74-ci overhead valve twin, Super Sport, hand shift.
Model 58-FLF: 74-ci overhead valve twin, Sport solo, foot shift.
Model 58-FL: 74-ci overhead valve twin, Sport solo, hand shift.
(F series motorcycles designated Duo-Glide, equipped with swinging arm and twin rear shocks.)
Model 58-Hummer: 125-cc single-cylinder, two-stroke.
Model 58-ST: 165-cc single cylinder, two-stroke.
Model 58-STU: 165-cc single cylinder, two-stroke, modified carburetor.

1959

Model 59-XL: Sportster, 55-ci overhead valve twin, medium compression.
Model 59-XLH: Sportster, 55-ci overhead valve twin, high compression.
Model 58-XLCH: Sportster, 55-ci overhead valve twin, high compression.
Model 58-FLHF: 74-ci overhead valve twin, Super Sport, foot shift.
Model 58-FLH: 74-ci overhead valve twin, Super Sport, hand shift.
Model 58-FLF: 74-ci overhead valve twin, Sport solo, foot shift.
Model 58-FL: 74-ci overhead valve twin, Sport solo, hand shift.
Model 59-Hummer: 125-cc single-cylinder, two-stroke.

Model 59-ST: 165-cc single cylinder, two-stroke.

Model 59-STU: 165-cc single cylinder, two-stroke, modified carburetor.

1960

Model 60-XLH, Super H Sportster: 55-ci overhead valve twin.

Model 60-XLCH, Super CH Sportster: 55-ci overhead valve twin.

Model 60-FLF: 74-ci overhead valve twin, Super Sport, foot shift.

Model 60-FLH: 74-ci overhead valve twin, Super Sport, hand shift.

Model 60-FLF: 74-ci overhead valve twin, Sport solo, foot shift.

Model 60-FL: 74-ci overhead valve twin, Sport solo, hand shift.

Model 60-BT, Super 10: 165-cc single-cylinder, two-stroke, 9 horsepower.

Model 60-BTU, Super 10: 165-cc single-cylinder, two-stroke, 5 horsepower with carburetor restrictor.

Model 60-A, Topper scooter: 165-cc single-cylinder, two-stroke, belt drive, automatic transmission, 9 horsepower.

Model 60-AU, Topper scooter: 165-cc, single-cylinder, two-stroke, belt drive, automatic transmission, 5 horsepower with carburetor restrictor.

1961

Model 61-XLH, Super H Sportster: 55-ci overhead valve twin.

Model 61-XLCH, Super CH Sportster: 55-ci overhead valve twin.

Model 61-FLHF: 74-ci overhead valve twin, Super Sport, foot shift.

Model 60-FLH: 74-ci overhead valve twin, Super Sport, hand shift.

Model 60-FLF: 74-ci overhead valve twin, Sport solo, foot shift.

Model 60-FL: 74-ci overhead valve twin, Sport solo, hand shift.

Model 61-BT, Super 10: 165-cc single-cylinder, two-stroke, 9 horsepower.

Model 61-BTU, Super 10: 165-cc single-cylinder, two-stroke, 5 horsepower with carburetor restrictor.

Model 61-AH, Topper scooter: 165-cc single-cylinder, two-stroke, belt drive, automatic transmission, 9 horsepower.

Model 61-AU, Topper scooter: 165-cc, single-cylinder, two-stroke, belt drive, automatic transmission, 5 horsepower with carburetor restrictor.

Model 61-C Sprint: 250-cc single-cylinder four-stroke.

Model 61-KR and KRTT: 45-ci side valve racing motorcycle.

Model 61-XLRTT: 45-ci side valve TT racing motorcycle.

Model 61-CRTT: 250-cc single cylinder overhead valve four-stroke motor, 9.5:1 compression ratio, four-speed transmission, battery ignition, off-road racing motorcycle.

1962

Model 62-KR and KRTT: 45-ci side valve racing motorcycle.

Model 62-XLRTT: 45-ci side valve TT racing motorcycle.

Model 62-FLHF: 74-ci overhead valve twin, Super Sport, foot shift.

Model 62-FLH: 74-ci overhead valve twin, Super Sport, hand shift.

Model 62-FLF: 74-ci overhead valve twin, Sport solo, foot shift.

Model 62-FL: 74-ci overhead valve twin, Sport solo, hand shift.

Model 62-BT Pacer: 175-cc single-cylinder two-stroke.

Model 62-BTH Scat: 175-cc single-cylinder two stroke.

Model 62-BTF Ranger: 165-cc single-cylinder two-stroke.

Model 62-BTU Pacer: 165-cc single-cylinder two-stroke, 5 horsepower with carburetor restrictor.

Model 62-H Sprint H: 250-cc single-cylinder four-stroke.

Model 62-C Sprint: 250-cc single-cylinder four-stroke.

Model 62-CRTT: 250-cc single-cylinder, four-stroke road racer.

Model 62-AH, Topper scooter: 165-cc single-cylinder, two-stroke, belt drive, automatic transmission, 9 horsepower.

Model 62-AU, Topper scooter: 165-cc, single-cylinder, two-stroke, belt drive, automatic transmission, 5 horsepower with carburetor restrictor.

1963

Model 63 XLH, super H Sportster: 55-ci overhead valve twin.

Model 63-XLCH, Super CH Sportster: 55-ci overhead valve twin.

Model 63-KR: 45-ci side valve twin, four-speed transmission, magneto ignition, designed for flat-track racing.

Model 63-KRTT: 45-ci side-valve twin, four-speed transmission, magneto ignition, designed for TT racing.

Model 63-XLRTT: 55-ci overhead valve twin, four-speed transmission, magneto ignition, 9:1 compression ratio.

Model 63-FLHF: 74-ci overhead valve twin, Super Sport, foot shift.

Model 63-FLH: 74-ci overhead valve twin, Super Sport, hand shift.

Model 63-FLF: 74-ci overhead valve twin, Sport solo, foot shift.

Model 63-FL: 74-ci overhead valve twin, Sport solo, hand shift.

Model 63-AH, Topper scooter: 165-cc single-cylinder two-stroke, belt drive, automatic transmission, 9 horsepower.

Model 63-AU, Topper scooter: 165-cc single-cylinder two-stroke, belt drive, automatic transmission, 5 horsepower with carburetor restrictor.

Model 63-BT, Pacer: 175-cc single-cylinder two-stroke, three-speed transmission, street model.

Model 63-BTH, Scat: 175-cc single-cylinder two-stroke, three-speed transmission, trail model.

Model 63-BTU, Pacer: 175-cc single cylinder two-stroke, three-speed transmission, 5 horsepower with carburetor restrictor.

Model 63-C, Sprint: 250-cc single-cylinder, four-cycle.

Model 63-H, Sprint: 250-cc single-cylinder, four-cycle, trail model.

Model 63-CRTT: 250-cc Single-cylinder, four-stroke road racer.

1964

Model 64-KR: 45-ci side-valve twin, four-speed transmission, magneto ignition.

Model 64-XLRTT: 55-ci overhead valve twin, four-speed transmission, magneto ignition, 9:1 compression ratio.

Model 64-CRTT: 250-cc Single-cylinder, four-stroke road racer.

Model 64-XLH, Super H, Sportster: 55-ci overhead valve twin.

Model 64-XLCH, Super CH, Sportster: 55-ci overhead valve twin.

Model 64-FLHF: 74-ci overhead valve twin, Super Sport, foot shift.

Model 64-FLH: 74-ci overhead valve twin, Super Sport, hand shift.

Model 64-FLF: 74-ci overhead valve twin, Sport solo, foot shift.

Model 64-FL: 74-ci overhead valve twin, Sport solo, hand shift.

Model 64-BT, Pacer: 175-cc single-cylinder, two-stroke, three-speed transmission, street model.

Model 64-BTH, Scat: 175-cc single-cylinder, two-stroke, three-speed transmission, trail model.

Model 64-BTU, Pacer: 175-cc single-cylinder, two-stroke, three-speed transmission, 5 horsepower with carburetor restrictor.

Model 64-C, Sprint: 250-cc single-cylinder, four-stroke.

Model 64-H, Sprint: 250-cc single-cylinder, four-stroke, trail model.

Model 64-AH, Topper scooter: 165-cc, single-cylinder, two-stroke, belt drive, automatic transmission, 9 horsepower.

Model 64-AU, Topper scooter: 165-cc, single cylinder, two-stroke, belt drive, automatic transmission, 5 horsepower with carburetor restrictor.

1965

Model 65-XLH, Super H, Sportster: 55-ci overhead valve twin.

Model 65-XLCH, Super CH, Sportster: 55-ci overhead valve twin.

Model 65-FLHFB: 74-ci overhead valve twin, Super Sport, foot shift.

Model 65-FLHB: 74-ci overhead valve twin, Super Sport, hand shift.

Model 65-FLFB: 74-ci overhead valve twin, Super solo, foot shift.

Model 65-FLB: 74-ci overhead valve twin, Super solo, hand shift.

(All F models were equipped with electric starting and designated Electra Glides. Last year for the Panhead motor.)

Model 65-BT, Pacer: 175-cc single-cylinder, two-stroke, three-speed transmission, street model.

Model 65-BTH, Scat: 175-cc single-cylinder, two-stroke, three-speed transmission, trail model.

Model 65-C, Sprint: 250—cc, single-cylinder, four-stroke.

Model 65-H, Sprint: 250-cc, single-cylinder, four-stroke, trail model.

Model 65 M-50: 50-cc Single-cylinder, two-cycle, three-speed transmission.

Model 65-AH, Topper scooter: 165-cc, single-cylinder, two-stroke, belt drive, automatic transmission, 9 horsepower. Designated high compression.

1966

Model 66-FLHFB: 74-ci overhead valve twin, Super Sport, foot shift.

Model 66-FLHB: 74-ci overhead valve twin, Super Sport, hand shift.

Model 66-FLFB: 74-ci overhead valve twin, Super solo, foot shift.

Model 66-FLB: 74-ci overhead valve twin, Super solo, hand shift.

Model 66-XLH, Super H, Sportster: 55-ci overhead valve twin.

Model 66-XLCH, Super CH, Sportster: 55-ci overhead valve twin.

Model 66-C, Sprint: 250-cc single-cylinder, four-stroke.

Model 66-H Sprint: 250-cc single-cylinder, four-stroke, trail model.

Model 66-BTH, Bobcat: 175-cc single-cylinder, two-stroke, three-speed transmission, offered in standard (street) and trail models without separate model designation.

Model 66-M-50: 50-cc single-cylinder, two-stroke, three-speed transmission, magneto ignition.

Model 66-M-50 Sport: 50-cc single-cylinder, two-stroke, three-speed transmission, magneto ignition.

1967

Model 67-XLH, Super H, Sportster: 55-ci overhead valve twin.

Model 67-XLCH, Super CH, Sportster: 55-ci overhead valve twin.

Model 67-FLHFB: 74-ci overhead valve twin, Super Sport, foot shift.

Model 67-FLHB: 74-ci overhead valve twin, Super Sport, hand shift.

Model 67-FLFB: 74-ci overhead valve twin, Super solo, foot shift.

Model 67-FLB: 74-ci overhead valve twin, Super solo, hand shift.

Model 67-H, Sprint: 250-cc single-cylinder, four-stroke, trail model.

Model 67-SS, Sprint: 250-cc, single-cylinder, four-stroke.

Model 67-M-65: 65-cc, single-cylinder, two-cycle, three-speed transmission.

Model 67-M-65, Sport: 65-cc, single-cylinder, two-cycle, three-speed transmission.

Model 67-M-50: 50-cc single-cylinder, two-cycle, three-speed transmission.

1968

Model 68-XLH, Super H, Sportster: 55-ci overhead valve twin.

Model 68-XLCH, Super CH, Sportster: 55-ci overhead valve twin.

Model 68-FLHFB: 74-ci overhead valve twin, Super Sport, foot shift.

Model 68-FLHB: 74-ci overhead valve twin, Super Sport, hand shift.

Model 68-FLFB: 74-ci overhead valve twin, Super solo, foot shift.

Model 68-FLB: 74-ci overhead valve twin, Super solo, hand shift.

Model 68-H, Sprint: 250-cc single-cylinder, four-stroke, trail model.

Model 68-SS, Sprint: 250-cc, single-cylinder, four-stroke.

Model 68-M-125, Rapido: 125-cc single cylinder, two-stroke, four-speed transmission.

Model 68-M-65: 65-cc single-cylinder, two-cycle, three-speed transmission.

Model 68-M-65 Sport: 65-cc single-cylinder, two-cycle, three-speed transmission.

Model 68-M-50, Sport: 50-cc, single-cylinder, two-cycle, three-speed transmission.

1969

Model 69-XLH, Super H, Sportster: 55-ci overhead valve twin.

Model 69-XLCH, Super CH, Sportster: 55-ci overhead valve twin.

Model 69-XLRTT: 55-ci overhead valve twin, 9:1 compression ratio, four-speed transmission, magneto ignition.

Model 69-FLHFB: 74-ci overhead valve twin, Super Sport, foot shift.

Model 69-FLHB: 74-ci overhead valve twin, Super Sport, hand shift.

Model 69-FLFB: 74-ci overhead valve twin, Super solo, foot shift.

Model 69-FLB: 74-ci overhead valve twin, Super solo, hand shift.

Model 69-SS, Sprint: 350-cc, single-cylinder, four-stroke.

Model 69-ERS, Sprint Scrambler: 350-cc overhead valve, four-cycle, four-speed transmission, magneto ignition.

Model 69-ML-125, Rapido: 125-cc single-cylinder, two-stroke (1,000 street models built; Rapido then continued as a trail model).

Model 69-M-65: 65-cc single-cylinder, two-stroke.

Model 69-M-65 Sport: 65-cc single-cylinder, two-stroke.

1970

Model 70-FLHF: 74-ci overhead valve twin, Super Sport, foot shift.

Model 70-FLH: 74-ci overhead valve twin, Super Sport, hand shift.

Model 70-FLPF: 74-ci overhead valve twin, Super solo, foot shift.

Model 70-FLP: 74-ci overhead valve twin, Super solo, hand shift.

Model 70-XLH, super H, Sportster: 55-ci overhead valve twin.

Model 70-XLCH, Super CH, Sportster: 55-ci overhead valve twin.

Model 70-SS, Sprint: 350-cc single-cylinder, four-stroke.

Model 70-MLS, Rapido: 125-cc single-cylinder, two-stroke.

Model 70-M-65 Sport, Leggero: 65-cc single-cylinder, two-stroke.

Model 70-ERS Sprint Scrambler: 350-cc overhead valve, four-cycle.

Model 70-MSR, Baja: 100-cc single-cylinder, two-cycle, four-speed transmission.

1971

Model 71-FLHF: 74-ci overhead valve twin, Super Sport, foot shift.

Model 71-FLH: 74-ci overhead valve twin, Super Sport, hand shift.

Model 71-FLPF: 74-ci overhead valve twin, Super solo, foot shift.

Model 71-FLP: 74-ci overhead valve twin, Super solo, hand shift.

Model 71-FX, Super Glide: 74-ci overhead valve twin, foot shift.

Model 71-XLH, Super H, Sportster: 55-ci overhead valve twin.

Model 71-XLCH, Super CH, Sportster: 55-ci overhead valve twin.

Model 71-SX, Sprint: 350-cc single-cylinder, four-cycle, off-road model.

Model 71-SS, Sprint: 350-cc single-cylinder, four-cycle.

Model 71-MLS Rapido: 125-cc single-cylinder, off-road bike.

Model 71-M-65 Sport, Leggero: 65-cc single-cylinder, two-cycle.

Model 71-ERS, Sprint Scrambler: 350-cc overhead valve, four-cycle.

Model 71-MSR, Baja: 100-cc single-cylinder, two-cycle.

1972

Model 72-FLHF: 74-ci overhead valve twin, Super Sport, foot shift.

Model 72-FLH: 74-ci overhead valve twin, Super Sport, hand shift.

Model 72-FLPF: 74-ci overhead valve twin, Super solo, foot shift.

Model 72-FLP: 74-ci overhead valve twin, Super solo, hand shift.

Model 72-FX, Super Glide: 74-ci overhead valve twin, foot shift.

Model 72-XLH, Super H, Sportster: 1000-cc V-twin.

Model 72-XLCH, Super CH, Sportster: 1000-cc V-twin.

Model 72-MLS Rapido: 125-cc, single-cylinder, two-cycle.
Model 72-M-65 Sport, Leggero: 65-cc single-cylinder, two cycle.
Model 72-ERS, Sprint Scrambler: 350-cc overhead valve four-cycle.
Model 72-MSR, Baja 100L (lights): 100-cc Single-cylinder, two-cycle.
Model 72-MSR Baja 100 (no lights): 100-cc Single-cylinder, two-stroke.
Model 72-MC-65, Shortster minicycle: 65-cc single-cylinder, two stroke.

1973
Model 73-FL: 74-ci overhead valve twin.
Model 73-FLH: 74-ci overhead valve twin.
Model 73-XLH, Super H, Sportster: 1000-cc V-twin.
Model 73-XLCH, Super CH, Sportster: 1000-cc V-twin.
Model 73-FX, Super Glide: 74-ci overhead valve twin.
Model 73-SS, Sprint: 350-cc single-cylinder, four-stroke, electric start.
Model 73-SX, Sprint: 350-cc single-cylinder, four-stroke, electric start.
Model 73-TX: 125-cc.
Model 73-Z-90: 90-cc single-cylinder, two-stroke, automatic gas-oil mix.
Model 73-X-90: 90-cc single-cylinder, two-stroke, automatic gas-oil mix.
Model 73-SR-100: 100-cc single-cylinder, two-stroke, automatic gas-oil mix.
Model 73-XRTT: 45-ci aluminum engine, racing motorcycle.

1974
Model 74-FLH-1200: 74-ci overhead valve twin.
Model 74-FLHF: 74-ci overhead valve twin.
Model 74-FL Police: 74-ci overhead valve twin.
Model 74-FX, Super Glide: 74-ci overhead valve twin.
Model 74-FXE, Super Glide: 74-cc Electric start, overhead valve twin.
Model 74-XLH, Super H, Sportster: 1000-cc V-twin.
Model 74-XLCH, Super CH, Sportster: 1000-cc V-twin.
Model 74-SS 350: 350-cc single-cylinder, four-cycle.
Model 74-SX 350: 350-cc single-cylinder, four-cycle.
Model 74-SX 175: 175-cc single-cylinder, four-cycle.
Model 74 SX 125: 125-cc single-cylinder, four-cycle.
Model 74-Z-90: 90-cc single-cylinder, two-cycle.
Model 74-X-90: 90-cc single-cylinder, two-cycle.
Model 74-SR-100: 100-cc single-cylinder, two-cycle, off-road bike.
Model 74-XR: 45-ci racing motorcycle.

1975
Model 75-FLH-1200: 74-ci overhead valve twin.
Model 75-FLHF: 74-ci overhead valve twin.
Model 75-FL Police: 74-ci overhead valve twin.
Model 75-FX, Super Glide: 74-ci overhead valve twin.
Model 75-FXE, Super Glide:74-cc Electric start, overhead valve twin.
Model 75-XLH, Super H, Sportster: 1000-cc V-twin.
Model 75-XLCH, Super CH, Sportster: 1000-cc V-twin.
Model 75-SX 175: 175-cc single-cylinder, four-cycle.
Model 75-SX 125: 125-cc single-cylinder, four-cycle.
Model 75-Z-90: 90-cc single-cylinder, two-cycle.
Model 75-X-90: 90-cc single-cylinder, two-cycle.
Model 75-XR: 45-ci racing motorcycle.
Model 75-SX-250: 250-cc single-cylinder, two-cycle, five-speed transmission.
Model 75-RC-125: 125-cc single-cylinder, two-cycle.
Model 75-SS-250: 250-cc single-cylinder, two-cycle, five speed transmission.

1976
Model 76-FLH-1200: 74-ci overhead valve twin.
Model 76-FX, Super Glide: 74-ci overhead valve twin.
Model 76-FXE, Super Glide: Electric start, 74-ci overhead valve twin.
Model 76-XLH, Super H, Sportster: 1000-cc V-twin.
Model 76-XLCH, Super CH, Sportster: 1000-cc V-twin.
Model 76-SS-250: 250-cc single-cylinder, two-cycle.
Model 76-SX-250: 250-cc single-cylinder, two-cycle, off-road.
Model 76-SXT-125: 125-cc single-cylinder, two-cycle.
Model 76-SS-175: 175-cc single-cylinder, two-cycle.
Model 76-SS-125: 125-cc single-cylinder, two-cycle.
Model 76-MX-250: 250-cc single-cylinder, off-road racing cycle.
Model 76-RR-250: 250-cc two-cylinder, liquid-cooled racing cycle.

1977
Model 77-FLH-1200: 74-ci overhead valve twin.
Model 77-FLHS: 74-ci overhead valve twin.
Model 77-FX, Super Glide: 74-ci overhead valve twin.
Model 77-FXE, Super Glide: Electric start, 74-ci overhead valve twin.
Model 77-FXS, Low Rider: 74-ci overhead valve twin.
Model 77-XLT, Sportster: Electric start, 1000-cc V-twin.
Model 77-XLCR: Café Racer, 1000-cc V-twin.
Model 77-XLH, Super H, Sportster: 1000-cc V-twin.
Model 77-XLCH, Super CH, Sportster: 1000-cc V-twin.
Model 77-SS-250: 250-cc single-cylinder, two-cycle.
Model 77-SX-250: 250-cc single-cylinder, two-cycle, off-road.
Model 77-SXT-125: 125-cc single-cylinder, two-cycle.
Model 77-SS-175: 175-cc single-cylinder, two-cycle.
Model 77-SS-125: 125-cc single-cylinder, two-cycle.
Model 77-RR-250: 250-cc two-cylinder, liquid-cooled racing cycle.

1978
Model 78-FLH-1200: 74-ci overhead valve twin.
Model 78-FLH Anniversary: 74-ci overhead valve twin.
Model 78-FLH 80, Electra Glide: 80-ci overhead valve twin.
Model 78-FX, Super Glide: 74-ci overhead valve twin.
Model 78-FXE, Super Glide: Electric start, 74-ci overhead valve twin.
Model 78-FXS, Low Rider: 74-ci overhead valve twin.
Model 78-XLH, Super H, Sportster: 1000-cc V-twin.
Model 78-XLH Anniversary, Sportster: 1000-cc V-twin.
Model 78-XLCH, Super CH, Sportster: 1000-cc V-twin.
Model 78-SX 250: 250-cc single-cylinder, two-cycle.
Model 78-XLT, Sportster: Electric start, 1000-cc V-twin.
Model 78-XLCR, Café Racer: 1000-cc V-twin.
Model 78-XLS, Roadster: 1000-cc V-twin.
Model 78-XR 750: 45-ci V-twin flat-track racer.

1979
Model 79-FLT, Tour Glide: 80-ci V-twin, solid-state ignition.
Model 79-FLHC, Electra Glide Classic: 80-ci V-twin, solid-state ignition, 16-spoke wheels, MT90 x 16-inch rear tire; TourPak standard.
Model 79-FLHC with sidecar, Electra Glide Classic, sidecar standard.
Model 79-FLH 80, Electra Glide: 80-ci V-twin; fairing/windshield, saddle bags with safety guards, luggage rack, passing lights, safety bars, running boards, all standard.
Model 79-FLH-1200, Electra Glide 74: 1200-cc V-twin; fairing/windshield, saddle bags with safety guards, luggage rack, passing lights, safety bars, running boards, all standard.

Model 79-FLH 80, Police: 80-ci police motorcycle.
Model 79-FLH 1200, Police: 74-ci police motorcycle.
Model 79-FXS 1200 Low Rider: 1200-cc V-twin, solid-state ignition, two-into-one exhaust; stash pouch, sissy bar standard.
Model 79-FXS 80, Low Rider: 80-ci V-twin, solid-state ignition, two-into-one exhaust; stash pouch, sissy bar standard.
Model 79-FXEF 1200, Fat Bob Super Glide: 1200-cc V-twin, solid-state ignition, buckhorn handlebars.
Model 79-FXEF 80, Fat Bob Super Glide: 80-ci V-twin, solid-state ignition, 3.5-gal twin gas tanks with instrument pod in middle, two-into-one exhaust.
Model 79-FXE 1200, Super Glide: 1200-cc V-twin, solid-state ignition, two-into-one exhaust.
Model 79-XLH, Sportster: 1000-cc V-twin, XR750-derived frame, 16-inch rear tire, nine-spoke aluminum wheels, buckhorn bars.
Model 79-XLCH, Sportster: 1000-cc V-twin, XR750-derived frame, 16-inch rear tire, nine-spoke aluminum wheels, buckhorn bars.
Model 79-XLCR, Café Racer: 1000-cc V-twin.
Model 79-XLS, Roadster: 1000-cc V-twin, solid-state ignition, siamesed exhaust system, cast aluminum wheels, 16-inch drag-style rear tire, tooled leather stash pouch, highway pegs; termed by factory "a Sportster version of the FXS Low Rider."

1980
Model 80-FLT, Tour Glide: 80-ci V-twin, solid-state ignition.
Model 80-FLHC, Electra Glide Classic: 80-ci V-twin, solid-state ignition.
Model 80-FLHC with sidecar, Electra Glide Classic.
Model 80-FLH 80, Electra Glide: 80-ci V-twin, solid-state ignition.
Model 80-FLH 1200, Electra Glide: 1200-cc V-twin, solid-state ignition.
Model 80-FLHS, Electra Glide: 80-ci V-twin, solid-state ignition.
Model 80-FLH 80, Police: 80-ci police motorcycle.
Model 80-FLH 1200, Police: 74-ci police motorcycle.
Model 80-FXB, Sturgis: 80-ci V-twin, solid-state ignition, primary and secondary belt drive.
Model 80-FXWG, Wide Glide: 80-ci V-twin, solid-state ignition.
Model 80-FXS 1200, Low Rider: 1200-cc V-twin, solid-state ignition.
Model 80-FXS 80, Low Rider: 80-ci V-twin, solid-state ignition.
Model 80-FXEF 80, Fat Bob Wide Glide: 80-ci V-twin, solid-state ignition.
Model 80-FXE 1200, Super Glide: 1200-cc V-twin, solid-state ignition.
Model 80-XLS Roadster: 1000-cc V-twin, solid-state ignition, spoke wheels standard, cast wheels extra.
Model 80-XLH, Sportster: 1000-cc V-twin, solid-state ignition, spoke wheels standard, cast wheels extra.

1981
Model 81-FLTC, Tour Glide Classic: 80-ci V-twin, solid-state ignition, crossover exhaust system.
Model 81-FLT Tour Glide: 80-ci V-twin, solid-state ignition, crossover exhaust system.
Model 81-FLHC. Electra Glide Classic: 80-ci V-twin, belt drive, four-speed transmission, 7-inch quartz halogen headlight; TourPak and back rest standard.
Model 81-FLHC with sidecar, Electra Glide Classic: 80-ci overhead valve V-twin, belt drive, four-speed transmission, 7-inch quartz halogen headlight; TourPak and back rest standard.
Model 81-FLH 80, Electra Glide: 80-ci V-twin, solid-state ignition.
Model 81-FLHS, Electra Glide: 80-ci V-twin, solid-state ignition.
Model 81-Heritage, Electra Glide: 80-ci V-twin, solid-state ignition.

Model 81-FLH 80 Police: 80-ci police motorcycle.
Model 81-FXB, Sturgis: 80-ci engine, primary and secondary belt drive.
Model 81-FXWG, Wide Glide: 80-ci V-twin.
Model 81-FXS 80, Low Rider: 80-ci V-twin.
Model 81-FXEF 80, Fat Bob: 80-ci V-twin.
Model 81-FXE 80, Super Glide: Electric start, 80-ci V-twin.
Model 81-XLS, Roadster: 1000-cc V-twin.
Model 81-XLH, Sportster: 1000-cc V-twin.

1982
Model 82-FLT, Tour Glide: 80-ci V-twin.
Model 82-FLT Classic, Tour Glide: 80-ci V-twin.
Model 82-FLH, Electra Glide: 80-ci V-twin.
Model 82-XLS, Roadster: 61-ci V-twin.
Model 82-FXS, Low Rider: 80-ci V-twin.
Model 82-FXWG, Wide Glide: 80-ci V-twin.
Model 82-XLH, Sportster: 61-ci V-twin.
Model 82-FXE, Super Glide: 80-ci V-twin.
Model 82-FXB, Sturgis: 80-ci V-twin, primary and secondary belt drive.
Model 82-FXR, Super Glide II: 80-ci V-twin, five-speed transmission.
Model 82-FXRS, Super Glide II: 80-ci V-twin, five-speed transmission, computer-designed frame.
Model 82-FLH 80: 80-ci police motorcycle.

1983
Model 83-FLHT, Electra Glide: 80-ci motor, fork-mounted fairing, halogen headlamp and dual spot lamps, tubeless tires, five-speed transmission.
Model 83-FLHT Classic, Electra Glide: 80-ci motor, fork-mounted fairing, halogen headlamp and dual spot lamps, tubeless tires, five-speed transmission, TourPak standard.
Model 83-FLT, Tour Glide: 80-ci motor, adjustable footboards, tubeless tires, rear fender engine vents, 22-amp alternator, spin-on oil filter.
Model 83-FLT Classic Tour Glide: 80-ci motor, adjustable footboards, tubeless tires, rear fender engine vents, 22-amp alternator, spin-on oil filter.
Model 83-FLH, Electra Glide: 80-ci motor, secondary belt drive, automotive type spin-on oil filter.
Model 83-XLH, Sportster: 61-ci motor, two-stage ignition, 8.8:1 compression ratio, oval air box, 3.3-gal gas tank, ribbed primary chain cover.
Model 83-XLS, Roadster: 61-ci motor, two-stage ignition, 8.8:1 compression ratio, oval air box, 3.8 gal Fat Bob-style gas tank, nine-spoke cast wheels.
Model 83-XLX-61: 61-ci motor, two-stage ignition, 8.8:1 compression ratio, oval air box, peanut gas tank, nine-spoke cast wheels.
Model 83-FXSB Low Rider: 80-ci motor, four-speed transmission.
Model 83-FXWG, Wide Glide: 80-ci motor, four-speed transmission.
Model 83-FXE, Super Glide: 80-ci motor, four-speed transmission.
Model 83-FXR, Super Glide: 80-ci motor, five-speed gearbox, low-maintenance calcium alloy grid battery, spin-on oil filter.
Model 83-FXRS, Super Glide II: 80-ci motor, five-speed gearbox, low-maintenance calcium alloy grid battery, spin-on oil filter.
Model 83-FLH 80: 80-ci police motorcycle.

1984
FLHT Electra Glide: 80 ci V-twin, four-speed gearbox, electronic ignition.
FLH Electra Glide Belt Drive: 80-ci V-twin, four-speed gearbox, electronic ignition.
FLHTE-80 Electra Glide Classic: 80-ci V-twin, four-speed gearbox, electronic ignition.

FLT-80 Tour Glide: 80-ci V-twin, four-speed gearbox, electronic ignition.

FLTC-80 Tour Glide Classic: 80-ci V-twin, four-speed gearbox, electronic ignition.

FXE-80 Super Glide: 80-ci V-twin, four-speed transmission, electronic ignition.

FXSB-80 Low Rider Belt: 80-ci V-twin, four-speed transmission, electronic ignition.

FXR Super Glide II: 80-ci V-twin, five-speed transmission, electronic ignition.

FXWG-80 Wide Glide: 80-ci V-twin, four-speed transmission, electronic ignition.

FXRS-80 Low Glide: 80-ci V-twin, five-speed transmission, electronic ignition.

FXRT-80 Sport Glide: 80-ci V-twin, five-speed transmission, electronic ignition.

FXRP-80 Sport Glide Police: 80-ci V-twin, five-speed transmission, electronic ignition.

FXEF-80 Fat Bob: 80-ci V-twin, four-speed transmission, electronic ignition.

XLX-61 Sportster Standard: 61-ci V-twin, four-speed transmission, electronic ignition.

XLH Sportster: 61-ci V-twin, four-speed transmission, electronic ignition.

XLS-1000 Roadster: 61 ci, V-twin, four-speed transmission, electronic ignition.

XR-1000 Sportster: 61-ci V-twin, four-speed transmission, electronic ignition.

1985
FLHTE-80 Electra Glide Classic: 80-ci V-twin, five-speed transmission.
FLTC-80 Tour Glide Classic: 80-ci V-twin, five-speed transmission.
FXEF-80 Fat Bob: 80-ci V-twin, four-speed transmission.
FXSB-80 Low Rider Belt: 80-ci V-twin, four-speed transmission.
FXWG-80 Wide Glide: 80-ci V-twin, four-speed transmission.
FXRS-80 Low Glide: 80-ci V-twin, five-speed transmission.
FXRT-80 Sport Glide: 80-ci V-twin, five-speed transmission.
FXST-80 Softail: 80-ci V-twin, four-speed transmission.
XLH-1000 Sportster: 61-ci V-twin, four-speed transmission.
XLX-61 Sportster Standard: 61-ci V-twin, four-speed transmission.
XLS-1000 Roadster: 61-ci V-twin, four-speed transmission.
XR-1000 Sportster: 61-ci V-twin, four-speed transmission.

1986
FLHT-80 Electra Glide: 80-ci V-twin, five-speed transmission.
FLHTC-80 Electra Glide Classic: 80-ci V-twin, five-speed transmission.
FLTC-80 Tour Glide Classic: 80-ci V-twin, five-speed transmission.
FXR-80 Super Glide: 80-ci V-twin, five-speed transmission.
FXRS-80 Low Rider: 80-ci V-twin, five-speed transmission.
FXRS SP-80 Low Rider Sport Edition: 80-ci V-twin, five-speed transmission.
FXRT-80 Sport Glide: 80-ci V-twin, five-speed transmission.
FXRD-80 Sport Glide Grand Tour: 80-ci V-twin, five-speed transmission.
FXST-80 Softail: 80-ci V-twin, five-speed transmission.
FXSTC-80 Softail Custom: 80-ci V-twin, five-speed transmission.
XLH-883 Sportster: 61-ci V-twin, four-speed transmission.
XLX-883 Sportster Deluxe: 61-ci V-twin, four-speed transmission.
XLH-1100 Sportster: 1100-cc V-twin, four-speed transmission.
XLH-1200 Sportster: 74-ci four-speed transmission.

1987
FLHT Electra Glide: 80-ci V-twin five-speed transmission.
FLHTC Electra Glide Classic: 80-ci V-twin, five-speed transmission.

FLTC Tour Glide Classic: 80-ci V-twin, five-speed transmission.
FXRT Sport Glide: 80-ci V-twin, five-speed transmission.
FXR Super Glide: 80-ci V-twin, five-speed transmission.
FXRS Low Rider: 80-ci V-twin, five-speed transmission.
FXRS Low Rider Sport Edition: 80-ci V-twin, five-speed transmission.
FXLS Low Rider Custom: 80-ci V-twin, five-speed transmission.
FXST Softail: 80-ci V-twin, five-speed transmission.
FXSTC Softail Custom: 80-ci V-twin, five-speed transmission.
FLST Heritage Softail: 80-ci V-twin, five-speed transmission.
XLH Sportster 883: 55-ci V-twin, four-speed transmission.
XLH Sportster Deluxe: 1100-cc V-twin, four-speed transmission.

1988
FLHS Electra Glide Sport: 80-ci V-twin, five-speed transmission.
FLTC Tour Glide Classic: 80-ci V-twin, five-speed transmission.
FLHTC Electra Glide Classic: 80-ci V-twin, five-speed transmission.
FXR Super Glide: 80-ci V-twin, five-speed transmission.
FXST Softail: 80-ci V-twin, five-speed transmission.
FXSTC Softail Custom: 80-ci V-twin, five-speed transmission.
FLST Heritage Softail: 80-ci V-twin, five-speed transmission.
FLSTC Heritage Softail Classic: 80-ci V-twin, five-speed transmission.
FXRT Sport Glide: 80-ci V-twin, five-speed transmission.
FXRS Low Rider: 80-ci V-twin, five-speed transmission.
FXLR Low Rider Custom: 80-ci V-twin, five-speed transmission.
FXRS Sp, Low Rider Sport: 80-ci V-twin, five-speed transmission.
XLH Sportster 883 Solo: 55-ci V-twin, four-speed transmission.
XLH Sportster 883 Hugger: 55-ci V-twin, four-speed transmission.
XLH Sportster 883 Deluxe: 55-ci V-twin, four-speed transmission.
XLH Sportster 1200: 74-ci V-twin, four-speed transmission.

1989
FLHS Electra Glide Sport: 80-ci V-twin, five-speed transmission.
FLHTC Electra Glide Classic: 80-ci V-twin, five-speed transmission.
FLHTU Ultra Classic Electra Glide: 80-ci V-twin, five-speed transmission.
FLTC Tour Glide Classic: 80-ci V-twin, five-speed transmission.
FLTU Ultra Tour Glide Classic: 80-ci V-twin, five-speed transmission.
FXR Super Glide: 80-ci V-twin, five-speed transmission.
FXRS Low Rider: 80-ci V-twin, five-speed transmission.
FXRT Sport Glide: 80-ci V-twin, five-speed transmission.
FXRS Sport, Low Rider Sport: 80-ci V-twin, five-speed transmission.
FXLR Low Rider Custom: 80-ci V-twin, five-speed transmission.
FXST Softail: 80-ci V-twin, five-speed transmission.
FXSTC Softail Custom: 80-ci V-twin, five-speed transmission.
FXSTS Springer Softail: 80-ci V-twin, five-speed transmission.
FLST Heritage Softail: 80-ci V-twin, five-speed transmission.
FLSTC Heritage Softail Custom: 80-ci V-twin, five-speed transmission.
XLH Sportster 883 Solo: 55-ci V-twin, four-speed transmission.
XLH Sportster 883 Deluxe: 55-ci V-twin, four-speed transmission.
XLH 883 Hugger: 55-ci V-twin, four-speed transmission.
XLH Sportster 1200: 74-ci V-twin, four-speed transmission.

1990
FLHS Electra Glide Sport: 80-ci V-twin, five-speed transmission.
FLHTC Electra Glide Classic: 80-ci V-twin, five-speed transmission.
FLHTC Ultra Classic Electra Glide: 80-ci V-twin, five-speed transmission.
FLTC Tour Glide Classic: 80-ci V-twin, five-speed transmission.
FXR Super Glide: 80-ci V-twin, five-speed transmission.
FLSTF Fat Boy: 80-ci V-twin, five-speed transmission.

FLST Heritage Softail: 80-ci V-twin, five-speed transmission.
FLSTC Heritage Softail Classic: 80-ci V-twin, five-speed transmission.
FXST Softail: 80-ci V-twin, five-speed transmission.
FXSTC Softail Custom: 80-ci V-twin, five-speed transmission.
FXSTS Springer Softail: 80-ci V-twin, five-speed transmission.
FXRS Convertible, Low Rider Convertible: 80-ci V-twin, five-speed transmission.
FXRS Sport, Low Rider Sport Edition: 80-ci V-twin, five-speed transmission.
FXLR Low Rider Custom: 80-ci V-twin, five-speed transmission.
FXRS Low Rider: 80-ci V-twin, five-speed transmission.
XLS Sportster 883: 55-ci V-twin, four-speed transmission.
XLS Sportster 883 Hugger: 55-ci V-twin, four-speed transmission.
XLS Sportster 1200: 74-ci V-twin, four-speed transmission.
XLS Sportster 883 Deluxe: 55-ci V-twin, four-speed transmission.

1991

FLHS Electra Glide Sport: 80-ci V-twin, five-speed transmission.
FLHTC Electra Glide Classic: 80-ci V-twin, five-speed transmission.
FLHTCU Ultra Classic Electra Glide: 80-ci V-twin, five-speed transmission.
FLTC Tour Glide Classic: 80-ci V-twin, five-speed transmission.
FLTCU Ultra Classic Tour Glide: 80-ci V-twin, five-speed transmission.
FXR Super Glide: 80-ci V-twin, five-speed transmission.
FXRS Low Rider: 80-ci V-twin, five-speed transmission.
FXRT Sport Glide: 80-ci V-twin, five-speed transmission.
FXRS Sport, Low Rider Sport Edition: 80-ci V-twin, five-speed transmission.
FXRS Convertible, Low Rider Convertible: 80-ci V-twin, five-speed transmission.
FXLR Low Rider Custom: 80-ci V-twin, five-speed transmission.
FXDB Sturgis Dyna Glide: 80-ci V-twin, five-speed transmission.
FXSTC Softail Custom: 80-ci V-twin, five-speed transmission.
FLSTF Fat Boy: 80-ci V-twin, five-speed transmission.
FXSTS Springer Softail: 80-ci V-twin, five-speed transmission.
FLSTC Heritage Softail Classic: 80-ci V-twin, five-speed transmission.
XLH Sportster 883: 55-ci V-twin, five-speed transmission.
XLH Sportster 883 Deluxe: 55-ci V-twin, five-speed transmission, belt drive.
XLH Sportster 883 Hugger: 55-ci V-twin, five-speed transmission.
XLH Sportster 1200: 74-ci V-twin, five-speed transmission, belt drive.

1992

FLHS Electra Glide Sport: 80-ci V-twin, five-speed transmission.
FLHTC Electra Glide Classic: 80-ci V-twin, five-speed transmission.
FLHTCU Electra Glide Ultra Classic: 80-ci V-twin, five-speed transmission.
FLTC Tour Glide Classic: 80-ci V-twin, five-speed transmission.
FLTCU Ultra Classic Tour Glide: 80-ci V-twin, five-speed transmission.
FXR Super Glide: 80-ci V-twin, five-speed transmission.
FXRS Low Rider: 80-ci V-twin, five-speed transmission.
FXRT Sport Glide: 80-ci V-twin, five-speed transmission.
FXRS Sport, Low Rider Sport Edition: 80-ci V-twin, five-speed transmission.
FXRS Convertible, Low Rider Convertible: 80-ci V-twin, five-speed transmission.
FXLR Low Rider Custom: 80-ci V-twin, five-speed transmission.
FXDB-Sturgis Dyna Glide: 80-ci V-twin, five-speed transmission.
FXSTC Softail Custom: 80-ci V-twin, five-speed transmission.
FLSTF Fat Boy: 80-ci V-twin, five-speed transmission.
FXSTS Springer Softail: 80-ci V-twin, five-speed transmission.
FLSTC Heritage Softail Classic: 80-ci V-twin, five-speed transmission.
XLH Sportster 883: 55-ci V-twin, five-speed transmission.
XLH Sportster 883 Deluxe: 55-ci V-twin, five-speed transmission.

XLH Hugger: 55-ci V-twin, five-speed transmission.
XLH Sportster 1200: 74-ci V-twin, five-speed transmission.

1993

FLHR Electra Glide Road King: 80-ci V-twin, five-speed transmission.
FLHS Electra Glide Sport: 80-ci V-twin, five-speed transmission.
FLHTC Electra Glide Classic: 80-ci V-twin, five-speed transmission.
FLHTCU Ultra Classic Electra Glide: 80-ci V-twin, five-speed transmission.
FLTCU Ultra Classic Tour Glide: 80-ci V-twin, five-speed transmission.
FXD Super Glide: 80-ci V-twin, five-speed transmission.
FLSTC Heritage Softail Classic: 80-ci V-twin, five-speed transmission.
FLSTN Heritage Softail Nostalgia: 80-ci V-twin, five-speed transmission.
FLSTF Fat Boy: 80-ci V-twin, five-speed transmission.
FLXR Low Rider Custom: 80-ci V-twin, five-speed transmission.
FXDL Dyna Low Rider: 80-ci V-twin, five-speed transmission.
FXDWG Dyna Wide Glide: 80-ci V-twin, five-speed transmission.
FXRS Sport, Low Rider Sport Edition: 80-ci V-twin, five-speed transmission.
FXSTC Softail Custom: 80-ci V-twin, five-speed transmission.
FXSTS Springer Softail: 80-ci V-twin, five-speed transmission.
FXDS Convertible, Dyna Low Rider Convertible: 80-ci V-twin, five-speed transmission.
XLH Sportster 883: 55-ci V-twin, five-speed transmission.
XLH Sportster Hugger: 55-ci V-twin, five-speed transmission.
XLH Sportster 1200: 74-ci V-twin, five-speed transmission.

1994

FLHR Electra Glide Road King: 80-ci V-twin, five-speed transmission.
FLHTC Electra Glide Classic: 80-ci V-twin, five-speed transmission.
FLHTCU Ultra Classic Electra Glide: 80-ci V-twin, five-speed transmission.
FXD Super Glide: 80-ci V-twin, five-speed transmission.
FXLR Low Rider Custom: 80-ci V-twin, five-speed transmission.
FXDL Dyna Wide Glide: 80-ci V-twin, five-speed transmission.
FXDWG Dyna Wide Glide: 80-ci V-twin, five-speed transmission.
FXDS Convertible: 80-ci V-twin, five-speed transmission.
FLSTN Heritage Special: 80-ci V-twin, five-speed transmission.
FLSTC Heritage Softail Classic: 80-ci V-twin, five-speed transmission.
FXSTS Springer Softail: 80-ci V-twin, five-speed transmission.
FXSTC Softail Custom: 80-ci V-twin, five-speed transmission.
FLSTF Fat Boy: 80-ci V-twin, five-speed transmission.
XLH Sportster 883: 55-ci V-twin, five-speed transmission.
XLH Sportster Hugger: 55-ci V-twin, five-speed transmission.
XLH Sportster 1200: 74-ci V-twin, five-speed transmission.

1995

FLHR Electra Glide Road King: 80-ci V-twin, five-speed transmission.
FLHT Electra Glide Standard: 80-ci V-twin, five-speed transmission.
FLHTC Electra Glide Classic: 80-ci V-twin, five-speed transmission.
FLHTU Ultra Classic Electra Glide: 80-ci V-twin, five-speed transmission.
FLTCU Ultra Classic Tour Glide: 80-ci V-twin, five-speed transmission.
FXD Dyna Super Glide: 80-ci V-twin, five-speed transmission.
FXDS Convertible, Dyna Convertible: 80-ci V-twin, five-speed transmission.
FXDWG Dyna Wide Glide: 80-ci V-twin, five-speed transmission.
FXDL Dyna Low Rider: 80-ci V-twin, five-speed transmission.
FXSTC Softail Custom: 80-ci V-twin, five-speed transmission.
FXSTS Springer Softail: 80-ci V-twin, five-speed transmission.
FXSTB Bad Boy: 80-ci V-twin, five-speed transmission.
FLSTC Heritage Softail Classic: 80-ci V-twin, five-speed transmission.
FLSTN Heritage Special: 80-ci V-twin, five-speed transmission.

XLH Sportster 883 Standard: 55-ci V-twin, five-speed transmission.
XLH Sportster 883 Hugger: 55-ci V-twin, five-speed transmission.
XLH Sportster 883 Deluxe: 55-ci V-twin, five-speed transmission.
XLH Sportster 1200: 74-ci V-twin, five-speed transmission.

1996
FLHTU Ultra Classic Electra Glide: 80-ci V-twin, five-speed transmission.
FLHTUI Ultra Classic Electra Glide EFI: 80-ci V-twin, five-speed transmission.
FLHTC Electra Glide Classic: 80-ci V-twin, five-speed transmission.
FLHTCI Electra Glide EFI: 80-ci V-twin, five-speed transmission.
FLHT Electra Glide Standard: 80-ci V-twin, five-speed transmission.
FLSTF Fat Boy, 80-ci V-twin: five-speed transmission.
FLSTC Heritage Softail Classic: 80-ci V-twin, five-speed transmission.
FLSTN Heritage Softail Special: 80-ci V-twin, five-speed transmission.
FXSTB Bad Boy: 80-ci V-twin, five-speed transmission.
FXSTS Springer Softail: 80-ci V-twin, five-speed transmission.
FXSTC Softail Custom: 80-ci V-twin, five-speed transmission.
FXDWG Dyna Wide Glide: 80-ci V-twin, five-speed transmission.
FXDS Convertible, Dyna Convertible: 80-ci V-twin, five-speed transmission.
FXDL Dyna Low Rider: 80-ci V-twin, five-speed transmission.
FXD Dyna Super Glide: 80-ci V-twin, five-speed transmission.
XLH Sportster 883: 55-ci V-twin, five-speed transmission.
XLH Sportster Hugger 883: 55-ci V-twin, five-speed transmission.
XLH Sportster 1200: 74-ci V-twin, five-speed transmission.
XL 1200C Sportster Custom: 74-ci V-twin, five-speed transmission.
XL 1200S Sportster Sport: 74-ci V-twin, five-speed transmission.

1997
FLHTCUI Ultra Classic Electra Glide: 80-ci V-twin, five-speed transmission.
FLHTCU Ultra Classic Electra Glide: 80-ci V-twin, five-speed transmission.
FLHTC Electra Glide Classic: 80-ci V-twin, five-speed transmission.
FLHT Electra Glide Standard: 80-ci V-twin, five-speed transmission.
FLHR Road King: 80-ci V-twin, five-speed transmission.
FLSTF Fat Boy: 80-ci V-twin, five-speed transmission.
FLSTC Heritage Softail Classic: 80-ci V-twin, five-speed transmission.
FLSTS Heritage Springer: 80-ci V-twin, five-speed transmission.
FXSTB Bad Boy: 80-ci V-twin, five-speed transmission.
FXSTS Springer Softail: 80-ci V-twin, five-speed transmission.
FXSTC Softail Custom: 80-ci V-twin, five-speed transmission.
FXDWG Dyna Wide Glide: 80-ci V-twin, five-speed transmission.
FXDS Convertible, Dyna Convertible: 80-ci V-twin, five-speed transmission.
FXDL Dyna Low Rider: 80-ci V-twin, five-speed transmission.
FXD Dyna Super Glide: 80-ci V-twin, five-speed transmission.
XLH Sportster 883: 55-ci V-twin, five-speed transmission.
XLH Sportster Hugger 883: 55-ci V-twin, five-speed transmission.
XLH Sportster 1200: 74-ci V-twin, five-speed transmission.
XL 1200C Sportster Custom: 74-ci V-twin, five-speed transmission.
XL 1200S Sportster Sport: 74-ci V-twin, five-speed transmission.

1998
N/A

1999
N/A

2000
N/A

2001
XLH Sportster 883: 883-cc overhead valve Evolution engine, carburetor, five-speed transmission, staggered shorty dual exhausts, 60-inch wheelbase, 489 pounds dry weight.
XLH Sportster 883 Hugger: 883-cc overhead valve Evolution engine, carburetor, five-speed transmission, staggered shorty dual exhausts, 59-inch wheelbase, 486 pounds dry weight.
XL 883C Sportster 883 Custom: 883-cc overhead valve Evolution engine, carburetor, five-speed transmission, staggered shorty dual exhausts, 60-inch wheelbase, 489 pounds dry weight.
XLH Sportster 1200: 1200-cc overhead valve Evolution engine, carburetor, five-speed transmission, staggered shorty dual exhausts, 60-inch wheelbase, 491 pounds dry weight.
XL 1200S Sportster 1200 Sport: 1200-cc overhead valve Evolution engine, carburetor, five-speed transmission, black staggered shorty dual exhausts, 60.2-inch wheelbase, 501 pounds dry weight.
XL 1200C Sportster 1200 Custom: 1200-cc overhead valve Evolution engine, five-speed transmission, staggered shorty dual exhausts, 60-inch wheelbase, 491 pounds dry weight.
FXD Dyna Super Glide: 88-ci twin-cam engine, carburetor, five-speed transmission, staggered shorty duals, 62.5-inch wheelbase, 612 pounds dry weight.
FXDX Dyna Super Glide Sport: 88-ci twin-cam engine, carburetor, five-speed transmission, black staggered shorty dual exhausts, 63.2-inch wheelbase, 619 pounds dry weight.
FXDXT Dyna Super Glide T-Sport: 88-ci twin-cam engine, carburetor, five-speed transmission, staggered shorty dual exhausts, 63.2-inch wheelbase, 642 pounds dry weight.
FXDL Dyna Low Rider: 88-ci twin-cam engine, carburetor, five-speed transmission, staggered shorty dual exhausts, 65.5-inch wheelbase, 614 pounds dry weight.
FXDWG Dyna Wide Glide: 88-ci twin-cam engine, carburetor, five-speed transmission, staggered shorty dual exhausts, 66.1-inch wheelbase, 612 pounds dry weight.
FXST/FXSTI Softail Standard: 88-ci twin-cam engine, carburetor, five-speed transmission, staggered shorty dual exhausts, 66.9-inch wheelbase, 628 pounds dry weight.
FXSTB/FXSTBI Night Train: 88-ci balanced twin-cam engine, carburetor or fuel injection, five-speed transmission, staggered shorty dual exhausts, 66.9-inch wheelbase, 629 pounds dry weight.
FXSTD/FXSTDI Softail Deuce: 88-ci balanced twin-cam engine, carburetor or fuel injection, five-speed transmission, over/under shotgun dual exhausts, 66.6-inch wheelbase, 644 pounds dry weight.
FXSTS/FXSTSI Springer Softail: 88-ci balanced twin-cam engine, carburetor or fuel injection, five-speed transmission, staggered shorty dual exhausts, 65.4-inch wheelbase, 652 pounds dry weight.
FLSTF/FLSTFI Fat Boy: 88-ci balanced twin-cam engine, carburetor or fuel injection, five-speed transmission, over/under shotgun dual exhausts, 64.5-inch wheelbase, 665 pounds dry weight.
FLSTC/FLSTCI Heritage Softail Classic: 88-ci balanced twin-cam engine, carburetor or fuel injection, five-speed transmission, staggered shorty dual exhausts, 64.5-inch wheelbase, 695 pounds dry weight.
FLSTS/FLSTSI Heritage Springer: 88-ci balanced twin-cam engine, carburetor or fuel injection, five-speed transmission, crossover dual fishtail exhausts, 64.2-inch wheelbase, 716 pounds dry weight.
FLHT Electra Glide Standard: 88-ci vibration isolation-mounted engine, carburetor, five-speed transmission, crossover dual blunt-cut exhausts, 63.5-inch wheelbase, 758 pounds dry weight.

FLHTC/FLHTCI Electra Glide Classic: 88-ci vibration isolation-mounted engine, carburetor or fuel injection, five-speed transmission, crossover dual blunt-cut exhausts, 63.5-inch wheelbase, 776 pounds dry weight.

FLHTCUI Ultra Classic Electra Glide: 88-ci vibration isolation-mounted engine, carburetor or fuel injection, five-speed transmission, crossover dual blunt-cut exhausts, 63.5-inch wheelbase, 788 pounds dry weight.

FLHR/FLHRI Road King: 88-ci vibration isolation-mounted engine, carburetor or fuel injection, five-speed transmission, crossover dual blunt-cut exhausts, 63.5-inch wheelbase, 723 pounds dry weight.

FLHRCI Road King Classic: 88-ci vibration isolation-mounted engine, fuel injection, five-speed transmission, crossover dual slash-cut exhausts, 63.5-inch wheelbase, 710 pounds dry weight.

FLTR/FLTRI Road Glide: 88-ci vibration isolation-mounted engine, carburetor or fuel injection, five-speed transmission, crossover dual blunt-cut exhausts, 63.5-inch wheelbase, 731 pounds dry weight.

Buell Cyclone M2: 1203-cc V-twin, Keihin CV carburetor, five-speed transmission, Showa front forks, aluminum arc swingarm, 55-inch wheelbase, 435 pounds dry weight.

Buell Lightning X1: 1203-cc V-twin, fuel injection, five-speed transmission, Showa inverted front forks, aluminum arc swingarm, 55-inch wheelbase, 440 pounds dry weight.

Buell Thunderbolt S3: 1203-cc V-twin, fuel injection, five-speed transmission, Showa inverted front forks, aluminum arc swingarm, 55-inch wheelbase, 450 pounds dry weight.

Buell Thunderbolt S3T: 1203-cc V-twin, fuel injection, five-speed transmission, Showa inverted front forks, aluminum arc swingarm, 55-inch wheelbase, 465 pounds dry weight.

Buell Blast: 492-cc single-cylinder engine, five-speed transmission, Showa forks, gas-charged shock absorbers, 55.3-inch wheelbase, 360 pounds dry weight.

2002

Buell Cyclone M2: 1203-cc overhead valve V-twin, carburetor, 91 horsepower, 2-into-1 collector exhaust, three-spoke cast wheels, 435 pounds dry weight.

Buell Lightning X1: 1203-cc overhead valve V-twin, fuel injection, 101 horsepower, 2-into-1 exhaust, three-spoke cast wheels, 440 pounds dry weight.

Buell X1 White Lightning: 1203-cc overhead valve V-twin, fuel injection, 101 horsepower, 2-into-1 exhaust, three-spoke cast wheels, 440 pounds dry weight.

Buell Firebolt XB9R: 984-cc overhead valve V-twin, fuel injection, 92 horsepower, 2-into-1 exhaust, six-spoke cast wheels, 385 pounds dry weight.

Buell Thunderbolt S3T: 1203-cc overhead valve V-twin, fuel injection 101 horsepower, 2-into-1 exhaust, three-spoke cast wheels, 465 pounds dry weight.

Buell Blast: 492-cc overhead valve four-stroke single-cylinder, carburetor, 34 horsepower, tuned resonance chamber exhaust, five-spoke wheels, 360 pounds dry weight.

XLH883 Sportster: 883-cc air-cooled V-twin, carburetor, 60.0-inch wheelbase, single disc brakes front and rear, 489 pounds dry weight.

XLH883H Hugger: 883-cc air-cooled V-twin, carburetor, 59.0-inch wheelbase, single disc brakes front and rear, 486 pounds dry weight.

XL883C Sportster 883 Custom: 883-cc V-twin, carburetor, 60.0-inch wheelbase, single disc brakes front and rear, 489 pounds dry weight.

XLH1200 Sportster 1200: 1200-cc V-twin, carburetor, 60.0-inch wheelbase, single disc brake front and rear, 491 pounds dry weight.

XL1200C Sportster 1200 Custom: 1200-cc V-twin, carburetor, 60.0-inch wheelbase, single disc brake front and rear, 491 pounds dry weight.

XL1200S Sportster 1200 Sport: 1200-cc V-twin, carburetor, 60.2-inch wheelbase, single disc brake front and rear, 501 pounds dry weight.

XL883R Sportster 883R: 883-cc V-twin, carburetor, 60.0-inch wheelbase, single disc brake front and rear, 501 pounds dry weight.

VRSCA V-Rod: 1130-cc 60-degree liquid-cooled V-twin, fuel injection, 67.5-inch wheelbase, dual disc front, single disc rear brake, 595.7 pounds dry weight.

FXD Dyna Super Glide: 1450-cc V-twin, carburetor, 62.5-inch wheelbase, single disc brake front and rear, 612 pounds dry weight.

FXDX Dyna Super Glide Sport: 1450-cc V-twin, carburetor, 63.2-inch wheelbase, dual disc front, single disc rear brake, 619 pounds dry weight.

FXDL Dyna Low Rider: 1450-cc V-twin, carburetor, 65.5-inch wheelbase, single disc brake front and rear, 614 pounds dry weight.

FXDXT Dyna Super Glide T-Sport: 1450-cc V-twin, carburetor, 63.2-inch wheelbase, dual disc front, single disc rear brake, 542 pounds dry weight.

FXDWG Dyna Wide Glide: 1450-cc V-twin, carburetor, 66.1-inch wheelbase, single disc brake front and rear, 612 pounds dry weight.

FXST/Fuel Injection Softail Standard: 1450-cc V-twin, fuel injection, 66.9-inch wheelbase, single disc brake front and rear, 628.6 pounds dry weight.

FXSTB/I Night Train: 1450-cc V-twin, fuel injection, 66.9-inch wheelbase, single disc brake front and rear, 629.6 pounds dry weight.

FXSTS/I Springer Softail: 1450-cc V-twin, fuel injection, 65.4-inch wheelbase, single disc brake front and rear, 652.6 pounds dry weight.

FXSTD/I Softail Deuce: 1450-cc V-twin, fuel injection, 66.6-inch wheelbase, single disc brake front and rear, 644.6 pounds dry weight.

FLSTF/I Fat Boy: 1450-cc V-twin, fuel injection, 64.5-inch wheelbase, single disc brake front and rear, 665.6 pounds dry weight.

FLSTC/I Heritage Softail Classic: 1450-cc V-twin, fuel injection, 64.5-inch wheelbase, single disc brake front and rear, 695.6 pounds dry weight.

FLSTS/I Heritage Springer: 1450-cc V-twin, fuel injection, 64.2-inch wheelbase, single disc brake front and rear, 716.6 pounds.

FLHT Electra Glide Standard: 1450-cc V-twin, carburetor, 63.5-inch wheelbase, dual disc front, single disc rear brake, 758 pounds dry weight.

FLHR/I Road King: 1450-cc V-twin, fuel injection, 63.5-inch wheelbase, dual disc front, single disc rear brake, 723 pounds dry weight.

FLHRCI Road King Classic: 1450-cc V-twin, fuel injection, 63.5-inch wheelbase, dual disc front, single disc rear brake, 710 pounds.

FLTR/I Road Glide: 1450-cc V-twin, fuel injection, 63.5-inch wheelbase, dual disc front, single disc rear brake, 731 pounds dry weight.

FLHTC/I Electra Glide Classic: 1450-cc V-twin, fuel injection, 63.5-inch wheelbase, dual disc front, single disc rear brake, 776 pounds dry weight.

FLHTCUI Ultra Classic Electra Glide: 1450-cc V-twin, fuel injection, 63.5-inch wheelbase, dual disc front, single disc rear brake, 768 pounds dry weight.

FLHRSEI Screamin' Eagle Road King: 1550-cc V-twin, fuel injection, 63.5-inch wheelbase, dual disc front, single disc rear brake, 741 pounds dry weight.

FXDWG3: 1450-cc V-twin, carburetor, 65.3-inch wheelbase, single disc brake front and rear, 647.5 pounds dry weight.

2003

Buell Firebolt XB9R: 984cc OHV V-twin, fuel injection, 92 horsepower, 2-into-1 exhaust, six-spoke cast wheels, 385 lbs. dry weight, $9,995 msrp.

Buell Lightning XB9S: 984cc OHV V-twin, fuel injection, 92 horsepower,

2-into-1 exhaust, six-spoke cast wheels, 385 lbs. dry weight, $9,995 msrp.

Buell Blast: 492cc OHV four-stroke single-cylinder, carburetor, 34 horsepower, tuned resonance chamber exhaust, five-spoke wheels, 360 lbs. dry weight, $4,595 msrp.

883R—XL Sportster: 883cc V-twin, carburetor, 60.0 in. wheelbase, single disc brake front and rear, 503 lbs. dry weight, $6,795 msrp.

883—XLH Sportster: 883cc air-cooled V-twin, carburetor, 60.0 in. wheelbase, single disc brakes front and rear, 489 lbs. dry weight, $5,975-$6,145 msrp.

883 Custom—XL Sportster: 883cc V-twin, carburetor, 60.0 in. wheelbase, single disc brakes front and rear, 489 lbs. dry weight, $7,075-$7,690 msrp.

883 Hugger—XLH Sportster: 883cc air-cooled V-twin, carburetor, 59.0 in. wheelbase, single disc brakes front and rear, 486 lbs. dry weight, $6,435-$6,595 msrp.

XLH 1200 Sportster: 1200cc V-twin, carburetor, 60.0 in. wheelbase, single disc brake front and rear, 491 lbs. dry weight, $8,255-$8425 msrp.

1200 Custom—XL 1200C: 1200cc V-twin, carburetor, 60.0 in. wheelbase, single disc brake front and rear, 491 lbs. dry weight, $9,425-$10,040 msrp.

1200 Sport—XL 1200S: 1200cc V-twin, carburetor, 60.2 in. wheelbase, single disc brake front and rear, 501 lbs. dry weight, $8,960-$9,130 msrp.

VRSCA V-Rod: 1130cc 60-degree, liquid-cooled V-twin, fuel injection, 67.5 in. wheelbase, dual disc front, single disc rear brake, 595.7 lbs. dry weight, $17,995-$18,695 msrp.

FXDL Low Rider: 1450cc V-twin, carburetor, 65.5 in. wheelbase, single disc brake front and rear, 632 lbs. dry weight, $15,185-$16,090 msrp.

FXD Super Glide: 1450cc V-twin, carburetor, 62.5 in. wheelbase, single disc brake front and rear, 622 lbs. dry weight, $12,255-$12,490 msrp.

FXDWG Wide Glide: 1450cc V-twin, carburetor, 66.1 in. wheelbase, single disc brake front and rear, 639 lbs. dry weight, $16,310-$17,215 msrp.

FXDX Super Glide Sport: 1450cc V-twin, carburetor, 63.2 in. wheelbase, dual disc front, single disc rear brake, 632 lbs. dry weight, $14,275-$14,510 msrp.

FXDXT Super Glide T-Sport: 1450cc V-twin, carburetor, 63.2 in. wheelbase, dual disc front, single disc rear brake, 662 lbs. dry weight, $15,370-$15,520 msrp.

FXSTD/I Softail Deuce: 1450cc V-twin, fuel injection, 66.6 in. wheelbase, single disc brake front and rear, 645 lbs. dry weight,$16,965-$17,870 msrp.

FXSTB/I Night Train: 1450cc V-twin, fuel injection, 66.9 in. wheelbase, single disc brake front and rear, 633 lbs. dry weight, $15,425-$15,575 msrp.

FXST/Fuel Injection Softail Standard: 1450cc V-twin, fuel injection, 66.9 in. wheelbase, single disc brake front and rear, 632 lbs. dry weight, $13,635-$13,870 msrp.

FLSTF/I Fat Boy: 1450cc V-twin, fuel injection, 64.5 in. wheelbase, single disc brake front and rear, 669 lbs. dry weight, $16,195-$17,100 msrp.

FXSTS/I Springer Softail: 1450cc V-twin, fuel injection, 65.4 in. wheelbase, single disc brake front and rear, 656 lbs. dry weight, $16,395-$16,630 msrp.

FLSTS/I Heritage Springer: 1450cc V-twin, fuel injection, 64.2 in. wheelbase, single disc brake front and rear, 721 lbs., $17,795-$18,615 msrp.

FLSTC/I Heritage Softail Classic: 1450cc V-twin, fuel injection, 64.5 in. wheelbase, single disc brake front and rear, 699 lbs. dry weight, $16,965-$17,870 msrp.

FLHR/I Road King: 1450cc V-twin, fuel injection, 63.5 in. wheelbase, dual disc front, single disc rear brake, 723 lbs. dry weight, $16,215-$16,650 msrp.

FLHRCI Road King Classic: 1450cc V-twin, fuel injection, 63.5 in. wheelbase, dual disc front, single disc rear brake, 710 lbs, $17,405-$18,310 msrp.

FLTRI Road Glide: 1450cc V-twin, fuel injection, 63.5 in. wheelbase, dual disc front, single disc rear brake, 731 lbs. dry weight, $17,450-$18,520 msrp.

FLHT/I Electra Glide Standard: 1450cc V-twin, carburetor, 63.5 in. wheelbase, dual disc front, single disc rear brake, 758 lbs. dry weight, $14,710 msrp.

FLHTC/I Electra Glide Classic: 1450cc V-twin, fuel injection, 63.5 in. wheelbase, dual disc front, single disc rear brake, 776 lbs. dry weight, $16,765-$18,070 msrp.

FLHTCUI Ultra Classic Electra Glide: 1450cc V-twin, fuel injection, 63.5 in. wheelbase, dual disc front, single disc rear brake, 788 lbs. dry weight, $19,760-$21,065 msrp.

Screamin' Eagle Road King: 1690cc V-twin, fuel injection, 63.5 in. wheelbase, dual disc front, single disc rear brake, 745 lbs. dry weight, $27,995 msrp.

Screamin' Eagle Deuce: 1550cc V-twin, fuel injection, 66.6-in. wheelbase, dual disc front, single disc rear brake, 677 lbs. dry weight, $25,995 msrp.

The Harley-Davidson Motor Company

Appendix B

H-D Production 1903-2000

The following figures were gleaned from several sources, all linked to the corporation. It should be noted that figures for the first half of Harley-Davidson's existence are known to be inaccurate, because a long-time recorder apparently confused model years and fiscal years with conventional years. Totals that are more complete are available only from the Harley-Davidson, Inc., service department, which has a master record of serial numbers. Harley-Davidson declined to make these figures available.

Year		Year		Year	
		1914	16,284	1931	10,500
		1915	16,645	1932	6,841
		1916	17,439	1933	3,703
		1917	19,763	1934	10,231
		1918	19,359	1935	10,368
		1919	24,292	1936	9,812
1903	1	1920	28,189	1937	11,674
1904	2	1921	10,202	1938	9,934
1905	8	1922	12,759	1939	8,355
1906	50	1923	18,430	1940	10,855
1907	150	1924	13,996	1941	18,428
1908	450	1925	16,929	1942	29,603
1909	1,149	1926	23,354	1943	29,243
1910	3,168	1927	19,911	1944	17,006
1911	5,625	1928	22,350	1945	11,978
1912	9,571	1929	21,142	1946	15,554
1913	12,904	1930	17,422	1947	20,392

1948	31,163
1949	23,740
1950	18,355
1951	14,580
1952	17,250
1953	14,050
1954	12,250
1955	9,750

1956

FL	836
FLE	671
FLH	224
FLF	1,578
FLEF	162
FLHF	2,315
(Total F series	5,786)
G 467	
GA	736
KHK	714
KH	539
KR29	
KRTT	18
XL1	
KHRTT	13
ST2,219	
B 1,384	
TOTAL	**11,906**

1957

FL	1,579
FLH	164
FLF	1,259
FLHF	2,614
(Total F series	5,616)
G 518	
GA	674
KH	90
XL1,983	
XLA	418
(Total XL series	2,401)
KR16	
KRTT	9
KHRTT	4
ST2,401	
B 1,350	
TOTAL	**13,079**

1958

FL	1,591
FLH	195
FLF	1,299
FLHF	2,953
(Total F series	6,038)
G	283

GA	643
XL579	
XLH	711
XLCH	239
(Total XL series	1,529)
KRTT	26
KR9	
XLRTT	26
ST2,445	
B	1,677
TOTAL	**12,676**

1959

FL	1,201
FLH	121
FLF	1,222
FLHF	3,223
(Total F series	5,767)
G	288
GA	524
XL42	
XLH	942
XLCH	1,059
XLR	5
XLRTT	13
(Total XL series	2,061)
KR10	
KRTT	23
ST2,311	
B	1,285
A 73	
TOTAL	**12,342**

1960

A	3,801
74 5,967	
Servi-Car	707
XLH	2,765
B, BT	2,488
TOTAL	**15,728**

1961

A	1,341
74 4,927	
Servi-Car	628
XLH	2,014
BT1,587	
TOTAL	**10,497**

1962

74 5,184	
45 1,276	
XLSS	1,998
G, GE	703
B	1,983
TOTAL	**11,144**

1963

BT824	
BTU	39
BTH	877
AH	972

AU	6	*(Total F series*	*7,800)*
XLH	432	BTH	1,150
XLCH	1,001	XLCH	3,900
(Total XL series	*1,433)*	XLH	900
KR80		*(Total XL series*	*4,800)*
FL	1,096	GE	625
FLF	950	KR10	
FLH	100	KRTT	10
FLHF	2,100	XLRTT	25
Sprint C	150	CR	50
Sprint H	1,416	CRS	350
TOTAL	**10,043**	Sprint H	4,700
		Sprint C	600
		M50	5,700
		M50S	10,500
		TOTAL	**36,310**

(Factory reported 10,407 bikes produced;
no reason given for discrepancy.)

1964

FL	2,775
FLH	2,725
(Total FL series	*5,500)*
BT600	
BTH	800
BTU	50
AH	800
AU	25
XLCH	1,950
XLH	810
XLA	100
(Total XL series	*2,860)*
GE	725
XLRTT	30
KRTT	30
KR20	
CR	50
Sprint C	230
Sprint H	1,550
TOTAL	**13,270**

1965

FL	2,130
FLH	4,800
(Total F series	*6,930)*
BT500	
BTH	750
AH	500
XLCH	2,815
XLH	955
(Total XL series	*3,770)*
GE	625
XLRTT	25
KRTT	10
KR8	
CR	35
CRS	175
Sprint H	2,500
Sprint C	500
M50	9,000
TOTAL	**25,328**

1966

FL	2,175
FLH	5,625

1967

FL	2,150
FLH	5,600
(Total F series	*7,750)*
XLCH	2,500
XLH	2,000
(Total XL series	*4,500)*
GE	600
Sprint H	2,000
Sprint SS	7,000
CRTT	35
CRS	50
M65	2,000
M-65 Sport	**3,267**
TOTAL	**27,202**

1968

FL	1,718
FLH	5,354
XLH	1,995
XLCH	4,889
GE	617
M-65	1,200
M-65 Sport	1,700
SS-350	4,150
ML	5,000
ERS	125
TOTAL	**26,748**

1969

FL	1,800
FLH	5,500
XLH	2,700
XLCH	5,100
GE	475
M-65	950
M-65 Sport	1,750
SS-350	4,575
ML	1,000
MLS	3,275
ERS	250
TOTAL	**27,375**

1970

FL	1,706

FLH	5,909
XLH	3,033
XLCH	5,527
GE	494
M-65 Sport	2,080
SS-350	4,513
MLS	4,059
ERS	102
MSR-100	1,427
TOTAL	**28,850**

1971

FL 1,200	
FLH	5,475
XLH	3,950
XLCH	6,825
GE	500
M-65 Sport	3,100
SS-350	1,500
MLS	5,200
ERS	50
MSR-100	1,200
FX4,700	
SX-350	3,920
TOTAL	**37,620**

1972

FL	1,600
FLH	8,100
XLH	7,500
XLCH	10,650
GE	400
M-65 Sport	3,708
SS-350	3,775
MLS	6,000
ERS	50
MSR-100	900
FX6,500	
SX-350	2,525
XR200	
MC	8,000
TOTAL	**59,908**

1973

FL	1,025
FLH	7,750
XLH	9,875
XLCH	10,825
GE	425
SS-350	4,137
FX7,625	
SX-350	2,431
MC	95
TX-125	9,225
Z-90	8,250
X-90	8,250
SR-100	986
XRTT	10
TOTAL	**70,903**

1974

FLH-1200	5,166

FX3,034	
FXE	6,199
XLH	13,295
XLCH	10,535
SS-350	2,500
SX-350	2,085
SX-175	3,612
SX-125	4,000
Z-90	7,168
X-90	7,019
SR-100	1,396
XR100	
FLHF	1,310
FL-Police	791
TOTAL	**68,210**

1975

FLH-1200	7,400
FX3,060	
FXE	9,350
XLH	13,515
XLCH	5,895
SX-175	8,500
SX-125	2,500
Z-90	2,562
X-90	1,586
XR100	
FLHF	1,535
FL-Police	900
SX-250	11,000
RC-125	4,500
SS-250	3,000
TOTAL	**75,403**

1976

FLH-1200	11,891
FX3,857	
FXE	13,838
XLH	12,844
XLCH	5,238
SX-250	3,125
SS-250	1,416
SXT-125	6,056
SS-175	1,461
SS-125	1,560
MX-250	87
RR-250	2
TOTAL	**61,375**

1977

FLH-1200	8,691
FX2,049	
FXE	9,400
XLH	12,742
XLCH	4,074
SX-250	558
SS-250	144
SXT-125	48
SS-175	110
SS-125	488
RR-250	5
FLHS	535

FXS	3,742		FXWG Wide Glide	5,166
XLT	1,099		FXS-80 Low Rider	7,223
XLCR	1,923		FXEF-80 Fat Bob	3,691
TOTAL	**45,608**		FXE-80 Super Glide	3,085
			XLS-1000 Roadster	1,660
1978			XLH-1000 Sportster	8,442
FLH-1200	4,761		**TOTAL**	**40,268**
FX1,774				
FXE	8,314		**1982**	
XLH	11,271		FLH-80 Electra Glide	1,491
XLCH	2,758		FLHC-80 Electra Glide Classic	N/A
XLH Anniversary	2,323		FLT-80 Tour Glide	1,196
SX-250	479		FLTC Tour Glide Classic	833
FXS	9,787		FXE-80 Super Glide	1,617
XLT	6		FXR Super Glide II	3,065
XLCR	1,201		FXRS Super Glide II	3,190
FLH-80	2,525		FXEF-80 Fat Bob	N/A
XLS	2		FXS-80 Low Rider	1,816
XR750	80		FXB-80 Sturgis	1,833
FLH-1200 Anniversary	2,120		FXWG Wide Glide	2,348
TOTAL	**47,401**		XLH 1000 Sportster	5,015
			XLS-1000 Roadster	1,261
1979			**TOTAL (estimate)**	**28,665**
FLT	19			
FLHC	4,368		**1983**	
FLHC and sidecar	353		FLHT Electra Glide	1,426
FLH-80	3,429		FLHC-80 Electra Glide Classic	1,302
FLH-1200	2,612		FLH Electra Glide Belt Drive	1,272
FLH-80 Police	84		FLT-80 Tour Glide	565
FLH-1200 Police	596		FLTC Tour Glide Classic	475
FXS-1200	3,827		FXE-80 Super Glide	1,215
FXS-80	9,433		FXR Super Glide II	1,413
FXEF-1200	4,678		FXWG Wide Glide	2,873
FXEF-80	5,264		FXS-80 Low Rider	3,277
FXE-1200	3,117		FXEF-80 Fat Bob	N/A
XLCH	141		XLX-61 Sportster	4,892
XLCR	9		XLH-1000 Sportster	2,230
XLS	5,123		XLS-1000 Roadster	1,616
XLH	6,525		**TOTAL (estimate)**	**25,056**
TOTAL	**49,578**			
			1984	
1980			FLHT Electra Glide	208
FLHC Electra Glide Classic	2,480		FLH Electra Glide Belt Drive	2,686
FLH-80 Electra Glide	1,625		FLHTE-80 Electra Glide Classic	
FLH-1200 Electra Glide	1,111		N/AFLT-80 Tour Glide	N/A
FLT-80 Tour Glide	4,480		FLTC-80 Tour Glide Classic	1,301
FXB-80 Sturgis	1,970		FXE-80 Super Glide	2,606
FXWG Wide Glide	6,085		FXSB-80 Low Rider Belt	N/A
FXS-80 Low Rider	5,922		FXR Super Glide II	N/A
FXEF-80 Fat Bob	4,773		FXWG-80 Wide Glide	N/A
FXE-1200 Super Glide	3,169		FXRS-80 Low Rider	2,227
XLS-1000 Roadster	2,926		FXRT-80 Sport Glide	2,030
XLH-1000 Sportster	11,841		FXRP-80 Sport Glide Police	820
TOTAL	**46,382**		FXEF-80 Fat Bob	N/A
			XLX-61 Sportster Standard	4,281
1981			XLS-1000 Roadster	1,135
FLHC-80 Electra Glide Classic	1,472		XR-1000 Sportster	759
FLH-80 Electra Glide	2,131		**TOTAL (estimated)**	**25,000**
FLHS Electra Glide	1,062			
FLTC-80 Tour Glide Classic	1,157		**1985**	
FLT-80 Tour Glide	1,636		FLHTE-80 Electra Glide Classic	N/A
FXB-80 Sturgis	3,543		FLTC-80 Tour Glide Classic	1,847

FXEF-80 Fat Bob	2,324	
FXSB-80 Low Rider Belt	2,359	
FXWG-80 Wide Glide	4,171	
FXRS-80 Low Glide	3,476	
FXRT-80 Sport Glide	1,252	
FXST-80 Softail	4,529	
XLH-1000 Sportster	4,074	
XLX-61 Sportster Standard	1,824	
XLS-1000 Roadster	616	
XR-1000 Sportster	N/A	
TOTAL (estimated)	**27,000**	

1986

Sportsters	11,959	
Customs	18,398	
Touring	6,378	
TOTAL	**36,735**	
of which	*6,825*	*were exported.*

1987

Sportsters	14,249	
Customs	20,865	
Touring	8,201	
TOTAL	**43,315**	
of which	*8,586*	*were exported.*

1988

Sportsters	17,491	
Customs	23,232	
Touring	9,794	
TOTAL	**50,517**	
of which	*11,576*	*were exported.*

1989

Sportsters	17,838	
Customs	27,461	
Touring	13,626	
TOTAL	**58,925**	
of which	*15,288*	*were exported.*

1990

Sportsters	16,119	
Customs	34,579	
Touring	11,760	
TOTAL	**62,458**	
of which	*19,320*	*were exported.*

1991

Sportsters	18,735	
Customs	39,550	
Touring	10,341	
TOTAL	**68,626**	
of which	*21,633*	*were exported.*

1992

Sportsters	17,623	
Customs	48,177	
Touring	10,695	
TOTAL	**76,495**	
of which	*23,253*	*were exported.*

1993

Sportsters	22,247	
Customs	49,004	
Touring	10,445	
TOTAL	**81,696**	
of which	*24,513*	*were exported.*

1994

Sportsters	26,466	
Customs	52,046	
Touring	17,299	
TOTAL	**95,811**	
of which	*29,313*	*were exported.*
Buell	576	

1995

Sportsters	29,625	
Customs	54,456	
Touring	21,023	
TOTAL	**105,104**	
of which	*32,076*	*were exported.*
Buell	1,407	

1996

Sportsters	31, 173	
Customs	63,198	
Touring	24,400	
TOTAL	**118,771**	
of which	*34,657*	*were exported.*
Buell	2,762	

1997

Sportsters	31,453	
Customs	70,724	
Touring	30,108	
TOTAL	**132,285**	
of which	*36,069*	*were exported.*
Buell	4,415	

1998

Sportsters	33,892	
Customs	77,434	
Touring	39,492	
TOTAL	**150,818**	
of which	*39,916*	*were exported.*

1999

Sportsters	41,870	
Customs	87,806	
Touring	47,511	
TOTAL	**177,817**	
of which	*41,573*	*were exported.*
Buell	7,767	

2000

Sportsters	46,213	
Customs	100,875	
Touring	57,504	
TOTAL	**204,592**	
of which	*45,775*	*were exported.*
Buell (excluding Blast)	5,043	
Blast	5,416	

Appendix C

Champions

AMA National Champions

1946	Chet Dykgraff; Grand Rapids, MI; Norton
1947	Jimmy Chann; Bridgeton, NJ; H-D
1948	Jimmy Chann; Bridgeton, NJ; H-D
1949	Jimmy Chann; Bridgeton, NJ; H-D
1950	Larry Headrick, San Jose; CA, H-D
1951	Bobby Hill; Grove City, OH; Indian
1952	Bobby Hill; Grove City, OH; Indian
1953	Bill Tuman; Rockford, IL; Indian, Norton
1954	Joe Leonard; San Jose, CA; H-D
1955	Brad Andres; San Diego, CA; H-D
1956	Joe Leonard; San Jose, CA; H-D
1957	Joe Leonard; San Jose, CA; H-D
1958	Carroll Resweber; Cedarburg; WI; H-D
1959	Carroll Resweber; Cedarburg; WI; H-D
1960	Carroll Resweber; Cedarburg, WI; H-D
1961	Carroll Resweber; Cedarburg, WI; H-D
1962	Bart Markel; Flint, MI; H-D
1963	Dick Mann; Richmond, CA; BSA, Matchless
1964	Roger Reiman; Kewanee, IL; H-D
1965	Bart Markel; Flint, MI; H-D
1966	Bart Markel; Flint, MI; H-D
1967	Gary Nixon; Cockeysville, MD; Triumph
1968	Gary Nixon; Cockeysville, MD; Triumph
1969	Mert Lawwill; San Francisco, H-D
1970	Gene Romero; San Luis Obispo, CA; Triumph
1971	Dick Mann; Richmond, CA; BSA
1972	Mark Brelsford; Woodside, CA; H-D
1973	Kenny Roberts; Modesto, CA; Yamaha
1974	Kenny Roberts; Modesto, CA; Yamaha
1975	Gary Scott; Springfield, OH; H-D
1976	Jay Springsteen; Lapeer, MI; H-D
1977	Jay Springsteen; Lapeer, MI; H-D
1978	Jay Springsteen; Lapeer, MI; H-D
1979	Steve Eklund; San Jose, CA; Yamaha
1980	Randy Goss; Hartland, MI; H-D
1981	Mike Kidd; Euless, TX; Yamaha
1982	Ricky Graham; Seaside, CA; H-D
1983	Randy Goss; Hartland, MI; H-D
1984	Ricky Graham; Seaside, CA; Honda
1985	Bubba Shobert; Carmel Valley, CA; Honda
1986	Bubba Shobert; Carmel Valley, CA; Honda
1987	Bubba Shobert; Carmel Valley, CA; Honda
1988	Scott Parker; Swartz Creek, MI; H-D
1989	Scott Parker; Swartz Creek, MI; H-D
1990	Scott Parker; Swartz Creek, MI; H-D
1991	Scott Parker; Swartz Creek, MI; H-D
1992	Chris Carr; Valley Springs, CA; H-D
1993	Ricky Graham; Salinas, CA; Honda
1994	Scott Parker; Swartz Creek, MI; H-D
1995	Scott Parker; Swartz Creek, MI; H-D
1996	Scott Parker; Swartz Creek, MI; H-D
1997	Scott Parker; Swartz Creek, MI; H-D
1998	Scott Parker; Swartz Creek, MI; H-D
1999	Chris Carr; Fleetwood, PA; H-D
2000	Joe Kopp; Mica, WA; H-D
2001	Chris Carr; Fleetwood, PA; H-D

AMA Nationals Wins *(Ten or more wins; make most often ridden is listed first)*

1.	Scott Parker; H-D; 94 wins
2.	Chris Carr; H-D, ATK, Rotax; 52 wins
3.	Jay Springsteen; H-D; 43 wins
4.	Ricky Graham; Honda , H-D; 39 wins *
5.	Bubba Shobert; Honda, H-D; 34 wins
6.	Kenny Roberts; Yamaha; 33 wins
7.	Will Davis; H-D, Honda; 32 wins *
8.	Bart Markel; H-D; 28 wins
9.	Dick Mann; BSA; Matchless, Yamaha, Ossa, Honda; 24 wins
10.	Joe Leonard; H-D; 23 wins
11.	Steve Morehead; H-D; 23 wins
12.	Gary Scott; H-D; 19 wins
13.	Gary Nixon; Triumph, Kawasaki, Suzuki; 18 wins
14.	Hank Scott; H-D; 17 wins
15.	Steve Eklund; Yamaha, H-D, Can-Am, Rotax; 17 wins *
16.	Carroll Resweber; H-D; 17 wins
17.	Randy Goss; H-D; 16 wins
18.	Michael Baldwin; Honda; 16 wins
19.	Mert Lawwill; H-D; 15 wins
20.	Gene Romero; Triumph, Yamaha; 13 wins
21.	Mike Kidd; H-D, Triumph, Honda, Yamaha; 12 wins
22.	Brad Andres; H-D; 12 wins *
23.	Kevin Atherton; H-D; 12 wins
24.	Jim Rice; BSA, H-D; 12 wins
25.	Cal Rayborn; H-D; 11 wins
26.	Fred Nix; H-D; 11 wins *
27.	Rich King; H-D; 11 wins
28.	Terry Poovey; H-D, Bultaco, Honda, Rotax; 11 wins
29.	Everett Brashear; H-D; 10 wins
30.	Ronnie Jones; Honda, Yamaha; 10 wins
31.	Alex Jorgensen; Can-Am, Norton, BSA, H-D, Rotax, Wood-Rotax; 10 wins

(Deceased)*

Appendix D

Timeline

(From a brochure offered by York as part of the factory tour.)

1903   21-year-old William S. Harley and 20-year-old Arthur Davidson make available to the public the first production Harley-Davidson motorcycle. The factory is a 10 x 15-foot wooden shed with the words "Harley-Davidson Motor Company" crudely scrawled on the door.

1906   The first factory is built on the Chestnut Street site, later re-named Juneau Avenue.

1909   The 6-year-old company introduces its first V-twin engine motorcycle. With a displacement of 49.5 ci, the bike provided 7 horsepower. The image of two cylinders in a 45-degree configuration would become one of the most enduring icons of H-D history.

1914   Sidecars are made available to Harley-Davidson buyers. The Motor Company also enters motorcycle racing.

1915   Harley-Davidson motorcycles are made available with three-speed transmissions.

1918   All Harley-Davidson motorcycles produced are sold for use by the U. S. military in World War I. At war's end, it is estimated that the Army used some 20,000 motorcycles, most of which were Harleys.

1919   The 37-ci opposed twin-cylinder Sport model is introduced and gains great popularity overseas.

1921   The first 74-ci V-twin engine is introduced. This motorcycle was called the F-head.

1925   Gas tanks on all models now have a distinct teardrop shape. This basic appearance for H-D motorcycles would never vary.

1929   The 45-ci V-twin engine is introduced.

1930   The flathead engine is introduced.

1936   Harley introduces the 61-ci bike. The motorcycle quickly earns the nickname of "Knucklehead," because of the shape of its rocker boxes. The company also introduces an 80-ci side valve engine.

1942   H-D produces the unique XA 750, a motorcycle with horizontally opposed cylinders and shaft drive.

1945   At the end of World War II, H-D had produced 88,000 WLA models for military use, as well as 1,000 XA models.

1948   The 61- and 74-ci overhead valve engines were introduced and nicknamed "Panhead."

1949   Hydraulic front forks appear on the new Hydra-Glide models.

1952   The K model is introduced with an integrated transmission. The K will evolve into the Sportster.

1953   H-D celebrates its 50th anniversary in style. Its new logo depicts a "V" with a bar overlaid reading "Harley-Davidson" and the words "50 years—American made."

1957   The Sportster is introduced with a 55-ci overhead valve engine.

1959   The H-D Topper motor scooter is introduced.

1962   Harley purchases facilities in Tomahawk, Wisconsin.

1964   The three-wheel Servi-Car is the first H-D to receive electric start.

1965   Duo-Glide name is changed to Electra-Glide and is updated with electric start.

1966   The "Shovelhead" is introduced.

1969   Harley-Davidson merges with AMF.

1971   The FX 1200 Super Glide is introduced.

1973   All assembly operations are moved to a 400,000-square-foot plan in York, Pennsylvania.

1977   The FXS Low Rider and the Café Racer are introduced.

1981   In June, 13 H-D executives purchased the company from AMF. The phrase, "The Eagle soars alone," becomes a rallying cry.

1983   Harley Owners Group, or H.O.G., is established.

1984   The 1340-cc V2 Evolution engine is introduced on five models. The Softail design debuts.

1986   H-D releases the Heritage Softail.

1990   The legendary Fat Boy is introduced.

1993   H-D celebrates its 90th anniversary.

1995   The Ultra Classic Electra Glide becomes the first model with fuel injection.

1997   The new 330,000-square-foot plant in Kansas City produces its first Sportster.

1998   H-D celebrates its 95th anniversary and introduces the Twin Cam 88, the first new engine since 1984.

1999   Twin Cam B, which reduces vibration, is put into the 2000 Softail family. The Softail Deuce is introduced. More than 177,000 cycles are shipped.

2002   The V-Rod, with a 60-degree V-twin, 115 horsepower, and a dragster look is introduced.

Appendix E

Index